Internet Security: Hacking, Counterhacking, and Society

Kenneth Einar Himma

Seattle Pacific University

JONES AND BARTLETT PUBLISHERS

Sudbury, Massachusetts

BOSTON   TORONTO   LONDON   SINGAPORE

World Headquarters

Jones and Bartlett
  Publishers
40 Tall Pine Drive
Sudbury, MA 01776
978-443-5000
info@jbpub.com
www.jbpub.com

Jones and Bartlett
  Publishers Canada
6339 Ormindale Way
Mississauga, Ontario
L5V 1J2
CANADA

Jones and Bartlett
  Publishers International
Barb House, Barb Mews
London W6 7PA
UK

Jones and Bartlett's books and products are available through most bookstores and online booksellers. To contact Jones and Bartlett Publishers directly, call 800-832-0034, fax 978-443-8000, or visit our website www.jbpub.com.

Substantial discounts on bulk quantities of Jones and Bartlett's publications are available to corporations, professional associations, and other qualified organizations. For details and specific discount information, contact the special sales department at Jones and Bartlett via the above contact information or send an email to specialsales@jbpub.com.

Production Credits
Acquisitions Editor: Tim Anderson
Production Director: Amy Rose
Editorial Assistant: Laura Pagluica
Production Assistant: Jamie Chase
Manufacturing Buyer: Therese Connell
Marketing Manager: Andrea DeFronzo
Composition: Northeast Compositors, Inc.
Cover Design: Kristin E. Ohlin
Cover Image: © Vasil Vasilev / ShutterStock, Inc.
Cover Image: © Melissa King / ShutterStock, Inc.
Printing and Binding: Malloy, Inc.
Cover Printing: Lehigh Press

Library of Congress Cataloging-in-Publication Data

Internet security : hacking, counterhacking, and society / Kenneth
  Einar Himma. – 1st ed.
    p. cm.
  Includes index.
  ISBN-13: 978-0-7637-3536-4
  ISBN-10: 0-7637-3536-1
    1. Internet–Security measures. 2. Computer security–Moral and
ethical aspects. 3. Computer hackers.   I. Himma, Kenneth Einar.
TK5105.875.I57I574 2006
005.8–dc22

                             2006014412

6048

Printed in the United States of America
10 09 08 07 06   10 9 8 7 6 5 4 3 2 1

Introduction

From North America to South America to Asia, computer-related misconduct is posing an ever-growing problem in the public and the private sectors for several reasons. First, nearly every nation, industrial and developing, is becoming increasingly reliant on new digital information technologies to perform legitimate commercial and governmental functions. While these new information technologies have impacted social well-being in a variety of beneficial ways, they have also exposed a number of important interests to possible intrusion or attack. For example, a reasonably sophisticated distributed denial of service attack can take a commercial Web site down for hours, potentially resulting in the loss of revenue, value to shareholders, and, ultimately, jobs that may be spread across the globe. The effects on the global economy are potentially significant.

Second, the frequency of digital attacks and intrusions directed at private commercial interests has been steadily increasing over the years as the number of people with the appropriate motivations and technical skills continues to grow. Compounding the problem is the increasing availability on the Web of easy-to-use hacker tools that can be used by comparatively unskilled users — so-called script kiddies — to stage malicious attacks and intrusions against private networks. These tools are available to anyone, anywhere in the world, who has access to the Internet.

Third, at this point in time, not a single nation has adequate law-enforcement resources to pursue investigations into the vast majority of computer intrusions involving that nation. But even in those occasions where a nation has sufficient resources to warrant intervention, the response is likely to come long after the damage is done. It is uncontroversial that law enforcement agencies have not been able to keep pace with the rapidly growing problems posed by digital attackers.

Hackers believe that, at the very least, non-malicious intrusions are morally permissible and have offered a number of arguments purporting to justify such intrusions. Some hackers believe, for example, these intrusions are justified by consequentialist considerations because they result

in an increase in humanity's stock of knowledge about the relevant technologies. This, therefore, promotes the development of technologies that
will ultimately help make the Internet more secure. Some hackers believe
that any barriers to information are morally illegitimate and hence deserve
no respect, including barriers that separate the information on an individual's computer from another individual's computer.

Recently, a number of writers have begun to suggest that attacks on government and corporate sites might be justified as a form of political
activism. On this influential line of analysis, acts that are otherwise ethically impermissible or unlawful might be morally and legally acceptable
if motivated by a political concern to protest unjust laws or institutions.
Similarly, digital attacks that might otherwise be legally or morally objectionable are legally and morally permissible if they are politically-motivated acts of civil disobedience or "hacktivism."

Not surprisingly, victims of such attacks disagree and have begun to
respond to digital attacks with measures that have been characterized as
"hacking back" or "active defense." These measures are distinguished
from other kinds of private intrusion responses in that they are noncooperative and reasonably calculated to causally impact remote systems (i.e., those that belong to other persons or entities). While active
defense measures are not necessarily "uncooperative," in the sense of
being deliberately contrary to the wishes of other parties, they are undertaken unilaterally in situations where the interests of other parties are
infringed and are thus reasonably characterized as non-cooperative in
nature.

Active defense measures exhibit varying levels of force. Some of these
responses are aggressive in the sense of being intended to inflict the same
kind of harm on the attacker's machine or network as the attack intended to inflict on the victim's machine or network. Some active defense measures are, however, intended simply to gather intelligence about the attack
and are significantly less aggressive in character. One increasingly common active defense measure involves an attempt to follow an attack path
in reverse through intermediate networks and systems in order to identify the parties ultimately culpable for that attack. While there are more
benign, cooperative tactics for tracing the path of an attack, these more
invasive traceback technologies follow attack paths by entering into
machines and networks involved in the attack.[1]

---

[1] Another related issue of theoretical interest arises in connection with the so-called Good Samaritan Worm—a worm that
was designed to eliminate a security vulnerability to a more malicious worm and then was released onto the Internet where
it was unwittingly downloaded by thousands of users.

Many individuals have come to believe that private persons and firms have a right to protect themselves against hacker attacks because (1) such attacks are, contrary to the arguments of hackers, unjustified and (2) law enforcement is currently unable to protect them. For example, Tim Mullen argues that the right to self-defense implies a right on the part of firms to adopt even aggressive active defense in response to a digital attack:

> I propose that we have the right to defend our systems from attack. I am not talking about some vigilante strike upon script kiddies at the drop of a packet. I am not talking about a rampant anti-worm. I am talking about neutralizing an attacking machine in singularity when it is clearly and definitively infected with a worm that will continue to attack every box it can find until stopped.... The moment that I begin to incur costs, or the integrity of services that I pay for is reduced by any degree, is the moment that I have the right to do something about it.... It is simply self-defense. (Security Focus, 2003)

Somewhat different issues arise in connection with the proliferation of a large number of "e-organisms," such as viruses and Internet worms. Whereas a person need not perform any affirmative acts to be victimized by a hacker attack, he or she must perform some sort of act, such as opening an email attachment, to be victimized by a virus or a worm. Some people have suggested that such acts amount to a form of "implied consent" that immunizes the writer of the virus or worm from moral and legal culpability. Further, some commentators argue that benevolent e-organisms, those designed to install a helpful fix or patch of some kind, are morally justified.

There are, of course, other important Internet security issues that arise directly from unwanted computer intrusions. These intrusions, for example, are becoming increasingly common in the growing world of on-line gaming, which poses a host of security risks—some more important and some less important. For example, a breach of security within an on-line gaming community might lead to something as serious as identity theft or it might, less seriously, lead to one person's hijacking another's resources to play a game under the latter's on-line name. Gamers, in every nation, are unfortunately vulnerable.

Still other important security problems are indirectly related to unwanted computer intrusions. For example, one concern pertains to the growing number of Web sites all over the world that are devoted to discussing code contrived to facilitate the commission of such intrusions. Indeed, some Web sites will publish code that can be used/abused to commit these very intrusions. One might legitimately ask whether the authors of such Web content should be criminally or civilly liable for the intrusions and associated harms that foreseeably result from them.

Other problems arise in connection with certain technologies that have been developed to protect persons from these various intrusions—technologies that raise a host of ethical questions themselves. There are many technologies, such as encryption and steganography, that enable a person to conceal the content of certain messages from potential hackers and crackers. These technologies, however, can also be used in ways that have social costs, raising the issue of whether, and to what extent, they may permissibly be used.

In any event, the problems associated with unwanted computer intrusions are of significant interest to ethicists and policymakers because they implicate a variety of morally significant considerations across the globe. Digital attacks, for example, not only affect the financial and privacy interests of victims, they can also affect other important interests. At best, a digital intrusion forces its immediate victim to shift resources from more productive uses to less productive security uses, costs that are passed on to consumers in the form of higher prices. At worst, a coordinated digital attack that takes key commercial firms offline for significant periods can result in millions of dollars in lost revenue and employment. These costs impact our collective material well-being in a variety of ethically significant ways. Unfortunately, such costs are likely to increase along with the frequency and severity of such incidents.

Not surprisingly, the various problems posed by unwanted computer intrusions are of growing concern to public officials and policymakers in every nation who are struggling to assess the costs, benefits, and legitimacy of coercive regulation. Public officials must attempt to weigh the risks and impacts of the various intrusions against the impacts of regulating such intrusions on morally legitimate speech, property, and privacy interests, along with the costs to taxpayers of ensuring efficacious regulation. As is evident by the controversial character of the various debates, there are no obvious answers to these problems.

This book considers the ethical issues that arise in connection with unwanted computer intrusions. The collection begins with a chapter by Tom Forester and Perry Morrison, "Hacking and Viruses," that provides a general overview of some of the important issues regarding unwanted intrusions. In "The Conceptual and Moral Landscape of Computer Security," Herman Tavani articulates some general conceptual and ethical issues that must be addressed before proceeding to an evaluation of specific problems associated with unwanted computer intrusions.

Part Two is concerned with hacking, hacktivism, and counterhacking. The section begins with two chapters, Eugene Spafford's chapter "Are Computer Hacker Break-ins Ethical?" and Mark Manion and Abby Goodrum's chapter "Terrorism or Civil Disobedience: Toward a Hacktivist Ethic." The former chapter considers whether hacking motivated by curiosity and other benign purposes is morally permissible, while the latter considers whether politically-motivated hacking is morally permissible. It continues with two contributions by myself—one on whether hacktivism can be justified as a form of electronic civil disobedience and the other on whether it is permissible for victims of a digital attack to hack back at the perpetrators. This section ends with Dorothy Denning's chapter, "A View of Cyberterrorism 5 Years Later."

Part Three considers ethical issues that arise in connection with professionalism and design. Don Gotterbarn and David Tarnoff discuss certain ethical issues that arise in connection with computer professionalism in "Internet Development: Professionalism, Profits, Ethics, or Sleaze?" The chapter focuses primarily on the need to "professionalize" Internet development. Next is a chapter on informed consent and value sensitive design by Batya Friedman, Daniel Howe, and Edward Felten. Richard Epstein closes Part Three by exploring general issues of professionalism in development in "The Impact of Computer Security Concerns on Software Development." This chapter will be particularly valuable to software developers.

The book concludes with Part Four, which considers a number of miscellaneous problems associated with Internet security. The first chapter in this section is an in-depth discussion of steganography by Frances Grodzinsky, Keith Miller, and Marty Wolf, entitled "The Ethical Implications of the Messenger's Haircut: Steganography in the Digital Age." It continues with a chapter on the security issues associated with on-line gaming by Kai Kimppa, Andy Bissett, and N. Ben Fairweather, entitled, appropriately enough, "Security in On-line Games." Adam Moore's contribution discusses the relationship between putative justifications for hacking and intellectual property and privacy rights. Last, but not least, Maria Canellopoulou-Bottis discusses the issue of whether, and to what extent, software vulnerabilities may permissibly be exposed and publicized by third-parties in the chapter "Disclosing Software Vulnerabilities."

I am optimistic that the wide range and high quality of these chapters ensures that this book will be a valuable addition to the library of anyone who is concerned about the growing number of problems associated with unwanted computer intrusions.

Classroom Use

This volume can be used in a variety of classroom settings for a variety of courses at nearly every level. It is suitable as a principal text for courses concerned with security issues in computer science departments, information schools, philosophy departments, and even law schools. The interdisciplinary character of the volume, of course, mirrors the multidisciplinary interests of the authors. It is also suitable as a supplemental text for general courses in information ethics, which tend to gloss over security issues—despite their growing importance. Additionally, it can be used at both the beginning undergraduate and advanced graduate level; the theorizing, while always demanding and sophisticated, is uniformly clear and well-written. The diversity of uses to which this text can be put, I believe, makes it a valuable addition to academic and professional literature.

About the Author

Kenneth Einar Himma teaches philosophy at Seattle Pacific University. He formerly taught in the Philosophy Department, the Information School, and the Law School at the University of Washington. His specialties are legal philosophy and information ethics. He is the author of more than 100 scholarly articles, encyclopedia entries, book reviews, and op-ed newspaper pieces. He is on the editorial boards of *International Review of Information Ethics* and the forthcoming *INSEIT Journal*.

Acknowledgments

"Are Computer Break-ins Ethical?" originally appeared in the *Journal of Systems Science* (1992, Vol 17). "Hacking and Viruses" originally appeared in the book *Computer Ethics: Cautionary Tales and Ethical Dilemmas in Computing, Second Edition* (MIT Press, 1994). "Terrorism or Civil Disobedience: Toward a Hacktivist Ethic" originally appeared in *Computers and Society* (2000, Vol 30). "Informed Consent in the Mozilla Browser: Implementing Value-Sensitive Design" originally appeared at the *Proceedings of the Thirty-Fifth Annual Hawai'i International Conference on System Sciences* (IEEE Computer Society: Los Alamitos, CA). I am grateful to the authors and to the publishers for allowing me to republish these essays here.

Table of Contents

Introduction   iii

Part I   **Preliminaries 1**

Chapter 1   Tom Forester and Perry Morrison, "Hacking and Viruses"   3

Chapter 2   Herman Tavani, "The Conceptual and Moral Landscape of Computer Security"   29

Part II   **Hacking, Hacktivism, and Active Defense   47**

Chapter 3   Eugene Spafford, "Are Computer Break-ins Ethical?"   49

Chapter 4   Mark Manion and Abby Goodrum, "Terrorism or Civil Disobedience: Toward a Hacktivist Ethic"   61

Chapter 5   Kenneth Einar Himma, "Hacking as Politically Motivated Digital Civil Disobedience: Is Hacktivism Morally Justified?"   73

Chapter 6   Kenneth Einar Himma, "The Ethics of 'Hacking Back': Active Response to Computer Intrusions"   99

Chapter 7   Dorothy Denning, "A View of Cyberterrorism 5 Years Later"   123

Part III   **Ethical Issues in Professionalism and Design   141**

Chapter 8   Don Gotterbarn and David Tarnoff, "Internet Development: Professionalism, Profits, Ethics, or Sleaze?"   143

Chapter 9   Batya Friedman, Daniel Howe, and Edward Felten, "Informed Consent in the Mozilla Browser: Implementing Value-Sensitive Design"   153

Chapter 10   Richard Epstein, "The Impact of Computer Security Concerns on Software Development"   171

Part IV   **Other Security Issues   203**

Chapter 11   Frances Grodzinsky, Keith Miller, and Marty Wolf, "The Ethical Implications of the Messenger's Haircut: Steganography in the Digital Age"   205

Chapter 12   Kai Kimppa, Andy Bissett, and N. Ben Fairweather, "Security in On-line Games"   221

Chapter 13   Adam Moore, "Privacy, Intellectual Property, and Hacking: Evaluating Free Access Arguments"   235

Chapter 14   Maria Canellopoulou-Bottis, "Disclosing Software Vulnerabilities"   255

Index   269

Part 1: Preliminaries

This volume is concerned with ethical issues arising in connection with acts involving unauthorized computer intrusions. The growing number of such intrusions has impacted our economic and social life in a variety of different ways. Software, for example, is more expensive than it otherwise would be because of the need to cover the costs of trying to ensure that the relevant code is secure. Computer intrusions also have psychological costs; the less confidence we have in the security of information technologies, the more vulnerable we feel to security breaches, diminishing our subjective sense of well-being. These effects, of course, are of ethical significance and deserve careful consideration.

This section is intended to set the stage for the rest of the volume. The two chapters in this section provide an overview of the empirical and ethical considerations that will figure prominently in one way or another in each of the other essays in the volume. These chapters therefore provide helpful contextual and background information that enable readers to get the most out of the materials in the rest of the book.

The first chapter contains Tom Forester and Perry Morrison's essay "Hacking and Viruses." The chapter begins with a brief explanation of the concept of hacking and then goes on to consider the motivations for hacking. Forester and Morrison describe many famous cases of hacker attacks and discuss some of the most important ethical issues raised by these acts. In addition, there is a very helpful discussion of the difference between worms, Trojan horses, and viruses. This essay is as good an introduction to the issues and problems surrounding hacking as I have seen.

The second chapter contains Herman Tavani's essay, "The Conceptual and Moral Landscape of Computer Security." Tavani, like many of the authors whose work appears in this volume, is one of the most well-known theorists in information ethics, and his broad grasp of the area is on display fully in this essay. Tavani explains the concept of security and its application in computing contexts. He then goes on to explain a variety of different ethical issues arising in connection with computer security. While the first chapter focuses on the empirical and technical dimensions of the hacking problem, Tavani's chapter focuses on the ethical dimensions. These two chapters together provide the needed material for the reader to understand all that is to follow.

Chapter 1: Hacking and Viruses

Tom Forester and Perry Morrison

On April 27, 1987, viewers of the Home Box Office (HBO) cable TV channel in the United States witnessed a historically significant event, variously described as the first act of high-tech terrorism or the world's most widely viewed piece of electronic graffiti. On that evening, watchers of HBO's satellite transmission of *The Falcon and the Snowman* saw their screens go blank and the following message appear:

> *Good Evening HBO from Captain Midnight. $12.95 a month?*
> *No way!*
> (Show-time/Movie Channel, Beware!)

This transmission lasted for some 4 minutes. It represented a protest against HBO's decision to scramble its satellite signal so that backyard dish owners were forced to buy or hire decoders to view HBO's programs. More significantly—and in the most impressive way—it illustrated the vulnerability of satellites and other communications services to malicious interference.

The search for and apprehension of Captain Midnight took several months and a certain amount of luck. Investigators initially reasoned that the captain had used a commercial satellite uplink facility to overcome HBO's intended signal, but to their dismay, they discovered that there were some 2,000 such facilities. Fortunately for them, only a much smaller number (580) used the kind of character generator that Captain Midnight used to create his text message, and of these only 12 were available that night for jamming purposes. Of the remaining suitable facilities, records showed that they had all been involved in normal activities.

A breakthrough in the case did not occur until a Wisconsin tourist happened to overhear a man talking about the Captain Midnight prank while using a public telephone in Florida. The tourist reported the man's license number, and this information eventually led police to the culprit—John MacDougall, a satellites dish salesman, electronics engineer, and part-time employee at the Central Florida Teleport satellite uplink facility in Ocala. MacDougall was subsequently charged with transmitting without a license and sentenced to 1 year's probation and a $5,000 fine ("Conclusion," 1986).

Since the Captain Midnight episode, however, several other instances of uplink video piracy have occurred, including a November 1987 incident in which WGN-TV (Channel 9 in Chicago) was overridden for approximately 1.5 seconds. That same evening, WTTW (Channel 11 in Chicago) was also overridden by a 90-second transmission, this time by a man in a Max Headroom mask smacking his exposed buttocks with a fly swatter (*Software Engineering Notes* [SEN], 1988a). As a result of these incidents, the U.S. Congress passed a law making satellite hacking a felony, and the first person convicted under that law was Thomas M. Haynie, an employee of the Christian Broadcasting Network, who in 1987 generated a religious message on the Playboy Channel (*SEN*, 1991).

Yet the most important aspect of the Captain Midnight hack and other similar incidents is not immediately obvious. MacDougall caused mild annoyance to a large number of viewers and probably, at worst, a severe case of embarrassment to HBO. Yet the fact that this individual was able to broadcast a particular message into the homes of thousands and to take control of a sophisticated satellite transponder demonstrates a much more significant danger. What if, instead of being an angry satellite dish salesman, MacDougall had been an international terrorist and instead of interrupting a movie, he had begun to jam the telephone, facsimile, and data communications of a number of satellites? Further, we know that satellites are directed from the ground by using radio signals to control the functioning of their small maneuvering engines. What if MacDougall or somebody else had used these signals to move the satellite into a decaying orbit or caused it to enter the orbit of another satellite—perhaps a Soviet one—many of which carry small nuclear reactors as a power source?

Even worse, if MacDougall had been an employee of a city traffic authority, could he have used his knowledge of computer systems and traffic control to completely foul up a city's traffic lights during a peak traffic period? One does not need much imagination to think of the consequences of such an act for a city, say, the size of Los Angeles. Not only would the traffic snarls take days to untangle, but emergency services (police, fire, ambulance, etc.) would be incapacitated. Maintenance of sewage, lighting, power, and telephones would probably come to a halt, and inevitably there would be fatalities and an enormous insurance bill stemming from the hundreds of wrecked or damaged cars and injured or ill people. More important, security services would be hard pressed to deal with any additional terrorist acts such as a hijacking or a takeover of the city's water supply ("Enter the Technically-Competent Terrorist," 1986; Morrison, 1986b).

These kinds of concerns have been echoed in a recent report by the U.S. National Academy of Sciences, which stated that the United States has been "remarkably lucky" with its computer networks and that technically proficient thieves or terrorists could subvert some of the country's most critical computer systems. According to the report, these include telecommunications networks, aviation control systems, and financial systems (Charles, 1991).

1.1. What Is Hacking?

In the media, incidents such as the HBO prank are referred to as "hacking." Yet this term is not easy to define, nor is it a recent phenomenon. According to writers such as Steven Levy, author of *Hackers: Heroes of the Computer Revolution,* the earliest hackers were students at the Massachusetts Institute of Technology (MIT) in the late 1960s. These hackers specialized in putting together pieces of telephone circuitry and tracing the wiring and switching gear of the MIT network. Next came the phone "phreaks"—epitomized by the famous Captain Crunch (John T. Draper)—who discovered that a breakfast cereal of the same name supplied a toy whistle that generated a tone identical to the one used by the U.S. telephone network to access toll-free services. Eventually, instead of blowing the whistle into a pay phone mouthpiece, Draper and other resourceful individuals developed "blueboxes," electronic tone generators that could reproduce the full series of tones that the U.S. telephone network used in its call-routing system. With such devices, it was possible to call anywhere in the world for free. But, unfortunately, many "blueboxers" and even the ingenious Captain Crunch himself were convicted on various offenses and enjoyed several stints in jail.

According to Levy, hacking as we understand it—that is, involving the use of computers—began to emerge only with the development of time-shared systems. Hacking then spread quickly once virtual data toolkits (VDTs) allowed users to interact with a machine directly rather than through the remote mechanism of card-based batch processing. Yet, even then, hacking referred to a much more noble set of activities than the criminal acts that are described by the term today. Hacking was an elite art practiced by small groups of extremely gifted individuals. It generated its own set of folk heroes, huge rivalries, eccentricities, and cult rituals. But, above all, this early form of hacking was about intellectual challenge, not malicious damage. Levy portrays this period as a sort of golden era of hacking, which mainly took place at two major sites—MIT and Stanford University in California. For most hackers at this time, their chief interest lay in understanding the innards of a system down to the last chip and the last line of the operating system. The software they wrote was for public display, use, and further development and was their major source of self-esteem, challenge, and socialization.

In Levy's view, all of this began to change once huge commercial interests moved into the software industry and flexed their legal and commercial muscles. Suddenly, software was not for public use or refinement. It became the property of those who had paid for it to be written (and who did not always appreciate unauthorized revisions), and once this had happened, the golden age came to an end. Intellectual challenge was not enough. Like everywhere else, there was no free lunch in the world of hacking, either. Therefore, to some extent Levy indirectly blames the commercialization of software for the emergence of hacking in its criminal form. Having been introduced to the cut and thrust of the commercial world, the best and brightest may have taken on this different set of values—a set that has been augmented and made more sinister among the current crop of hackers. Then, armed with these different values and goals and empowered by the development of nationwide networks of computers (the ARPANET being the earliest of these), hackers began to break out of the confines of their local machines and to spread their interests across the United States, even using links to international networks to gain access to systems on the other side of the earth.

Back from the Ashes: The Reemergence of Phone Hacking

In recent years, the merging of the telephone network with computer systems and private automatic branch exchanges (PABXs) has provided hackers with easier and in some ways more tempting targets. Accessing peoples' voice mail, redirecting calls, and generally fouling up these systems is becoming more and more common (Brock, 1991).

- From April 1990, the switchboard of Palomar Hospital was intermittently jammed and even disconnected by an individual armed with a common touch-tone phone. The alleged offender, Rick Ivkovich, had operators in tears as he blocked calls to and from the hospital and connected hospital operators to outside lines, including 911 emergency numbers and the county jail (SEN, 1992a).
- In 1991, 10 students from the University of Kent, England, admitted in court to making around $1 million worth of calls from six unmodified call boxes (Blankensteijn, 1991).
- Lynne Doucette and a team of 17 break-in artists defrauded U.S. telephone companies of more than $1.6 million by using other people's credit cards and access codes. Around the same time, an independent attack was made on an office switch that redirected calls from the state parole board office to a New York phone sex line (The Australian, 1989).

U.S. phone companies are responding to the threat from phone hacking and credit card fraud by monitoring overseas calls for suspicious patterns, such as heavy utilization of calls to unusual destinations. If customers agree to pay for these services, the phone companies place ceilings on their liability in the event of an abuse being discovered (Lewyn, 1992).

Big losers in PABX fraud have included the New York City Human Resources Administration ($704,000), Proctor and Gamble ($300,000), Suitomo Bank ($97,000), Philadelphia Newspapers ($90,000), Tennessee Valley Authority ($65,000), and the Christian Broadcasting Network ($40,000) (Lewyn, 1992).[1]

Yet, even today, "hacking" has a wide range of meanings. To some, to hack is to roughly force a program to work, generally inelegantly. For others, a hack is a lever (generally small) program or program modification that displays unusual insight into a programming language or operating system. On the other hand, any scam or clever manipulation may also be termed a hack. For example, the famous stunt-card "switcheroo" at the 1961 Rose Bowl football game is often referred to as a *great hack* (Neumann, 1984). In this context, computer viruses (a topic we address short-

---

[1]See other interesting cases in SEN, 1988b.

ly) may represent a particular kind of malicious and destructive hack. Many more of us, though, tend to associate the term almost exclusively with attempts to use the telephone network to gain unauthorized access to computer systems and their data (some have preferred to call this *cracking*). Psychologists, sociologists, and others who concern themselves with the behavioral aspects involved, view hacking as mere computer addiction. Those suffering from the malady are regarded as being socially inept and unable to form a peer group through any medium other than that provided by the remoteness and abstraction of computing.

In their book *The Hacker's Dictionary*, authors Raymond et al. have outlined at least seven different definitions of a hacker:

1. A person who enjoys learning the details of computer systems and how to stretch their capabilities, as opposed to most users of computers, who prefer to learn only the minimum amount necessary.

2. One who programs enthusiastically or who enjoys programming rather than just theorizing about programming.

3. A person capable of appreciating *hack value*.

4. A person who is good at programming quickly.

5. An expert on a particular program or one who frequently does work using it or on it.

6. An expert of any kind.

7. A maliciously inquisitive meddler who tries to discover information by poking around. For example, a *password hacker* is one who tries, possibly by deceptive or illegal means, to discover other people's computer passwords. A *network hacker* is one who tries to learn about the computer network (possibly to improve it or possibly to interfere) (Neumann, 1984).

It is beyond the scope of this chapter to provide an exhaustive list of definitions of hacking and their associated behaviors. Although we attempt primarily to address those issues that most clearly pertain to ethics, this may involve covering incidents in all of the aforementioned categories. Hence, for our purposes, *hacking* is any computer-related activity that is not sanctioned or approved of by an employer or owner of a system or network. We must distinguish it, however, from software piracy and computer crime, where the primary issue is the right of information ownership and the use of computer systems to perpetrate what, in any other arena, would simply be regarded as monetary theft or fraud. To some extent, this definition is rather broad and post hoc. Nevertheless, such a definition provides us with a rich load of cases and events that are very much at the heart of ethical issues in computing.[2]

---

[2]Interested readers can find a much more detailed account of hacking in Hafner and Markoff's *Cyberpunk: Outlaws and Hackers on the Computer Frontier* (1991). The authors provide a very readable account of major hacking cases with a rich background on the individual hackers.

1.2. Why Do Hackers Hack?

There are probably as many answers to the question of why hackers hack as there are different forms of hacking. Clearly, some amount of intellectual challenge may be involved. Rather like solving an elaborate crossword, guessing passwords and inventing means of bypassing file protections pose intriguing problems that some individuals go to enormous lengths to solve (Gill, 1987). In other cases, hacking involves acts of vengeance, usually by a disgruntled employee against a former employer. For others, hacking represents a lifestyle that rests on social inadequacy among otherwise intellectually capable individuals—the so-called "computer nerd syndrome," which particularly affects male adolescents between the ages of 14 and 16. These individuals tend to be self-taught, enjoy intellectual games, are not sexually active, and perhaps even neglect personal hygiene (Raymond, 1991). Indeed, a case of "computer psychosis" has even been reported in Copenhagen, Denmark. Apparently the young man concerned became so mesmerized by his computer that he was unable to distinguish between the real world and computer programs; he talked in programming language when carrying out ordinary everyday tasks (SEN, 1987).

For psychologists such as Sherry Turkel of MIT, hackers are individuals who use computers as substitutes for people because computers do not require the mutuality and complexity that human relationships tend to demand. Other researchers at Carnegie-Mellon University have provided evidence that partially supports this view: Sara Kiesler and her coworkers have investigated the social psychology of computer-mediated communication and found that this medium removes status cues (such as sitting at the head of the table) and body language (nods, frowns, etc.), and provides a kind of social anonymity that changes the way people make decisions in groups. Their investigations into computer conferencing and electronic mail showed that group decision-making discussions using this medium exhibited more equal participation and a larger coverage of issues (Kiesler, Siegel, and McGuire, 1984).

However, despite this benefit, the limited bandwidth of the computer screen (i.e., its lack of feedback in the form of body language, etc.) often has caused users to seek substitutes for physical cues. For example, in the absence of any other (nonverbal) mechanisms to communicate their emotions, electronic mail users often substitute depictions of their face to represent how they are feeling or how their message should be interpreted. The following keyboard characters are often used to represent a smile, a wink, and a sad face, respectively (view them sideways):

|:-) |;-) |:-(

Hence, the form of communication that computers require, even when communicating with other human beings, may be attractive to those who feel less competent in face-to-face settings, where the subtleties of voice, dress, mannerisms, and vocabulary are mixed in complex ways. Those who are less skilled in dealing with these sources of information therefore may retreat to more concrete and anonymous forms of interaction with a machine, and those who are limited by these communication modes attempt to extend them to incorporate more naturalistic features of communication when dealing remotely with other human beings.

In contrast to this, other commentators, such as Professor Marvin Minsky of MIT, have argued that there is nothing very special about hackers: They are simply people with a particular obsession that is no different from that of old-style "radio hams" or those addicted to certain sports, hobbies, cars, or any other popular kind of fascination (Robotham, 1989).

Yet this view ignores a very important difference between, say, an addiction to TV sports and an addiction to computers, particularly if the latter takes a malicious form. The amount of damage the TV sports enthusiast can cause is likely to be minimal, whereas hacking in its most malicious forms retains the potential to cause massive damage and perhaps even loss of life. The hypothetical scenarios presented in the introduction to this chapter depict some quite feasible applications of malicious hacking. Indeed, the power that we invest in computer systems sets them apart from conventional systems. This capability, allied with the remote and abstract nature of computing, provides the potential for individuals to cause massive damage with little understanding of the enormity of their acts, because the consequences are not fed back to the perpetrators in any meaningful way, and especially not in any form that emphasizes human costs.

Although this fact may contradict popular stereotypes about hackers, by far the greatest amount of hacking involves very little intellectual challenge or great intellectual ability ("NASA Hackers," 1987). Certainly, some system penetrations or hacks display incredible ingenuity. But, for the most part, hacking relies on some basic principles: excessive determination on the part of the hacker and reliance on human fallibility. For example, when faced with a new unpenetrated system, the most common form of attack is to guess passwords, because there is an amazing lack of variation in the kinds of passwords that users choose.

In addition, many systems have guest accounts that are used for display purposes, and these often have the log-in name "guest" with the same word used as a password as well. To assist their chances of penetrating a system, hackers often scan the waste baskets of computer centers looking for password clues, or they may attend computer exhibitions hoping to look over the shoulder of someone logging on to a remote system. The details of successful or partially successful penetrations are often listed on computer bulletin boards (electronic notice boards for posting and circulating information), and this information allows other hackers to further penetrate a system or to cooperate in exhausting the possible mechanisms for unauthorized entry.

Most hackers use only a small suite of equipment: generally a modem, a personal computer (PC), and some communications software. The modem converts digital pulses from the computer into analog (continuous) signals of the kind that the telephone network uses. Once on the telephone network, the PC is able to communicate with almost any machine that has a dial-in line—that is, a phone line that also has a modem connected to it. Once the hacker's modem has connected to the target machine's modem, both devices convert the analog phone signals back to digital ones and allow communication to proceed. Generally, the communications software that the hacker uses provides high-quality emulation of a range of popular terminal types (such as DEC's VT52 or VT100), and sometimes such packages have a number of built-in features that aid the hacker.

For example, some communications packages autodial telephone numbers within a particular numeric range. Thus, while the hackers sleep, watch TV, or whatever, their computers can target a particular region or suburb (where a large computer installation is believed to exist) by dialing all the numbers in that region until a computer is identified. Undoubtedly, a large number of these calls are answered by humans or facsimile machines, but every so often the carrier tone of a computer's modem is identified and the hacker can later begin work on gaining access to that system. Furthermore, if the calls are charged to a stolen credit card number or a telephone account (such numbers are freely circulated on many hacker bulletin boards), the hacker can make thousands of calls at no personal cost.

Yet, apart from guessing passwords, there are very few ways in which a hacker can penetrate a system from the outside, although the stereotyped passwords that many people use often maximize a hacker's chances of discovering a legitimate user name and password combination. Despite such flukes, most system penetrations are abetted by some form of inside assistance.

For example, a common trap in university computer laboratories is to leave a terminal switched on, waiting for an unwary user to log on to the system. In some cases, the terminal may still be running a program from the previous user that simulates a log-on procedure, thereby capturing the user's log-on name and password. The log-on procedure then aborts with the usual failure message, and normally such users assume that they made an error when typing in their password and try again. Unfortunately for these users, although the terminal appeared to be idle, the program already running on it captures their log-on details and then shuts down, so that the real system log-on procedure appears. Given the closeness of this sequence of events to a very common log-on error (everyone at some stage makes mistakes in logging on) and given some amount of naivete, in most instances it is unlikely that many users even suspect that they have been duped. Then, using the ill-gotten log-on name and password, the hacker can enter the system, thereby gaining full access to the data and programs of the legitimate user.

Indeed, some insider knowledge or partial access has proved to be an important part of the most spectacular break-ins that have occurred in recent years. For example, in 1986 a series of break-ins occurred at Stanford University in California. These were made possible by certain features of the UNIX operating system (one of the most popular operating systems in academic computing) as well as by the laxness of the systems programmers administering these systems (Reid, 1986). The weaknesses included the networking features of certain versions of UNIX and the fact that this operating system often allows users to log on using a guest account (usually with the same password, "guest"). Once into the first system, hackers were able to impersonate other users (again, knowing a couple of the classic weaknesses of UNIX) and gain access to other machines in the network that these same users had legitimate access to. The well-publicized hack carried out by Mathias Speer in 1988, in which he penetrated dozens of computers and networks across the world, also used many of these techniques to cross from machine to machine and from network to network.

In other cases, system and network inadequacies can sometimes be exploited to obtain access. For example, a persistent hacker sometimes can grab a line with legitimate privileges after a legitimate user has logged out. This can happen if the log-out sequence has not yet completed, so that the line the legitimate user has relinquished has not yet been hung up. If the hacker happens to log onto the system in those few microseconds, it is sometimes possible to grab the line and job of the legitimate user, who, more often than not, is preparing to walk away from the terminal ("More on Nonsecure Nonlogouts," 1986).

For those who are interested in further details of the techniques that hackers use, a particularly clear and comprehensive guide can be found in Hugo Cornwall's book, *Hacker's Handbook III*. Cornwall not only provides a potted history of hacking in the United Kingdom but also describes the principles of digital communication, radio transmissions, and datastreams. Another book that had a wide impact was Bill Landreth's *Out of the Inner Circle*. Landreth was a key figure in the legendary hacker group known as the Inner Circle. Some press articles have reported Landreth's disappearance, amid rumors that he planned to commit suicide on his 22nd birthday and fears that others in the Inner Circle were preparing to get their revenge on Landreth because he allegedly broke their code of silence (Lowe, 1987).

1.3. Hackers: Criminals or Modern Robin Hoods?

The mass media had tended to sensationalize hacking while soundly condemning it. But there are other points of view: For example, in many instances the breaching of systems can provide more effective security in the future, so that other (presumably less well-intentioned hackers) are prevented from causing real harm (Herschberg and Paans, 1984). A good illustration of this was the penetration of British Telecom's electronic mail system in 1984 by Steven Gold and Robert Schifreen, who left a rude message in the Duke of Edinburgh's account. This incident attracted enormous publicity and led directly to improved security arrangements for the whole of the Prestel system. Gold and Schifreen, therefore, were extremely indignant at being treated as criminals, and their attitude illustrates once again the discrepancy between what the law considers to be criminal behavior and how hackers perceive themselves. Although Gold and Schifreen were convicted under the Forgery Act and fined £2,350, an appeal saw the charges quashed. It was argued that because the hackers caused no damage and defrauded no one, they could not be held guilty of an offense ("Hacking Away," 1988; "Hackers Found Guilty," 1986; "Lords Clear British Hackers," 1988; "Hackers Appeal," 1989).

More recently, the U.K.-based National Westminster Bank and the merchant bank S.G. Warburg met with a number of hackers to discuss arrangements for these computer experts to test the banks' security systems. Using the American idea of a "tiger team"—putting hackers in a controlled environment and pitting them against the existing security—the banks hoped to identify their weaknesses and also to gain inside information from the hackers about what was happening in the hacking community and where potential threats might come from (Warren, 1990).

We might ask ourselves whether, for the sake of balance, a truly democratic society should possess a core of technically gifted but recalcitrant people. Given that more and more information about individuals is now being stored on computers, often without their knowledge or consent, is it not reassuring that some citizens are able to penetrate these databases to find out what is going on? Thus, it could be argued that hackers represent one way in which we can help to avoid the creation of a more centralized, even totalitarian, government. This is one scenario that hackers openly entertain. Indeed, we now know that at the time of the Chernobyl disaster, hackers from the West German Chaos Computer Club released more information to the public about developments than did the West German government. All of this information was gained by illegal break-ins carried out by government computer installations.

Given this background and the possibility of terrorist acts becoming increasingly technologically sophisticated, perhaps we also can look to hackers as a resource to be used to foil such acts and to improve our existing security arrangements. To some extent, this development is already happening: In the United States, convicted hackers are regularly approached by security and intelligence organizations with offers to join them in return for amelioration or suspension of sentence. Other hackers have used their notoriety to establish computer security firms and to turn their covertly gained knowledge to the benefit of commercial and public institutions (Caseby, 1989; Peterzell, 1989; "Open Season," 1989).

Perhaps we should recognize that in a fair and open society there is a tension between the capabilities of government and the capabilities of individuals and groups of concerned citizens. As the communications theorist Harold Innes stated in the 1930s, in terms of information control, there is a constant struggle between centralizing and decentralizing forces. Clearly, total centralization of information poses significant problems for the rights of individuals and for the proper conduct of a democratic government.

On the other hand, total decentralization of information resources can lead to gross inefficiencies and even to the denial of services or aberrations in the quality of services provided by government. As long as this tension exists and as long as things do not become unbalanced, we can remain reasonably assured that the society we live in and the government we elect are fairly effective and equitable. Perhaps, with the advent of digital computers and telecommunications, hacking represents an expansion of this struggle into a different domain.

Admittedly, hacking has the potential to cause enormous harm by utilizing resources that have tremendous power. Yet we should not forget that there are other, equally powerful and much older ways in which similar powers can be unleashed. Leaks to the press, espionage of all kinds, and high-quality investigative journalism (such as that which uncovered Watergate and Iran Contra affair) have the power to break a government's control over the flow of information to the public and can even destroy corporations or governments that have been shown to be guilty of unethical or criminal acts.

Perhaps, therefore, the hallmark of democracy is its capacity to tolerate people of all kinds, from different ethnic backgrounds, cultural beliefs, and religions, as well as those with radically opposing political views. It remains to be seen whether hacking in all its forms will be banned as a criminal offense in most modern democracies or whether some forms of it will be tolerated. From an ethical perspective, is the outlawing of hacking equivalent to criminalizing investigative journalism (journalists have been known to bribe officials or to obtain information unlawfully)? As always, a balance must be struck between the ethical difficulties that are attached to activities such as investigative journalism and hacking, and the greater public good that may (or may not) arise from them.

Indeed, to complete the analogy, we should bear in mind that a great deal of journalism is merely malicious muckraking that can damage a government or a company much more deeply than can some simple kinds of hacking. On the other hand, we need the muckrakers: The press is the principal institution that most democracies rely upon to ensure that the people are informed and that citizens remain aware of what is being done in their name.

1.4. The Hacker Crackdown

If any trend is evident in the world of hacking—apart from its increasing incidence—then it seems to involve the creation of stiffer penalties for hacking and a tighter legal framework classifying hacking as criminal behavior. For example, in August 1990, the United Kingdom introduced the Computer Misuse Act and identified three new offenses:

1. Unauthorized access: entry to a computer system knowing that the entry is unauthorized (6 months' jail term).
2. Unauthorized access in furtherance of a more serious crime, punishable by up to 5 years imprisonment.
3. Unauthorized modification of computer material (viruses, Trojan horses, malicious damage to files, etc.), punishable by up to 5 years imprisonment (SEN, 1990b).

The first person to be jailed under this legislation was Nicholas Whiteley (the so-called Mad Hacker). Whiteley, then a 21-year-old computer operator, was sentenced to a 4-month jail term with a further 8-month suspended sentence (*The Daily Telegraph*, 1990; Diddle, 1991; "Hacking Defined as Crime," 1990; "Hacker Takes up the Challenge," 1990; "Mad Hacker," 1990).

Elsewhere, similar calls for a crackdown on hacking have reached the popular press from concerned computing professionals or victims of hacking activity, and the number of prosecutions and convictions appears to be on the increase. In Pennsylvania, two men were charged with theft of service, unlawful computer use, and criminal conspiracy over the use of university computer facilities (SEN, 1990b). In Australia, three men are currently under investigation for their role in accessing the computers of NASA, the Smithsonian Institution, Melbourne University, and universities in the United States and Europe. As part of their hacking spree, the men allegedly accessed the computer of Clifford Stoll, the Harvard University astronomer who played a key role in tracking down a group of German hackers in search of top-secret data and files. Stoll published an account of this investigation in *The Cuckoo's Egg*, and the Australians apparently left a message for Stoll: "Now the cuckoo has egg on his face" (Stoll, 1990). However, the consequences for the accused hackers could be very serious. For illegal use of Australian government computers alone, they face a possible 10-year jail sentence (Charles and O'Neill, 1990; Rucci, 1990).

In July 1992 U.S. federal agents indicted five members of the group of computer hackers known as the Masters of Disaster. The gang members—who called themselves Phiber Optic, Corrupt, Outlaw, Acid Phreak, and Scorpion—were arrested on 11 charges, including conspiracy, wire fraud, unauthorized access to computers, unauthorized possession of access devices, and interception of electronic communications. In sum, the charges allege that the group broke into telephone switching computers of several Bell systems and engaged in phone phreaking and computer tampering. It is alleged that the defendants gained access to Bell Tymenet computers and intercepted data communications on a network owned by the Bank of America. In addition, it is alleged that the gang accessed credit reporting services such as TRW, Trans Union, and Information America.[3]

Hacker cooperation seems unaffected by distance. In one noteworthy case, an 18-year-old Israeli and a 24-year-old man from Colorado jointly penetrated NASA and U.S. Defense Department computers during the Desert Storm Gulf War operation. Of even greater interest than the distance involved was the sophistication of the Israeli teenager's phone phreaking equipment and the evidence of his involvement in an international credit card forgery ring ("Arrested Israeli 'Genius'," 1991; " 'Harmless' Hacker," 1991).

In mid-1991, Scotland Yard announced that it had cracked the world's largest (a term they left undefined) computer hacking ring. Karl Strickland, an 18-year-old computer programmer from Liverpool; Neil Woods, 23 and unemployed; and Paul Bedworth, a 17-year-old student from Yorkshire, were charged under the Computer Misuse Act with offenses in at least nine countries that included making financially devastating alterations to computers at Edinburgh, Lancaster, Bath, London, Strathclyde, and Oxford universities. Scotland Yard revealed that the investigation involved eight police forces and a surveillance team from British Telecom, and that it cost U.K. and European companies millions of pounds (*Computer Talk*, 1991).

But perhaps the clearest indication of a new hard-line approach to hacking occurred in 1990 when U.S. Secret Service agents instigated a national computer fraud investigation known as *Operation Sundevil*. This operation involved 150 agents simultaneously executing 28 search warrants on 16 U.S. citizens and the seizure of 42 computer systems, including 23,000 computing disks (*Detroit News*, 1990). However, by mid-1991 it became clear that the operation had produced only one indictment as a result of a combination of lack of evidence and lack of the high-tech savvy needed for present gumshoe law enforcement officers to find such evidence (Lewyn, 1991). Two of the most publicized victims of Operation Sundevil included Craig Neidorf and Steve Jackson of Steve Jackson Games, both of whom had systems and computer-related property seized by the Secret Service as a result of various charges involving wire fraud, computer fraud, and interstate transportation of stolen property. Eventually Neidorf stood trial but was acquitted,

---

[3]Various reports form the Internet-circulated *Computer Underground Digest,* July 1992.

although he was forced to bear the $100,000 in costs incurred in making his defense (Denning, 1991).

Yet, in contrast to these growing demands to bring hackers to account, a number of commentators have argued that these law enforcement efforts are misplaced. The threat from hackers, they argue, is overblown, and the major threat to computer installations remains what it always has been—not outside intruders, but inside employees (Charles, 1990). Sociologist Richard Hollinger argues that hackers are simply the easiest target: isolated individuals pitted against massive corporate and government interests forced into a judicial system that finds it difficult to understand the offense, let alone make judgments on it. Yet, faced with the need to be seen to be doing something against the tide of "computer-related criminal activities," law enforcement officials find hackers easy, high-profile targets compared to the hidden, often forgiven, or paid-off inside computer criminals (Hollinger, 1991).

Worms, Trojan Horses, and Bombs

New terms are entering the nomenclature of computing, many of them borrowed form other domains and many of them with sinister connotations. The following definitions may assist the reader in identifying the differences and similarities among some of these terms.

Trojan Horse
A program that allows access to an already penetrated system—for example, by establishing a new account with superuser privileges. This tactic helps to avoid overuse of the system manager's (superuser) account, which may show up on system statistics. It can also refer to a program that gathers the log-in names and passwords of legitimate users so that those who already have penetrated a system can log in under a wider variety of accounts. Sometimes confused with a *trap door*, which is generally a secret entry that system designers build into their systems so that once they have left, they may gain access at any time without fear of discovery. The principle of the Trojan horse relies on successful penetration and creation of alternative entry paths.

Logic Bomb or Time Bomb
A program that is triggered to act upon detecting a certain sequence of events or after a particular period of time has elapsed. For example, a popular form of logic bomb monitors employment files and initiates system damage (such as erasure of hard disks or secret corruption of key programs) once the programmer's employment has been terminated. A simple variation on the theme is a logic bomb virus—that is, a virus that begins to replicate and destroy a system once triggered by a time lapse, a set of preprogrammed conditions coming into existence, or a remote control using the appropriate password.

Virus
A self-replicating program that causes damage—generally hard disk erasure or file corruption—and infects other programs, floppy disks, or hard disks, by copying itself onto them (particularly onto components of the operating system or boot sectors of a disk). Viruses use a variety

of strategies to avoid detection. Some are harmless, merely informing users that their systems have been infected without destroying components of the systems. Most are not benign, and identification of their creators can be virtually impossible, although some have been quite prepared to identify themselves.

Vaccine or Disinfectant

A program that searches for viruses and notifies the user that a form of virus has been detected in the system. Some are general-purpose programs that search for a wide range of viruses, whereas others are more restricted and are capable only of identifying a particular virus type. Some are capable of eradicating the virus, but there are relatively few such programs. Other forms of virus protection include isolation of the infected system(s), use of nonwritable systems disks so that viruses cannot copy themselves there, and trying out unknown software (particularly public domain software downloaded from the bulletin boards) on a minimal, isolated system.

Worm

A self-replicating program that infects idle workstations or terminals on a network. The earliest worms were exploratory programs that demonstrated the concept itself and were generally not destructive, although they often replicated to the point at which a network would collapse. The latter phenomenon was used to good effect as the basis of the science fiction book, *Shockwave Rider* by John Brunner. Worms tend to exist in memory and are not permanent, whereas viruses tend to reside on disk where they are permanent until eradicated. In addition, worms are network oriented, with segments of the worm inhabiting different machines and being cognizant of the existence of other segments in other nodes of the network. Worms actively seek out idle machines and retreat when machine load increases. Viruses (at present) have none of these capabilities.

Tempest

A term that refers to the electronic emissions that computers generate as they work. With the right equipment, these transmissions can be monitored, stored, and analyzed to help discover what the computer is doing. As would be expected, most security agencies throughout the world are interested in this phenomenon, but up to now it has not been the mechanism for any known hack. But given time, who knows?

1.5. The Virus Invasion

Software viruses are the most recent computer phenomenon to hit the headlines. Hardly a day goes by without reports of new viruses or accounts of virus attacks that have resulted in the destruction of data and the shutdown of networks.

Yet the concept of a virus is not altogether new. Its precursor—the worm—was created in the early 1980s, when computer scientists John Scoch and Jon Hupp devised a program that would spread from machine to machine, steadily occupying the idle resources of the Xerox Palo Alto Research Center's network (Scoch and

Hupp, 1982). These early worms were fairly harmless and released only at night when network traffic was low and the machines were unlikely to be used in any case. Whatever maliciousness was embedded in worm-type programs lay in their tendency to consume resources—particularly memory—until a system or network collapsed. Nevertheless, worms almost never caused any permanent damage. To rid a machine or network of a worm, all one had to do was to restart the machine or reboot the network.

The conceptualization and development of viruses had a longer gestation period. Other precursors to the virus included a number of experimental computer games, including the game program known as *Core Wars* (Dewdney, 1984, 1985). This game operates by setting aside an area of machine memory (which in the earliest days of computing was often called the *core*) as a battleground for programs to compete for territory and to attempt to destroy each other. To understand how Core Wars works and its relationship to the virus concept, we need to understand a little about the structure and nature of computer memory and Core Wars programs themselves.

To begin with, computer memory can be regarded as a series of pigeonholes or boxes in which an instruction, some data, or another memory address can be located. The following schematics represent a typical Core Wars battle:

IMP A's Turn

The letters A and B identify the location of the two combatants. The contents of address 2 in the preceding schematic is a machine code instruction that is a Core Wars program called *IMP*. Address 5 also contains an IMP program—the first IMP's adversary. (There are many kinds of Core Wars programs; IMP is among the simplest, but also one of the most powerful.) The battle proceeds like this: It is IMP A's turn and its program is executed: MV01 (the IMP program) means "move the contents of an address that is 0 addresses away (that is, the current address, address 2) into an address that is 1 address away" (that is, address 3). Essentially, this instruction copies the contents of address 2 (the IMP program) to address 3. In other words, IMP A has replicated itself.

When this has been done and it is IMP B's turn, IMP A has copied itself to address 3 and IMP B moves to address 4 (by executing its own program). This state of affairs is represented below:

IMP B's Turn

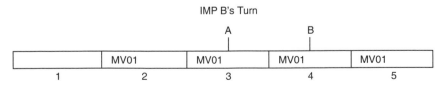

When it is IMP A's turn again, it already occupies address 3 (as well as its prior addresses), and IMP B occupies addresses 4 and 5. On IMP A's second turn (which we need not show here), it copies itself into address 4 (again by executing its MV01 instruction), which is where the current IMP B resides. Hence, by overwriting IMP B, IMP A has won the battle.

The bulk of Core Wars programs (and battles) are not this simple. Many of the more complex programs have facilities for repairing themselves and for totally relocating themselves in memory (i.e., evading enemy programs), and can even detect the approach of other programs by having sentinels. What is most important about Core Wars, however, and indeed this whole genre of game programs, such as the games LIFE and Wa-Tor (both games that demonstrate the evolution of "life forms" in a computer-generated environment), is their common notion of reproduction in a computer-based system.

This concept of a program reproducing itself began to fascinate many people and, in particular, the notion that a program could spread itself beyond the boundaries of a single machine or network attracted a growing interest. The acknowledged originators of the virus concept were Fred Cohen and Len Adleman (who conceived of the term *virus*). At a computer security conference sponsored by the International Federation of Information Processing in 1984, they publicly announced the results of a range of different networks and host machines (Cohen, 1984). Their experiments showed how easily isolated machines and even whole networks could succumb to simple viral forms. In fact, their experiments were so successful that they often were banned from carrying out further experiments by the administrators of various systems. Yet, despite this and other public warnings of the future threat of software viruses, the first viral epidemics took much of the computing world by surprise (Dembart, 1984; Morrison, 1986a).

By far the most obvious (and common) way to virally infect a system is to piggyback a virus onto bona fide programs so that it can be transported on storage media such as tapes, floppy disks, and hard disks. In addition, a virus can be transported via network links and electronic mail. So long as the virus either appears to be a legitimate program or is capable of attaching itself to legitimate programs (such as the operating system), then its spread to other system users and countries can be almost assured. It should be noted, though, that although most of the current crop of viruses are maliciously destructive, a number of viruses have been released that are quite harmless; these usually inform the user that the virus has only occupied a few bytes of disk space. More common viruses tend to erase the entire contents of a user's hard disk or else corrupt programs and data to the point where they are irretrievably damaged and quite useless.

Perhaps the most widely reported virus attack occurred in October 1987, when large numbers of microcomputer users throughout the United States began to report problems with their data disks. A quick inspection of the volume labels of these disks (a volume label is a user-supplied name for the disk, such as "cash flow figures") showed that they all possessed the same volume label: "© Brain." For these reasons, the identified virus is often referred to as the Brain virus or as the Pakistani Brain virus after the authors' Pakistan address, which is revealed if the boot sector of the disk is inspected. Although this virus caused some loss, procedures were soon implemented that effectively eliminated the virus. These included using only system disks that were write protected so that the virus could not copy itself from one system disk to another, as well as programs that identified an infected disk and rewrote the boot sector so that the virus was destroyed (Webster, 1989).

Shortly before Thanksgiving 1987, a further virus was discovered at Lehigh University in Bethlehem, Pennsylvania (and hence called the *Lehigh virus*). This virus appeared to be particularly malicious in that it totally destroyed a disk's contents once the disk had been copied four times. Unlike the Brain virus, which spread when an infected disk was totally copied, the Lehigh virus was much more virulent and intelligent. Once it had infected a disk, this virus checked all other disks inserted into the machine. If they were bootable (that is, if they carried a copy of the operating system on them), the virus then checked whether the disk was already infected; if it was not, the virus copied itself onto the new disk. Fortunately, the same kinds of countermeasures that were effective against the Brain virus were also effective against the Lehigh virus, and it now appears to have been eradicated (van Wyck, 1989).

And in yet another incident, Israeli PCs showed signs of viral infection in December 1987, when programs that had been run thousands of times without incident suddenly became too large to fit within available memory. This virus, which was disassembled by computer scientists at the Hebrew University of Jerusalem, exhibited a somewhat different modus operandi. It appeared to work by copying itself into memory and then attaching itself to any other program that the user might subsequently execute. The author of this virus also had been clever enough to program the virus so that it exhibited different effects over several months (almost a form of time bomb). In 1988, the virus waited 30 minutes after the machine had been booted up, then it slowed the machine down by a factor of around five, and portions of the screen would be uncontrollably scrolled. More important, though, if the date was Friday the 13th (any Friday the 13th after 1987), any program that was executed was erased from the disk. It was soon found that the virus was extremely widespread in both the Jerusalem and Haifa areas, with an estimated infection base of between 10,000 and 20,000 disks. But, once again, antiviral software was written to identify infected files and kill the virus, and another program was written to act as a sentinel, warning users if an attempt had been made to infect their disks (Radai, 1989).

Since the late 1980s, hundreds of viruses have been created and have caused varying amounts of damage around the world. In 1990, it was even reported that 10% of the computers in China had been affected by only three strains of virus (SEN, 1990a). Now internationally recognized virus guru John McAfee has placed the number of different viruses at more than 1,200, with 10 to 15 new strains being found each week (Cribb, 1992). And perhaps the worst offenders are former Eastern Bloc programmers; some Russian experts estimate that there are 300 to 400 Russian strains alone ("Russian Viruses," 1992). Many of these viruses are variations on a theme in the sense that they rely on well-understood techniques for propagating themselves and infecting systems. However, new vaccine techniques are constantly being developed, and the vaccine development industry becomes more lucrative every year as its software products attempt to immunize systems from large-scale data loss to the annoying refrains of Barry Manilow hits. Yes, the Barry Manilow virus plays "Mandy" and "Copacabana" in endless succession! ("News Track," 1992b).

Unfortunately, not all self-replicating software is so innocuous. In November 1988, a 23-year-old Cornell University computer science student, Robert Morris, devised a worm program that crippled the network connecting MIT, the RAND Corporation, NASA's Ames Research Center, and other American universities. This virus was said to have spread to 6,000 machines before being detected. In June 1989, Morris was suspended from college after having been found guilty of violating the university's code of academic integrity. The FBI also carried a 6-month investigation into this remarkable virus attack, and Morris was later charged under the Computer Fraud and Abuse Act of 1986 with unauthorized access to government computers ("Cornell Suspends Student Hacker," 1989; "Cornell Virus Suspect," 1989).

Eventually, Morris was convicted, sentenced to 400 hours of community service, and fined $10,000 (Brock, 1990). But despite the fate of Morris, other Cornell students since have been accused of using computer viruses to cause malicious damage. For example, in February 1992 sophomores David Blumenthal and Mark Pilgrim were accused of implanting infected game programs into a Stanford University public computer archive (Daniels, 1992).

Conceptually speaking, it is possible for viruses and worms to achieve much more sophisticated disruption than the cases reported so far, and it is quite likely that the next generation of software viruses will exhibit a quantum jump in intelligence and destructiveness. For example, it might be possible to develop a virus that only affects a particular user on a particular network. In other words, given sufficient technical expertise, instead of affecting all users, the virus would wait until a particular user ID executed an infected program. Then the virus would copy itself into the disk area of that user and begin to wreak havoc.

Alternatively, viruses may have a range of effects that they carry out on a random schedule, such as slowing a system down, deleting electronic mail, fuzzing the screen (which almost certainly would be attributed to a hardware problem), and encrypting files with a randomly selected encryption key (this would effectively deny users access to their own files until the key was discovered—an almost impossible task). Such strategies would delay the identification of a viral infection for an extended period, because the set of symptoms would be large and extremely variable.

At least one recent virus appears to use such a strategy. The Twelve Nasty Tricks virus generates a random number to determine which of 12 different actions to take. Its repertoire includes a low-level format of a PC's hard disk, reversing upper and lower characters in print output, eliminating the printers' line feed, blanking out the monitor, and affecting the computer's clock (Tellzen, 1990).

Even more worrying is the fact that commercially distributed software has been contaminated by viruses. In one well-publicized case, desktop publishing specialist Aldus shipped several thousand shrink-wrapped disks that were infected with the Peace virus (Jinman, 1990b). The concern generated by the advent of increasingly sophisticated and powerful viruses has prompted some notable members of the computing community to call for new computers to be fitted with antiviral protection (both in software and hardware) as a standard feature (Hoffman, 1990).

The next generation of viruses probably will be more selective, not only in whom they act upon and in the acts they carry out, but also in their objectives. This prospect raises a number of interesting questions and hypothetical scenarios. For example, could viruses be used for espionage purposes, not only infiltrating an enemy's machines to delete their files but gathering intelligence data that would be mailed back (electronically) or eventually gathered as versions of the virus filter back to the virus authors? Could viruses become another facet of military capabilities in much the same way that research into cryptography currently is? (A science fiction book has encapsulated this theme. *Softwar: La Guerre Douce* by French authors Thierry Breton and Denis Beneich depicts this scenario in pre-Glasnot days.) Given the remarkable swiftness with which new viruses appear to spread around the world, their potential uses as a weapon should not be underestimated (Hebditch, Anning, and Melvern, 1984; Rothwell, 1988).

Such speculation seems to have some foundation from reports emerging out of the Gulf war. Citing a new book, *Triumph without Victory: The Unreported History of the Persian Gulf War*, U.S. News and World Report writer Philip R. Karn claimed that U.S. intelligence agents placed a virus in one of the microchips used in a model of printer and shipped it to Baghdad via Amman, apparently with devastating effects ("Operation Virus," 1991; SEN, 1992b). Other reports indicate that the U.S. Army is very interested in the possibilities of computer viruses and has even awarded a $50,000 preliminary study to a company known as Software and Electrical Engineering (Lewyn, 1990).

Some other developments also suggest that virus warfare is not mere speculation. Already, the analogy of a computer system as an organism and a virus as an infection has been extended to incorporate the developments of virus-killing programs called *vaccines*. These programs look for virus symptoms and notify users that their systems have been infected. Some of the better vaccines seek out the virus and kill it by repairing infected files. Furthermore, just as we would expect to eliminate a virus in humans by the use of quarantine procedures, when dealing with infected systems and media these procedures work equally well.

But for many virus attacks the only solution—provided that a vaccine does not work—is to erase the hard disk as well as any other media (tapes, floppy disks) that might have come into contact with the virus (almost like burning linen and other possibly infected items). Then, clean copies of the system and backup disks are reloaded onto the hard disk. Until this is done, the computer should not be used for any other purpose and the trading of storage media is extremely unwise.

Yet perhaps the best form of defense against viruses is to make them much more difficult to write. Some experts have argued that the way to do this is to place the operating system on a read-only disk or in ROM (read-only memory composed of chips, which cannot be altered and hence infected). Other procedures include carrying out parity checks on software (basically an arithmetic calculation, such as an addition, on a file; if the calculation yields the correct result, it is unlikely that the file has been tampered with); making each copy of an operating system different in its physical layout (that is, its pattern of storage on disk); and, whenever one uses a disk for the first time, making sure that the operating system on disk matches that in memory (Dellinger, 1988).

Because of the risks that virus attacks pose to the knowledge assets of large companies and corporations, and because of their lack of experience in dealing with them, a number of security firms and consulting companies have sprung up to exploit this rich commercial niche (Schwartz and Rothfeder, 1990). Furthermore, the development of hardware forms of viruses has fueled the demand for such firms, particularly since the discovery of the device known as Big Red. This small electronic gadget is surreptitiously installed in a computer installation by an insider or commercial saboteur. Like software viruses, this device is parasitic in that it interfaces with the host computer's operating system and converts encrypted files into "invisible" ones that can be inspected easily by other users, if they know where the files are and what to look for. At least 50 Big Reds have been found in the United States, the United Kingdom, and Australia in banking and transaction-handling systems ("Local Crime Team," 1987; "What To Do," 1988).

Unfortunately, like system penetrations and computer crimes, it is often difficult to gather data on the incidence of virus attacks because these may have important consequences for share prices and investor confidence. However, a recent survey of 600 U.S. and Canadian companies and government agencies revealed that 63% had experienced at least one virus in 1991, compared to only 25% in 1990. Furthermore, 40% of these institutions had at least one virus incident in the last quarter of 1991, with networks being the most common form of propagation ("News Track," 1992a). Other independent surveys by Coopers & Lybrand Deloitte suggest that of the top 500 U.K. companies, 24% had suffered a virus attack in the last 3 years (Charlton, 1991). The U.S. National Security Agency has revealed that two thirds of the companies it surveyed had reported at least one virus in their computers and that 10% of the 600 government agencies and businesses it polled had experienced an attack sufficient to shut down 25 or more computers (Boswell, 1991).

But perhaps even more worrying is the effect that viruses may have on large, extremely complex, and potentially dangerous systems, such as those that manage air traffic control systems, hydroelectric dams, and nuclear plants. Already at least one nuclear power plant has been affected by the introduction of a computer virus. In early 1992, an employee of the atomic power plant in Ignalina, Lithuania, infected his system in the hope that he would be paid handsomely to fix the damage. As a result of the incident, both reactors were shut down and the Swedish government announced that it would pay to correct the 20 "small problems" that had emerged (SEN, 1992c).

Other potentially life-threatening virus attacks include infections in three Michigan hospitals that delayed patient diagnosis and threatened data loss and even a mix-up of patient records ("Virus Hits Hospital Computers," 1989). And like any powerful technology, viruses have been used by the mentally unbalanced to cause monumental harm. Perhaps the most serious case involved Dr. Joseph Popp, an AIDS researcher who had worked in Africa for 10 years, who distributed 20,000 infected computer disks labeled "AIDS Information" to organizations obtained from an AIDS-related mailing list. Unfortunately, Popp's mental state deteriorated to such an extent that he was unable to stand trial for his offenses (Siddle, 1991). These and other incidents have prompted calls for both preventive measures and highly responsive emergency teams who can act quickly to limit the viral damage caused to sensitive systems. One example of this is the U.S. Defense Department's Initiative in creating Computer Emergency Response Teams to fight viruses and other computer-based security threats ("Defence Departments Team up," 1990; Jinman, 1990a).

1.6. Ethical Issues Arising from Hacking

Some of the ethical difficulties associated with hacking and viruses are already quite well known; other, more hypothetical, ones have yet to emerge. With regard to hacking or system penetration, the legal position in different countries is often confusing and is sometimes contradictory. But the central issues involved in hacking remain almost universal.

When a hacker gains access to a system and rummages around in a company's files without altering anything, what damage has been caused? Has the hacker simply stolen a few cents worth of electricity? Indeed, if the hacker informs a company of its lax security procedures, is he or she creating a public benefit by performing a service that the company otherwise might have to pay for? In some countries, such as Canada, it is not an offense to walk into somebody's residence, look around, and leave, as long as nothing has been altered or damaged. Can a hacker's walk through a system be considered in similar terms?

Unfortunately, the legal basis applied to system break-ins languishes in the dark ages of real locks and doors and physical forms of information such as blueprints and contracts. Equally, the law as it applies to breaking and entering—the destruction of physical locks—and the theft of information in paper form is a poor analogy when applied to the electronic locks that modems and password systems provide and the highly mutable forms of information that computer files represent. After all, when one breaks into a system, nothing has been broken at all; hence, there is no obvious intent to cause harm. When a file has been copied or selectively viewed, what has been stolen? The information is still there. And if one happens to try out a few programs while browsing through a system, is this almost analogous to seeing someone's bicycle, riding it for a while, and then putting it back? Again, what harm has been caused, what crime has been committed? In the eyes of many hackers, only in the most trivial sense could this kind of use be considered unlawful.

On the other hand, where malicious damage of information does occur (such as the destruction of patients' records in a health administration system), then a form of criminal act clearly has occurred. The problem lies in determining the extent of the damage and the degree to which the act was premeditated. Unfortunately, in a complex and perhaps poorly understood computer system, it is quite easy to cause unintentional damage, yet it is extremely difficult to determine the extent to which the act was maliciously premeditated. In addition, for those figuring out a system for the first time, it is difficult to estimate the consequences of some acts or the extent to which a command sequence may alter the functionality of a system. Is this an example of ignorance of the law and is it equally unacceptable as a defense?

Perhaps what is central to the ethical debate regarding hacker behavior is the different conceptualizations of systems by their owners and by would-be hackers. For system owners, the system is their property (as suggested by the legal framework)—physical, touchable collections of central processors and disk drives—bought, paid for, and maintained for the use of authorized individuals to carry out authorized functions for the company's benefit. Any unauthorized person or even an authorized person who uses the system for unauthorized purposes is therefore guilty of a form of unlawful use, a criminal act in the eyes of the owners. For hackers, however, a system is an abstract resource at the end of a telephone line. It is a challenging talisman, an instrument they can borrow for a while and then return, probably without any damage done and without anybody being the wiser.

We enter a different arena, however, when we encounter acts of theft and willful damage. Clearly, the theft of credit card numbers and their circulation to other hackers are criminal acts, as is their use to obtain free telephone calls or to charge other goods and services. The destruction of information or its intentional alteration on a computer system can be regarded in similar terms. Yet, to return to our earlier point, should we regard browsing through a system as a criminal act? Perhaps the answer depends on the nature of the information and who owns it. Undoubtedly, the operators of a military installation would prosecute over any unauthorized access, even if the system were concerned with the control of the army's laundry requirements. The government and the military have the right to deny access to certain information if they believe that it is central to the nation's defense or to its continued good government. Yet, is a laundry service central to national security or good government? Once again, we encounter a familiar dilemma: Who owns this information and who should or should not have access to it?

In the private sector, we might even ask, What right does a company have to hold information on individuals and what right does it have to deny individuals access to that information? For example, many commercial institutions tap into databases that hold the credit ratings of hundreds of thousands of people. The providers of these databases have collected information from a huge range of sources and organized it so that it constitutes a history and an assessment of our trustworthiness as debtors. Who gave these companies the right to gather such information? What gave them the right to sell it (which they do, along with subscription lists, names, and addresses)? What limits are there on the consequences of this information for the quality of our lives? What rights should we have to ensure that our particulars are correct? Suppose that a hacker penetrates a system to correct the records of those who have been denied correction of incorrect data. Which of these entities—the database owners or the hacker—has committed the greatest ethical error? Or are both equally guilty?

Perhaps the final issue is that concerning information ownership: Should information about me be owned by me? Or should I, as a database operator, own any information that I have paid to have gathered and stored? On the other hand, given that the storage of information is so pervasive and that the functioning of our modern society relies on computer-based data storage, does the public have the right to demand absolute security in these systems? Finally, should some hackers be regarded as our unofficial investigative journalists—finding out who holds what information on whom and for what purpose; checking whether corporations are adhering to the data protection laws; and exposing flagrant abuses that the government cannot or will not terminate?

Many organizations in modern society claim to possess rights to the gathering and maintenance of information and its application in the form of computer-based information systems. In addition, apart form the dangers of the centralization of government power and authority, the centralization of information in powerful computer systems increases their influence in running our societies and, in turn, makes us more reliant upon them, thereby increasing their influence even further. In this milieu, the hacker represents a dangerous threat. Yet, like the corporations and institutions hackers act against, they also claim certain rights in terms of information access and ownership.

For many commentators, these issues should be resolved in the legal domain by determining the rights and responsibilities of information holders and the legal status of information and information systems. But such an approach may be too limited. Hacker activities can be deterred not only by punitive legislation but by making systems secure in the first place; that is, by making them secure in their design, in their technological implementation, and in the procedures and practices that are used in running them. And, in turn, that protection also implies inculcating security habits among employees and system managers.

There is an important role for ethics education in clearly identifying unethical practices and areas of ethical conflict. Unfortunately, the abstract nature of computing often removes it from its real-life consequences, and what appears to some to be an innocent act can cause untold harm if it goes wrong. By increasing the sensitivity of computing professionals and students to the ethical implications of their conduct, the amount of hacking might be reduced. This three-pronged approach of revising existing laws, building and running more secure systems, and sensitizing individuals to ethical issues has been advocated in more recent writings by Peter Denning and other authorities (Denning, 1990). Even representatives of IBM have spoken of the limitations of technical measures against hacking and viruses and have suggested that the greatest gains might be made in simply convincing people that high-tech high jinks are wrong ("Viruses Give Legislators a Headache," 1990).

References

"Arrested Israeli 'Genius' Saw Hacking as a Challenge." (1991, September 10). *The Australian.*

Blankensteijn, Herbert. (1991). "Dutch Phone Phreaks Dial the World for Free," *New Scientist,* 8 June, p. 19.

Boswell, Bryan. (1991, December 7). "Fired Workers Take Revenge," *The Australian.*

Breton, Thierry, and Denis Beneich. (1984). *Softwar: La Guerre Douche.* France: R. Laffont.

Brock, Ben. (1990, May 8). "'Benign' Nature of Crime Spares Hacker From Prison," *The Australian.*

Brock, Ben. (1991, April 2). "Hackers Besiege U.S. Voice-Mail," *The Australian.*

Brunner, John. (1975). *Shockwave Rider.* New York: Harper & Row.

Caseby, Richard. (1989, June 12). "Worried Firms Pay Hush Money to Hacker Thieves," *South China Morning Post.* (Reprinted from *The Times.*)

Charles, Dan. (1990, July 21). "Crackdown on Hackers May Violate Civil Rights," *New Scientist*, p. 8.

Charles, Dan. (1991). "Can We Stop the Databank Robbers?" *New Scientist*, 26 January, pp. 12–13.

Charles, Dan, and Graeme O'Neill. (1990, April 20). "Hackers Plan Revenge for Police Clampdown on Computer Crime," *New Scientist*.

Charlton, John. (1991, June 2). "Dons Confounded by Spanish Virus," *Computer Talk*.

Cohen, Fred. (1984). "Computer Viruses: Theory and Experiments." In: J. H. Finch, and E.G. Dougall, eds., *Computer Security: A Global Challenge*. North Holland: Elsevier, pp. 143–157.

Computer Talk (1991, July 8).

"Conclusion of the HBO Captain Midnight Saga." (1986, October). *Software Engineering Notes*, Vol. 11, No. 5, pp. 24–25.

"Cornell Suspends Student Hacker." (1989, June 12). *Computing Australia*.

"Cornell Virus Suspect Suspended for Violation." (1989, June 6). *The Australian*.

Cornwall, Hugo. (1988). *Hackers Handbook III*. London: Century Hutchinson Limited.

Cribb, Julian. (1992, February 12). "Computer Virus Due to Strike in March," *The Australian*.

The Daily Telegraph (UK). (1990, June 8).

Daniels, Lee A. (1992, February 25). *The New York Times*.

"Defence Departments Team up for Virus/Hack War." (1990, November). *Computing Australia*.

Dellinger, Joe. (1988, January). "Virus Protection Strategies," *Software Engineering Notes*, Vol. 13, No. 1.

Dembart, Lee. (1984, November). "Attack of the Computer Virus." *Discover*, pp. 90–92.

Denning, Dorothy. (1991, March). "ATE vs. Craig Neidorf," *Communications of the ACM*, Vol. 34, No. 3, pp. 23–43.

Denning, Peter, ed. (1990). *Computers Under Attack: Intruders, Worms and Viruses.* New York: ACM Press/Addison-Wesley.

Dewdney, A. K. (1984, May). "Computer Recreations," *Scientific American*, pp. 14–19.

Dewdney, A. K. (1985, March). "Computer Recreations," *Scientific American*, pp. 14–19.

Detroit News. (1990, May 10).

Diddle, Richard. (1991, April 8). "Freed Hacker in Lords Quest," *Computer Talk*.

"Enter the Technically-Competent Terrorist." (1986, April 8). *The Australian*.

Gill, Stuart. (1987, October 16). "Hi-Tech's Hubcap Thieves Are in it for the Buzz," *Computing Australia*, pp. 33–34.

"Hacker Takes up the Challenge and Pays." (1990, June 4). *Computer Australia*.

"Hackers Appeal on Prestel Conviction." (1989, September 18). *Computing Australia*.

"Hackers Found Guilty After Cracking Duke's Code. (1986, April). *The Australian*.

"Hacking Away at Security." (1988, January). *The Australian*.

"Hacking Defined as Crime." (1990, July 16). *Computing Australia*.

Hafner, Katie, and John Markoff. (1991). *Cyberpunk: Outlaws and Hackers on the Computer Frontier.* New York: Simon & Schuster.

" 'Harmless' Hacker under Jail Threat." (1991, October 7). *Computer Talk.*

Hebditch, David, Nick Anning, and Linda Melvern. (1984). *Techno–Bandits.* Boston: Houghton Mifflin.

Herschberg, I. S., and R. Paans. (1984). "The Programmer's Threat: Cases and Causes." In: J. H. Finch and E. G. Dougall, eds. *Computer Security: A Global Challenge.* North Holland: Elsevier, pp. 409–423.

Hoffman, Lance J., ed. (1990). *Rogue Programs: Viruses, Worms, and Trojan Horses.* New York: Van Nostrand Reinhold.

Hollinger, Richard. (1991). "Hackers: Computer Heroes or Electronic Highwaymen?" *Computers and Society*, Vol. 21, No. 1, pp. 6–16.

Jinman, Richard. (1990a, May 29). "Army Makes No Secret of Strong Need for Security." *The Australian.*

Jinman, Richard. (1990b, June 5). "US Author Attacks Virus Spread Theory," *The Australian.*

Kiesler, Sara, Jane Siegel, and Timothy McGuire. (1984). "Social Psychological Aspects of Computer-Mediated Communication," *American Psychologist*, Vol. 39, No. 10, pp. 1123–1134.

Landreth, Bill. (1985). *Out of the Inner Circle: A Hacker's Guide to Computer Security.* Bellevue: Microsoft Press.

Levy, Steven. (1985). *Hackers: Heroes of the Computer Revolution.* New York: Doubleday.

Lewyn, Mark. (1990, July 23)."Killer Viruses: An Idea Whose Time Shouldn't Come," *Business Week.*

Lewyn, Mark. (1991, April 22). "Why the 'Legion of Doom' Has Little Fear of the Feds," *Business Week*, p. 62.

Lewyn, Mark. (1992, July 13). "Phone Sleuths Are Cutting off the Hackers," *Business Week*, p. 90.

"Local Crime Team Crack the Riddle of Big Red." (1987, April 14). *The Australian.*

"Lords Clear British Hackers." (1988, April 28). *New Scientist.*

Lowe, Peter. (1987, February). "Still No Trace of High-Profile Hacker Author," *The Australian.*

"Mad Hacker Jailed in UK Legal First." (1990, June 12). *The Australian.*

"More on Nonsecure Nonlogouts." (1986, October). *Software Engineering Notes*, Vol. 11, No. 5.

Morrison, Perry. (1986a, March–April). "Computer Parasites: Software Disease May Cripple Our Computers," *The Futurist*, Vol. 20, No. 2, pp. 36–38.

Morrison, Perry. (1986b). "Limits to Technocratic Consciousness: Information Technology and Terrorism as Example," *Science, Technology and Human Values*, Vol. 11, No. 4, pp. 4–16.

"NASA Hackers Weren't as Smart as It Seems." (1987, July 13). *Computing Australia.*

Neumann, Peter G. (1984, January). *Software Engineering Notes*, Vol. 9, No. 1, pp. 12–15.

"News Track." (1992a, February). *Communications of the ACM*, Vol. 35, No. 2, p. 12.

"News Track." (1992b, June 6). *Communications of the ACM*, Vol. 35, No. 6, p. 10.

"Open Season for Hackers." (1989, September 18). *Computing Australia.*

"Operation Virus." (1991, November 18). *The Australian.*

Peterzell, Jay. (1989, March 20). "Spying and Sabotage by Computer," *Time.*

Radai, Yisrael. (1989). "The Israeli PC Virus," *Computers and Security*, Vol. 8, pp. 111–113.

Raymond, Eric S., ed, and Guy L. Steele, Jr. (1991). *The New Hackers Dictionary.* Cambridge, MA: MIT Press.

Reid, Brian. (1986, October). "Lessons from the UNIX Break-ins at Stanford," *Software Engineering*, Vol. 11, No. 5.

Robotham, Rosemarie. (1989, January 31). "Putting Hackers on the Analyst's Couch," *The Australian*, pp. 30–34.

Rothwell, Nicholas. (1988, June 4). "Computer AIDS: The Hitech Disease That is Spreading Worldwide," *The Weekend Australian*.

Rucci, Michelangelo. (1990, March 27). "Vic Pair Hacked into Top US Sites," *The Australian*.

"Russian Viruses in Global Epidemic." (1992, November 2). *The Australian*.

Scoch, J. F., and J. A. Hupp. (1982). "The Worm Programs—Early Experiences with Distributed Computation," *Communications of the ACM*, Vol. 25, No. 3, pp. 172–180.

Schwartz, Evan I., and Jeffrey Rothfeder. (1990, August 6). "Viruses? Who You Gonna Call? 'Hackbusters,' " *Business Week*, pp. 48–49.

Siddle, Richard. (1991, December 9). "U.S. Virus Creator Unfit for Trial," *Computer Talk*.

Software Engineering Notes. (1987, October). Vol. 12, No. 4, p. 9.

Software Engineering Notes. (1988a, January). Vol. 13, No. 1, p. 7.

Software Engineering Notes. (1988b, October). Vol. 13, No. 4, p. 14–16.

Software Engineering Notes. (1990a, January). Vol. 15, No. 1, p. 13.

Software Engineering Notes. (1990b, October). Vol. 15, No. 5, p. 12.

Software Engineering Notes. (1991, January). Vol. 16, No. 1, pp. 13.

Software Engineering Notes. (1992a, April). Vol. 17, No. 2, p. 15.

Software Engineering Notes. (1992b, April). Vol. 17, No. 2, p. 17.

Software Engineering Notes. (1992c, April). Vol. 17, No. 2, p. 19.

Stoll, Clifford. (1990). *The Cuckoo's Egg.* New York: Doubleday.

Tellzen, Roland. (1990, May 29). " 'Malicious' New Strain of Viruses the Next Threat," *The Australian*.

Thomas, Jim, and Gordon Meyer, eds. (1992, July 11). "MOD Busts in New York," *Computer Underground Digest*.

van Wyck, Kenneth R. (1989). "The Lehigh Virus," *Computers and Security*, Vol. 8, pp. 107–110.

"Virus Hits Hospital Computers." (1989, March 27), *Los Angeles Times*.

"Viruses Give Legislators a Headache." (1990, March 13). *The Australian*.

Warren, Peter. (1990, October 22). "Unholy Alliance," *Computer Talk*.

Webster, Anne. (1989). "University of Delaware and the Pakistani Virus," *Computers and Security*, Vol. 8, pp. 103–105.

"What To Do About Computer Viruses." (1988, December 5). *Fortune*, p. 16.

Chapter 2: The Conceptual and Moral Landscape of Computer Security

Herman T. Tavani

What is *computer security?* What kinds of moral issues arise because of security concerns involving computers? This chapter[1] addresses both questions, beginning with an analysis of the concept of computer security. Following a brief examination of some standard computer security definitions, I propose a comprehensive definition that takes into account three distinct kinds of security concerns affecting computers: data security, system security, and network security. Next, I examine aspects of computer security that are frequently associated with crime and privacy in cyberspace. In particular, I try to show how these concepts overlap and intersect at some points, but are also distinguishable in other respects. I then examine moral aspects of computer security, identifying some of the moral issues that arise in the context of security in cyberspace. In the final section, I examine two kinds of moral dilemmas affecting computer security, one having to do with hacker break-ins intended either to accomplish some good or prevent some harm, and another involving counterhacking activities aimed either at thwarting off or preempting hacker attacks. I conclude by showing why both kinds of dilemmas are difficult to resolve.

2.1. The Concept of Security in a Computing Context

As in the case of many concepts associated with computers and cybertechnology,[2] *security* has no universally agreed upon definition. Until we try to define it, we might assume that the concept of computer security is fairly clear and unam-

---

[1] In composing this chapter, I have drawn from material in the first and second editions of my book *Ethics and Technology: Ethical Issues in an Age of Information Communication Technology* (Hoboken: John Wiley & Sons, 2004, 2007). I have also drawn from material in five additional works: Tavani (2000a, 2000b, 2004, 2006) and Spinello and Tavani (2004).

[2] I use *cybertechnology* to refer to a wide range of computing/information and communication technologies that include stand-alone computers, privately owned computer networks, and the Internet itself (Tavani, 2004).

biguous. The notion of security in computing contexts is often associated with concerns involving availability, reliability, integrity, and so forth.[3] Sometimes concerns involving computer security are also examined vis-à-vis privacy issues.[4] However, few definitions of computer security capture the wide range of concerns involving security in cyberspace.

According to Garfinkel and Spafford (1996), a computer is secure when two conditions are satisfied: (a) you can depend on it, and (b) its software behaves as you expect. Kizza (2003), however, believes that three elements comprise computer security: *confidentiality*, *integrity*, and *availability*. He notes that "confidentiality," in computer security contexts, aims at protecting information from unauthorized disclosure, while "integrity" is concerned with preventing unauthorized modification of files. "Availability" can be understood as preventing unauthorized withholding of information from those who need it when they need it.

Both Kizza's and Garfinkel and Spafford's classic definitions identify key aspects of computer security, but neither captures the full range of concerns. Garfinkel and Spafford's definition attends to aspects of security involving dependability and reliability, but it does not specifically address concerns involving data integrity and confidentiality. Kizza's definition, on the contrary, captures the role that security plays in preserving the confidentiality and integrity of data, but it says little about the roles of dependability and reliability, especially with respect to the critical roles each can play in protecting systems and networks from attacks by what some security analysts refer to as "programmed threats" (e.g., Spafford et al., 1989) and others call "malicious programs."

I believe that an adequate definition of computer security needs to account for three distinct kind of vulnerabilities: (1) unauthorized access to *data*, which can reside in or be exchanged between computer systems; (2) attacks on *system resources* (hardware and software systems), and (3) attacks on *computer networks*, including privately owned networks as well as the Internet itself, which can include vandalism and cyberterrorism (Spinello and Tavani, 2004; Tavani, 2007). We refer to the first of these three categories of security concerns as "data security," the second as "system security," and the third as "network security." We briefly describe some security concerns associated with each category.

2.1.1. Data Security and the Integrity of Information

Data security aims at protecting information against unauthorized access. It is also concerned with ensuring the *integrity* of data, which either can be stored as electronic records in proprietary databases or can be exchanged between computers, as in the case of e-mail communications. As we will see in Section 2.2.2, concerns

---

[3] Another notion that is frequently discussed in security contexts is "risk" and "risk assessment." However, we do not examine this concept in the present chapter. For some excellent discussions of risk analysis as it relates to computer security, see Gotterbarn (2004) and Schneier (2000).

[4] In this sense, security is very much like privacy, which is also a very elusive concept that defies a clear and universally agreed upon definition. We examine some similarities and differences between security and privacy in Section 2.2.

involving data security sometimes overlap with concerns about confidentiality and privacy in cyberspace.[5]

Describing some of the key elements involved in ensuring the integrity of data, Spinello (2000) argues that integrity requires that "information being transmitted is not altered in form or content and cannot be read by unauthorized parties." This information is often either proprietary or sensitive; whereas proprietary information is legally protected and thus "owned" by corporations or by individuals, sensitive information includes personal medical and financial records that are generally considered to be intimate or confidential in nature. Spinello also notes that to ensure integrity, "all information being disseminated or otherwise made accessible through Web sites and on-line data repositories is as accessible and reliable as possible." In other words, the information must be secured from tampering and alteration by unauthorized parties. Spinello also points out that the information must be readily accessible to authorized parties. Moreover, this information, which can reside in a computer database or in a password-protected Web site, must be available on demand to authorized users.

2.1.2. System Security and the Vulnerability of System Resources

System security aims at protecting against a cluster of vulnerabilities involving computer systems themselves. These include vulnerabilities to attacks directed at a computer system's resources, such as its operating system software, applications programs, disk drives, and so forth. Specifically, the focus of system security is on providing measures that protect against a computer system's vulnerability to the kinds of damage and destruction caused by programmed threats such as viruses and worms.

How can viruses and worms be distinguished? Rosenberg (1997) defines a computer *virus* as a "program that can insert executable copies of itself into programs." He distinguishes a virus from a *worm*, which he defines as a program or program segment that "searches computer systems for idle resources and then disables them by erasing various locations in memory." Power (2000) differentiates between a virus and a worm in the following way: A *virus* is a "program that can 'infect' other programs by modifying them to include a possibly evolved copy of itself." A *worm*, on the other hand, is an "independent program that replicates from machine to machine across network connections often clogging networks and information systems as it spreads." [6]

The names of certain notorious worms and viruses, such as the *Michelangelo*, *Melissa*, and *ILOVEYOU* viruses, have become have become familiar to many users.

---

[5]For a discussion of some similarities and differences between issues involving data security and on-line privacy, see Tavani (2000a).

[6]Some security analysts suggest that worms and viruses can be further differentiated by pointing out that the former are generally less virulent than the latter. For example, they note that worms often do less harm to computers than viruses, and that some worms can be destroyed or eliminated by turning off and rebooting an infected machine. However, worms can also spread more quickly than viruses. Unlike worms, viruses are not typically able to run on their own, but instead are inserted into other programs. In many cases, viruses are activated when an unsuspecting user opens an e-mail attachment.

Some security analysts suggest that we can further differentiate categories of disruptive programs to include *Trojan horses*, *logic bombs*, and *bacteria*.[7] Thus, it seems that distruptive programs can take many forms. However, not all security experts care about the nuances of such distinctions and subtleties when it comes to understanding and responding to these various programmed threats that disrupt system software. Following Branscomb (1990), we can refer to all flavors of programmed threats, including the various forms of worms and viruses, simply as "rogue computer programs," and we can refer to those who write them as "computer rogues."

2.1.3. Network Security and the Threat of Cyberterrorism

Network security aims at securing computer networks—from privately owned computer networks (such as LANs and WANs) to the Internet itself—against cyberattacks that are designed to disrupt the flow of information. In recent years, the Internet's infrastructure, consisting of the set of protocols that makes communication across individual computer networks possible, has been the victim of several cyberattacks. Through the launching of various kinds of rogue computer programs, some computer rogues (from malicious hackers to individuals who claimed their intentions were benign) have severely disrupted activities on the Internet. In some cases, they have also have rendered the Internet inoperable. In 1988, users realized how vulnerable the Internet was to these kinds of attacks when Robert Morris unleashed a program, later described as the "Internet worm," that brought activity on the Internet to a virtual standstill. Since then, numerous Internet disruptions caused by various kinds of rogue computer programs have occurred.

Recent concerns about protecting computer networks have included worries related to *cyberterrorism*, which Denning (2004) defines as the "convergence of cyberspace and terrorism."[8] In 2002, the U.S. House of Representatives passed a bill (HR 3394) that expanded research on protecting computer networks from terrorist attacks. Proponents of this bill argued that because the war against terrorism needs to focus on threats other than hijackings and bombings, congressional funding should be also allocated for university research into terrorist threats involving the use of cybertechnology.

We should note that it is not always easy to determine whether a major computer network disruption is the result of the work of cyberterrorists or whether it might be due to a system failure (a failure either in the hardware or software of a computer system).[9] Thus, in some cases, it is difficult to separate acts of comput-

---

[7]While these distinctions are useful for some security experts, they are not pursued in this chapter.

[8]According to Denning, cyberterrorism refers to a wide range of politically motivated hacking activities that are intended to cause "grave harm." When successful, these activities can result in either loss of life or severe economic loss, or both.

[9]Consider, for example, an incident that occurred in January 1990, when the AT&T long distance telephone service experienced a "mysterious" power outage due to a network crash. Was this incident due to a software glitch in the programming code, or was it, as some have speculated, the first attack of cyberterrorism in the U.S.?

er hacking and "cybervandalism" from cyberterrorism.[10] We should also note that cyberterrorism, like other forms of mischief and vandalism in cyberspace, raises security issues that often overlap with concerns analyzed within the topical area of computer crime.

2.2. Security, Crime, and Privacy in the Context of Computing: Some Similarities and Differences

Sometimes issues involving computer security overlap and intersect with concerns pertaining to crime; other times they are associated with issues involving privacy. In this section, we examine some ways in which security issues can be connected with both kinds of concerns.

2.2.1. Computer Security Versus Computer Crime

In one sense, issues involving security and crime in cyberspace may seem to be so closely related that no useful distinctions between them would be worth drawing. Consider that virtually every violation of security involving computers and cybertechnology is also criminal in nature.[11] We should not assume, however, that every instance of crime in cyberspace necessarily involves a breach or violation of security.

Imagine three different kinds of computer-related crimes[12] that have no direct implications for computer security: (i) someone uses one or more stand-alone computers to make unauthorized copies of proprietary software programs; (ii) a person uses a networked computer to stalk[13] one or more individuals in cyberspace; and (iii) a pedophile uses the Internet to solicit sex with young children. Even though these activities are all criminal, and thus illegal, it is not clear that any of these crimes are the result of insecure computers.

Additionally, individuals and organizations can use cybertechnology to engage in a host of other kinds of illegal activities that are not aided by security flaws involving computers. For example, criminal activities such as distributing child pornography, trafficking in drugs, and illegal gambling can be carried out on perfectly secure computers. However, one might argue that stronger security mechanisms for computers and computer networks could help to deter would-be cybercriminals, and

---

[10]It is also sometimes difficult to separate cyberterrorism from what Manion and Goodman (2000) call "hacktivism," which is the use of computer hacking techniques to engage in political activism, including acts of civil disobedience. However, cyberterrorism goes beyond hacktivism in that it covers politically motivated actions that can result in loss of life, severe economic loss, or both (Denning, 2004).

[11]Ken Himma has pointed out that what counts as a cybercrime is determined by law, and that the law often lags behind in permitting cyber behavior. Thus it is conceivable that some new way of breaching security will be discovered that isn't covered by an existing law. So I need to stress the point that I wish only to claim that *virtually* every breach of computer security is criminal, because there could be some kind of security breach that is not yet (or perhaps will never be) explicitly covered by law.

[12]Elsewhere (Tavani, 2000b), I distinguish between "genuine" computer crimes and "computer-related" crimes. The former are crimes that can be committed only with a computer or some form of cybertechnology. In this chapter, however, I will use "computer-related crime" in a more generic sense to cover both kinds of crimes.

[13]For a discussion of whether cyberstalking should be viewed as a special kind of computer crime, see Grodzinsky and Tavani (2001). For a discussion of broader ethical implications of cyberstalking, see Grodzinsky and Tavani (2002).

that such mechanisms could help law enforcement agencies to detect criminals as they carry out their illegal activities (in "real time") in cyberspace. However, it is important to note that cyber-related crimes involving pedophilia, stalking, and pornography do not typically occur because of security flaws in computer systems.

Not only are concerns involving computer security frequently associated and identified with issues pertaining to computer crime, they are also associated (and sometimes confused) with issues involving privacy in cyberspace. We next consider some ways in which issues pertaining to security in cyberspace are different, in significant respects, from those involving privacy.

2.2.2. Security Versus Privacy

The notions of privacy and security are not always easy to distinguish, even in contexts other than computers and cybertechnology. In some cases, the two concepts overlap; in others, they intersect at various points. Consider that in the United States, for example, arguments for a right to privacy that refer to the Fourth Amendment to the Constitution have often been made on the basis of securing the person from physical intrusion in the form of unwarranted searches and seizures. Thompson (2001) believes that in the United States, many claims alleging a right to privacy are rooted in the concept of security. He further believes such claims are often better understood as arguments having to do with a "right to being secure." The idea that a privacy right involves "being secure from intrusion into one's personal space" can be traced back to Warren and Brandies' analysis of privacy in their seminal article on the right to privacy in the *Harvard Law Review*, published in 1890.

At first glance, it may not seem easy to differentiate between privacy and security issues in cyberspace. Issues affecting the two concepts are nonetheless worth distinguishing both for pragmatic and conceptual purposes. But how can we disentangle these concepts and the corresponding issues surrounding them? According to Moor (1997), privacy can be understood as an "articulation of security," which Moor defines as a *core value* and which Moor believes is essential for human flourishing in all societies. Moor also suggests that as computers insinuate themselves more and more into the fabric of our daily lives, privacy is threatened as security becomes increasingly vulnerable. So, in Moor's scheme, preserving security in a computerized world requires that we establish safeguards against privacy violations made possible by computer technology.[14]

Consider some additional ways that security concerns can be differentiated from privacy concerns. For one thing, privacy concerns involving computers and cybertechnology often arise because individuals are concerned about losing control over ways in which personal information about them that can be accessed both by individuals and organizations (especially businesses and government agencies). Some individuals and organizations have a legitimate need for that information in order to make important decisions. Concerns about cyber-related security, on the contrary, often arise because of fears held by many individuals and organiza-

---

[14]Because of this vulnerability, Moor argues for stronger privacy policies.

tions with respect to how their data could be accessed by those who have no legitimate need for, or right to, such information.[15]

In one sense, it would seem that the objectives of privacy and security complement each other. Consider that many individuals wish to control the manner in which information about them in computer databases can be accessed by others (they desire personal privacy). Securing personal information stored in computer databases, then, is an important element in helping individuals to achieve and maintain their privacy. Here, the objectives of privacy protection and security seem compatible, and possibly even complementary.

In another sense, however, the objectives of achieving privacy and security seem to be at odds with one another because of one or more tensions that also exist between these two notions. Consider that ratcheting up the level of security in computer systems can result in less privacy for users, especially those who wish to be anonymous while on-line. So in some cases, security and privacy interests conflict because the objectives and means used to protect each are opposed. At other times, the objectives—for example, those concerned with confidentiality and data integrity—are the same for both privacy and security.

2.2.2.1. Distinguishing Between Security and Privacy Violations

In March 2005, an incident occurred that can help us to think about some distinctions, as well as some overlapping concerns, involving privacy and security concerns vis-a-vis cybertechnology. According to the Dean of the Graduate Business School at Stanford University, 41 individuals applying for admission to the school's MBA Program gained unauthorized access to Stanford's admissions database. These applicants discovered a security flaw in the Apply Yourself software program used by Stanford in its admissions process. Although the applicants were able to access their electronic files, they were not able to determine whether they had been admitted to the program. Furthermore, they were able to view only their own files; they were unable to access the files of others. We can ask whether any privacy violations had occurred in this incident.

One line of defense used by some applicants who were caught in the break-ins is that they were not guilty of any privacy violations. These applicants argued that they had viewed only their own files and not those of other applicants. And some also argued that because the information in the files they viewed was about them, as individual persons, they were the legal owners of that information. Because the information at issue here pertained to these persons as individuals, does it follow that no privacy violations occurred in this incident?[16]

Regardless of whether any privacy violations had technically occurred, it is quite clear that the security of Stanford University's computer system had been breached because individuals had gained unauthorized access to information in

---

[15]Recall our discussion of "data security" in Section 2.1.1.

[16]Ken Himma has raised an interesting point with respect to this claim by noting that if the files accessed by these individuals contained information supplied by the universities, the intrusion might also involve a clear privacy violation. As Himma notes, an applicant might be entitled to information she supplies to the university, but she is not entitled to the university's thoughts about that information.

the university's database. So a security violation had clearly resulted. We should also note that, independent of whether the information residing in Stanford's database is information about individual persons (in this case the applicants to the MBA program), that information resides in a proprietary database that is not open to public access.

Perhaps an analogy in physical space can help us to reflect on some key issues in this case. Consider the case of Sam, who learns that Sally has a phone directory in her house that contains information about him. Sam breaks into Sally's house and removes a portion of a page from a phone book that he finds located on a table in Sally's kitchen. When Sally returns home, she sees that the phone directory on her table is open and that a portion of a page of the directory has been torn out. She decides to call the police, who discover that it was Sam who broke into Sally's home. Sam is then arrested on charges of breaking and entering. However, Sam argues that he has done nothing wrong because he simply removed a portion of a page in a phone book that contained personal information about him, which included his name, address, and phone number. Because the information was about Sam as a person—his personal information—Sam argues that he is the owner of this information and that he has the right to do with it as he pleases. In Sam's view, this right would include going into someone's private home, if necessary. However, neither Sally nor the police are impressed with Sam's argument. From their point of view, Sam clearly violated the law by entering Sally's home without her permission, regardless of whatever information about him happened to reside there. So in this case, a security violation has indeed occurred, irrespective of whether it could be shown that no privacy violation also occurred.

2.3. Moral Aspects of Computer Security

Thus far, our discussion has focused on aspects of computer security that are essentially descriptive in nature. For example, we have differentiated among three distinct elements or components of computer security and we have contrasted cybersecurity issues with concerns involving both crime and privacy in cyberspace. In this section, we examine some moral aspects of computer security.

First, we should define what is meant by *morality* and *moral issue*. We can begin by drawing an important distinction between the terms *ethics* and *morality*, which often tend to be used interchangeably in ordinary discourse. For our purposes, *ethics* is the study of morality. In this scheme, ethics is one perspective for studying morality (or a "moral system"), which, in turn, can be understood as a system of rules and principles.[17]

We should note that the terms *morals* and *moral values* have recently begun to take on a distinct, and arguably narrow, meaning in their popular or colloquial usage.

---

[17]These distinctions are developed more fully in Tavani (2004). There, morality is viewed as a "system" comprised of two key components: (1) rules that guide our conduct, and (2) principles and values that provide standards for evaluating the action-guiding rules. A moral system can be analyzed from multiple vantage points, three of which include legal, religious, and philosophical/ethical perspectives. However, for purposes of this chapter, our focus is on the analysis of moral issues from the vantage point of philosophical ethics.

This trend may have been influenced by the way in which members of many—though by no means all—conservative religious organizations and conservative political groups use these expressions. Often, representatives of these groups use *moral* in a very limited sense of the term, to refer almost exclusively to concerns involving reproductive and sexual issues. These concerns typically include abortion, cloning, and stem cell research, as well as issues involving gay marriage and extramarital sex. Although these issues deserve ethical analysis, they do not exhaust the list of moral concerns that warrant serious and sustained consideration (Tavani, 2006).

As many ethicists and philosophers would quickly point out, the domain of moral issues that warrant ethical analysis is much more robust than the one portrayed by some conservative thinkers and organizations. Thus we need to expand on the narrow scheme of morality used by many conservatives—a scheme that also currently tends to be reinforced, perhaps unwittingly, in the popular media.[18]

A wide range of social concerns having to do with equity of, and access to, resources also need to be identified and analyzed as *moral* issues. For example, grossly unequal distributions of wealth—and especially unequal distributions of vital human resources between and within nations—also generate moral concerns that warrant ethical analysis. However, moral issues of this type are not examined in this chapter because, like those moral issues identified by many conservatives, they are beyond the scope of computer security. I mention them here only to show the broad range of moral issues that deserve attention on the part of ethicists.

In this chapter, our focus is on moral issues that arise because of concerns involving computer security. In particular, we examine moral issues that can arise because of two different kinds of concerns affecting security in cyberspace: (1) computer systems that are not sufficiently secure, and (2) computer systems that are maximally secure. Whereas insufficiently secure systems can facilitate certain kinds of behavior on the part of some individuals that result in harm to computer users, maximally secure systems can (potentially at least) deprive ordinary individuals of autonomy and freedom.

2.3.1. Moral Issues Involving Non-Sufficiently Secure Computing Environments

Computing contexts that are not sufficiently secure enable some individuals to exploit the computer systems of others for their own ends. This behavior can result in harm to users at all levels—from individual users of personal computers to users in large organizations. We saw in Section 1 that the integrity of data and the reliability of system resources can be compromised because of inadequate computer security. Security concerns of this kind are often discussed under the general category of computer hacking. But what, exactly, is meant by the expression "hacking?" We should note that many different definitions have been put forth to

---

[18]Perhaps the media has been responsible for engendering this view because of the way it tends to describe the positions of conservative vs. liberal politicians with respect to controversial issues. When reporting on the 2004 U.S. presidential elections, for example, the media suggested that people who voted for Geroge Bush were swayed by the "moral values" argument. This description of events may unintentionally have painted candidates in both political parties inaccurately, by wrongly suggesting that (1) liberals do not care about moral values and that (2) conservatives only consider a subset of moral issues to be real moral issues.

describe "hacking," "hackers," and the "hacker ethic."[19] We should also note that the expressions "hacker" and "hacking" themselves have become emotionally charged terms,[20] influencing some computer security experts to advocate for distinctions between the following kinds of paired concepts: "hacking" and "cracking;" "hacking for fun" and "hacking for profit;" "white hat" hackers and "black hat" hackers; and so on. However, we do not pursue those distinctions here. Because our main concern in this section is with identifying moral aspects of computer security and not in differentiating many of the subtle nuances that could be articulated with respect to hacking activities, we use "hacking" in a loose sense to refer to behavior pertaining to unauthorized access to computer systems.

Why are hacking activities that involve unauthorized access, or "break-ins," to computers immoral? Many computer security experts believe that the answer is quite straightforward: Hacker break-ins, no matter how innocuous they might seem, are never harmless. Spafford (1992), in a classic essay, offers a very thoughtful and careful analysis of why this is so. Spafford puts forth a series of counterexamples to show the logical flaws in much of the rhetoric surrounding hacking activities, including hacker clichés such as "information should be totally free" and "hackers are doing computer users a favor" by breaking into computer systems to show the vulnerabilities of those computers. Although some hacker break-ins may initially seem harmless, Spafford argues that they are always unethical even if no obvious damage results. We return to Spafford's arguments for this view in Section 2.4.1.

Some of those who defend hacking activities involving unauthorized access to computer systems argue that no "real" harm results from computer break-ins because cyberspace, unlike physical space, is merely a virtual space. And because "virtual" is contrasted with "real" (as in "virtual reality" versus actual reality), no real harm results from activities that occur in cyberspace. In this scheme, it is argued that hackers, at most, are guilty only of causing virtual harm. Moor (2001) notes this kind of thinking illustrates what he calls the "virtuality fallacy."[21] Because harm occurs in virtual space, does it follow that this harm is any less real than harm occurring in physical space? For example, imagine that someone receives an offensive letter that insults her. Whether she receives this message via e-mail (in virtual space) or as a hardcopy letter in physical space, is the psychological harm she experiences any more or any less real in either space? Assuming that the content is identical in both letters, it would seem that the psychological harm experienced in both spaces will be the same.

So, it seems that activities conducted in cyberspace can indeed result in real harm to real people. And because causing (unjustified) harm to others is morally wrong,

---

[19]For some excellent discussions of this topic, see Himanen (2001), Kapor (1991), and Levy (1984).

[20]Helen Nissenbaum (2005) points out that the term hacker has been "hijacked" by the media to stand for something it did not originally mean.

[21]For a description of this fallacy, see Tavani (2004). Moor (2001) has described this fallacy in the following way: "X exists in cyberspace; cyberspace is not real; therefore, X is not real."

it follows that hacking activities involving break-ins (which involve trespass and thus are not harmless) raise moral issues. To the extent that nonsecure computers facilitate harm caused by hackers to users, computer security issues have moral implications.

2.3.2. Moral Issues Arising Because of Fully Secure Computing Environments

Whereas non-fully secure computers have moral implications because of harm that can result to users, fully secure[22] computers can raise a different set of moral concerns. In the latter case, secure computers could potentially deprive users of autonomy, freedom, and civil liberties. First, consider a key connection between issues affecting computer security and individual autonomy. To realize autonomy, individuals need to be able to have some say about—retain some control over—information about them that resides in computer databases. Computer security is essential in enabling users to realize this objective. So, secure computers seem to be critical in supporting individual autonomy. However, placing too much emphasis on preserving individual autonomy could also, unwittingly perhaps, undermine security in cyberspace. For example, certain security measures that would provide an optimal level of security for a computer system might not be implemented because of anticipated resistance from civil liberties groups who fear that individual autonomy and freedom would be compromised by those measures. Thus, a natural tension arises between security interests and issues of individual autonomy in cyberspace.

Another tension arises because of concerns about user anonymity,[23] which is closely related to issues of privacy in cyberspace. Consider that certain forms of anonymous behavior, made possible by "anonymity tools,"[24] enable users to navigate the Web without having to reveal their true identities. Although this might help to protect an individual's privacy, it also poses a potential risk for computer security. So, the cost of providing more secure computer systems may mean less (or possibly no) anonymity for individual users. Some security experts argue that concerns involving user anonymity, as well as individual freedom and autonomy, will have to yield to concerns involving public safety and security. But critics of this

---

[22]For lack of a better term, I use *fully secure* to describe computers that have been made so secure that they can negatively impact the movement of users in a system. These systems are contrasted with *non-fully secure* computers, which may be secure enough in one sense to withstand most threats but are not as completely secure as they could possibly be.

[23]For some excellent discussions of anonymity issues, see Johnson (1997), Nissenbaum (1999), and Wallace (1999).

[24]One popular anonymity tool is the *Anonymizer*. For more information about this tool, including a discussion of ethical issues surrounding anonymity tools of this type, see Tavani (2000a).

[25]These technologies enable the biological identification of a person through an analysis of one's eyes, retina patterns, fingerprints, handwritten signatures, and so forth. For some excellent discussions of tensions involving biometrics from an ethical perspective, see Brey (2004) and van der Ploeg (1999).

[26]*Encryption* is a technique used to ensure the confidentiality and integrity of information transmitted over the Internet, as in the case of e-mail communications.

position, including civil libertarians, worry about individuals being forced to give up too much freedom for the sake of security.

Some technologies that have been used to make computers more secure—for example, the use of biometric technologies,[25] encryption technologies,[26] and keystroke monitoring[27] technologies—have also raised concerns that have moral implications. Initially, the use of biometric technologies met with considerable resistance from civil liberties groups. Since September 11, 2001, however, support for the use of these technologies, especially in large public venues such as airports and sports stadiums, has increased significantly among U.S. citizens. Although biometric technologies are still perceived by many to infringe on basic civil liberties, ongoing concerns about attacks from terrorists have strongly tilted public opinion in favor of security interests versus concerns involving individual freedoms such as anonymity and privacy.

The use of encryption technologies and keystroke monitoring tools by the federal government in the United States has caused some tensions involving individual freedom and security. Law enforcement agencies use "packet sniffing" technologies such as Carnivore in their attempt to trace the movements of terrorists as well as the activities of members of organized crime syndicates. Encryption technologies such as the Clipper Chip[28] have also fueled a debate between advocates of civil liberties and proponents of computer security. Members of the former group have argued that with a technology like the Clipper Chip, the U.S. government could monitor private citizens and thus deprive them of their basic civil liberties, including a presumption of innocence.[29] Proponents of Clipper, however, argued that this technology was necessary for national security.

So, moral issues involving computer security can arise when systems are fully secure, as well as when they are insufficiently secure. Whereas the former set of concerns has to do with worries about the loss of individual freedom and autonomy that can occur when computers are maximally secure, the latter set of concerns arise because of the kinds of harm that can result from hacker activities involving break-ins.

2.4. Moral Dilemmas Involving Computer Security

In Section 2.3, we saw how moral concerns involving security arise both in fully secure and in non-fully secure computer systems. In some cases, moral *dilemmas* can also arise in the context of computer security. We briefly identify two such dilemmas, which can be expressed in the form of the following questions: (1) Is it ever morally permissible to break into a computer system, especially if doing so will prevent some harm? and (2) Is it ever morally permissible to counterhack (or "hack back") at hackers as a form of self-defense?

---

[27]*Keystroke monitoring software* is a tool that enables every keystroke entered by a user, and every character of the response that the system returns to the user, to be tracked.

[28]The Clipper Chip was a controversial encryption system proposed by the Clinton Administration in the 1990s.

[29]It is interesting to note that the critics of Clipper included groups and individuals as diverse as the American Civil Liberties Union and Rush Limbaugh.

2.4.1. Can Computer Break-ins Ever Be Justified on Moral Grounds?

Recall that Spafford (1992) argues that computer break-ins, which are never harmless, are unethical. Yet, Spafford also claims that in some—albeit highly unusual—cases, breaking into a computer might be "the right thing to do." How can Spafford defend a position that some might find contradictory—sometimes it could be right to do something that is unethical? To explain how this is possible, Spafford provides a scenario in which vital medical information that resides in a computer is needed in an emergency to save someone's life. In this scenario, those who are authorized to access the information cannot be located. Here, Spafford suggests that breaking into that computer system would be the "right thing to do," even if break-ins are unethical. If Spafford's rationale were based simply on the notion that a greater harm would result if the break-in were not carried out, his argument is then compatible with a utilitarian system of ethics.

However, Spafford does not appeal to a utilitarian argument; instead, he defends his view on deontological (duty-based or non-consequentialist) grounds. Spafford rejects utilitarianism because he believes that morality is ultimately determined by actions, not by consequences or results. He rejects theories that attempt to evaluate the morality of actions on the basis of results because we cannot "know the full scope of those results," that are part of what he describes as the "sum total of all future effect" (Spafford, 1992). So, in Spafford's scheme, the moral justification of a course of action cannot be determined on the basis of the results of the act. Elsewhere (Tavani, 2007), I have shown that Spafford's position can be defended as a variation of an ethical theory called *Act Deontology* (along the lines of an ethical framework introduced by philosopher David Ross). According to this theory, the circumstances affecting each moral dilemma have to be weighed carefully in terms of conflicting duties in order to determine the morally appropriate course of action in that situation. Although many ethicists, especially utilitarians, disagree with the strategy used by deontologists, most would agree with the conclusion that Spafford reaches in this particular case. However, some critics of Act Deontology argue that this ethical theory does not provide us with a general principle or rule for determining which kinds of extraordinary cases justify breaking into a computer.

Consider a hypotherical case involving an employee named Bill, who is about to depart on an important business flight to London, where he will represent his company at a very important business meeting. Imagine, that because of heightened security concerns affecting international travel, all business travelers are required to supply the airlines with security access codes from their employers. To board his plane, Bill needs to present a document that contains his employer's security code, which he has misplaced on the way to the airport. Bill knows that a copy of this code is also stored in a file, in a restricted area of his employer's computer database, that he is not authorized to access. He also realized that if he does not provide the security code to the flight security attendant, he cannot board the plane.

Bill tries to reach employees at his company who are authorized to access the code, but is unsuccessful. However, Bill figures out a way to break into his employer's database and to access the security code that is stored there. Should he break into the system (solely for the purpose of getting the necessary information)? Consider the consequences—the harm that can result—if he does not, but also consider the claim that no computer break-ins are harmless. If Bill misses the plane, he will be unable to attend a critical business meeting in London the next morning. If so, Bill's company could lose millions of dollars in potential revenue, that could eventually result in the demise of the company. In this case, is Bill justified in breaking into his employer's computer database to get the security code?

Because the future existence of Bill's company may turn on his decision, the dilemma that faces Bill is clearly not trivial. Can we apply Spafford's model, based on Act Deontology, here? Consider that the kind of computer break-ins that Spafford justifies affected the life of one of the individuals involved. The case involving Bill does not; is that relevant? Utilitarians and other critics would likely point out, that because no general rule or principle has been established for determining which kinds of exemptions would justify breaking into a computer, we are required to resolve dilemmas of this kind on a case-by-case basis. So it appears that the dilemma involving Bill's situations is not easily resolved.

2.4.2. Can Counterhacking Be Justified on Moral Grounds?

What, exactly, is *counterhacking* or *hacking back*—sometimes also referred to as *active defense hacking*? Are individuals and corporations ever ethically justified in "hacking back" against hackers who seek to cause harm to them? Some view counterhacking as a form of self-defense; others, however, see it as more of an instance of "two wrongs to make a right." Perhaps the most controversial form of this kind of behavior involves preemptive attacks. Some suggest that preemptive attacks could be justified on consequentialist grounds such as utilitarianism, because less overall harm would result from these attacks.

Appealing to a utilitarian justification in counterhacking activities, however, presents us with many of the same difficulties we faced in the preceding section in our attempt to arrive at a justification for computer break-ins. Perhaps another kind of ethical theory could be used to justify active defense hacking. Himma (2004) examines a line of reasoning that is based on the so-called necessity principle.[30] He points out that according to this principle, "it is morally right for one person to infringe the rights of an innocent person if doing so is necessary to achieve a greater moral good." Himma shows how, in the case of hacking back against those who engage in activities such as launching distributed denial of service (DDOS) attacks,[31] many innocent persons are adversely affected because the attacks are routed through their computer systems. Perpetrators of DDOS attacks use "host computers," which often include the computers of innocent persons, to initiate the DDOS attacks. This

---

[30]Himma begins his analysis by examining the impact for individuals and "entities" (organizations including corporations, but not governmental agencies, which are subject to different criteria). Although Himma acknowledges the point that individuals may have a right to fight back in terms of self defense, he also worries about the rights of innocent people who may have their rights violated in the process.

[31]He questions whether victims (and potential victims) of DDOS attacks are justified in "attacking back" by redirecting the attack back to the originator of the DDOS attack.

gives the victims the sense that the attacks are originating from the host computer, as opposed to the computer of the initiator of the attack. Thus, when the victim hacks back, he can unintentionally cause the intermediate computer to be assaulted by bogus requests for service.[32]

Himma rejects the justification for counterhacking based on the necessity principle, but he does not conclude that hacking back is never justified. Instead, he argues that a rationale other than the necessity principle is needed to justify hacking back on ethical grounds. Could such a rationale possibly be found in natural law theory? In the classic view of natural law theory advanced by Thomas Aquinas, it is never permissible to intentionally carry out a bad act to bring about some good. (So, initially, that might seem to rule out counterhacking.) However, it is permissible to carry out a good act, even though one foresees that some harm could result. But Aquinas's theory would be useful only if we could show that both (1) hacking back is essentially a good thing, even though some harm could result to others including innocent persons; and (2) although the harm could be foreseen, the intent was not to cause harm but to eliminate something bad.[33] However, such an argument would need to be worked out in much more detail than is described here.

Of course, other possible lines of defense for counterhacking might also be constructed. But we should note that to date, no clear or noncontroversial resolution to the dilemma involving counterhacking can be found in the computer ethics literature.

2.5. Concluding Remarks

We began this chapter by examining various definitions of computer security, and we differentiated among three distinct aspects of security in the context of computers and cybertechnology: data security, system security, and network security. Next, we showed how issues involving computer security can be distinguished from concerns associated with related topics such as crime and privacy in cyberspace. We then examined some moral aspects of computer security. We saw that whereas some moral issues arise because of harms caused by insufficiently secure computers, other issues can emerge as a result of fully secure computer systems. Finally, we examined two different kinds of moral dilemmas that can arise in the context of computer security: one having to do with hacker break-ins intended either to accomplish some good or prevent some harm, and another involving counterhacking activities aimed either at thwarting off or preempting hacker attacks. We also showed why neither kind of dilemma is easily resolved.

References

Branscomb, Anne W. (1990). "Rogue Computer Programs and Computer Rogues: Tailoring the Punishment to Fit the Crime," *Rutgers Computer and Technology Law Journal*, Vol. 16, pp. 1–6.

---

[32]Also see Dittrich and Himma (2005) for an analysis of concerns involving active defense hacking.

[33]We should note that if counterhacking is justified by either principles of self-defense or by the necessity principle, then it would not be inconsistent with Aquinas's principle.

In: D. G. Johnson and H. Nissenbaum, eds. *Computing, Ethics and Social Values*, Englewood Cliffs, NJ: Prentice Hall, pp. 89–115.

Brey, Philip. (2004). "Ethical Aspects of Facial Recognition Systems in Public Places." In: R. A. Spinello and H. T. Tavani, eds. *Readings in CyberEthics*. 2nd ed. Sudbury, MA: Jones and Bartlett, 585–600.

Dittrich, David, and Kenneth E. Himma. (2005). "Active Response to Computer Intrusion." In: H. Bidgoli, ed. *The Handbook of Information Security*. Hoboken, NJ: John Wiley and Sons.

Denning, Dorothy E. (2004). "Cyberterrorism." In: R. A. Spinello and H. T. Tavani, eds. *Readings in CyberEthics*. 2nd ed. Sudbury, MA: Jones and Bartlett, pp. 536–541.

Garfinkel, Simson, and Eugene Spafford. (1996). *Practical UNIX and Internet Security*. 2nd ed. Cambridge, MA: O'Reilly & Associates, Inc.

Gotterbarn, Don. (2004). "Reducing Software Failures: Address Ethical Risks with Software Development Impact Statements." In: R. A. Spinello and H. T. Tavani, eds. *Readings in CyberEthics*. 2nd ed. Sudbury, MA: Jones and Bartlett, pp. 674–689.

Grodzinsky, Frances S., and Herman T. Tavani. (2001). "Is Cyberstalking a Special Type of Computer Crime?" In: T. Bynum, et al., eds. *Proceedings of the Fifth Ethicomp Conference*. Vol. 2, Gdansk, Poland: Mikom Publishers, pp. 73–85.

Grodzinsky, Frances S., and Herman T. Tavani. (2002). "Ethical Reflections on Cyberstalking," Computers and Society, Vol. 32, No. 1, pp. 22–32. In: R. A. Spinello and H. T. Tavani, eds. *Readings in CyberEthics*. 2nd ed. Sudbury, MA: Jones and Bartlett, pp. 561–570.

Himanen, Pekka. (2001). *The Hacker Ethic: A Radical Approach to the Philosophy of Business*. New York: Random House.

Himma, Kenneth E. (2004). "Targeting the Innocent: Active Defense and the Moral Immunity of Innocent Persons from Aggression," *Journal of Information, Communication, and Ethics in Society*, Vol. 2, No. 1, pp. 31–40.

Johnson, Deborah G. (1997). "Ethics On-line," *Communications of the ACM*, Vol. 40, No. 1, pp. 60–69. In: R. A. Spinello and H. T. Tavani, eds. *Readings in CyberEthics*. 2nd ed. Sudbury, MA: Jones and Bartlett, pp. 30–39.

Kizza, Joseph M. (2003). *Ethical and Social Issues in the Information Age*. 2nd ed. New York: Springer-Verlag.

Levy, Steve. (1984). *Hackers: Heroes of the Computer Revolution*. Garden City, NY: Doubleday.

Manion, Mark, and Abby Goodrum. (2000). "Terrorism or Civil Disobedience: Toward a Hacktivist Ethic," *Computers and Society*, Vol. 30, No. 2, pp. 14-19. In: R. A. Spinello and H. T. Tavani, eds. *Readings in CyberEthics*. 2nd ed. Sudbury, MA: Jones and Bartlett, pp. 525–535.

Moor, James H. (1997). "Towards a Theory of Privacy for the Information Age," *Computers and Society*, Vol. 27, No. 3, pp. 349-359. In: R. A. Spinello and H. T. Tavani, eds. *Readings in CyberEthics*. 2nd ed. Sudbury, MA: Jones and Bartlett, pp. 407–417.

Moor, James H. (2001, February 21). "Just Consequentialism and Computing." Presented at the 2000–2001 Humanities Lecture Series, Rivier College, Nashua NH.

Nissenbaum, Helen. (1999). "The Meaning of Anonymity in an Information Age," *The Information Society*, Vol. 15, No. 2, pp. 141–144. In: R. A. Spinello and H. T. Tavani, eds. *Readings in CyberEthics*. 2nd ed. Sudbury, MA: Jones and Bartlett, pp. 555–560.

Nissenbaum, Helen. (2005). "Hackers and the Contested Ontology of Cyberspace." In: R. Cavalier, ed. *The Impact of the Internet on Our Moral Lives*. Albany: State University of New York Press, pp. 139–160.

Power, Richard. (2000). *Tangled Web: Tales of Digital Crime from the Shadows of Cyberspace*. Indianapolis, IN: Que Corp.

Rosenberg, Richard S. (1997). *The Social Impact of Computers*. 2nd ed. San Diego: Academic Press.

Schneier, Bruce. (2000). *Secrets and Lies: Digital Security in a Networked World*. New York: John Wiley and Sons.

Spafford, Eugene H. (1992). "Are Computer Hacker Break-Ins Ethical?" *Journal of Systems Software*, Vol. 17, pp. 41–47. In: D. G. Johnson and H. Nissenbaum, eds. *Computing, Ethics and Social Values*. Englewood Cliffs, NJ: Prentice Hall, pp. 125–134.

Spafford, Eugene H., Kathleen A. Heaphy, and David J. Ferbrache. (1989). *Computer Viruses: Dealing With Electronic Vandalism and Programmed Threats*. Arlington, VA: ADAPSO Press.

Spinello, Richard A. (2000). "Information Integrity." In: D. Langford, ed. *Internet Ethics*. London: Macmillan Publishers, pp. 158–180.

Spinello, Richard A., and Herman T. Tavani. (2004). "Security and Crime in Cyberspace." In: R. A. Spinello and H. T. Tavani, eds. *Readings in CyberEthics*. 2nd ed. Sudbury, MA: Jones and Bartlett, pp. 501–512.

Tavani, Herman T. (2000a). "Privacy and Security." In: D. Langford, ed. *Internet Ethics*. New York: St. Martin's Press, pp. 65–95.

Tavani, Herman T. (2000b). "Defining the Boundaries of Computer Crime: Piracy, Break-Ins, and Sabotage in Cyberspace," *Computers and Society*, Vol. 30, No. 3, pp. 3–9. In: R. A. Spinello and H. T. Tavani, eds. *Readings in CyberEthics*. 2nd ed. Sudbury, MA: Jones and Bartlett, pp. 513–524.

Tavani, Herman T. (2004). *Ethics and Technology: Ethical Issues in an Age of Information and Communication Technology*. Hoboken: John Wiley and Sons.

Tavani, Herman T., ed. (2006). *Ethics, Computing, and Genomics*. Sudbury, MA: Jones and Bartlett.

Tavani, Herman T. (2007). *Ethics and Technology: Ethical Issues in an Age of Information and Communication Technology*. 2nd ed. Hoboken: John Wiley and Sons.

Thompson, Paul B. (2001). "Privacy, Secrecy, and Security," *Ethics and Information Technology*, Vol. 3, No. 1, pp. 13–19.

van der Ploeg, Irma. (1999). "The Illegal Body: Eurodac and the Politics of Biometric Identification," *Ethics and Information Technology*, Vol. 1, No. 4, pp. 295–302.

Wallace, Kathleen A. (1999). "Anonymity," *Ethics and Information Technology*, Vol. 1, No. 1, pp. 22–35.

Warren, Samuel, and Louis Brandeis. (1890). "The Right to Privacy," *Harvard Law Review*, Vol. 14, No. 5, pp. 193–220.

Part 2: Hacking, Hacktivism, and Active Defense

This section explores the ethical issues associated with "hacking"—defined as "the commission of an unauthorized computer intrusion"—and considers a number of potential moral justifications for such behavior. Most people believe that the decisions they make are morally justified, and people who commit such intrusions are presumably no exception. These intrusions have been justified on a variety of different grounds. For example, people have argued that the following sorts of hacking activities are justified: intrusions that cause no harm and are motivated by simple curiosity, intrusions that are intended as acts of political activism, and intrusions that are committed in response to wrongful hacker attacks. The chapters in this section develop and evaluate these lines of argument in more detail.

The first chapter of the section is Eugene Spafford's article "Are Computer Break-ins Ethical?" In this seminal piece—perhaps the first rigorous examination of hacking rationales—Spafford considers a variety of arguments that have been made to justify garden-variety intrusions not motivated by political or defensive purposes. Spafford ultimately concludes that, while there may be situations in which an unauthorized intrusion is justified, most intrusions are morally impermissible and violate rights to property and privacy.

The second chapter considers the issue of politically motivated intrusions, or "hacktivism," as it has come to be known. Mark Manion and Abby Goodrum distinguish ordinary intrusions from intrusions that are committed as a means of protesting some significant injustice. According to Manion and Goodrum, these intrusions can be both socially useful and morally justified, provided that they are not intended to cause harm to the victim or result in financial gain to the persons committing the intrusions.

In the third chapter, Ken Himma takes up the issue of whether hacktivism is morally justified as a form of electronic civil disobedience. Himma begins the discussion with an analysis of the concepts of civil disobedience and hacktivism, and from there attempts to identify the moral principles that govern civil disobedience. While Himma argues that acts of civil disobedience are frequently justified, he points to a number of key differences between the civil rights sit-ins of the 1960s—paradigmatic instances of justified civil disobedience—and acts of hacktivism. The latter, unlike the former, are anonymous and likely to result in significant harm to parties other than the intended targets.

The fourth chapter, "The Ethics of 'Hacking Back': Active Response to Computer Instrusions," takes up the topic of active defense. Because law-enforcement agencies seem to many to be unable to protect adequately against hacker attacks, some victims respond to such attacks with intrusions of their own. These "counterhacks" or "active defense measures" are sometimes intended to stop the attacks and are sometimes intended to gather information about the attack and identity of the responsible persons. In this chapter, Ken Himma considers the question of whether and when active defense is morally permissible.

The final chapter in the section is an update of Dorothy Denning's assessment of the threat of cyberterrorism, which she presented to the Special Oversight Panel on Terrorism of the Committee on Armed Services to the United States House of Representatives. Denning's original analysis was published shortly after the terrorist attacks of September 11, 2001. The updated analysis provides a detailed assessment of the threat of cyberterrorism in a post 9/11 world.

Chapter 3: Are Computer Hacker Break-ins Ethical?

Eugene H. Spafford

Recent incidents of unauthorized computer intrusion have brought about discussion of the ethics of breaking into computers. Some have argued that as long as no significant damage results, break-ins may serve a useful purpose. Others counter with the expression that the break-ins are almost always harmful and wrong.

This chapter lists and refutes many of the reasons given to justify computer intrusions. It is the author's contention that break-ins are ethical only in extreme situations, such as a life critical emergency. The chapter also discusses why no break-in is "harmless."

3.1. Introduction

On November 2, 1988, a program was run on the Internet that replicated itself on thousands of machines, often loading them to the point where they were unable to process normal requests (Seeley, 1989; Spafford, 1989a, 1989b). This Internet Worm program was stopped in a matter of hours, but the controversy engendered by its release raged for years. Other recent incidents, such as the "wily hackers" [1] tracked by Cliff Stoll (1989), the "Legion of Doom" members who are alleged to have stolen telephone company 911 software (Schwartz, 1990), and the growth of the computer virus problem (Denning, 1991; Hoffman, 1990; Spafford, Heaphy, and Ferbrache, 1989; Stang, 1990) have added to the discussion. What constitutes improper access to computers? Are some break-ins ethical? Is there such a thing as a "moral hacker" (Baird, Baird, and Ranauro, 1987).

It is important that we discuss these issues. The continuing evolution of our technological base and our increasing reliance on computers for critical tasks suggests that future incidents may well have more serious consequences than those we have seen to date. With human nature as varied and extreme as it is, and with the technology as available as it is, we must expect to experience more of these incidents.

---

[1] I realize that many law-abiding individuals consider themselves hackers—a term formerly used as a compliment. The press and general public have coopted the term, however, and it is now commonly viewed as a pejorative. Herein, I use the word as the general public now uses it.

In this chapter, I introduce a few of the major issues that these incidents have raised, and present some related arguments. For clarification, I have separated a few issues that often have been combined when debated; it is possible that most people are in agreement on some of these points once they are viewed as individual issues.

3.2. What Is Ethical?

Webster's Collegiate Dictionary defines *ethics* as: "The discipline dealing with what is good and bad and with moral duty and obligation." More simply, it is the study of what is right to do in a given situation—what we ought to do. Alternatively, it is sometimes described as the study of what is good and how to achieve that good. To suggest whether an act is right or wrong, we need to agree on an ethical system that is easy to understand and apply as we consider the ethics of computer break-ins.

Philosophers have been trying for thousands of years to define right and wrong, and I will not make yet another attempt at such a definition. Instead, I suggest that we make the simplifying assumption that we can judge the ethical nature of an act by applying a deontological assessment: Regardless of the effect, is the act itself ethical? Would we view that act as sensible and proper if everyone were to engage in it? Although this may be too simplistic a model (and it can certainly be argued that other ethical philosophies also may be applied), it is a good first approximation for purposes of discussion. If you are unfamiliar with any other formal ethical evaluation method, try applying this assessment to the points I raise later in this paper. If the results are obviously unpleasant or dangerous in the large, then they should be considered unethical as individual acts.

Note that this philosophy assumes that right is determined by actions and not by results. Some ethical philosophies assume that the ends justify the means; our current society does not operate by such a philosophy, although many individuals do. As a society, we profess to believe that "it isn't whether you win or lose, it's how you play the game." This is why we are concerned with issues of due process and civil rights, even for those espousing repugnant views and committing heinous acts. The process is important no matter the outcome, although the outcome may help to resolve a choice between two almost equal courses of action.

Philosophies that consider the results of an act as the ultimate measure of good are often impossible to apply because of the difficulty in understanding exactly what results from any arbitrary activity. Consider an extreme example: The government orders a hundred cigarette smokers, chosen at random, to be beheaded on live nationwide television. The result might well be that many hundreds of thousands of other smokers would quit "cold turkey," thus prolonging their lives. It might also prevent hundreds of thousands of people from ever starting to smoke, thus improving the health and longevity of the general populace. The health of millions of other people would improve because they would no longer be subjected to secondary smoke. The overall impact on the environment would be very favorable; tons of air and ground pollutants would no longer be released by smokers or tobacco companies.

Yet, despite the great good this might hold for society, everyone, except for a few extremists, would condemn such an act as immoral. We would likely object even if only one person was executed. It would not matter what the law might be on such a matter; we would not feel that the act was morally correct, nor would we view the ends as justifying the means.

Note that we would be unable to judge the morality of such an action by evaluating the results, because we would not know the full scope of those results. Such an act might have effects, favorable or otherwise, on issues of law, public health, tobacco use, and TV shows for decades or centuries to follow. A system of ethics that considered primarily the results of our actions would not allow us to evaluate our current activities at the time when we would need such guidance; if we are unable to discern the appropriate course of action prior to its commission, then our system of ethics is of little or no value to us. To obtain ethical guidance, we must base our actions primarily on evaluations of the actions and not on the possible results.

More to the point of this chapter, if we attempt to judge the morality of a computer break-in based on the sum total of all future effect, we would be unable to make such a judgement, either for a specific incident or for the general class of acts. In part, this is because it is so difficult to determine the long-term effects of various actions and to discern their causes. We cannot know, for instance, if increased security awareness and restrictions are better for society in the long term, or whether these additional restrictions will result in greater costs and annoyance when using computer systems. We also do not know how many of these changes are directly traceable to incidents of computer break-ins.

One other point should be made here: It is undoubtedly possible to imagine scenarios where a computer break-in would be considered to be the preferable course of action. For instance, if vital medical data were on a computer and necessary to save someone's life in an emergency, but the authorized users of the system could not be located, breaking into the system might well be considered the right thing to do. However, that action does not make the break-in ethical. Rather, such situations occur when a greater wrong would undoubtedly occur if the unethical act were not committed. Similar reasoning applies to situations such as killing in self-defense. In the following discussion, I assume that such conflicts are not the root cause of the break-ins; such situations should very rarely present themselves.

3.3. Motivations

Individuals who break into computer systems or who write vandalware usually use one of a few rationalizations for their actions. (See, for example, Landreth [1984] and the discussion in Adelaide et al. [1990].) Most of these individuals would never think to walk down a street, trying every door to find one unlocked, then search through the drawers of the furniture inside. Yet, these same people seem to give no second thought to making repeated attempts at guessing passwords to accounts they do not own, and once on to a system, browsing through the files on disk.

These computer burglars often present the same reasons for their actions in an attempt to rationalize their activities as morally justified. I present and refute some of the most commonly used justifications in what follows; motives involving theft and revenge are not uncommon, and their moral nature is simple to discern, so I do not include them here.

3.3.1. The Hacker Ethic

Many hackers argue that they follow an ethic that both guides their behavior and justifies their break-ins. This hacker ethic states, in part, that all information should be free (Baird et al., 1987). This view holds that information belongs to everyone, and there should be no boundaries or restraints to prevent anyone from examining information. Richard Stallman (1986) states much the same thing in his GNU Manifesto. He and others have further stated in various forums that if information is free, it logically follows that there should be no such thing as intellectual property, and no need for security.

What are the implications and consequences of such a philosophy? First and foremost, it raises some disturbing questions of privacy. If all information is (or should be) free, then privacy is no longer a possibility. For information to be free to everyone, and for individuals to no longer be able to claim it as property, means that anyone may access the information if they please. Furthermore, as it is no longer property of any individual, that means that anyone can alter the information. Items such as bank balances, medical records, credit histories, employment records, and defense information all cease to be controlled. If someone controls information and controls who may access it, the information is obviously not free. But without that control, we would no longer be able to trust the accuracy of the information.

In a perfect world, this lack of privacy and control might not be a cause for concern. However, if all information were to be freely available and modifiable, imagine how much damage and chaos would be caused in our real world by such a philosophy! Our whole society is based on information whose accuracy must be ensured. This includes information held by banks and other financial institutions, credit bureaus, medical agencies and professionals, government agencies such as the IRS, law enforcement agencies, and educational institutions. Clearly, treating all their information as "free" would be unethical in any world where there might be careless and unethical individuals.

Economic arguments can be made against this philosophy, too, in addition to the overwhelming need for privacy and control of information accuracy. Information is not universally free. It is held as property because of privacy concerns, and because it is often collected and developed at great expense. Development of a new algorithm, program, or collection of a specialized database may involve the expenditure of vast sums of time and effort. To claim that it is free or should be free is to express a naive and unrealistic view of the world. To use this as a justification for computer break-ins is clearly unethical. Although not all information currently treated as private or controlled as proprietary needs such protection, that does not justify unauthorized access to it or to any other data.

3.3.2. The Security Arguments

These arguments are the most common ones within the computer community. One common argument was the same one used most often by people attempting to defend the author of the Internet Worm program in 1988: Break-ins illustrate security problems to a community that will otherwise not note the problems.

In the Worm case, one of the first issues to be discussed widely in Internet mailing lists dealt with the intent of the perpetrator—exactly why the Worm program had been written and released. Explanations put forth by members of the community ranged from simple accident to the actions of a sociopath. A common explanation was that the Worm was designed to illustrate security defects to a community that would not otherwise pay attention. This was not supported by the testimony during the author's trial, nor is it supported by past experience of system administrators.

The Worm author, Robert T. Morris, appears to have been well-known at some universities and major companies, and his talents were generally respected. Had he merely explained the problems or offered a demonstration to these people, he would have been listened to with considerable attention. The month before he released the Worm program on the Internet, he discovered and disclosed a bug in the file transfer program ftp; news of the flaw spread rapidly, and an official fix was announced and available within a matter of weeks. The argument that no one would listen to his report of security weaknesses is clearly fallacious.

In the more general case, this security argument is also without merit. Although some system administrators might have been complacent about the security of their systems before the Worm incident, most computer vendors, managers of government computer installations, and system administrators at major colleges and universities have been attentive to reports of security problems. People wishing to report a problem with the security of a system need not exploit it to report it. By way of analogy, one does not set fire to the neighborhood shopping center to bring attention to a fire hazard in one of the stores, and then try to justify the act by claiming that firemen would otherwise never listen to reports of hazards.

The most general argument that some people make is that the individuals who break into systems are performing a service by exposing security flaws, and thus should be encouraged or even rewarded. This argument is severely flawed in several ways. First, it assumes that there is some compelling need to force users to install security fixes on their systems, and thus computer burglars are justified in "breaking and entering" activities. Taken to extremes, it suggests that it would be perfectly acceptable to engage in such activities on a continuing basis, so long as they might expose security flaws. This completely loses sight of the purpose of the computers in the first place—to serve as tools and resources, not as exercises in security. The same reasoning implies that vigilantes have the right to attempt to break into the homes in my neighborhood on a continuing basis to demonstrate that they are susceptible to burglars.

Another flaw with this argument is that it completely ignores the technical and economic factors that prevent many sites from upgrading or correcting their software. Not every site has the resources to install new system software or to correct existing software. At many sites, the systems are run as turnkey systems, employed as tools and maintained by the vendor. The owners and users of these machines simply do not have the ability to correct or maintain their systems independently, and they are unable to afford custom software support from their vendors. To break into such systems, with or without damage, is effectively to trespass into places of business; to do so in a vigilante effort to force the owners to upgrade their security structure is presumptuous and reprehensible. A burglary is not justified, morally or legally, by an argument that the victim has poor locks and was therefore "asking for it."

A related argument has been made that vendors are responsible for the maintenance of their software, and that such security breaches should immediately require vendors to issue corrections to their customers, past and present. The claim is made that without highly visible break-ins, vendors will not produce or distribute necessary fixes to software. This attitude is naive, and is neither economically feasible nor technically workable. Certainly, vendors should bear some responsibility for the adequacy of their software (McIlroy, 1990), but they should not be responsible for fixing every possible flaw in every possible configuration.

Many sites customize their software or otherwise run systems incompatible with the latest vendor releases. For a vendor to be able to provide quick response to security problems, it would be necessary for each customer to run completely standardized software and hardware mixes to ensure the correctness of vendor-supplied updates. Not only would this be considerably less attractive for many customers and contrary to their usual practice, but the increased cost of such "instant" fix distribution would add to the price of such a system—greatly increasing the cost borne by the customer. It is unreasonable to expect the user community to sacrifice flexibility and pay a much higher cost per unit simply for faster corrections to the occasional security breach. That assumes it was even possible for the manufacturer to find those customers and supply them with fixes in a timely manner, something unlikely in a market where machines and software are often repackaged, traded, and resold.

The case of the Internet Worm is a good example of the security argument and its flaws. It further stands as a good example of the conflict between ends and means valuations of ethics. Various people have argued that the Worm's author did us a favor by exposing security flaws. At Mr. Morris's trial on federal charges stemming from the incident, the defense attorneys also argued that their client should not be punished because of the good the Worm did in exposing those flaws. Others, including the prosecuting attorneys for the government, argued that the act itself was wrong no matter what the outcome. Their contention has been that the result does not justify the act itself, nor does the defense's argument encompass all the consequences of the incident.

This is certainly true; the complete results of the incident are still not known. There have been many other break-ins and network worms since November 1988, perhaps inspired by the media coverage of that incident. More attempts will possibly be made, in part inspired by Mr. Morris's act. Some sites on the Internet have restricted access to their machines, and others were removed from the network; I have heard of sites where a decision has been made not to pursue a connection, even though this will hinder research and operations. Combined with the many decades of person-hours devoted to cleaning up afterward, this seems to be a high price to pay for a claimed "favor."

The legal consequences of this act are also not yet known. For instance, many bills were introduced into Congress and state legislatures in subsequent years as a (partial) result of these incidents. One piece of legislation introduced into the House of Representatives, HR-5061, entitled "The Computer Virus Eradication Act of 1988," was the first in a series of legislative actions that had the potential to affect significantly the computer profession. In particular, HR-5061 was notable because its wording would have prevented it from being applied to true computer viruses.[2] The passage of similar well-intentioned but poorly defined legislation could have a major negative effect on the computing profession as a whole.

3.3.3. The Idle System Argument

Another argument put forth by system hackers is that they are simply making use of idle machines. They argue that because some systems are not used at any level near their capacity, the hacker is somehow entitled to use them.

This argument is also flawed. First of all, these systems usually are not in service to provide a general-purpose user environment. Instead, they are in use in commerce, medicine, public safety, research, and government functions. Unused capacity is present for future needs and sudden surges of activity, not for the support of outside individuals. Imagine if large numbers of people without a computer were to take advantage of a system with idle processor capacity: The system would quickly be overloaded and severely degraded or unavailable for the rightful owners. Once on the system, it would be difficult (or impossible) to oust these individuals if sudden extra capacity was needed by the rightful owners. Even the largest machines available today would not provide sufficient capacity to accommodate such activity on any large scale.

I am unable to think of any other item that someone may buy and maintain, only to have others claim a right to use it when it is idle. For instance, the thought of someone walking up to my expensive car and driving off in it simply because it is not currently being used is ludicrous. Likewise, because I am away at work, it is not proper to hold a party at my house because it is otherwise not being used. The related positions that unused computing capacity is a shared resource, and that my privately developed software belongs to everyone, are equally silly (and unethical) positions.

3.3.4. The Student Hacker Argument

Some trespassers claim that they are doing no harm and changing nothing—they are simply learning about how computer systems operate. They argue that computers are expensive, and that they are merely furthering their education in a cost-effective

---

[2] It provided penalties only in cases where programs were introduced into computer systems; a computer virus is a segment of code attached to an existing program that modifies other programs to include a copy of itself (Spafford et al., 1989).

manner. Some authors of computer viruses claim that their creations are intended to be harmless, and that they are simply learning how to write complex programs.

There are many problems with these arguments. First, as an educator, I claim that writing vandalware or breaking into a computer and looking at the files has almost nothing to do with computer education. Proper education in computer science and engineering involves intensive exposure to fundamental aspects of theory, abstraction, and design techniques. Browsing through a system does not expose someone to the broad scope of theory and practice in computing, nor does it provide the critical feedback so important to a good education (see Denning et al., 1989; Tucker et al., 1991). Neither does writing a virus or worm program and releasing it into an unsupervised environment provide any proper educational experience. By analogy, stealing cars and joyriding does not provide one with an education in mechanical engineering, nor does pouring sugar in the gas tank.

Furthermore, individuals "learning" about a system cannot know how everything operates and what results from their activities. Many systems have been damaged accidentally by ignorant (or careless) intruders; most of the damage from computer viruses (and the Internet Worm) appear to be caused by unexpected interactions and program faults. Damage to medical systems, factory control, financial information, and other computer systems could have drastic and far-ranging effects that have nothing to do with education, and certainly could not be considered harmless.

A related refutation of the claim has to do with knowledge of the extent of the intrusion. If I am the person responsible for the security of a critical computer system, I cannot assume that any intrusion is motivated solely by curiosity and that nothing has been harmed. If I know that the system has been compromised, I must fear the worst and perform a complete system check for damages and changes. I cannot take the word of the intruder, for any intruder who actually caused damage would seek to hide it by claiming that he or she was "just looking." To regain confidence in the correct behavior of my system, I must expend considerable energy to examine and verify every aspect of it.

Apply our universal approach to this situation and imagine if this "educational" behavior was widespread and commonplace. The result would be that we would spend all our time verifying our systems and never would be able to trust the results fully. Clearly, this is not good, and thus we must conclude that these "educational" motivations are also unethical.

3.3.5. The Social Protector Argument

One last argument, more often heard in Europe than in the United States, is that hackers break into systems to watch for instances of data abuse and to help keep "Big Brother" at bay. In this sense, the hackers are protectors rather than criminals. Again, this assumes that the ends justify the means. It also assumes that the hackers are actually able to achieve some good end.

Undeniably, there is some misuse of personal data by corporations and by the government. The increasing use of computer-based record systems and networks may lead to further abuses. However, it is not clear that breaking into these systems will aid in righting the wrongs. If anything, it will cause those agencies to become even more secretive and use the break-ins as an excuse for more restricted access. Break-ins and vandalism have not resulted in new open records laws, but they have resulted in the introduction and passage of new criminal statutes. Not only has such activity failed to deter "Big Brother," but it has also resulted in significant segments of the public urging more laws and more aggressive law enforcement—the direct opposite of the purported goal.

It is also not clear that these are the individuals we want "protecting" us. We need to have the designers and users of the systems—trained computer professionals—concerned about our rights and aware of the dangers involved with the inappropriate use of computer monitoring and recordkeeping. The threat is a relatively new one, as computers and networks have become widely used only in the last few decades. It will take some time for awareness of the dangers to spread throughout the profession. Clandestine efforts to breach the security of computer systems do nothing to raise the consciousness of the appropriate individuals. Worse, they associate that commendable goal (heightened concern) with criminal activity (computer break-ins), discouraging proactive behavior by the individuals in the best positions to act in our favor. Perhaps it is in this sense that computer break-ins and vandalism are most unethical and damaging.

3.4. Concluding Remarks

I have argued here that computer break-ins, even when no obvious damage results, are unethical. This must be the considered conclusion even if the result is an improvement in security, because the activity itself is disruptive and immoral. The results of the act should be considered separately from the act itself, especially when we consider how difficult it is to understand all the effects resulting from such an act.

Of course, I have not discussed every possible reason for a break-in. There might well be an instance where a break-in might be necessary to save a life or to preserve national security. In such cases, to perform one wrong act to prevent a greater wrong may be the right thing to do. It is beyond the scope or intent of this chaper to discuss such cases, especially as no known hacker break-ins have been motivated by such instances.

Historically, computer professionals as a group have not been overly concerned with questions of ethics and propriety as they relate to computers. Individuals and some organizations have tried to address these issues, but the whole computing community needs to be involved to address the problems in any comprehensive manner. Too often, we view computers simply as machines and algorithms, and we do not perceive the serious ethical questions inherent in their use.

When we consider, however, that these machines influence the quality of life of millions of individuals, both directly and indirectly, we understand that there are broader issues. Computers are used to design, analyze, support, and control applications that protect and guide the lives and finances of people. Our use (and misuse) of computing systems may have effects beyond our wildest imagining. Thus, we must reconsider our attitudes about acts demonstrating a lack of respect for the rights and privacy of other people's computers and data.

We must also consider what our attitudes will be toward future security problems. In particular, we should consider the effect of widely publishing the source code for worms, viruses, and other threats to security. Although we need a process for rapidly disseminating corrections and security information as they become known, we should realize that widespread publication of details will imperil sites where users are unwilling or unable to install updates and fixes.[3] Publication should serve a useful purpose; endangering the security of other people's machines or attempting to force them into making changes they are unable to make or afford is not ethical.

Finally, we must decide these issues of ethics as a community of professionals and then present them to society as a whole. No matter what laws are passed, and no matter how good security measures might become, they will not be enough for us to have completely secure systems. We also need to develop and act according to some shared ethical values. The members of society need to be educated so that they understand the importance of respecting the privacy and ownership of data. If locks and laws were all that kept people from robbing houses, there would be many more burglars than there are now; the shared mores about the sanctity of personal property are an important influence in the prevention of burglary. It is our duty as informed professionals to help extend those mores into the realm of computing.

References

Adelaide, John Perry Barlow, Robert Jacobson Bluefire, Russell Brand, Clifford Stoll, Dave Hughes, Frank Drake, Eddie Joe Homeboy, Emmanuel Goldstein, Hank Roberts, Jim Gasperini JIMG, Jon Carroll JRC, Lee Felsenstein, Tom Mandel, Robert Horvitz RH, Richard Stallman RMS, Glenn Tenney, Acid Phreak, and Phiber Optik. (1990). "Is Computer Hacking a Crime?" *Harper's Magazine*, Vol. 280, No. 1678, pp. 45–57.

Baird, Bruce J., Lindsay L. Baird Jr., and Ronald P. Ranauro. (1987). "The Moral Cracker?" *Computers and Security*, Vol. 6, No. 6, pp. 471–478.

Denning, Peter J., ed. (1991). *Computers Under Attack: Intruders, Worms, and Viruses.* New York: ACM Books/Addison-Wesley.

Denning, P. J., D. E. Comer, D. Gries, M. C. Mulder, A. Tucker, A. J. Turner, and P. R. Young. (1989). "Computing as a Discipline." *Communications of the ACM*, Vol. 32, No. 1, pp. 9–23.

Hoffman, Lance, ed. (1990). *Rogue Programs: Viruses, Worms, and Trojan Horses.* New York: Van Nostrand Reinhold.

Landreth, Bill. (1984). *Out of the Inner Circle: A Hacker's Guide to Computer Security.* New York: Microsoft Press.

McIlroy, M. Douglas. (1990). "Unsafe at Any Price." *Information Technology Quarterly*, Vol. IX, No. 2, pp. 21–23.

Schwartz, John. (1990). "The Hacker Dragnet." *Newsweek*, Vol. 65, No. 18.

---

[3]To anticipate the oft-used comment that the "bad guys" already have such information: Not every computer burglar knows or will know every system weakness, unless we provide them with detailed analyses.

Seeley, Donn. (1989, January). "A tour of the worm." In *Proceedings of the Winter 1989 Usenix Conference*. The Usenix Association.

Spafford, Eugene H. (1989a). "An analysis of the Internet Worm." In C. Ghezzi and J. A. McDermid, eds. *Proceedings of the 2nd European Software Engineering Conference*, New York: Springer-Verlag, pp. 446–468.

Spafford, Eugene H. (1989b). "The Internet Worm: Crisis and Aftermath." *Communications of the ACM*, Vol. 32, No. 6, pp. 678–698.

Spafford, Eugene H., Kathleen A. Heaphy, and David J. Ferbrache. (1989). *Computer Viruses: Dealing with Electronic Vandalism and Programmed Threats.* Arlington, VA: ADAPSO.

Stallman, Richard. (1986). "The GNU Manifesto." In *GNU EMacs Manual*, Free Software Foundation, pp. 239–248.

Stang, David J. (1990). *Computer Viruses,* 2nd ed. Washington, DC: National Computer Security Association.

Stoll, Clifford. (1989). *Cuckoo's Egg.* New York: Doubleday.

Tucker, Allen B., Bruce H. Barnes, Robert M. Aiken, Keith Barker, Kim B. Bruce, J. Thomas Cain, Susan E. Conry, Gerald L. Engel, Richard G. Epstein, Doris K. Lidtke, Michael C. Mulder, Jean B. Rogers, Eugene H. Spafford, and A. Joe Turner. (1991). *Computing Curricula 1991.* IEEE Society

Chapter 4: Terrorism or Civil Disobedience: Toward a Hacktivist Ethic

Mark Manion and Abby Goodrum

In this era of global commerce via the Internet, strikes against the hegemony of bureaucratic capitalism and the commercialization of the Internet will inevitably be carried out on the Internet. In fact, recent proliferation of hacking activity has shocked the commercial Internet world. On February 8, 2000, hackers attacked Yahoo, Amazon, eBay, CNN.com, and Buy.com, closing them for several hours. Through "denial of service" attacks originating from hundreds of independent computers, these sites were flooded with millions of simultaneous requests. This increase in fake service requests effectively blocked legitimate users from accessing the sites.

Such hacks have led to widespread speculation regarding the motivation of the perpetrators. Are they mere nuisance attacks perpetrated by malicious teenagers, more serious acts of cyberterrorism, or evidence of growing outrage over an increasingly commodified Internet? Although at present no individuals or groups have officially claimed responsibility, MSNBC reported receipt of an 18-page letter claiming responsibility by an individual who angrily criticized the sites for their "capitalization of the Internet." Hundreds of reports in the popular press have portrayed the hackers as vandals, terrorists, and saboteurs, yet no one seems to have considered the possibility that this might be the work of electronic political activists or "hacktivists."

Perhaps these attacks are evidence of a new form of civil disobedience, which unites the talents of the computer hacker with the social consciousness of the political activist. Adapting a variation of civil disobedience, with its practices of "trespass" and "blockade" to the electronic age, participants in what has been called *electronic civil disobedience*, or *hacktivism*, can attack the Web sites of any individual, corporation, or nation that is deemed responsible for oppressing the ethical, social, or political rights of others. Through an investigation of hacktivism, this chapter seeks to elucidate the cooperative and liberal ideology of the originators of the "electronic frontier," speaking in the name of social justice, political decentralization, and freedom of information, and the more powerful counteracting moves to reduce the Internet to one grand global "electronic marketplace."

Hacktivism has the potential to play an active and constructive role in the overcoming of political injustice; to educate, inform, and be a genuine agent of positive political and social change. However, there is the fear that cyberactivism could reduce to more radical and violent forms of cyberterrorism (Arquilla and Ronfeldt, 1993). How governments and societies react to this new form of social activism have not been sufficiently addressed in the computer ethics literature. Researchers concerned with ethical issues in computing, policy makers, and computer professionals must come to terms with the complex set of issues surrounding the potential power of hacktivism.

4.1. Background

Hacktivism is the (sometimes) clandestine use of computer hacking to help advance political causes. Hacktivist groups such as the Electronic Disturbance Theater, the Cult of the Dead Cow, and the Hong Kong Blondes have used electronic civil disobedience to help advance the Zapatista rebellion in Mexico, protest nuclear testing at India's Bhabba Atomic Research Center, attack Indonesian Government Web sites over the occupation of East Timor, and protest antidemocratic crackdowns in China. In addition, hacktivism has been used to inveigh against the corporate domination of telecommunications and mass media, the rapid expansion of dataveillance, and the hegemonic intrusion of the "consumer culture" into the private lives of average citizens.

These concerns give rise to two institutional forces that hactivist protests aim to confront: the commodification of the Internet at the hands of corporate profiteers and violations of human rights at the hands of oppressive governments. Hacktivism thus poses a potential threat at two levels: the private industry/intellectual property level and the national government/national security level. Both of these issues are discussed herein.

4.2. Electronic Civil Disobedience

Civil disobedience entails the peaceful breaking of unjust laws. It does not condone violent or destructive acts against its enemies, focusing instead on nonviolent means to expose wrongs, raise awareness, and prohibit the implementation of perceived unethical laws by individuals, organizations, corporations, or governments. In a civil society, it is the responsibility of all ethical individuals to take a stand against oppression, inequality, and injustice (Honderich, 1997). Civil disobedience is a technique of resistance and protest whose purpose is to achieve social or political change by drawing attention to problems and influencing public opinion. Breaking specific laws, which are unjust, constitutes direct acts of civil disobedience. Symbolic acts of civil disobedience are accomplished by drawing attention to a problem indirectly. Sit-ins and other forms of blockade and trespass are examples of symbolic acts of civil disobedience.

The Internet has created a brave new world of digital activism by providing forums for organizing, communicating, publishing, and taking direct action. The use of the computer as a tool of civil disobedience has been termed *electronic civil disobedience* (ECD) (Wray, 1998). Electronic civil disobedience comes in many forms, ranging from conservative acts such as sending e-mail and publishing Web sites, to breaking into computer systems. A distinction must be made between the use of computers to support ECD, and the use of computers as an act of ECD. If a U.S. citizen wishes to speak out against the government's actions in Kosovo, it is legal to publish a Web site or host mailing lists or chat rooms for this purpose. This activity does not constitute an act of civil disobedience, electronic or otherwise. These types of activity are usually referred to as *electronic activism*, which uses the Internet in fully legitimate ways to publish information, coordinate effective action, and to directly lobby policy makers. Running a program such as FloodNet, however, that posts the reload command to a Web site hundreds of times a minute, constitutes an act of symbolic ECD because the intended aim of such programs is to create an electronic disturbance akin to a sit-in or blockade.

The effect of hundreds of persons reloading a targeted page on the "Web" thousands of times effectively blocks entrance by outsiders and may even shut down the server, as occurred in the attacks on the commercial Web sites of Yahoo and Amazon.com. In 1998, pro-Zapatista activists took this kind of action against Mexican government Web sites (Cleaver, 1998). This is easily seen as a symbolic act of ECD because it tries to draw attention to a perceived violation of rights, rather than attacking the suspected violator(s) directly. The purpose of most ECD is to disrupt the flow of information into and out of institutional computer systems. The point is not to destroy information or systems, but to block access temporarily. This results in virtual sit-ins and virtual blockades. Because institutions today are no longer localized in physical structures but exist in the decentralized zones of cyberspace, electronic blockades can cause financial stress that physical blockades cannot (Critical Art Ensemble, 1994).

The changing nature of authoritative and repressive power has necessitated qualitative changes in resistance to this power. Power/capital, having constituted itself in a new electronic form in cyberspace, requires that opposition movements have to invent new strategies and tactics that counter this new nomadic power of capital. This entails that certain old ways of trespass and blockade—such as street demonstrations—are being modified through electronic civil disobedience, or hacktivism, to meet the new conditions (Critical Art Ensemble, 1996).

4.3. Hacktivism and Electronic Civil Disobedience

Nothing has fired debate about ECD so heatedly as the issue of hacktivism. The central question is whether hacking can reasonably be defined as an act of civil disobedience. Now the refusal to obey governmental commands, even if it entails breaking the law, is often morally sanctioned if certain preconditions are met. Even though philosophers often disagree as to when the breaking of a law actually constitutes an act of civil disobedience, most would agree on the following set of core principles as forming the necessary conditions, and hence ethical justification, for acts considered civilly disobedient. They are:

- No damage done to persons or property
- Nonviolent
- Not for personal profit

- Ethical motivation—the strong conviction that a law is unjust, unfair, or to the extreme detriment of the common good
- Willingness to accept personal responsibility for the outcome of actions

Are acts of hacktivism consistent with the philosophy of civil disobedience? For hacking to qualify as an act of civil disobedience, hackers must be clearly motivated by ethical concerns, be nonviolent, and be ready to accept the repercussions of their actions. Examined in this light, the hack by Eugene Kashpureff clearly constitutes an act of ECD. Kashpureff usurped traffic from InterNIC to protest domain name policy. He did this nonanonymously and went to jail as a result. Further evidence of ethical motivation for hacktivism can also be seen in the messages left behind at hacked sites (Harmon, 1998):

- "China's people have no rights at all, never mind human rights..."
- "Save Kashmir" overlaid with the words "massacre" and "extra-judicial execution."
- "Free East Timor" with hypertext links to Web sites describing Indonesian human rights abuses in the former Portuguese colony.

To justify hactivism's direct action praxis and to legitimate its theoretical foundations, two things must be demonstrated. First, it must be shown that hacktivism is not the work of curious teenagers with advanced technical expertise and a curiosity for infiltrating large computer networks for mere intellectual challenge or sophomoric bravado. Moreover, the justification of hacktivism entails demonstrating that its practitioners are neither "crackers"—those who break into systems for profit or vandalism (Anonymous, 1998)—nor are they cyberterrorists—those who use computer technology with the intention of causing grave harm such as loss of life, severe economic losses, or destruction of critical infrastructure (Denning, 1999). Hacktivism must be shown to be ethically motivated. Second, politicized hacking must be shown to be some form of civil disobedience—a form of civil disobedience that is morally justified. To determine the motivations of hactivists, one place to look is what hactivists themselves claim is their motivation.

On October 12, 1998, the Web site of Mexican president Erenesto Zedillo was attacked. From all accounts, the Zedillo hack was not the work of bored teens. It was a political act, according to the Electronic Disturbance Theatre, to "demonstrate continued resistance to centuries of colonization, genocide, and racism in the western hemisphere and throughout the world" (Harmon, 1998). In August of the same year, the hactivist group "X-Ploit" hacked the Web site of Mexico's finance ministry, defacing it by replacing the contents with the face of the revolutionary hero Emiliano Zapata, in sympathy with the Zapatista rebellion in the Chipas region of southern Mexico. These acts are political protests, which draw attention to what is perceived to be grave social injustice. The reason for these actions is clear: they are motivated by a socioeconomic system that perpetuates discrimination, racism, and economic inequality, not the mere thrill and challenge of breaking into networks for fun.

In June of 1998 the hactivists group "MilwOrm" hacked India's Bhabba Atomic Research Centre to protest against recent nuclear tests. Later, in July of that year,

"MilwOrm" and the group "Astray Lumberjacks" orchestrated an unprecedented mass hack of more than 300 sites around the world, replacing Web pages with antinuclear statements and images of mushroom clouds. Not surprisingly, the published slogan of MilwOrm is: "Putting the power back in the hands of the people" (Hesseldhal, 1999). The groups responsible for these hacks seem to be motivated by belief in the positive forces of democracy and freedom rather than the mere thrill of vandalism or the nihilism of "cyberterrorism."

Mail bombs were delivered and several other Chinese government Web sites were hacked to protest the targeting of Chinese and Indonesian citizens for torture, rape, and looting during the anti-Suharto riot in May of 1998 (Hesseldhal, 1999). On August 1, the Portuguese group "Kaotik Team" hacked 45 Indonesian government Web sites, altering Web pages and calling for full autonomy of East Timor and the cessation of the harsh military crackdown on dissidents (Hesseldhal, 1999). Again, fighting for social justice and human rights is motivated by ethics, not anarchy. Many, many other hactivist activities can be sited to demonstrate the ethical motivation behind this new form of political activism.

These messages, and many others like them, demonstrate a striking change from hacker messages of the past. Prior hacks have had little if any sociopolitical content, and bear a closer resemblance to "tagging" and other forms of boasting graffiti. There has been a certain juvenile style to messages left by hackers in the past. The hacks listed above, however, represent a new breed of hacker: one who is clearly motivated by the advancement of ethical concerns and who believes such actions should be considered a legitimate form of (electronic) civil disobedience.

4.4. Hacktivism and Cyberterrorism

If hacktivism can be defined as an act of electronic civil disobedience, then the punitive outcomes must be brought into alignment with other forms of civil disobedience. Traditional penalties for civil disobedience are mild compared to penalties for hacking. Penalties for hacktivism are meted out with the same degree of force as for hacking in general, regardless of the motivation for the hack or the political content of messages left at hacked sites. Most governments do not recognize hacking as a political activity, and the penalties for breaking into computers can be extreme (Jaconi, 1999). For example, the hack of the Chinese government's Web site by the Hong Kong Blondes, attacks on Indonesian Government Web sites regarding policy in Kashmir, attacks on India's nuclear weapons research center Web sites to protest nuclear testing, as well as the hacks on the commercial Web sites of Yahoo and CNN, are all subject to felony prosecution. All of these examples provide convincing evidence in support of our thesis that hacktivism should be considered a legitimate form of civil disobedience, and not the work of "cybervandals" or "cyberterrorists." Under U.S. law, *terrorism* is an act of violence for the purpose of intimidating or coercing a government or civilian population. Hacktivism clearly does not fall into this category; it is fundamentally nonviolent.

Because many acts of hacktivism have been perpetuated against government Web sites, however, hacktivism is increasingly being equated with acts of information warfare and cyberterrorism (Furnell and Warren, 1999; Kovacich, 1997). In August of 1998, the Center for Intrusion Control was established by a coalition of various government agencies to respond to these "cyberwarfare threats" (Glave, 1998). Similarly, organizations such as RAND and the NSA have categorically denied the existence of hacktivism as an act of civil disobedience and repeatedly refer to all acts of hacking as *cyberwar* or *cyberterrorism* in an attempt to push for stronger penalties for hacking, regardless of ethical motivations (Bowers, 1998; Gompert, 1998).

To determine the kinds and range of threats to its critical infrastructures posed by possible cyberterrorists, the U.S. government established the President's Commission on Critical Infrastructure Protection (PCCIP). The PCCIP findings have led to the development of the National Infrastructure Protection Center, the Critical Infrastructure Assurance Office, the National Infrastructure Assurance Council, and the Joint Task-Force Computer Network Defense, established by the Department of Defense. The threat posed by cyberterrorism is very real. However, it is a mistake to identify cyberterrorism with hacktivism. As we have established, acts of hacktivism are more akin to acts of civil disobedience than to acts of terrorism, and it is important to keep this distinction clear.

In fact, potential acts of cyberterrorism are explicitly condemned by hacktivists. During a December 1998 press conference, one member of a hacktivist group, which call themselves the Legion of the Underground (LoU), declared "cyberwar" on the information infrastructures of China and Iraq. This declaration of war prompted a coalition of hacktivist groups to condemn the "irresponsible" declaration of war. In a "Joint Statement by 2600, The Chaos Computer Club, The Cult of the Dead Cow, !Hispahack, L0pht Heavy Industries, Phrack and Pulhas," the leaders of the hacktivist community denounced the LoU declaration of war, saying:

> We strongly oppose any attempt to use the power of hacking to threaten or destroy the information infrastructure of any country, for any reason. Declaring "war" against anyone, any group of people, or any nation is a most deplorable act... this has nothing to do with hacktivism or the hacker ethic and is nothing a hacker can be proud of. (Hackernews, 12/29/98)

This immediately prompted a quick response from the leaders of LoU, who issued a statement saying that the declaration of war did not represent the position of the group. The letter states:

> The LoU does not support the damaging of other nations' computers, network or systems in any way, nor will the LoU use their skills, abilities or connections to take any actions against the systems, network or computers in China or Iraq which may damage or hinder in any way their operations. (Hackernews, 01/7/99)

Why is it, then, that a growing number of experts refuse to make this distinction, and insist on conflating hacktivism and cyberterrorism? It may be that describing hacktivists as criminals helps to entrench a certain conception of, and control over, intellectual property, and obscures the larger critique about the ownership of information, and the legal system's need to protect the powerful economic interests of corporations attempting to dominate and completely commercialize the Internet. Moreover, labeling the hacktivist as a national security threat provides further legitimation for the erasure of individual privacy at the hands of the national security state, which compiles and stores vast databases on hundreds of thousands of citizens each year. The demonization of the hacker may also be an attempt to obscure the violation of our privacy at the hands of corporations. As one critic put it

> Through the routine gathering of information about transactions, consumer preferences, and creditworthiness, a harvest of information about an individual's whereabouts and movements, tastes, desires, contacts, friends, associates, and patterns of work and recreation become available in the form of dossiers sold on the tradable information market, or is endlessly convertible into other forms of intelligence through computer matching. Advanced pattern recognition technologies facilitate the process of surveillance, while data encryption protects it from public accountability. (Ross, 1998)

Hence, one rationalization for the vilification of hacktivism is the need for the power elite to rewrite property law to contain the effects of the new information technologies. As a result of the newly evolving intellectual property laws, information and knowledge can now be held as capital. The existence of these laws effectively curtails the widest possible spread of this new form of wealth. However, unlike material objects, information can be shared widely without running out. As two experts put it

> Intellectual property is not a tangible, material entity. It is nothing more than a volatile pattern of electrons arrayed in patterns of open and closed gates to form intelligible numerical or textual symbols. Information, documents, and data reside inside computers in a form that can be "stolen" without ever being removed, indeed, without ever being touched by a would-be thief, or depriving the "owner" from still using and profiting off of the "property." (Michalowski and Pfuhl, 1991)

Although the information inside computers is clearly of value, the form of this value is both intangible and novel. Its character as "property" remained legally ambiguous until a rapid proliferation of computer crime laws took place to create the legal environment that helped to define and delimit the debate over the nature of intellectual property. These laws and rulings ultimately served to protect the immediate financial interests of the corporate techno-elite, and directed the state to protect the profit potential of telecommunications industries, financial investors, and entrepreneurs capitalizing on the Internet.

Ironically, this rapid proliferation of computer laws during the 1980s, which saw 47 states enact computer crime laws, as well as two Congressional pieces of computer crime legislation that entered the legal system at the same time, resulted in relatively few arrests or prosecutions. For example, "Operation Sundial," the largest FBI sting on suspected hackers, led to no serious charges. A few hackers pled guilty and paid a total of $233,000 in fines (Halbert, 1997). This rapid criminalization of computer abuse represents, moreover, an exception to the gradual and reformist nature of typical law formation in common law jurisprudence (Hollinger and Lanza-Kaduce, 1988). Michalowski and Pfuhl (1991) conclude from this that "the violations of computer security posed a broad challenge to the hegemonic constructions of property and authority relations, and it was this challenge, more than the concrete losses resulted from unauthorized computer access, that created a climate of fear about computer crime that led to the swift and non-controversial passage of computer crime laws."

The power elite, often synergistically intertwined with the design and operation of information technologies, will always come to the aid and defense of technologies of control, making revolt difficult and reform hard. Intellectual property laws attest to this, as do the excessively stringent laws against hacking. Nevertheless, if we say we support civil disobedience as a legitimate form of social protest, then we must support the computerization of these efforts as well. This means bringing penalties for hacktivism, or electronic civil disobedience, in line with penalties for traditional mechanisms used for the breaking of what are perceived to be unethical laws.

4.5. Toward a Hacktivist Ethic

Every technology releases opposing possibilities toward either emancipation or domination, and information technology is no different. The new information technologies are often portrayed as the utopian promise of total human emancipation and freedom. However, the promise of freedom from work, e-democracy, and global community, once hailed as the hallmarks of the computer revolution, are nowhere to be found. As critics are quick to point out, the only entities that seem to benefit from the Internet are large transnational business corporations.

For such critics, advanced information technology threatens to turn into an Orwellian nightmare of totalitarian domination and control, a dystopia of complete repression of free thought. They remind us that the Internet is quickly becoming subordinated to the pecuniary interests of the techno-elite, who merely pay lip service to the growth of electronic communities and participatory democracy. These interests are devoted to shutting down the anarchy of the Net in favor of virtualized commercial exchange. Hence, the power elite must destroy the public cybersphere for its own survival. This may account for the vilification of hacktivists, as well as why the charges against hacktivism are so high.

As is well known, however, the lifeblood of the hacker ethic has always been the freedom of information and the full democratization of the public sphere. The core principles of the hacker ethic were spelled out in Steven Levy's book, *Hackers: Heroes of the Computer Revolution* (Levy, 1984). Three of these principles are relevant here. They are:

1. Access to computers—and anything that might teach you something about the way the world works—should be unlimited and total. Always yield to the Hands-On Imperative!

2. All information should be free.

3. Mistrust Authority—Promote Decentralization

Hackers prioritize the freedom of information and are suspicious of centralized control or private ownership of information. Hackers question why a few corporations can own and sell huge databases of information about others and control information helpful to the public at large. Hackers are frustrated to discover that their coveted "electronic agora," a true marketplace for the free play of ideas, which was the original ideal behind the formation of the Internet, has been invaded and taken over by avaricious and enterprising entrepreneurs who prefer dollars to the free flow of information and knowledge. In sum, this ethic puts hackers on a collision course with the commercial–industrial complex who wish to own and control the Internet.

One of the most pervasive popular arguments against the panoptical intentions of the "Captains of Technology" is that their system does not work. Every successful hack in some way reinforces the popular perception that the rise of the total panoptic surveillance society is not inevitable. Hence, the hacker ethic, libertarian and anarchist in its right-to-know principles and its advocacy of decentralized technology, is a principled attempt to challenge the tendency to use technology to form information elites.

The debate over the control of intellectual property demands that we address issues of social justice such as wealth distribution and equality of opportunity. Politically, the resistance to corporate domination of the Internet must force not only the questions of privacy and property, but it must also place the critique of the technological society itself into the center of public consciousness and debate. Hacktivist activities put these issues of technocontrol on the political agenda, by performing acts of symbolic electronic civil disobedience.

Furthermore, resistance to political oppression and corporate manipulation must be embedded in a well-articulated theory, one that is morally informed and widely shared. Movements acting out of outrage often dissipate. They need to be durable and sustain a commitment, to the higher good that lasts even against repression. This leads to the necessity of creating a form of technocultural activism that can bring to reality the ideas of human emancipation. Activism today is no longer a case of putting bodies on the picket line; it requires putting minds and virtual bodies "on-line." This is the promise of hacktivism, the fusion of the political consciousness of the activist with the technical expertise of the computer "hacker."

4.6. Conclusion

Hacktivism is in its infancy, but, given the ubiquity and democratizing possibility of the Internet, we will certainly bear witness to the movement's growing pains and increasing maturity. One thing is sure, however. Incidents of cyberactivism are on the rise, and will continue to be on the rise in the near future.

Never in the long and often turbulent history of political and social activism have dissidents had at their disposal a tool as far-reaching and potentially effective as the Internet. Sadly, this inherently civil strategy of disobedience is being deliberately and officially misconstrued through misinformation as cyberterrorism, which it is clearly not. Steps must be taken to separate political direct action in cyberspace from organized criminality or cyberterrorism.

When is it legitimate to practice direct action on the Internet? Some inevitably argue that electronic civil disobedience is never justifiable, whereas others argue that it is always justified. What are the limits of political protest in cyberspace? How far can activists go without infringing on the legitimate rights of the people and institutions against whom they are protesting? These questions demand a more extensive argument that extends beyond the scope of this chapter. One way or another, for hacktivism to become a legitimate form of social protest, it must be provided sound ethical foundations. This, in turn, means expanding the ethical justification of civil disobedience to include acts of hacktivism.

As we envision the possibilities of resistance taking place increasingly on the Internet, it is important to remember that civil disobedience has been a vital part of the history of political growth and change in the United States, from the Boston Tea Party to the Civil Rights movement to contemporary environmental activism. However, although it is useful to consider the role that the theory and practice of civil disobedience has taken up until now, we must demand more than the right to speak; we must demand the right to act in the "wired world" on behalf of the public good. If we lose the right to protest in cyberspace in the coming Information Age, we are in jeopardy of losing the greater part of our individual and collective freedom.

References

Anonymous. (1998). "The Language of Hacking," *Management Review*, Vol. 87, No. 9, pp. 18–21.

Arquilla, J., and D. Ronfeldt. (1993). "Cyberwar Is Coming," *Comparative Strategy*, Vol. 12, No. 2, pp. 141–165.

Bowers, S. (1998, August). "Information Warfare: The Computer Revolution Is Altering How Future Wars Will Be Conducted," *Armed Forces Journal International*, pp. 38–49.

Cleaver, H. (1998). "The Zapatistas and the Electronic Fabric of Struggle." Available at www.eco.utexas.edu/faculty/Cleaver/zaps.htm. Accessed 5/18/99.

Critical Art Ensemble. (1994). *The Electronic Disturbance.* Brooklyn, NY: Autonomedia.

Critical Art Ensemble. (1996). *Electronic Civil Disobedience and Other Unpopular Ideas.* Brooklyn, NY: Autonomedia.

Denning, Dorothy. (1999). *Activism, Hacktivism, and Cyberterrorism: The Internet as a Tool for Influencing Foreign Policy.* Paper presented at the Internet and International Systems: Information Technology and American Foreign Policy Decisionmaking Workshop, Georgetown University, Washington, D.C.

Furnell, S., and Warren M. (1999). "Computer hacking and cyberterrorism: The real threats in the new millennium," *Computers and Security*, Vol. 18, pp. 28–34.

Glave, J. (1998). "Hacker raises stakes in DOD attacks." *Wired News.* Available at http://www.wired.com/news/technology/1,1282,10713,00.html. Accessed 5/27/06.

Gompert, D. (1998). "National Security in the Information Age," *Naval War College Review*, Vol. 51, No. 4, pp. 22–41.

Hackernews. Available at http://www.hackernews.com/archive.html. Accessed 5/27/06.

Halbert, D. (1997). "Disclosures of Danger and the Computer Hacker," *The Information Society*, Vol. 13, pp. 361–374.

Harmon, A. (1998, October 31). "Hacktivists of all Persuasions Take their Struggle to the Web," *The New York Times*, p. 1 col. 5.

Hesseldhal, Arik. (1999, May 21). "Hacking for Human Rights?" *Wired News*. Available at http://www.wired.com/news/politics/0,1283,13693,00.html. Accessed 5/27/06.

Hollinger, R., and L. Lanza-Kaduce. (1988). "The Process of Criminalization: The Case of Computer Crime Laws," *Criminology*, Vol. 26, No. 1, pp. 101–126.

Honderich, T. (1997). "Hierarchic Democracy and the Necessity of Mass Civil Disobedience." In: R. Bontekoe, ed. *Justice and Democracy: Cross-cultural Perspectives.* Honolulu: University of Hawaii Press.

Jaconi, J. (1999). Federal Cybercrime Law, Section 1030 "Computer Fraud & Abuse Act." www.antionline.com. Accessed 6/17/99.

Kovacich, G. (1997). "Information Warfare and the Information Systems Security Professional," *Computers & Security*, Vol. 16, pp. 14–24.

Levy, Stephen. (1984). *Hackers: Computer Heroes of the Computer Revolution*. New York: Delta.

Michalowski, R., and E. Pfuhl. (1991). "Technology, Property and Law: The Case of Computer Crime."

Ross, Andrew. (1998). "Hacking Away at the Counterculture." In: C. Penley and A. Ross, eds. *Technoculture*. Minneapolis: University of Minnesota Press; p. 126.

Wray, S. (1998). "Electronic Civil Disobedience and the World Wide Web of Hacktivism: A Mapping of Extraparliamentarian Direct Action Net Politics. Available at http://www.nyu.edu/projects/wray/www.hack.html. Accessed 5/27/06.

Chapter 5: Hacking as Politically Motivated Digital Civil Disobedience: Is Hacktivism Morally Justified?

Kenneth Einar Himma

Hackers believe that nonmalicious intrusions are morally permissible and have offered a number of arguments purporting to justify such intrusions. Some hackers believe, for example, these intrusions are justified because they increase humanity's stock of knowledge about the relevant technologies and thereby promote research that will ultimately make the Internet more secure. Some believe that any barriers to information are morally illegitimate and hence deserve no respect—including barriers that prevent a person from accessing the information on another person's computer.

These arguments have not persuaded many theorists or laypersons.[1] To begin, it is not clear that unauthorized digital intrusions are necessary to increase the stock of knowledge; community-minded hackers could always produce the same good by hacking each other or by going to work for some software company. Further, the idea that all barriers to information are morally illegitimate is incompatible with the right to information privacy; if all information should be free, then our efforts to protect sensitive information about ourselves (like social security numbers) are morally wrong. But regardless of whether the premises of these arguments are correct, the conclusion does not follow because unauthorized digital intrusions involve a trespass on computers and networks belonging to other people and thereby violate the victims' rights to their physical (as opposed to intellectual) property.

Recently, a more plausible line of justification has emerged. According to this reasoning, attacks on government and corporate sites can be justified as a form of political activism. The argument is roughly as follows. Because civil disobedience is morally justifiable as a protest against injustice, it is permissible to commit digital intrusions as a means of protesting injustice. Insofar as it is permissible to stage a sit-in in a commercial or governmental building to protest, say, laws that violate human rights, it is permissible to intrude on commercial or government networks to protest such laws. Thus, digital intrusions that would otherwise be morally

---

[1] For a critical evaluation of these lines of argument, see Spafford (1992) and Himma and Dittrich (2006).

objectionable are morally permissible if they are politically motivated acts of electronic civil disobedience, or *hacktivism*, as such intrusions have come to be called.

In this chapter, I consider the issue of whether and when hacktivism is morally impermissible. First, I argue that the above line of reasoning wrongly presupposes that committing civil disobedience is morally permissible as a general matter of moral principle; in an otherwise legitimate state, civil disobedience is morally justified or excusable only in narrowly defined circumstances. Second, I attempt to identify a reliable framework for evaluating civil disobedience that weighs the social and moral values against the social and moral disvalues. Third, I apply this framework to acts of hacktivism. I argue that hacktivism is impermissible insofar as such acts result in significant harms to innocent third parties or insofar as the persons responsible for such acts conceal their identities to avoid the potential legal consequences.

5.1. Civil Disobedience and Morality

5.1.1. What Is Civil Disobedience?

It has come to be an article of faith among many activist-minded persons that acts of civil disobedience are, as a general moral matter, not only permissible but positively good. On this view, it is true not only that people who commit acts of civil disobedience violate no moral obligations, but also that such persons are actually producing something that counts as a moral good. Accordingly, these behaviors deserve praise rather than punishment.

This common view cannot be evaluated without saying something about the concept of civil disobedience. Although a comprehensive analysis of the concept of civil disobedience is beyond the scope of this paper, I think it is fair to say that, as a conceptual matter, acts of civil disobedience involve the following elements: (1) the open, (2) knowing (3) commission of some nonviolent act (4) that violates a law L (5) for the expressive purpose of protesting or calling attention to the injustice of L, some other law, or the legal system as a whole.[2] Because acts of civil disobedience are deliberately open so as to call attention to the putative injustice of the law or legal system, they are fairly characterized as "political expression."

Several comments about these elements are in order. First, as I have defined it, it is a necessary condition for an act to count as civil disobedience that it openly disobeys the law. Clandestine acts of disobeying law do not count as civil disobedience, even if they are motivated by a desire to protest the law. The openness of an act of civil disobedience signals to the public that the act is intended to call attention to the injustice of some element of the law or legal system; indeed, as we will see, this feature of civil disobedience helps to make it reasonable to think such acts are morally permissible.

---

[2]One might reasonably carve up the notion of civil disobedience in a slightly different manner. For example, one might take the position that civil disobedience requires no more than a political motivation; it does not require a politically expressive motivation. Nothing of substance turns on these issues. This analysis is offered primarily to establish the boundaries of the phenomena I wish to discuss in this paper. As long as it is roughly correct, the above definition is adequate to the purposes.

Second, it is a necessary condition for an act to count as civil disobedience that it be nonviolent; violent acts, regardless of motivation, do not count as "civil" disobedience. The notion of violence, however, has become contentious—in part because of the development of digital information technologies. As the notion is traditionally understood, a violent act is one that involves physical force and results in physical damage to physical property or harm to one's physical person. Some people have come to believe that the notion of violence does not apply to physical force directed at property. Although I do not find either conception plausible (and the second is especially implausible),[3] it is worth noting at the outset that the traditional understanding of violence seems to preclude the possibility of digital violence; unauthorized digital trespass is neither fairly characterized as "physical force" nor as resulting in "physical harm or damage."[4] A digital act might not be fairly characterized as "civil disobedience," but it will be for some other reason than that the act fails to satisfy the nonviolence element of civil disobedience according to the first two definitions.

Third, one need not be protesting the law that one violates as an act of civil disobedience. One might violate a curfew law, for example, as a means of calling attention to the injustice of some other law. In such cases, an act might count conceptually as a piece of civil disobedience without its being clear exactly which law is being protested; indeed, considerable confusion might result about the point of the act. Although this will not result in the act's being conceptually disqualified from counting as "civil disobedience," it might very well figure into determining whether the act is morally permissible.

Fourth, to count as civil disobedience, an act need not target a law or system that is unjust as an objective moral matter. It is enough that the actor is motivated by a belief that the law or system is unjust and that the act is contrived to protest it and call attention to its injustice. The conceptual elements of civil disobedience, then, imply a purely subjective element that makes reference to the beliefs and motivations of the relevant class of actors, rather than to the objective moral quality of the law or system.

It should be noted, however, that the subjective element is, as I have defined it, a necessary condition for civil disobedience. Someone who breaks the law for some other purpose than to protest or call attention to the injustice of a law is not committing an act of civil disobedience. Indeed, someone who believes the law unjust and disobeys it does not commit an act of civil disobedience if her violation of the law is motivated by some other desire than a desire to protest or call attention to

---

[3]For what it is worth, I think a more plausible conception encompasses cases in which a person uses digital force to cause digital damage; someone who hacks into my computer and destroys the irreplaceable seems, according to my intuitions, to have committed a violent act against me. Nothing turns, however, on my taking a position on this issue because, as we see, the framework I suggest for evaluating hacktivism and civil disobedience explicitly takes such damage into account—regardless of whether it is properly characterized as the result of "violence."

[4]I do not find the idea that violence is necessarily physical particularly plausible, but there is no reason to challenge it in this essay. Nothing turns on this idea.

its injustice. Acts of civil disobedience are, on this conception, expressive in the sense that the point is to communicate something to someone.

5.1.2. Are Acts of Civil Disobedience Morally Permissible?

It is tempting to infer from this analysis of the concept of civil disobedience, together with the claim that people have a moral right to free speech, that acts of civil disobedience, as political expression, are morally justified as an exercise of the moral right to free speech. On this line of analysis, the right to free speech entails a right to express one's political views about the legitimacy of the law. Because the very point of civil disobedience is to call attention to the illegitimacy of the law, it is a morally justified exercise of the right to free expression.

This line of reasoning is problematic. First, the claim that X has a right to express p does not imply that expressing p is morally permissible. One might have a right to express all sorts of things that it is morally wrong to express. For example, one might have a right to express racist ideas even though expressing these ideas is wrong. Rights like the right to free speech are negative rights that are constituted by obligations on the part of other persons or entities. My right to free speech, for example, is constituted by an obligation on the part of the state not to coercively interfere with my speech. But the claim that X has an obligation not to interfere with my saying p does not imply that my saying p is morally permissible; it just means that X should not threaten me or attack me to prevent me from saying p.

Second, civil disobedience might be expressive, but it is considerably more than that. Civil disobedience, by its nature, involves disobeying something that has the status of law. It is one thing to assert that a law is unjust; it is another thing to deliberately and openly behave in a manner that violates the law; the former is a pure speech act, whereas the latter is behavior. Civil disobedience, then, might be expressive conduct, but it is primarily conduct and secondarily expression.

Ordinary views about the moral right to free speech commonly distinguish between speech acts and expressive behavior. On these views, expressive behavior is subject to more stringent moral limits than those to which pure speech is subject. One might seek, for example, to make a point about sexual morality by having sex in public, but the moral right to free speech does not entail a right to have sex in public for the purpose of promoting some view about sexual morality. One has a moral right to express oneself, but the protection afforded by that right extends further with respect to pure speech acts than with respect to acts that are primarily conduct and secondarily expression.

The reason for this, of course, has something to do with the effects on other people of these different kinds of acts. As a general matter, pure speech acts are primarily calculated to affect only the mental states of the audience. A joke, for example, is primarily calculated to induce a sense of amusement in the listener. A sad story might seek to elicit sympathy from the listener.

Pure speech intended to advance or defend some sort of position is calculated to affect a different class of mental states. A pure speech act intended to advance a political or moral position is calculated to affect only doxastic states in any morally significant way. In particular, such acts are calculated to alter or reinforce the belief structure in the audience. My expression of outrage at some perceived injustice might serve a variety of emotional functions (e.g., release of stress), but it is primarily intended to persuade others to recognize that an injustice has occurred.

It is true, of course, that a speech act intended to express a position can have other effects; an obscene speech act can cause offense, shame, and perhaps something resembling emotional trauma to someone who witnesses it. It is also true that a pure speech act can have the same ultimate effect as physical conduct. A collection of abortion protesters might lead a woman to refrain from having an abortion as effectively by reasoning with her as by physically tackling her; however, the result in the former case will be the result of a change in volitions that is shaped by a change in doxastic states, whereas the result in the latter case will not bear such a relationship to some change in mental states.[5] Pure speech acts intended to express a position, as a general matter, tend to affect only the doxastic states of the audience; the point is to communicate something in order to persuade or induce belief in the audience.

In contrast, although conduct might frequently be intended to affect only doxastic states, conduct tends to have effects on other states in which a person has a strong interest. Someone who seeks to express anger with you by hitting you not only affects your doxastic states, but also runs the risk of causing you physical and emotional injury. Physical injury is just not a reasonably likely outcome from pure speech acts of just about any kind.

As is evident from these examples, these additional effects of conduct can implicate morally significant interests. Someone who injures another person because she expressed her anger violently has affected morally significant interests of the other person. Someone who causes great offense to another person by masturbating in front of her has affected interests that are morally significant. Conduct is far more likely than pure speech to implicate such interests precisely because it is reasonably calculated to have other effects than on doxastic states, which receive comparatively little moral protection. Conduct, unlike pure speech, is not the kind of thing with primary effects limited to doxastic states.

None of this, of course, should be construed to deny that violating the law might sometimes be morally permissible, and even obligatory, in certain circumstances. Legal and political philosophers are nearly unanimous in believing not only that there is no universal moral obligation to obey the law, but also that there is no general moral obligation to obey the law of even reasonably just states; even reasonably just states, like morally wicked states, might sometimes enact legal content so morally problematic that it does not generate a moral obligation to obey.

At an intuitive level, this is quite plausible. It seems clear, to begin, that citizens in Nazi Germany were morally obligated to violate many laws. But it seems also clear that citizens of the United States, a reasonably just state, were, at the very least, morally permitted to disobey Jim Crow laws because of their egregious injustice. In such circumstances, one need not justify such behavior by reference to the right to free speech.

---

[5] I am indebted to Don Gotterbarn for this very helpful example.

The circumstances in which one is permitted or obligated to disobey the law, however, are comparatively rare in a morally legitimate democratic system with a body of law that is largely, although not perfectly, just for a number of reasons. First, citizens have alternative channels through which to express their political views in morally legitimate democratic systems. Because such systems recognize a legal right of free speech against the state, citizens can express their views through pure speech acts and have a growing array of media available to them that can be used to express their views—including democratizing digital media, like Web sites and blogs. The easy availability of such avenues of speech operates to circumscribe the circumstances in which someone is permitted to take the law into her own hands, so to speak, by deliberately flouting it.

Second, one of the justifying features of democracy is that, properly administered, it affords each person an equal voice in determining what content becomes law. Someone who violates a democratically enacted law is arrogating to herself a larger role than that to which she is entitled in a democracy. It is presumptively (as opposed to conclusively) problematic to circumvent democratic procedures in this way—again, assuming that such procedures are legitimate and legitimately administered.

Third, morally legitimate democratic states have some latitude with respect to enforcing law that is morally problematic. Although legitimacy theorists once focused on trying to show that morally legitimate systems give rise to a general content-independent moral obligation to obey law and hence an absolute permission to enforce the law, this idea has fallen out of favor. It seems clear that even an otherwise just morally legitimate democratic state might produce legal content so patently unjust that it does not give rise to an obligation to obey and may not permissibly be enforced. I assume that this was the case with Jim Crow laws in the United States.

The consensus now seems to be that a morally legitimate state may, as a general (although not absolute) matter, permissibly enforce laws that are reasonably thought just. If this is true, then the law of a morally legitimate system will more often than not give rise to a moral obligation to obey the law. It is hard to make sense of the idea that the state is morally justified in coercively enforcing a law against a citizen (e.g., with threat of incarceration) if it is not morally wrong to disobey that law. It is reasonable to assume that a citizen may be punished for disobeying a law (either directly in the case of criminal law or indirectly in the case of civil law through use of the contempt sanction) only insofar as he or she is morally culpable for disobeying it. Because a person can be morally culpable for disobeying a law only insofar as he or she has a moral obligation to obey it, any law that is justifiably enforced by the state will give rise to a moral obligation on the part of citizens to obey it.

This suggests that citizens might be morally obligated to obey some laws that are morally mistaken. As long as the moral problems with the content of the law do not rise to some threshold level of egregiousness, the state may permissibly enforce that law against citizens. But this seems to imply that citizens are morally obligated to obey such laws, despite the moral problems.

Even so, the idea that there are limits on the scope of even a legitimate state's permission to coercively enforce the law suggests, rightly, that civil disobedience is sometimes morally justified. In cases where an otherwise legitimate state has enacted a sufficiently unjust law that falls outside the scope of its coercive authority, citizens have a qualified moral permission to disobey it. That is, in cases in which the state is not justified in coercively enforcing a law, citizens may permissibly disobey that law because it does not give rise to any moral obligation to obey.

But this permission is qualified by a number of factors. To begin, it is reasonable to think that acts significantly impinging on the interests of innocent third parties are not justified. There are moral limits on the extent of the costs one may permissibly impose on innocent third parties. Conduct that, for example, is reasonably calculated or likely to result in loss of innocent life is generally not permissible, regardless of whether the conduct is expressive. It is morally impermissible to yell "fire" in a crowded theater precisely because it is likely to result in a stampede that may result in significant harm to another person.

Moreover, it is reasonable to think that disobedience must be properly motivated to be justified. Even acts that are generally permissible might be morally problematic when motivated by malicious intentions. If I give you something fairly characterized as a "gift" with the intention of making you feel you have to do something for me down the line, I have done something morally wrong.

Finally, it makes a difference as to whether or not someone is willing to accept responsibility under the law for her acts. Willingness to accept responsibility goes beyond merely openly defying the law; one might openly defy a law but attempt to evade apprehension by the police by, say, leaving the country. Someone who, say, openly performs an act of civil disobedience knowing he or she will be arrested seems more deserving of moral respect than someone who disobeys the law and attempts to conceal his or her identity. Intuitively, there is a world of difference, for example, between someone who defaces a billboard in front of 15 police officers to protest its content and someone who does so in a clandestine manner hoping to avoid detection. One seems fairly characterized as vandalism; the other, even if ultimately unjustified, does not.

This is especially true of electronic civil disobedience. One worry that many theorists share about hacktivism is that it can be difficult to distinguish an act of electronic civil disobedience from an act of cyberterrorism. Huschle (2002) argues that hacktivists should make it a point to accept responsibility for their actions precisely to ensure that their acts are not mistaken for acts of cyberterrorism, which could cause significant disruption in the population beyond what was intended to result from their acts. Similarly, Manion and Goodrum (2000, pp. 15–16) contend:

> [T]he justification of hacktivism entails demonstrating that its practitioners are neither "crackers"—those who break into systems for profit or vandalism—nor are they cyberterrorists—those who use computer technology with the intention of causing grave harm such as loss of life, severe economic losses, or destruction of critical infrastructure. Hacktivism must be shown to be ethically motivated.

The acceptance of responsibility sends a strong signal that the act is motivated by a principled stand. The most obvious explanation for the behavior of someone who breaks a law knowing that she will suffer some unpleasant legal consequences—at least in circumstances in which she does not stand to gain some more significant material benefit—is that the act of disobedience is motivated by considerations we would intuitively regard as morally commendable. Such acts of disobedience might not succeed in expressing the particular principles motivating the act, but they generally succeed in expressing that the act is motivated by moral considerations, a feature that operates to legitimize these acts.

There is another reason that acceptance of responsibility is a necessary element in justifying an act of civil disobedience. Someone who breaks the law breaches the public peace and contributes to a public sense of vulnerability and insecurity; if someone is hacking into machines all around me, I respond with feelings of vulnerability and insecurity—feelings that are fairly characterized as constituting an injury. The willingness of the perpetrator to accept responsibility usually (although not necessarily) signals that the breach of the public peace is exceptional rather than part of a general pattern of misconduct and need not give rise to feelings of vulnerability and insecurity.

5.1.3. Should Unjustified Civil Disobedience Be Punished?

A second important moral issue regarding civil disobedience is whether the state should, as a moral matter, punish unjustified acts of civil disobedience. A couple of observations are helpful by way of clarification. First, the claim that it is permissible for a legitimate state to punish unjustified acts of civil disobedience does not imply that it is obligated to do so, or even that it should do so. The claim that act A is morally permissible, as a logical matter, is consistent with the claim that not-A is morally permissible.

Second, the claim that A is permissible does not imply that A is the best thing to do from a moral standpoint. In circumstances in which A and not-A are both permissible (which frequently occurs), only one of the two options can be the best from the moral standpoint. If, for example, giving to charity is not obligatory, then not giving is morally permissible. However, it seems clear that, absent exceptional circumstances, not giving is not ideal from a moral point of view. Other things being equal, it is better to give than not to give.

Accordingly, the issue of whether the state should punish civil disobedience is different from the issue of whether it is permissible for the state to punish civil disobedience, although it is crucial to note that there is some relationship between them. If it is not permissible for the state to punish civil disobedience, then it follows that the state should not punish civil disobedience; one should not do what is not permissible. But, as was seen, the two issues are logically distinct because the claim that it is permissible for the state to punish civil disobedience does not imply that it should; if not doing so is ideal, then the state should not punish such acts.

Though the issue of whether the state should punish civil disobedience is frequently conflated with the issue of whether it is morally permissible for individuals to engage in civil disobedience, the two are distinct issues. There might be any number of reasons why the state should tolerate an act that is morally impermissible. For example, lying is presumptively impermissible, but the social costs of enforcing perfect honesty (including those to privacy) seem to militate decisively against attempting to prohibit all instances of dishonesty. Advocating racist views is morally impermissible, but one might have a moral right to assert patently immoral views.

This raises the question of whether, and under what circumstances, a morally legitimate state should punish unjustified (as opposed to justified) acts of civil disobedience. Proponents of civil disobedience have offered a number of reasons for thinking that the law should not, as a general matter, punish even unjustified acts of civil disobedience. First, acts of civil disobedience, even unjustified ones, call attention to laws that ought to be changed because they are unjust or because they lack sufficient support among citizens. Like any other form of speech, acts of civil disobedience can promote moral dialogue and debate, which conduces to the benefit of all.

Second, proponents maintain that acts of civil disobedience do not typically result in morally significant harm to other persons. A sit-in at a local restaurant might inconvenience other patrons, but minor inconvenience does not justify punishing participants. Indeed, according to the proponent, the benefits of civil disobedience greatly outweigh the costs, and for this reason should not be punished.

Neither of these arguments is successful in justifying the general claim that civil disobedience ought not to be punished. For starters, it is true that civil disobedience can stimulate debate and presumably open minds, but it is also true that civil disobedience can close them as well because civil disobedience is not merely speech. Someone who commits an act of civil disobedience runs the risk of alienating people and thereby closing channels that would otherwise be available for debate. I doubt, for example, that anyone who burned American flags to protest laws prohibiting flag burning did much to change the minds of those who supported those laws. Indeed, I suspect that such behavior led supporters of laws prohibiting flag burning to believe that stiffer penalties should be authorized for violating those laws. Unlike the act of giving a reasoned argument, acts of civil disobedience are likely to alienate many members of the community.

Moreover, it is not necessarily true that acts of civil disobedience do not result in morally significant harm to a person. After citizens in the state of Washington passed an initiative prohibiting affirmative action in public institutions (an initiative I think is unjust and unfair), opponents marched onto a highway bridge and blocked traffic for hours. As far as I know, no one was significantly harmed by this protest, but it is not difficult to see that this could have resulted in significant harm: someone could have lost a job or, worse, been denied essential medical service because of the traffic jam caused by this act of civil disobedience. Injury to morally significant interests is always a possible result of civil disobedience.

5.1.4. An Epistemic Issue in Justifying Civil Disobedience
Supporters of civil disobedience also argue that the state should not punish civil disobedience because the motivation is laudable. Because acts of civil disobedience are, by definition, motivated by conscience, it is not entirely clear what the legitimating point of punishment would be. One might think, for example, that someone who commits an act of civil disobedience does not need to be either rehabilitated

or segregated for the protection of other people (which are two legitimating points of punishment). Further, persons who are willing to accept a proportional punishment and even court such punishment cannot be deterred by the threat of punishment (another legitimating point of punishment).

As it turns out, the mental state of someone who commits an act of civil disobedience is not entirely unproblematic from a moral point of view. Although such a person's motivations might be laudable, she will likely have another mental state that is not unproblematic from a moral point of view. Someone who commits an act of civil disobedience is usually acting on the strength of a conviction that is deeply contested in the society—and, indeed, one that is frequently a minority position.

This, by itself, can obviously be laudable in many circumstances. The courage to act on one's convictions and the willingness to sacrifice for one's convictions are both virtues. We encourage a child, for example, not to follow the crowd when doing so is wrong or foolish, knowing that such behavior will frequently result in unpleasant social consequences to the child, such as being ridiculed or ostracized. One who is willing to risk ridicule and ostracism to honor her moral convictions is courageous and deserves praise.

But there are clear moral limits on how far one can go in acting on a contestable moral conviction. To take an extreme case, Paul Hill argued that he was morally justified in murdering John Bayard Britton, an abortion provider, by the moral principle that allows deadly force in defense of the lives of innocent moral persons against culpable attack.[6] Because, according to Hill, fetuses are moral persons from the moment of conception and because murdering Britton was necessary to save the lives of fetuses he would culpably abort, he was justified in killing Britton in defense of others—just as he would be justified under that principle in killing someone who was trying to murder a newborn infant.[7]

Hill's violent act, however, cannot be justified under the moral principle allowing defense of others for an interesting reason. The fact that the issue of whether fetuses are moral persons from the moment of conception is so deeply contested in this society by intelligent persons of conscience shows that much more evidence and argument are needed to provide adequate reason to believe that fetuses have this special moral status from the moment of conception. Because Hill lacked morally adequate reason to believe that the principle allowing deadly force in defense of innocent persons applied to fetuses, he could not be justified under this principle in killing Britton and was rightly convicted of murder. As a general matter, a person who takes aggressive action against a person under a moral principle without adequate epistemic grounds for believing its application conditions are satisfied commits a moral wrong against that person.

The same principle applies to cases far less extreme than the Hill case. For example, those persons who effectively shut down traffic on the Washington state

---

[6]For Hill's tragically misguided views on the morality of killing abortion providers, see http://www.armyofgod.com/PHillonepage.html.

[7]Indeed, this is a very consequence of the claim that a fetus is a moral person. If a fetus has a full and equal set of moral rights, then murdering a fetus violates the same right to life that murdering a newborn infant violates and is just as grave a moral offense. This is why the issue of fetal personhood is so crucial to the abortion debate.

bridge deliberately caused significant inconvenience to other persons after having their position rejected at the polls. Although their position might have been the correct one, their willingness to cause such inconvenience to others on the strength of a view that might, or might not, have been particularly well reasoned (protesters, after all, need not be philosophers) is problematic from a moral point of view for exactly the same reason that Hill's violent act is problematic—even if, all things considered, the civil disobedience was justified. One must have adequate reason for believing that one's moral conviction is correct to be justified in imposing significant detriment on innocent third parties.[8]

The mental state of someone who deliberately imposes detriment on innocent third parties on the strength of a moral conviction that lacks adequate epistemic support is morally problematic in at least two possibly related ways. First, it evinces disregard for the interests of innocent third parties, a failure to appreciate the importance of other people. Second, it evinces an arrogant judgment about the importance and reliability of one's own judgments. It seems, at the very least, arrogant for one person to deliberately subject another to a risk of harm on the strength of an idea that lacks adequate support.[9]

One sign that a moral conviction lacks adequate epistemic support is that it is deeply contested among open-minded, reasonable persons of conscience in the culture. The idea that there are many open-minded reasonable persons of conscience on both sides of an issue suggests that both positions are reasonable in the sense that they are backed by good reasons that lack an adequate rebuttal. Insofar as a disagreement is reasonable in this sense, neither side can claim to have fully adequate support.

This helps to explain why Hill's act was morally wrong. Even on the assumption that Hill's view about fetal personhood is correct, the fact that so many reasonable persons of conscience—who otherwise agree on so much—disagree on fetal personhood should have told Hill that there were limits on how far he could go in acting on his conviction. Although he could legitimately protest abortion rights in a variety of ways, he could not legitimately act in ways that deliberately impose significant detriment on other persons.

This should not be construed as overlooking the possibility of a disagreement that continues because one side is unreasonable or not open to reasoned argument. It seems clear, for example, that persons who disagreed in the 1960s and 1970s with the idea that race-based segregation is wrong lacked even minimal support for a position that had been all but conclusively refuted by that juncture. Sometimes there are a lot of unreasonable, narrow-minded persons who simply refuse to see the light.

---

[8]Some of the motorists delayed by the protest surely voted against the initiative and shared the view of the protesters.

[9]This primarily applies to individuals; the state is in a somewhat different position because, in many cases, it cannot avoid taking a position on a contested issue by refraining from acting. If it refrains from prohibiting abortion, for example, the absence of a prohibition presupposes (at least to the extent that we presume the state is trying to do what is morally legitimate) that abortion does not result in murder. If it prohibits abortion, the prohibition presupposes either that a woman does not have a privacy right in her body or that abortion results in murder. Citizens are rarely in such a position.

In many instances, however, disagreement will be reasonable, calling into question whether persons on one side of an issue may legitimately impose morally significant costs on other persons for expressive purposes. In cases where a position is held by only a small minority of the people and dissenting views are reasonably held, the worry is greater. In such cases, it seems clear that, other things being equal, persons should refrain from deliberately imposing morally significant costs on innocent third parties as a means of protesting the majority view or calling attention to its injustice.

But even when a position is in play among reasonable persons, a person should be in cognitive possession of a reasonably thoughtful justification for the position before deliberately imposing detriment on third parties as a means of expressing support for that position (or opposition to the contrary position). Someone who deliberately impacts the morally significant interests of others to their detriment without anything that would count as a thoughtful justification might as well be acting on the basis of a coin flip. It seems clear that we have an obligation not to deliberately harm morally significant interests of innocent third parties unless we have some good reason for believing it is morally justified.

5.1.5. A Framework for Evaluating Acts of Civil Disobedience

The foregoing discussion suggests a useful framework for evaluating acts of civil disobedience. From the standpoint of morality, acts of civil disobedience have both pluses and minuses that have to be weighed. The moral value, for example, of a conscientious desire to call attention to injustice must be weighed against the moral disvalue of imposing costs on third parties.

Accordingly, the following considerations weigh in favor of finding that an act of civil disobedience against an otherwise legitimate state is justified (or excused) and should not be punished by the state. First, the act is committed openly by properly motivated persons willing to accept responsibility for the act. Second, the position is a plausible one that is, at the very least, in play among open-minded, reasonable persons in the relevant community.[10] Third, persons committing an act of civil disobedience are in possession of a thoughtful justification for both the position and the act. Fourth, the act does not result in significant damage to the interests of innocent third parties. Fifth, the act is reasonably calculated to stimulate and advance debate on the issue.

In contrast, the following considerations weigh in favor of finding that an act of civil disobedience against an otherwise legitimate state is not excused and ought to be punished. First, the act is not properly motivated or committed openly by persons willing to accept responsibility. Second, the position is implausible and not in play among most thoughtful, open-minded persons in the relevant

---

[10]It should be noted that this is a considerably stronger standard than the one that would naturally arise from the last section. I suggested there that one indication that a position lacked adequate epistemic support is that it is deeply contested among thoughtful persons of conscience in the culture. The claim that the position motivating civil disobedience be a plausible one in play among reasonable persons effectively gives people who commit civil disobedience the benefit of the doubt: The standard that a position must be in play is much easier to satisfy than the standard that a position must not be deeply contested. Positions held by a small minority satisfy the former, but not the latter.

community. Third, the people who have committed an act of civil disobedience lack a thoughtful justification for the position or the act. Fourth, the act results in significant harm to innocent third parties. Fifth, the act is not reasonably calculated to stimulate or advance debate on the issue.

Again, it is important to emphasize here that the context is a legitimate democratic state with laws that are generally just. It is reasonable to think that the moral calculus in an illegitimate state is radically different insofar as citizens of such a state have a right to openly rebel. How exactly one distinguishes legitimate from illegitimate states is a matter of dispute among political philosophers and theorists, but I assume that the readers of this paper live in states that are not illegitimate.

The civil rights sit-ins of the 1960s are paradigmatic examples of justified acts of civil disobedience under the framework described. Someone who refuses to leave segregated lunch counters until police arrive to remove her is clearly committing an open act of civil disobedience and is willing to accept the consequences of her behavior. The view that such segregation is wrong was not only in play among open-minded, reasonable persons of conscience, but had pretty much won the day by the time the mid-1960s arrived. The people who committed these acts justified them by reference to a principle of equality that open-minded, reasonable persons of conscience in the culture had nearly universally accepted. Lunch counter sit-ins had significant effects only on the owners who wrongly implemented policies of segregating blacks and whites. These sit-ins helped to call attention to the ongoing racial injustices in the southern United States.

In contrast, acts of vandalism by anarchists during the 1999 World Trade Organization (WTO) protests in Seattle were not justified acts of civil disobedience (assuming, of course, that these were nonviolent acts of civil disobedience and hence motivated by the right sort of considerations) under this framework. Anarchists who broke windows and set fires typically fled the scene as soon as the police arrived. Anarchism—especially the confused version to which this class of protesters subscribe—is not in play among reasonable, open-minded persons in the community. If televised interviews with some of the anarchists were any indication, they generally lacked a thoughtful justification for their views; most of them I saw were strikingly inarticulate. The cost of replacing a large plate glass storefront window is in excess of $10,000—a morally significant cost to innocent store owners. These acts of vandalism tend to alienate people and entrench them further in their opposition to anarchism, rather than provoke reasoned discussion.

These are, of course, fairly easy cases under the framework described (or, for that matter, any plausible framework for evaluating acts of civil disobedience) because all of the relevant factors point in the same direction. All of the factors in the civil rights case weigh in favor of justification, whereas all of the factors in the anarchism case weigh against justification.

One should not think this will always be the case. One would expect that there will many instances of civil disobedience, electronic or otherwise, in which there are elements that weigh in favor of justification, as well as elements that weigh against justification. These cases will be quite difficult to evaluate under this framework because there is no easy methodology for weighing the various factors against one another.

Still, it is reasonable to think that a couple of these factors define necessary conditions for an act of civil disobedience to be justified. It seems clearly impermissible to deliberately impose morally significant costs on other people for purely expressive purposes—at least in democratic societies in which one's point can openly be expressed in other ways without fear of reprisal; thus, it is a necessary condition for an act of civil disobedience to be justified in such societies that it not impose morally significant detriment on innocent third parties.

In addition, willingness to accept responsibility seems also to be a necessary condition for an act of civil disobedience to be justified—provided that the legal consequences are not unreasonably out of line with moral requirements. It would be absurd to demand that someone accept responsibility for disobeying a parking law if the legal consequence was life in prison. As we have seen, willingness to accept responsibility is needed to assure the public that the breach of the peace is exceptional and is a crucial factor in justifying civil disobedience.

5.2. What Is Hacktivism?

To determine whether or not hacktivism might be excused or justified as civil disobedience, we need a sense for what is involved in hacktivism. Insofar as hacktivism is a form of hacking, the word "hacktivism" is related to the word "hacking". The latter term, however, is a highly contentious term that means different things to different people. Consider, for example, the entry for "hacker" in the original *Hacker's Dictionary*[11]:

> HACKER n. 1. A person who enjoys learning the details of programming systems and how to stretch their capabilities, as opposed to most users who prefer to learn only the minimum necessary. 2. One who programs enthusiastically, or who enjoys programming rather than just theorizing about programming. 3. A person capable of appreciating hack value (q.v.). 4. A person who is good at programming quickly. Not everything a hacker produces is a hack. 5. An expert at a particular program, or one who frequently does work using it or on it; example: "A SAIL hacker". (Definitions 1 to 5 are correlated, and people who fit them congregate.) 6. A malicious or inquisitive meddler who tries to discover information by poking around. Hence "password hacker", "network hacker".

Although the first five clauses define "hacker" in terms of approbation, these usages are currently idiosyncratic at best. Definition 6 comes closest to expressing the current use of "hacker" now irrevocably associated with computer crime. A "hacker," on this usage, is a (1) malicious or inquisitive (2) meddler who (3) pokes around to

---

[11] http://www.dourish.com/goodies/jargon.html.

(4) discover information. Although many persons in the computer industry continue to use "hacker" to pick out programmers of distinction, "hacker" is now used by most persons only to pick out persons who intrude on systems and machines belonging to other people without any meaningful authorization (whether through the consent of the owners or through the legal process). Anyone who trespasses on someone else's system or network qualifies as a "hacker" according to this common usage. This is the definition that is presupposed in this chapter.

At the most general level, "hacktivism" is reasonably defined as politically-motivated hacking (Manion and Goodrum, 2000) or as hacking that is performed as political activism. Because hacking, as a conceptual matter, involves the commission of an unauthorized digital intrusion, "hacktivism" is more precisely defined as the commission of an unauthorized digital intrusion for the purpose of expressing a political position or for the purpose of achieving a political agenda. As a species of digital act, hacktivism does not involve the use of physical force (at least, as traditionally understood) and hence is nonviolent in nature. As a species of activism, hacktivism does not seek to achieve its political purposes, unlike terrorism, by inspiring general fear or terror among the population; it attempts to achieve these purposes by stimulating reasoned discussion and debate. Hacktivism is thus conceptually distinct from cyberterrorism, although the boundaries, as we will see, sometimes seem to overlap in practice.

What distinguishes hacktivism from ordinary hacking (as opposed to "cracking") is the motivation. Although the motivation of hackers (as opposed to crackers) is benign, a benign motivation does not necessarily involve one that is expressive of a political or moral view. Simple curiosity, for example, is benign, but not expressive of a political or moral view. Nor is a benign motivation necessarily a praiseworthy one. Simple curiosity is always benign, but not necessarily morally laudable; indeed, there are many things about which it is probably not good, from a moral point of view, to be curious (e.g., what it feels like to kill someone). In contrast, the motivation of the hacktivist is both expressive and praiseworthy: The motivation is to bring about some greater moral good by calling attention to injustice for the purpose of eliminating it. Accordingly, for purposes of this chapter, "hacktivism" is understood as involving unauthorized digital intrusions for the purpose of protesting some injustice or advancing some political agenda.

There are forms of digital activism that do not, strictly speaking, count as hacktivism. Posting a Web site in the United States with a petition protesting the Iraqi war is a form of digital activism, on this definition, but does not count as an act of hacktivism because it does not involve an unauthorized digital intrusion. Nor, for that matter, does such an act count as act of electronic civil disobedience because the posting of such content online breaks no laws; electronic civil disobedience, as a conceptual matter, is a form of civil disobedience and hence requires the violation of a valid law.

There are also forms of hacktivism that do not count as civil disobedience. Hacking into a government server for the purpose of bringing down a repressive regime counts as an instance of hacktivism; it clearly involves committing a digital intrusion for the purpose of advancing a political agenda. But it does not count as civil disobedience because it is not motivated by a desire to protest the injustice of the regime; the goal is political, but not politically expressive.[12]

In contrast, the following acts all count, on this analysis, as both hacktivism and civil disobedience: (1) a denial of service (DoS) attack launched against the WTO Web site to protest economic globalization and WTO policies[13]; (2) the altering of the content of a government Web site to express outrage over some policy of that government[14]; and (3) the unauthorized redirection of traffic intended for a KKK Web site to Hatewatch.[15] Each of these acts involves some unauthorized digital intrusion and hence counts as hacktivism because it is presumably intended as a piece of political activism.

5.3. Is Hacktivism Morally Justified as Civil Disobedience?

The issue of whether hacktivism is justified civil disobedience must be addressed on a case-by-case basis because acts of hacktivism vary with respect to morally relevant characteristics. Some hacktivists, for example, make no attempt to conceal their identity and evince a willingness to accept responsibility for their acts, whereas others conceal their identities to evade detection. Some acts involve no significant damage to innocent third parties (e.g., defacing a governmental Web site to protest its policies), whereas others do (e.g., shutting down commercial Web sites with distributed DoS [DDoS] attacks). Open acts of hacktivism that do not impact innocent third parties have a different moral quality than clandestine acts that harm innocent third parties.

In addition, there are a variety of positions that motivate hacktivism. Many acts of hacktivism are meant to advance the cause of universal human rights and intrude against governmental entities believed to be violating those rights. Others are motivated by a desire to protest the increasing commercialization of the Internet and commodification of information. Some of these positions are more plausible and better supported than others; acts of hacktivism motivated by well-supported plausible positions are, other things being equal, morally preferable to acts not motivated by well-supported plausible positions.

A comprehensive survey of hacktivist acts is not possible here. In what follows, I consider some of the factors relevant to the evaluation of hacktivism under the framework described and illustrate them with a couple of examples. For this rea-

---

[12]I am indebted to Keith Miller for making me see this. It is also worth noting here that insofar as such an act might be morally justified (as seems quite plausible), it is not a necessary condition for hacktivism to be justified that it qualify as a piece of civil disobedience. (We see an example of this in Section 4.) We have already seen in Section 1 that civil disobedience is not necessarily justified, which suggests that it is not a sufficient condition for hacktivism to be justified that it qualify as a piece of civil disobedience.

[13]In 1999, the Electrohippies attacked a WTO Web site for such reasons. For a summary of notable hacker attacks, see "Timeline of Hacker History," *Wikipedia*. Available at http://en.wikipedia.org/wiki/Infamous_Hacks.

[14]In 1996, hackers changed the content of the Department of Justice Web site, replacing "Justice" with "Injustice."

[15]Anonymous hackers did exactly this in 1999. Intriguingly, a Hatewatch press release characterized the act as "vandalism." See Hatewatch (1999).

son, the discussion below makes no claim to being complete or even comprehensive in scope.

5.3.1. How Much Harm Is Caused?

One of the key issues in evaluating whether an act of hacktivism is morally justified is the extent to which the act harms the interests of innocent third parties. In thinking about this issue, it is important to reiterate that the context being assumed here is a morally legitimate democratic system that protects the right of free speech and thus affords persons a variety of avenues for expressing their views that do not impact the interests of innocent third parties.

As the amount of harm varies from case to case and thus must be determined by empirical means, I briefly discuss some general issues that commonly arise in connection with evaluating the amount of harm.

5.3.1.1. Public, Private, Commercial, and Noncommercial Entities

How much harm is caused frequently depends on whether the target of the hack is a public, private, commercial, or noncommercial entity. Attacks on public noncommercial, purely informative Web sites, for example, tend to cause less damage than attacks on private, commercial Web sites. The reason for this is that attacks on commercial Web sites can result in significant business losses ultimately passed on to consumers in the form of higher prices (reflecting a higher cost of doing business) or to employees in the form of layoffs. If the information on a public Web site is nonessential information (i.e., unrelated to vital interests), an attack on that Web site is not likely to result in anything more serious than inconvenience to citizens who are not able to access that information.[16]

This should not be taken to suggest that hacktivist intrusions on public entities cannot result in significant harm to third parties. One can conceive of a depressingly large variety of acts that might very well cause significant damage to innocent third parties. A digital attack on a public hospital server might very well result in deaths. Of course, these more serious acts are probably not motivated by expressive purposes (and, I would argue, should be characterized as "violent acts"[17]) and, if so, would not count either as civil disobedience or as hacktivism as these notions are defined here.

Acts of hacktivism directed at private individuals can also have morally significant effects. A DoS attack, for example, that effectively denies access to a citizen's Web site can impact her moral rights. A DoS attack on a citizen site impacts her ability to express her views and hence infringes her moral right to free speech (as opposed to her legal right to speech, which is typically against only governmental

---

[16]The Electrohippies justify attacks on various public Web sites precisely on such grounds: "Neither the Whitehouse nor 10 Downing Street web site are [sic] essential services. For the most part they merely distribute the fallacious justifications in Iraq, as well as trying to promote the image of the two prime movers behind war in Iraq: Messrs. Bush and Blair" (Electrohippies, 2003). The idea here is that the harm caused by attacks that ultimately deny access to public Web sites not providing essential services result in no significant harm to innocent third parties.

[17]See footnote 4, *supra*.

entities). An attempt to gain access to files on a citizen's computer impacts her rights to privacy, as well as her property rights in her computer.

5.3.1.2. The Character of the Hack

How much harm is done depends not only on the character of the victim, but also on the nature of the attack.[18] In the area of physical attacks, this is, of course, obvious. Throwing a Molotov cocktail into an open window is, other things being equal, likely to cause significantly more harm than tagging the building with some sort of graffiti. The more forceful the attack, the more harm is likely to result.

It should be emphasized that this is not necessarily true. Someone might throw a Molotov cocktail into a building that is slated for destruction and save the owner the costs of tearing it down, and the owner of a property being tagged might have a heart attack as a result of the distress caused by someone vandalizing her property. Accordingly, an accurate determination of how much damage any particular attack, physical or digital, requires an empirical analysis that looks to the specific circumstances of the attack.

Still, as a general matter, some digital attacks are less likely to cause harm than others. Defacement of a Web site—or "e-graffiti" as sympathetic theorists sometimes call it—seems far less likely to cause significant harm than attacks that have the effect of denying access to the contents of a Web site. Changing "Department of Justice" on a government Web site, for example, to "Department of Injustice" is not likely to result in significant harm to third-party interests. At most, it causes embarrassment to the government agency running the site and perhaps some minor loss of confidence among citizens in the accuracy of the site's contents.

This should not, however, be taken to suggest that defacement of a Web site can never result in significant damage to innocent third parties. Publishing sensitive information about individuals, like social security numbers, as "e-graffiti" on a government Web site could obviously result in significant damage to those individuals. As is true of physical graffiti, one must look to the specific circumstances to evaluate the damage caused by digital graffiti to ensure an accurate assessment.

Nevertheless, it is reasonable to think that, as a general matter, DoS and DDoS attacks are calculated to cause more damage, other things being equal, than defacement of Web sites. These attacks are calculated to deny access of third parties to the content of a Web site, effectively shutting it down by overwhelming the server with sham requests for information. Although there are undoubtedly exceptions to any generalizations about the comparative harm caused by defacement of Web sites and DoS attacks, it seems reasonable to think that shutting down a Web site is a more harmful act than merely defacing it. For this reason, DoS attacks are harder to justify, as a general matter, as permissible electronic civil disobedience than defacement.

But, again, the amount of harm caused to innocent parties depends on a host of circumstances, including the character of the Web site being shut down. Other

---

[18]For a helpful discussion of various tactics, see Auty (2004). My discussion in this and the last section owes an obvious debt to Auty's discussion.

things being equal, DoS and DDoS attacks on commercial Web sites are likely to result in greater harm than such attacks on noncommercial public Web sites providing nonessential services or information. Still, as a general matter, these attacks should be regarded as one of the more aggressive tools currently employed by hacktivists and hence as more problematic, from the standpoint of morality, than other tools.

It is true, of course, that most civil disobedience affects third parties, but digital civil disobedience can potentially do much more damage to the interests of far more people than ordinary, nondigital civil disobedience. Although it could have been worse, the effect of the protest in Washington was that many persons might have been late to work, losses that are easily made up. An attack that shuts down a busy commercial Web site for a few hours can easily affect hundreds of thousands of people. If the Web site's activity is vital to its profit margin, this can translate into morally significant losses of revenue, which are usually shifted to employees and consumers.

Indeed, a coordinated and sustained attack on the largest commercial Web sites, which can be carried out by a fairly small group of highly skilled hackers, could result in the sort of economic downturn that affects millions of people. According to experts on terrorism, al Qaeda is exploring the possibility of large-scale cyberattacks on public and commercial networks precisely because a large enough attack might suffice to weaken confidence in e-commerce to such an extent as to precipitate a recession, or worse. Here it is worth noting that an increase of the unemployment rate in the United States from 5% to 6% means the loss of approximately one and a half million jobs (according to the U.S. government, there were 147 million people in the labor force in 2004), a consequence of grave moral significance.

As is readily evident, electronic civil disobedience can have a greater impact on the interests of the targeted entity and third parties than ordinary civil disobedience. This, of course, is part of what makes digital trespass appealing to politically minded hackers and explains why electronic civil disobedience raises more serious moral concerns than ordinary civil disobedience.

5.3.2. Are Hacktivists Prepared to Accept Responsibility?

One important factor contributing to justify an act of civil disobedience is that the persons committing the act are willing to accept responsibility for those acts. Manion and Goodrum (2000, p. 15), for example, assert that "[w]illingness [of participants] to accept personal responsibility for outcome of actions" is a necessary, although not sufficient, condition for the justification of an act of civil disobedience: "In order for hacking to qualify as an act of civil disobedience, hackers must be clearly motivated by ethical concerns, be non-violent, and be ready to accept the repercussions of their actions."

Nevertheless, there is a distinction between claiming responsibility for an act and being willing to accept the legal consequences of that act. One can claim responsibility without coming forward to accept the legal consequences of one's act. One could do this, I suppose, by giving one's real name and then attempting to conceal one's location to avoid facing those consequences. Or, more likely, one can do this by giving some sort of pseudonym instead of one's real name or by attributing the act to a particular group to which one belongs that protects the names of its members. Although such a claim of responsibility helps to signal an ethical motivation, this is not tantamount to be willing to accept responsibility.

The heroic civil rights activists of the 1960s who staged sit-ins went beyond merely claiming responsibility; they accepted, even invited, prosecution. It was part of their strategy to call attention to the injustice of Jim Crow laws in the South by voluntarily subjecting themselves to prosecution under those very laws. These courageous activists did not anonymously claim responsibility for the sit-ins from a safe distance: They continued the protests until the police arrived to arrest them.

Some noteworthy hacktivists evince a similar willingness to accept responsibility for their actions. As Manion and Goodrum (2000, p. 15) observe:

> Examined in this light, the hack by Euguene Kashpureff clearly constitutes an act of civil disobedience. Kashpureff usurped traffic from InterNIC to protest domain name policy. He did this non-anonymously and went to jail as a result.

But this seems to be the exception, not the rule. There are a variety of hacktivist groups, including Electrohippies, MilwOrm, and Electronic Disturbance Theatre, but these groups typically claim responsibility for acts as a group without disclosing the identities of any members to avoid prosecution. For example, MilwOrm and another group claimed responsibility for the defacement of approximately 300 Web sites (they replaced the existing content with a statement against nuclear weapons and a photograph of a mushroom cloud), but did not disclose the identities of members who belong to the group. As far as I can tell, persons committing acts of hacktivism typically attempt to conceal their identities to avoid detection and exposure to prosecution, even when claiming responsibility.

Anonymous hacktivist attacks impose significant costs on social well-being. First, such attacks, regardless of motivation, contribute to an increasing sense of anxiety among the population about the security of the Internet, which has become increasingly vital to economic and other important interests. Second, these attacks require an expenditure of valuable resources that could be allocated in more productive ways, to protecting computers against intrusions, costs that are passed on to consumers.

In any event, it is worth noting that terrorists typically claim responsibility as a group but attempt to evade the consequences of their actions by concealing their identities and locations. It is important, of course, not to make too much of this similarity: Terrorists deliberately attempt to cause grievous harm to innocent people; hacktivists do not. The point, however, is merely to illustrate that there is a morally significant difference between claiming responsibility and accepting responsibility. Accepting responsibility is, other things being equal, needed to justify an act of hacktivism.

5.3.3. Is the Political Agenda Plausible and Supported by Adequate Reasons?

The motivating agenda behind electronic civil disobedience, other things being equal, is not as transparently evident as the motivating agenda behind ordinary civil disobedience. Whereas the protesters who shut down the Washington state highway carried signs and alerted the press they were protesting a specific measure, the point of many putative acts of hacktivism is not clear. A DDoS attack, for example, directed against Amazon.com could mean any number of things, some of which have nothing to do with expressing a political view (e.g., a recently discharged employee might be taking revenge for her dismissal). The absence of any clear message is surely problematic from a moral standpoint.

In any event, I consider in this section what I take to be the two most common motivating agendas behind hacktivist acts to illustrate the above framework for evaluating acts of civil disobedience.

5.3.3.1. Hacktivism in Support of Human Rights

Acts of hacktivism are frequently motivated by a desire to protest the suppression and violation of human rights by oppressive nondemocratic regimes and are directed at servers maintained and owned by governmental entities in those regimes. Chinese governmental Web sites, for example, have been hacked to protest the oppression of both Chinese and Indonesian citizens.

There are a number of things worth noting about digital intrusions directed at oppressive governments that are motivated by a desire to protest violations of human rights, like torture of political dissidents. First, strictly speaking, many such acts do not count as civil disobedience. The reason for this is that many of these attacks are from people who live outside the repressive regime and are not subject to the legal consequences within the regime. But insofar as these legal consequences are draconian and drastically out of proportion to what is morally appropriate, acceptance of responsibility is not necessary for such acts to be justified. Accordingly, these attacks that originate from outside the target nation might be justified hacktivism, but they are not justified as civil disobedience.[19]

Second, the primary impact of such acts is on the parties culpable for committing violations of human rights. Defacing a governmental Web site that does not provide essential services or information, for example, is not likely to have any significant effects on innocent citizens.

Third, the regimes being targeted do not recognize or respect a right of free speech. These regimes forcefully repress political dissent, usually with the threat of incarceration or worse. It is reasonable to think that the moral calculus of civil disobedience is considerably different in states that systematically deny citizens the opportunity to express dissent without fear of reprisal.

Fourth, such acts of civil disobedience are frequently successful in calling attention to the injustice and stimulating debate. Although a digital defacement of a governmental Web site is easily addressed by the affected governmental entities, it is likely to receive worldwide attention from the press. Given the peaceful character of the act, it is more likely to inform citizens of the world and provoke thought and discussion than to alienate them.

---

[19]See footnote 12.

Finally, the position is probably a majority position among people in this culture and worldwide. It is fairly clear that, in Western cultures, support for universal human rights is, far and away, a majority position. But it is also reasonable to think that such support is also a majority position in non-Western cultures. In nations where citizens are denied human rights, those citizens frequently demand them. When liberated from oppressive regimes, moreover, citizens tend to behave in ways that were suppressed under those regimes. Women, for example, in Afghanistan adopted a Western style of dress and rejected the oppressive burqa after the Taliban was removed from power. People almost universally want speech rights, equality, and a right to be free from torture or political persecution.

Although theorists may disagree on some particulars, the philosophical literature in support of universal human rights is much more prevalent than the literature against it. One of the few objections to the idea that there are universal human rights is grounded in the normative ethical relativist position that there are no objective moral truths. There are two problems with this line of objection. First, it ignores the fact that people almost universally demand human rights. If we assume, quite reasonably, that reasonably conscientious people would not demand something unless they believed themselves morally entitled to it, then we have reason to believe that people are universally entitled to human rights on the assumption that normative ethical relativism is true. Second, normative ethical relativism is vulnerable to a host of external and internal criticisms (e.g., that the supposition that there are no objective moral truths is self-contradictory because such a supposition must be construed as an objective moral truth to be normatively relevant) and remains a minority position.[20]

5.3.3.2. Hacktivism in Support of the "Hacker Ethic"

Unlike the human rights agenda, other positions that commonly motivate hacktivism are fairly characterized as fringe positions not generally in play among thoughtful, open-minded members of the community. Consider, for example, the main tenets of the "hacker ethic" as summarized by Levy (1984):

1. Access to computers should be unlimited and total.
2. All information should be free.
3. Mistrust authority—promote decentralization.
4. Hackers should be judged by their hacking, not bogus criteria such as degrees, age, race, or position.
5. You create art and beauty on a computer.
6. Computers can change your life for the better.

---

[20]It is worth noting that relativists rarely argue for their moral positions the way one would expect of relativists. I have seen a fair number of relativists argue for a moral position without any reference to what people believe or accept in the relevant culture; this is not surprising in many of these cases because they argue for positions that would be rejected by the vast majority of people in the relevant culture. I have seen a number of them state something like, "we must, of course, avoid the mistake of assuming that there are objective moral truths" and then go on to commit that very mistake by arguing for a minority position without any attempt to evaluate existing social practices or conventions.

Whereas tenets 4 though 6 are largely uncontroversial (and so obvious they do not need to be stated), these are not the tenets that motivate acts of hacktivism. The tenets that are most likely to motivate acts of hacktivism are the first three.

It is hard to know what to say about tenet 3, as it is not entirely clear what it means, beyond pointing out that it is overly general (Should all doctors be mistrusted? Always?); however, tenets 1 and 2 are clearly fringe positions that are not really in play among open-minded, thoughtful people. Tenet 1 implies that people have no property rights in their own computers and hence may not permissibly exclude others from their machines, an implausible position that, consistently applied to other forms of property, would vitiate ownership in homes and automobiles.[21] Tenet 2 implies that people have no privacy rights in highly intimate information about themselves. Although many people are rightly rethinking their positions about information ethics in response to the new technologies, tenets 1 and 2 are simply too strong to be plausible because they are inconsistent with bedrock views about privacy and property rights. For this reason, neither is in play among open-minded, reasonable persons in the community.

One might reasonably think that these extreme positions are not exactly what hacktivists have in mind, but these are the positions that emerge most clearly from what is being said by and on behalf of politically minded hackers who commit acts of civil disobedience. Universal quantifiers, for example, are most naturally interpreted as, well, performing the function of universal quantifiers. "All information should be free" is naturally interpreted as meaning that all information should be free.

In any event, if these positions are not what hacktivists have in mind, then they need to make themselves clearer, and this is something that they are obligated to do before they undertake to commit acts of digital civil disobedience. It seems clear that, as a moral matter, one should know exactly what position one is attempting to further before one deliberately attempts to compromise networks and systems that belong to other people so as to cause inconvenience and damage to those persons.

5.3.4. Are Hacktivists in Cognitive Possession of a Plausible Justification for the Positions Motivating Their Acts?

It is not enough, according to this framework, that an act of hacktivism is motivated by a plausible position in play among thoughtful, reasonably conscientious persons; it is a necessary condition for an act of hacktivism to be justified that the actor be in cognitive possession of a reasonably plausible justification for that position.

As a general matter, there is little reason to think that the hacktivists themselves are in possession of a reasoned justification that would support the positions they take. It is reasonable to hypothesize that hacktivists are much better at solving the

---

[21]It should be noted that this issue pertains to property rights in physical objects, and not to intellectual property rights, which is a contentious subject. Even Marxists are prepared to allow that, in the ideal society, people will be able to exclude others from use of personal objects, regardless of whether they would characterize this as rising to the level of property rights.

technological problems associated with committing digital intrusions than they are at articulating and defending the positions that motivate them. Occasionally, they articulate their position with some sort of slogan, but rarely provide the position with the critical support it needs. Consider, for example, Manion's and Goodrum's (2000, p. 16) discussion of one such motivation:

> In order to determine the motivations of hacktivists, one place to look is what hacktivists themselves say is their motivation. . . . In June of 1998 the hacktivists group "MilwOrm" hacked India's Bhabba Atomic Research Centre to protest against recent nuclear tests. Later, in July of that year, "MilwOrm" and the group "Astray Lumberjacks," orchestrated an unprecedented mass hack of more than 300 sites around the world, replacing web pages with an anti-nuclear statements [sic] and images of mushroom clouds. Not surprisingly, the published slogan of MilwOrm is: "Putting the power back in the hands of people."

Again, one should say much more by way of justification for hacking 300 sites than just a vague slogan like "Putting the power back in the hands of people." The victims of such an attack, as well as the public whose peace has been breached, have a right to know exactly what position is motivating the attack and why anyone should think it is a plausible position.

The willingness to impose morally significant costs on other people to advance fringe positions that are neither clearly articulated nor backed with some sort of plausible justification is clearly problematic from a moral point of view. It seems clear that such behavior involves, at least in most cases, a fairly serious form of arrogance—a mental state that is problematic according to ordinary intuitions about morality. Indeed, it is exactly the sort of arrogance hacktivists attribute to their intended victims.

The foregoing argument should not, of course, be construed to condemn all acts of hacktivism. Nothing in the foregoing argument would justify a condemnation of narrowly targeted acts of electronic civil disobedience properly motivated and justified by a well-articulated plausible position that do not result in significant harm to innocent third parties. Acts of hacktivism that have these properties might very well be justified by the right to free speech, although, again, it bears emphasizing here that such acts are much harder to justify in societies with morally legitimate legal systems.

The problem, however, is that the most common (or at least the most widely reported) acts of digital civil disobedience are justifiably condemned by the foregoing arguments. Hacktivists simply have not done the kinds of things they ought to have done to make sure their acts are unproblematic from a moral standpoint. In their zealousness to advance their moral causes, they have committed acts that are far more obviously problematic from a moral point of view than the positions they seek to attack. If, as Manion and Goodrum (2000) suggest, hacktivists have been misunderstood by mainstream media and theorists, they have only themselves to blame.

5.4. Should Unjustified Hacktivism Be Punished?

As noted, the issue of whether civil disobedience should be punished by the state is different from the issue of whether civil disobedience is morally justified. Although it would presumably be wrong for the state to punish a morally justified act of civil disobedience, it is not as clear whether the state should punish unjustified acts of civil disobedience. Not every morally unjustified act should be punished by the state; ordinary lying, for example, should not be criminalized.

The issue of whether unjustified hacktivist acts should be punished by the state must be determined on a case-by-case basis. Whatever values might be served by punishing such acts must be weighed against the costs associated with punishment. Punishing an offender can be expensive and not really worth the costs if the act is comparatively innocuous and the offender's mental states are sufficiently blameless.

Even so, it is reasonable to think that the costs will sometimes be worth incurring. In cases where an unjustified act of hacktivism results in significant financial losses to individuals, offenders should be punished, at least where those losses are reasonably foreseeable. To begin, punishment in such cases seems pretty clearly deserved. It is simply wrong for an individual to take it upon herself to deliberately perform an act that is calculated to cause significant harm to others for expressive purposes. Further, culpable offenders stand in need of some rehabilitation (though our penal system is admittedly not particularly well-equipped to perform this legitimating feature of punishment). Finally, society has an interest in preventing and deterring morally unjustified behavior, but has an especially strong interest in preventing and deterring unjustified behavior reasonably calculated to cause significant harm to others.

Moreover, acts of electronic civil disobedience committed anonymously should be punished to the full extent under the law. Again, it is not enough to claim responsibility as a group; even terrorist organizations like al Qaeda do this much. The willingness of responsible individuals to come forward and accept the legal consequences of their behaviors helps to distinguish their acts from the acts of cyberterrorists; as such, their acts should be treated differently from the acts of cyberterrorists. For this reason, willingness to accept responsibility should be treated as a mitigating factor. In cases where no significant harm results from the act, willingness to accept responsibility might even be enough to warrant a dismissal of criminal charges.

In this connection, it is important to note that the boundaries between activism and terrorism are becoming increasingly blurred. Organizations such as the Earth Liberation Front and the Animal Liberation Front have adopted a particularly aggressive form of what they characterize as "activism." Targeting property, rather than people, these organizations have bombed animal research facilities in an attempt to induce the victims to adopt more environmentally and animal friendly policies and practices. The tactics of such organizations resemble the tactics of terrorists in that they frequently involve physical force, but are distinct in that they have attempted up to now to avoid human casualties.[22] These organizations, like

---

[22]They typically deny that such acts constitute violence on the ground that "violence" involves force directed at people, not property. As is evident, the terms "force" and "violence" are becoming increasingly contentious.

terrorist organizations, claim responsibility but never step forward to accept the legal consequences of their acts.

The effect of these and like-minded organizations have been to blur the distinction between activism and terrorism in the minds of the public, who increasingly view such anonymous acts as posing a serious threat to the public peace. For this reason, it is especially important that a legitimate legal system provide (1) an incentive for hacktivists to do more than just anonymously claim responsibility for their actions and (2) a significant deterrent to anonymous cyberattacks of any kind, no matter how well motivated they might be. Punishment of anonymous attacks to the full extent of the law is at least a step towards providing appropriate incentives and disincentives.

Acknowledgments

A shorter version of this paper was presented at ETHICOMP 2005 in Linkoping, Sweden. I am indebted to the participants for a lively conversation and for many helpful suggestions. In particular, I am especially indebted to Don Gotterbarn, Keith Miller, Kai Kiimpa, and Andrew K. Adams for their comments and criticisms.

References

Auty, Caroline. (2004). "Political Hacktivism: Tool of the Underdog or Scourge of Cyberspace?" *ASLIB Proceedings: New Information Perspectives*, Vol. 56, pp. 212–221.

Electrohippies, The. (2003). "A Response to Criticism of dDos Actions Online." Available at http://www.thehacktivist.com/print.php?sid=174. Accessed 5/27/06.

Hatewatch. (1999, September 4). "Press Release: Activism vs. Hacktivism." Available at http://archives.openflows.org/hacktivism/hacktivism01048.html. Accessed 5/27/06.

Himma, Kenneth Einar, and David Dittrich. (2006). "Hackers, Crackers, and Computer Criminals." In *The Handbook of Information Security*. New York: Wiley.

Huschle, Brian J. (2002). "Cyber Disobedience: When Is Hacktivism Civil Disobedience?" *International Journal of Applied Philosophy*, Vol. 16, No. 1, pp. 69–83.

Levy, Stephen. (1984). *Hackers: Computer Heroes of the Computer Revolution*. New York: Delta.

Manion, Mark, and Abby Goodrum. (2000, June). "Terrorism or Civil Disobedience: Toward a Hacktivist Ethic." *Computers and Society*, pp. 14–19.

Spafford, Eugene. (1992). "Are Computer Hacker Break-ins Ethical?" *Journal of Systems Software*, Vol. 17, No. 1, pp. 41–48.

Chapter 6: The Ethics of "Hacking Back": Active Response to Computer Intrusions

Kenneth Einar Himma

Victims of Internet-based hacker attacks are increasingly responding with a variety of "active responses." Some of these responses are aggressive in the sense that they are intended to inflict the same kind of harm on the attacker's machine or network as the attack is intended to have on the victim's machine or network. Conxion, for example, attempted to overload the network from which the Electrohippies staged a denial of service (DoS) attack by redirecting the incoming packets back to the network instead of simply dropping the packets at the router (see Radcliff, 2000). Some of these responses are, however, nonaggressive in the sense that there is no intent to inflict harm on the attacker's network. The point, for example, of implementing a traceback is just to identify the parties responsible for a digital attack by tracing the path of the attack back to its original source; traceback technologies are not ordinarily equipped or intended to inflict harm.

In this chapter, I attempt to determine whether it is ethically permissible for private persons or entities (as opposed to governmental persons or entities) to adopt these various forms of active response.[1] To this end, I distinguish three categories of active defense response according to the level of aggressiveness. Next, I identify the relevant ethical principles governing active response. Such principles include principles governing self-defense, negligence, waiver, and punishment. I then evaluate the various categories under these principles and conclude that all but the most benign of these responses should be presumed unethical.

A preliminary observation is in order here. The analysis does not presuppose any particular general ethical theory (e.g., utilitarianism). Instead, this analysis is grounded in general principles and specific judgments about cases that most people would accept and that, indeed, figure prominently in ordinary ethical judgments about such acts. Accordingly, the analysis in this paper begins by identifying moral

---

[1]State use of active defense raises a very different set of issues; a morally legitimate state can permissibly do many things that private individuals and entities cannot permissibly do, such as tax and punish private persons and entities.

principles commonly accepted in Western industrialized nations[2] and proceeds by attempting to identify the implications of those widespread commitments.

6.1. The Active Response Spectrum

The *active response continuum* defines a subcategory of intrusion response (i.e., digital response to unauthorized digital intrusions) and hence falls within a wide spectrum of potential responses by private entities.[3] At one end of the spectrum is the wholly passive, unknowing victim who relies entirely on the inherent capabilities of the software that comes with her computer and does not know when it is being attacked. At the other is the active, fully engaged victim who deliberately pursues a series of discrete tactics with a set of well-defined objectives in mind. As the term "active" indicates, active response measures fall towards the latter end of the spectrum.

As defined in this chapter, measures falling within the active response continuum have the following characteristics. First, these measures are, of course, *digitally based*; assaulting someone who is committing a digital trespass is not an instance of active response. Second, they are *reactive* in the sense that they are implemented following detection of an intrusion and are intended to counter it; as such, they are contrived to serve investigative, defensive, or punitive purposes. Third, they are *noncooperative* in that they are implemented without the consent of at least one of the parties involved in or affected by the intrusion. Finally, they usually have *causal impacts* on remote systems (i.e., those owned or controlled by some other person). These tactics range from more benign information-gathering measures (e.g., tracebacks) that impact remote systems without impairing their ongoing operations and functions to more aggressive measures (e.g., DoS counterattacks) expressly intended to inhibit or even stop the operations and functions of remote systems.

At an intuitive level, the definition of "active response" attempts to pick out digital acts that would be characterized as "hacking" if performed without provocation. Theorists and policymakers have become concerned with active responses precisely because of their resemblance to hacker attacks; it is, for this reason, that active responses are sometimes referred to as "counterhacking" or "hacking back." Although this definition of "active response" picks out some acts (e.g., scanning ports) that are not fairly characterized as "hacking," even those acts are minimally intrusive. Indeed, although they might very well be morally justified all things considered, they raise, at least initially, the same sorts of privacy and property concerns that are raised by acts that are fairly characterized as "hacking."

---

[2]It is worth noting that the principles identified herein are incorporated into the law of every Western industrialized nation. To the extent that most people accept those laws as legitimate, it is reasonable to conclude that most people believe they are just—and hence reflect the content of morality.

[3]This essay is limited to private intrusion responses. The response by public entities to digital intrusions raises very different technical, ethical, and legal issues.

This definition also attempts to incorporate the idea that these measures are taken in response to an unauthorized intrusion. The idea that such measures are reactive implies that measures intended to detect the occurrence of an intrusion do not fall within the active response continuum. As defined, reactive measures are deliberately contrived as a response to an intrusion that has previously been detected, although it is true, of course, that detection and response might sometimes proceed together as the intrusion continues.

Although many measures falling within the active response continuum are defensive, not all are. "Defense" is typically used to refer to measures reasonably calculated to stop either an ongoing attack or the harm it is causing; however, active response measures can serve a variety of purposes that are not, strictly speaking, defensive in either of these respects. For example, information-gathering efforts can be related to efforts to adopt measures calculated to stop an attack or its harmful effects, but they can also be directed at providing law enforcement agencies with sufficient evidence to prosecute culpable parties. In addition, some measures characterized as active response are motivated by a desire to punish or retaliate against an attack—with little regard for whether such measures actually bring about its cessation. Accordingly, although active response tactics are sometimes adopted for defensive purposes, they are also frequently adopted for investigatory and offensive purposes—and, indeed, can be employed in ongoing information warfare.

Thus conceived, measures falling within the active response continuum are compatible with the efforts of law enforcement agencies to investigate and prosecute computer crimes. As is readily apparent, efforts by private victims to gather and preserve information about the attack can assist law enforcement efforts to investigate and prosecute it. Such information can provide not only helpful investigatory leads, but can also form the foundation for the evidentiary base needed to successfully prosecute culpable parties.

Even so, it is worth emphasizing at the outset that active response measures are increasingly adopted by private firms as a substitute for involving law enforcement agencies. There are a variety of reasons for this. First, the resources available to law enforcement agencies for responding to digital intrusions have simply not kept pace with the frequency and severity of digital intrusions. The decreasing success rate of law enforcement efforts has led to a sense among private victims that it is far more efficient to respond without involving law enforcement. Second, and equally important, many commercial victims worry about the effects that publicizing an attack might have on their relationships with customers.[4] The concern is that their customers would become alarmed to learn of security breaches and ultimately respond by taking their business elsewhere. Such firms believe that the best way to minimize the risk of publicity and such deleterious effects is to respond internally to digital intrusions without involving law enforcement.

---

[4]See, e.g., Stevan D. Mitchell and Elizabeth A. Banker, "Private Intrusion Response," *Harvard Journal of Law & Technology*, vol. 11, no. 3 (Summer 1998).

6.2. Levels of Active Response

This section classifies various intrusion responses according to levels of "force." Although there are clearly differences between physically forceful actions and digitally intrusive actions, there are sufficient similarities to justify characterizing the latter as involving force of some kind. Although there are probably limits to the analogy between digital and physical force, these limits are of little importance here and can be safely disregarded.

6.2.1. Benign

Benign activities are those involving operations that have no direct causal effects on remote systems and are not adopted from a self-consciously noncooperative posture or attitude. Such measures include operations intended to gather information, as well as operations intended to address or correct vulnerabilities in the victim's networks. *Sniffing* (monitoring network traffic) is an example of a benign response.

6.2.2. Intermediate

Intermediate responses involve causal interaction with remote systems outside a defender's network, but are neither intended nor reasonably likely to cause harm to those systems. It is worth noting that noncooperative measures falling in this category are fairly characterized as active response as this notion was defined above, although one should not draw any substantive normative conclusions merely on the strength of a characterization of something as involving, or not involving, active response. This taxonomy can assist a normative analysis, but is no substitute for such an analysis.

One important example of an intermediate response is a *traceback*, which attempts to follow attack paths back to the ultimate source of an attack. If a victim knows (1) the attacker's methodology for using back doors and exposed network services for establishing stepping stones or proxy relays, (2) the passwords and/or account names favored by the attacker, and (3) the IP addresses used for entry/exit from the victim's network, the victim can follow the attacker's trails backward through the network. Tracebacks that proceed through third-party networks or servers are characterized as intermediate because they causally impact remote systems.

6.2.3. Aggressive

Aggressive responses are those reasonably likely to interfere with the availability, integrity, confidentiality, or authenticity of information systems outside of one's own network. Aggressive measures include those intended or highly likely to result in something that the target would regard as harm or damage. Aggressive actions are all fairly characterized as active response; conceptually, only a noncooperative act can be aggressive.

DoS responses are examples of aggressive measures. These responses typically attempt to overwhelm the target server or network with sham requests for information as a means of effectively shutting it down. A successful DoS attack on a Web site has the effect of denying third parties access to the site and thus "denies service" to the site. Such responses are characterized as aggressive because they are reasonably calculated to cause damage to remote systems or networks.

6.3. Relevant Substantive Ethical Principles

6.3.1. The Principle Allowing Force in Defense of Self and Others

It is generally accepted in every Western industrialized nation that a person has a moral right to use proportional force when necessary to defend herself against an attack of some kind. If, for example, A starts shooting at B without provocation and B cannot save her own life without shooting back at A, it is permissible, according to ordinary judgments, for B to shoot at A.

The first principle considered here, then, is a general principle that allows a person to use proportional force when necessary to defend against an attack:

> The Defense Principle: *It is morally permissible for one person to use force to defend herself or other innocent persons against an attack or threat provided that (1) such force is proportional to the force used in the attack or threat; (2) such force is necessary either to repel the attack or threat or to prevent it from resulting in harm of some kind; and (3) such force is directed only at persons who are the immediate source of the attack or threat.*

Although "force" has traditionally been used to describe violent physical attacks in which one person attempts to inflict physical harm on another person, this is because the occurrence of digital attacks is a comparatively new phenomenon. "Force" could plausibly (and perhaps should) be construed as applying to both physical and digital attacks.

Each of the elements of the defense principle states a necessary condition for the justified use of force. First, the defense principle justifies the use of only so much force as is proportional to the attack. Although this may allow the victim to use somewhat greater force than the attacker, it does not justify the use of significantly greater force. For example, if the defense principle allows a victim to ward off an attacker's fist by hitting the attacker with a small stick of some kind, it does not allow a victim to do so by shooting the attacker. The introduction of a gun involves a morally significant escalation of force that is not permitted by the defense principle.

Second, force must be necessary in the sense that the victim cannot either stop the attack or prevent further harm to herself without resorting to the use of force. As has frequently been pointed out, this seems to imply that victims have a duty to escape (at least when attacks occur outside the home) when they can end the attack by escaping. If I know that I can save myself from an attack simply by running in the other direction, then I have a duty to do so under this construction; resorting to force in this circumstance is not to be justified by the defense principle.

Third, and of special importance in the active defense context, is that the defense principle justifies the use of force only against persons who are the direct source of the attack or threat. In limited cases, this might permit the use of force against innocent persons. Many ethical theorists have argued that a person may justifiably use force to defend against an attacker who is psychologically incapable of instantiating a culpable mental state and is hence "innocent" of any wrongdoing. On this view, it would be permissible for a person to direct force against an attacker known to be psychotic, even though the attacker is not morally responsible for her actions. Nevertheless, it is crucial to note that the defense principle never justifies directing force against an innocent bystander. Under no circumstances, then, does it allow a person to defend against an attack by interposing an innocent bystander between herself and the attacker.

Before proceeding to a discussion of another potentially relevant ethical principle, it is worth noting how this last feature of the defense principle bears on evaluating active defense measures. The defense principle, at most, justifies forceful measures directed at the owners of innocent agent machines; such machines are fairly characterized as "innocent attackers" rather than "innocent bystanders." However, active defense measures that have significant impacts on innocent bystanders are problematic under the defense principle.

6.3.2. A Principle Allowing Otherwise Wrongful Acts to Secure Greater Moral Good

It is also generally accepted that morality allows the infringement (as opposed to violation) of an innocent person's rights when it is necessary to secure a significantly greater good.[5] For example, if A must enter onto the property of B without her permission to stop a murderer from escaping, it is morally permissible for A to do so. Although such an act constitutes a trespass and hence infringes B's property rights, it does not violate B's property rights because it is morally justified.

There are four considerations that explain this judgment. First, stopping a dangerous murderer from escaping into the general population where she may do more harm has great moral value. Second, it is not possible for A to achieve such moral value without coming onto B's land without her permission. Third, the threat to the interests of the public is, from a moral point of view, significantly greater than the threat to B's interests. Fourth, A's intent in committing the putative trespass is morally respectable (to save the public from such a grave risk) and is hence properly respectful toward B.

Putting these four features together suggests a second general principle that might be applicable in evaluating active defense:

> The Necessity Principle: *It is morally permissible for one person A to infringe a right ρ of a person B if and only if (1) A's infringing of ρ would result in great moral value; (2) the good that is protected by ρ is significantly less valuable, morally speaking, than the good A can*

---

[5] By definition, to say that a right has been "infringed" is to say only that someone has acted in a way that is inconsistent with the holder's interest in that right; strictly speaking, then, the claim that a right has been infringed is a purely descriptive claim that connotes no moral judgment as to whether or not the infringement is wrong. In contrast, to say that a right has been "violated" is to say that the right has been infringed by some act and that the relevant act is morally wrong. Accordingly, it is a conceptual truth that it can be permissible for an individual or entity to infringe a right, but it cannot be permissible to violate a right.

bring about by infringing ρ; (3) there is no other way for A to bring about this moral value that does not involve infringing ρ; and (4) A's attitude toward B's rights is otherwise properly respectful.

As was true of the defense principle, the necessity principle could (and perhaps should) be construed as applying in the context of physical and digital attacks and, thus construed, potentially justifies the use of physical or digital force that is ordinarily impermissible.

As was also true of the defense principle, each of the elements of the necessity principle states a necessary condition for the justified use of force. First, the use of force is not justified unless it results in a significantly greater good than the interest infringed by the force. Second, the use of force is not justified unless it is the only practicable way to bring about the greater moral good. Third, the use of force is not justified only to the extent that the person using the force is not doing so for morally impermissible reasons. Fourth, justified force must be used with an otherwise respectful attitude.

The necessity principle augments the defense principle by allowing some action that infringes on the rights of even innocent bystanders: The necessity principle seems to allow one person A to infringe on the right of an innocent bystander B if necessary to defend A or some other person from a culpable attack that would result in a significantly greater harm than results from infringing B's right. But insofar as the necessity principle requires the achievement of a significantly greater good, it does not allow a person to direct at an innocent bystander force that is proportional to the force of the attack.

Although the principles clearly overlap, their rationales are different. On one common view, the defense principle is justified because an attacker, whether innocent or culpable, "forfeits" her right not to be attacked. If I shoot at you, for example, I have forfeited my right not to be shot at. But this cannot be what justifies the necessity principle; one can forfeit a right only by doing something—and innocent bystanders have, by definition, done nothing. The most persuasive justification for the necessity principle is that the scope of a person's rights simply does not extend to situations in which a significantly greater good can be achieved only by infringing it. For example, my property right to exclude you from my land simply does not extend to a situation in which you can escape from a deadly attack only by running across my land.

Accordingly, unlike the defense principle, the necessity principle might potentially allow active defense measures that have significant impacts on innocent bystanders. However, it is clear that the necessity principle allows impacts on innocent bystanders only if the moral value of using the relevant active defense measures significantly outweighs the moral disvalue of such impacts.

6.3.3. Potential Principles Allowing Persons to "Even the Score"

It might be thought that victims of an attack have a moral right to retaliate against or punish their attackers by inflicting a proportional harm on their attackers. If, for example, A hits B in the face and then turns and runs away in an obvious attempt to escape, it is ethically permissible, on this view, for B to catch A and then hit him back in the face; such a measure is permissible either as retaliation or as punishment. Applied to the present context, such a principle permits the victim of a digital attack to respond with force as a means of "evening the score." Accordingly, there are two potential lines of justification here grounded in two distinct principles—one that allows retaliation and one that allows punishment.

It is worth noting that such principles, whatever their precise formulation, are pretty clearly independent of the defense principle. There is nothing in any principle allowing retaliation or punishment that requires the force be necessary to stop the attack or prevent any further harm. Indeed, in this example, it is clear that the retaliatory act is not needed to stop the attack; B is obviously fleeing the scene of assault. Accordingly, the application of any principle purporting to justify retaliation or punishment in an active defense context would not require the victim to even think about whether proportional force would be efficacious, much less necessary, in stopping the attack or preventing any further harm.

In contrast, the issue of whether principles allowing force as retaliation or punishment are logically related to the necessity principle is somewhat more complicated and involves a substantive moral evaluation of all of the relevant harms. In particular, resolving this issue depends on an evaluation of (1) whether the harm that is inflicted in the name of punishment or retaliation constitutes a moral good and (2) whether, if so, this moral good significantly outweighs corresponding moral evils. If retaliation/punishment is needed, as a general matter, to secure a significantly greater moral good, then a general ethical principle justifying retaliation/punishment is a corollary of the necessity principle. If not, then an ethical principle justifying retaliation/punishment—if there is one—is not a logical consequence of the necessity principle.

6.3.3.1. The Retaliation Principle

The first principle that "evens the score" allows persons to inflict proportional harm as a means of retaliating against an attacker:

> The Retaliation Principle: *It is morally permissible for one person A to inflict proportional harm on another person B in retaliation for a harm inflicted by B on A.*

Under the retaliation principle, various active defense measures are ethically justified as retaliation for the harms inflicted by attackers.

It should be noted that, as a logical matter, the retaliation principle is relevant only with respect to aggressive active defense intended to inflict a proportional harm. Assuming the retaliation principle is an ethical principle, it justifies only those acts intended to inflict harm as a means of retaliation. Because benign and intermediate active defense measures are neither intended to inflict harm on the targets nor reasonably likely to do so, they are not properly characterized as "retaliatory" in character. At best, the retaliation principle justifies aggressive measures that are intended, at least in part, to inflict harm as retaliation.

The problem with this line of justification, however, is that the retaliation principle is not regarded, on ordinary judgments, as a principle of morality at all. There is no requirement in the retaliation principle that B be morally culpable for having inflicted the harm or that the harm inflicted by B be morally wrongful. It is clearly wrong for one person to inflict harm on another person in retaliation for a morally justified act; such a principle would permit someone who has rightly been punished by the state to retaliate against some class of persons that might include jurors, judges, or prosecutors.

Of course, one might simply reformulate the retaliation principle to justify only retaliation against morally wrongful acts, but this does not rescue it. The act of inflicting injury on another person for no other reason than to even the score is nothing other than "revenge"; and revenge is generally regarded by most theorists and ordinary persons as morally wrong.

In this connection, it is important to note that it is no part of the related concepts of revenge and retaliation that harm be inflicted as a means of giving a person his just deserts. From the standpoint of someone who is attempting merely to retaliate or to get revenge, the point of the retaliatory act is not to satisfy some sort of abstract retributivist requirement of justice; that is, the point of retaliation is not to restore the balance of justice after it has been disturbed by a wrongful act. Rather, the point is simply to even the score: He did this to me, so I did it back to him. Indeed, someone who cares only about retaliation is indifferent to the argument that, for one reason or another, the target does not, as a moral matter, deserve the harm.

This has a couple of important consequences. First, it shows that even a reconfigured version of the retaliation principle cannot be justified as a consequence of the necessity principle. If a retaliatory objective is morally wrongful, then satisfying a retaliatory objective could not constitute a greater moral good under the necessity principle.

Second, it shows that the reconfigured version of the retaliation principle is false. As far as ordinary intuitions and practices are concerned, then, morality does not allow the infliction of harm on another person without regard for whether that harm is deserved in some way or serves some greater purpose than satisfying the actor's desire for vengeance. Accordingly, even a reconfigured version of the retaliatory principle that limits it to just morally wrongful acts does not justify aggressive active defense measures because it requires nothing more ethically respectable as rationale than a desire for vengeance—something that is insufficient as an ethical matter to justify the infliction of harm.

6.3.3.2. The Punishment Principle

The second principle is an ethical principle that allows the punishment of wrongdoing:

> The Punishment Principle: *It is morally permissible for society to punish a person for wrongdoing provided that there is adequate reason to think that she is guilty.*[6]

---

[6]Exactly what constitutes an ethically adequate reason is not entirely clear (and beyond the scope of this chapter), but this much is uncontroversial: Adequate reason requires much more than merely a preponderance of the available evidence.

On this line of analysis, active defense is justified as a means of punishing a wrongful digital attack.

As was true of the retaliation principle, the punishment principle has no application to benign and intermediate aggressive active defense. Again, because benign and intermediate active defense measures are neither intended to inflict harm on the targets nor reasonably likely to do so, they are not properly characterized as "punitive." At most, the punishment principle justifies aggressive measures intended, in part, to inflict harm as punishment for wrongdoing.

It is worth noting that, assuming that punishment is morally justifiable, the punishment principle can be logically derived from the necessity principle. Both of the two most important normative theories of punishment identify moral goods that are sufficiently important to justify the intentional infliction of discomfort that constitutes punishment. Retributivist theories justify punishment on the ground that it is necessary to give the wrongdoer her just deserts and hence to restore the balance of justice that is disturbed by a morally wrongful act[7]; on this view, the restoration of the balance of justice counts as a moral good that outweighs the moral evil involved in inflicting proportional pain on the wrongdoer, something that otherwise is morally impermissible. Consequentialist theories justify punishment on the ground that it is necessary to bring about some consequences that maximally promote well-being; on this view, general deterrence and rehabilitation of the offender jointly involve utilities (moral goods) that outweigh the disutilities (moral disvalue) involved in inflicting discomfort on the offender. On either line of justification, then, the punishment principle can logically be derived from the necessity principle together with the underlying assessments of value.[8]

Although most theorists reasonably believe that punishment is morally justified and hence that something like the punishment principle is a principle of morality, it does not justify private parties in adopting aggressive countermeasures to punish attackers. It is generally accepted that, in any society with a morally legitimate government, it is ethically impermissible for private citizens to punish wrongdoing. Mainstream political theorists are nearly unanimous in holding that it is the province of government—and not of private persons—in such societies to punish wrongdoers after they have been found guilty in a fair trial with just procedures. Indeed, vigilantism is universally condemned as morally wrong: So long as the state is reasonably effective in prosecuting and properly punishing wrongdoing, citizens are morally prohibited from recourse to forceful self-help.

Even so, it is important to recognize the importance of the assumption that the state is reasonably effective in protecting against the relevant class of wrongful acts and in detecting and punishing such acts. The state may legitimately claim a monopoly over the use of force only insofar as it does a reasonably credible job of

---

[7]When one person *A* violates an obligation owed to *B* and commits a wrong against *B*, she creates a moral debt to *B* that must, as a moral matter, be discharged in some way. Exactly what is needed to discharge such debts is not entirely clear; forgiveness, compensation, and punishment are all relevant, but it is not clear whether each is sufficient or whether some combination is needed.

[8]Similar reasoning is available to show the punishment principle is a logical corollary of the necessity principle if punishment is justified by consequentialist arguments. If, for example, punishment is justified in virtue of deterring crime, then deterring crime is a moral good that significantly outweighs the moral disvalue involved in inflicting punitive harm on the wrongdoer.

recognizing and protecting the rights of its citizens. A theory of legitimacy that presupposes, as most do, that the function of the state is to serve the interests of its citizens justifies state authority only to the extent that it adequately serves these interests. Thus, it is reasonable to think that a state that cannot provide adequate protection to citizens has no legitimate grounds to demand that citizens refrain from using force to protect themselves.

This is particularly relevant in the context of active defense because one might be tempted to argue that, at this time, the law is not sufficiently efficacious in protecting persons from digital attacks to justify requiring individuals and firms to refrain from protecting themselves. Although the frequency and intensity of attacks against private entities seem to be increasing, law enforcement successes remain comparatively rare. Because, on this line of reasoning, law enforcement success rates do not reach some minimally acceptable level, it is justifiable for private firms to adopt active defense measures as a means of deterring future attacks (as opposed to defending against present attacks) and thereby protecting against future economic losses.

There are at least two problems with this argument. First, the argument incorrectly presupposes that the state may legitimately preclude citizens from retaliating against a specific class of acts only to the extent that it punishes those acts. Most theorists take the position that the state is justified in monopolizing the use of coercive force if it is generally effective in recognizing and protecting the rights and legitimate interests of its citizens. On this view, the state may legitimately prohibit citizens from retaliating against any narrowly specified class C of acts (i.e., one that does not involve a wholesale failure to protect life, liberty, physical security, equality, or property) if it is generally effective in enforcing laws that purport to protect certain vital interests and moral rights. If the class C of relevant acts is sufficiently narrow, then the failure of the state to protect the relevant rights from infringements does not rise to a level that would justify citizen vigilantism.

Second, even if we assume that the state may prohibit citizens from resorting to self-help in punishing certain acts only to the extent it satisfies its moral duty to protect citizens from those acts, the argument is problematic because it is not clear that state efforts to protect against digital attacks do not satisfy its moral duty. It is true, as is widely reported, that law enforcement successes are extremely rare; very few illegal intrusions are successfully prosecuted and punished. But this is explained—at least in part—by a variety of factors that have nothing to do with the quality of law enforcement efforts. Steven Mitchell and Elizabeth Banker (1998) estimate that only about 1 in 10 successful intrusions are even detected by the victims and that only about 1 in 10 detected intrusions are actually reported by victims to law enforcement; thus, only about 1 in 100 successful intrusions reach law enforcement to begin with. Moreover, although studies are difficult to come by, it is reasonable to think that many of these latter intrusions do not result in significant harm to justify extensive state involvement.

This calls attention to two gaps in the argument. First, it is not clear exactly how much of the gap between the number of computer intrusions and the number of successful prosecutions should be attributed to the state. Second, it is not clear exactly what sort of success rate in solving and punishing reported cases would satisfy the state's duty. Addressing the first issue requires an empirical analysis that shows what percentage of reported cases are successfully prosecuted and punished by the state; addressing the second requires a moral analysis of the substance of the state's duty to protect citizens from unauthorized digital intrusions. Until these issues are resolved, however, the argument does not justify private firms in adopting aggressive active defense to punish attackers.[9] Accordingly, the argument fails.

Given the moral presumption against vigilantism, however, the burden of proof rests on the party proposing to adopt active defense measures. Until these normative and descriptive matters are settled, then, it is reasonable to presume that active defense cannot be justifiably adopted on the strength of ethical principles governing punishment and retaliation.

This, of course, should not be construed to support any general conclusions about active response. For starters, the retaliation and punishment principles do not even purport to reach benign or intermediate responses, which might be justified by the necessity principle. Further, aggressive measures might be justified by either the defense or the necessity principle. These further issues are explored next.

6.4. An Evidentiary Restriction for Justifiably Acting Under Ethical Principles

Most theorists and laypersons agree that we have a duty to make sure we have correctly identified and applied the ethically relevant facts and principle before taking action against a person on the strength of that principle. Suppose that A believes without good reason that B has wronged A in some way. If A takes action against B under a relevant principle P without having a minimally adequate reason for thinking that P applies because B has truly wronged A, then A has committed a wrong against B. A has a duty to be at least minimally justified in believing that P governs the situation; if A does not satisfy this duty, then she must give B the benefit of the doubt until A has better evidence.

There is thus another general principle that is relevant with respect to evaluating active defense measures—one that is evidentiary or "epistemic" in character: One can be morally justified in taking action under an ethical principle only to the extent that one has adequate reason to believe that its application conditions are satisfied:

> The Evidentiary Principle: *It is morally permissible for one person A to take action under an ethical principle P only if A has adequate reason for thinking that all of the necessary conditions for applying P are satisfied.*

The evidentiary principle defines a moral duty to ensure that one is epistemically justified in acting under the relevant moral principles. If one person A takes

---

[9]It is also worth noting that the argument assumes that aggressive active defense measures are sufficiently successful in punishing attackers to justify their use by private parties, a claim that also needs a defense that partly consists in an empirical analysis (to determine the success rate of aggressive active defense in punishing attackers) and partly consists of a normative analysis (to determine how much of a success rate would justify use of aggressive active defense by private parties).

aggressive action against another person B without having sufficient reason—whatever this ultimately amounts to—for believing that the application conditions of the relevant ethical principles have not been satisfied, A has committed a wrong against B.

A more concrete example is helpful here. Notice that the evidentiary principle explains, and other principles do not, why Paul Hill committed a grievous wrong when he murdered John Bayard Britton, an abortion provider. Hill argued that he was justified in doing so on the strength of the defense principle: Because fetuses are moral persons from conception and because killing Britton was the only way to prevent his killing fetuses by performing abortions, it was permissible to kill Britton. The problem, however, is Hill lacked adequate reason to think that the application conditions of the defense principle were satisfied because his view that fetuses are moral persons from the moment of conception is deeply contested in our culture. The fact of such deep and widespread disagreement shows that Hill lacked adequate reason to think the defense principle's application conditions were satisfied. For this reason, he was rightly convicted of murder.

Accordingly, the victim of a digital attack can permissibly adopt active defense measures only if she has adequate reason to think the application conditions of one of the relevant principles are satisfied. Under the defense principle, she must have adequate reason to believe that (1) whatever force is employed is proportional to the force used in the attack; (2) such force is necessary either to repel the attack or to prevent it from resulting in harm of some kind; and (3) such force is directed only at persons immediately responsible for the attack. Under the necessity principle, she must have adequate reason to believe that (1) the relevant moral value significantly outweighs the relevant moral disvalue; (2) there is no other way to achieve the greater moral good than to do A; and (3) doing A will succeed in achieving the greater moral good. If the victim of a digital attack lacks adequate evidence for these elements, she cannot justifiably act under the defense or necessity principle. If she nonetheless adopts active defense measures that infringe an innocent person's rights, she has wronged that person.

6.5. Evaluating Active Defense Under the Relevant Ethical Principles

In thinking about whether various active defense strategies are ethically permissible, it is important to realize that the risk that active defense measures will impact innocent persons and their machines is not purely "theoretical." As discussed above, sophisticated attackers usually conceal their identities by staging attacks from innocent machines that have been compromised through a variety of mechanisms. Most active responses have to be directed, at least in part, at the agent machines used to stage the attack. Accordingly, it is not just possible that any reasonably efficacious active defense strategy will impact innocent persons; it is nearly inevitable—something that anyone sophisticated enough to mount an even partly successful active defense strategy is fairly presumed to realize.

Given that innocent persons enjoy a general (although not unlimited) moral immunity against forceful attack, the likelihood of impacting innocent persons with an active defense response is of special ethical concern. For this reason, the impacts of active responses on innocent parties occupies a central role in the ethical evaluation of those responses. It is true, of course, that some of the principles above allow force against innocent parties; however, it is also true that such force is allowed in only a narrow range of circumstances. An adequate evaluation of each response must thus determine whether the particular impact on innocent parties falls within the relevant range of circumstances.

6.5.1. Aggressive Measures

Aggressive active defense responses are distinguished from other responses in that the former are capable of inflicting some sort of harm, physical or financial, on the immediate targets. As defined, *aggressive responses* are intended to interfere with the availability, integrity, or authenticity of the information systems that are the immediate (as opposed to ultimate) targets. Such interference is caused primarily by digital inputs that effectively alter the targeted system in some way (e.g., data may be erased, changed, or corrupted) and hence physically "damage" it in some sense. Further, such interference can itself have a variety of harmful effects, which include financial effects deriving from loss of business. Aggressive responses include attempts to corrupt data, to disable services on remote systems, and to overwhelm targeted networks with incoming data (as occurs in a DoS or a DDoS attack).

6.5.1.1. The Defense Principle

In many instances, aggressive active defense cannot be justified by the defense principle. Consider, for example, the well-publicized response to a DoS attack by the Electrohippies on World Trade Organization (WTO) servers a few years ago. Instead of simply dropping the incoming packets at the router, the host of those servers, Conxion, sent those packets back to the Electrohippies' server. Because dropping the packets at the router would have sufficed to end the harmful effects of the Electrohippies attack, Conxion's response was not "necessary" and hence not justified under the defense principle.

Calling such measures "defense" radically mischaracterizes them. The primary point of the more aggressive response cannot accurately be characterized as defensive; it was not needed to stop the attack. Indeed, the reason that Conxion adopted the more aggressive response was that it wished to inflict exactly the same kind of harm on the Electrohippies' servers that the Electrohippies intended to inflict on the WTO servers. For this reason, Conxion's objective in mounting the aggressive response is more accurately characterized as punitive or retaliatory.

Even if it is sometimes permissible for a private party to punish an attack, Conxion's response is nonetheless ethically problematic. The Electrohippies were concerned with making a political statement against the WTO and made no effort to conceal their identity by staging the attack from compromised innocent machines—something that was presumably evident to Conxion from the obviously political character of the attack. Because the identity of the culpable attacker was easily identified, there was simply no reason to think that the state could not adequately vindicate Conxion's rights by identifying and prosecuting the

Electrohippies. In such circumstances, it is clearly the province of the state—and not the aggrieved individuals—to pursue punitive or retaliatory measures.

Additional ethical issues are raised by aggressive defense to attacks staged from innocent agent machines. Because the identity of the culpable attacker is generally unknown in such cases, any aggressive response invariably is directed at the innocent agents that have been compromised by the attacker, which compounds the harms done to the owners of those machines. As noted, theorists disagree about whether the defense principle allows a forceful response to an innocent attacker; some theorists believe that it is always wrong to direct force at an innocent person. If such theorists are correct, then the defense principle does not allow aggressive defense to attacks in which it is evident to the victim that the identity of the attacker has been concealed.

Moreover, aggressive defense in such cases is not justified under the defense principle if it is not necessary to prevent the harm or to stop the attack. If there is any nonaggressive way for the victim of the attack to avoid the attack or the damage that is caused by the attack, then an aggressive response cannot be justified under the defense principle. This, however, does not mean that the victim is obligated to escape the attack by any means possible. Although it is always possible to escape a digital attack by taking the target offline, such measures can result in significant damage (e.g., if the target is a Web-based business) that the defense principle does not require victims to accept. Victims have a duty to escape attacks only insofar as this can be done without incurring injuries that are comparable to those caused by the attack itself.

6.5.1.2. The Necessity Principle

As it turns out, aggressive defense is problematic under the necessity principle for a different reason. The necessity principle allows acts that would otherwise be wrong if necessary to achieve a significantly greater moral good. Even if we assume that an aggressive response is evidently necessary to achieve the moral good of preventing the damage caused by an attack and that this good significantly outweighs the harms done to the owners of the innocent agent machines, there is an evidentiary problem: For all that we can be presumed to know, an aggressive response might result in unpredictable harms that outweigh the relevant moral goods.

The problem here arises because machines can be linked via a network to one another in a variety of unpredictable ways, making it impossible to identify all the harmful effects of an aggressive response in advance. Indeed, a variety of intranational and international worst-case scenarios are unfortunately possible. Suppose, for example, that an attacker compromises machines on a university network linked to a university hospital. If hospital machines performing a life-saving function are linked to the network, an aggressive response against that network might result in a loss of human life. Even worse, suppose that an attacker compromises machines used by one nation's government to attack private machines in another nation. If the two nations are hostile toward each other, an aggressive response by the private victim could raise international tensions—a particularly chilling prospect if the two nations are nuclear powers.

The point here is not that we have reason to think that these worst-case scenarios are very likely; rather, the point is that we do not have any reliable way to determine how likely they are. A victim contemplating an aggressive response has no reliable way to estimate the probabilities of such scenarios in the short time available to her. Because the victim cannot reliably assess these probabilities, she lacks adequate reason to think that the application conditions of the necessity principle are satisfied. Thus, under the evidentiary principle, she may not justifiably adopt aggressive measures.

6.5.2. Intermediate Measures

Intermediate measures are typically concerned with identifying culpable attackers and are neither intended nor obviously likely to result in physical damage to affected machines. These responses typically include exploratory tracebacks that attempt to identify culpable attackers by following attack paths in reverse through innocent agent machines (if any) to the ultimate source of the attack, as well as devices that allow entry into a remote system for the purpose of gathering information. As is evident, the point of such measures is neither defensive nor punitive: The intent is to gather information to identify the attacker, not to stop or punish the attack. Indeed, this purpose typically requires the victim to ensure that the data and logs on remote machines remain largely (if not completely) uncorrupted.

Even so, intermediate responses are potentially problematic insofar as they require physical entry onto remote machines. Of course, this does not pose any obvious ethical problems when the remote machines are located within the victim's network or when the victim has sufficient permission to enter these machines from someone morally authorized to allow entry. But unauthorized entry onto innocent agent machines is presumptively problematic from an ethical standpoint; it involves what appears to be a trespass onto the property of an innocent person.

The only ethical principle clearly applicable to intermediate responses involving a trespass on innocent machines is the necessity principle. Because intermediate responses neither punish attackers nor defend against attacks, the ethical principles allowing defense or punitive measures are irrelevant. But because the greater moral goods that would justify an otherwise wrongful action under the necessity principle are not limited to defense or punishment, the fact that intermediate responses neither punish nor defend against attacks does not preclude justifying such responses under the necessity principle. As long as one can identify a moral good that significantly outweighs the moral disvalue of trespassing against innocent machines, one can justifiably adopt intermediate responses under the necessity principle if necessary to produce this greater moral good.

Intermediate responses can be contrived to secure an important moral good. Criminal attacks are traditionally regarded as offenses against the general public because they violate the legitimate expectations of the public and thereby breach the peace against the public. Like the victim, then, the public has a compelling reason to ensure that the criminal offender is brought to trial and punished as a matter of restoring the peace—a good of considerable moral significance. To the extent that invasive tracebacks can reliably be used to identify the culpable source of a digital attack for the purpose of prosecuting the responsible parties, they function to secure the important moral good of restoring the public peace by bringing wrongdoers to justice. Accordingly, intermediate responses motivated by such an objective are intended to secure an obviously important moral value.[10]

Moreover, it also seems clear that such goods are important enough to justify comparatively minor trespasses onto the property of innocent persons. If the only way that a private security officer can apprehend a robbery suspect is to commit a trespass against the property of an innocent person, it seems clear that she is justified in doing so under the necessity principle. The moral value of bringing the offender to justice and thereby restoring the public peace greatly outweighs the moral disvalue of a simple trespass onto the land of an innocent party.

The problem with intermediate responses, however, is that it is often unclear whether they are reasonably calculated to succeed in identifying culpable parties. As is now familiar, any reasonably sophisticated hacker attempts to conceal her identify by staging the attack from innocent agent machines. Indeed, it is possible for a sophisticated attacker to further insulate herself from discovery by compromising one set of innocent machines to control another set of innocent machines that will be used to stage the attack, a process that can be iterated several times. In such cases, the attacker interposes several sets of innocent machines between herself and the victim. But the greater the number of layers (or hops in the chain) between attacker and victim, the less likely intermediate responses will succeed in identifying the culpable party. Although intermediate responses can be highly effective in identifying the culpable parties in attacks staged directly from the hacker's machine, the probability of success drops dramatically with each layer of machines between attacker and victim. Indeed, it is fair to say that the likelihood of identifying the culpable parties in sophisticated attacks by intermediate responses is morally negligible.

This means that the expected moral value (the magnitude of the good multiplied by the probability of realizing it) to be achieved by using invasive tracebacks is a lower value than is desirable. In contrast, the expected moral disvalue (the magnitude of the bad multiplied by the probability of realizing it) is significant; although it may be difficult to quantify the magnitude of the evil involved in a trespass, the probability of committing a trespass in using invasive tracebacks against any reasonably sophisticated attack will be close to 1. This militates against the claim that the amount of moral value that will be achieved by using invasive tracebacks is significantly greater than the amount of moral disvalue that will be achieved.

Moreover, the use of intermediate response can also have significant impacts that are undesirable from a moral point of view. The use of invasive tracebacks can result in damage to a variety of important trust relationships. A private firm that implements a traceback in an attack staged from the machines of other competing businesses can damage not only trust relationships between those businesses, but also could precipitate a response that damages trust relationships between consumers and businesses, potentially resulting in economic losses passed on to

---

[10]Not all intermediate responses are motivated by a desire to prosecute the wrongdoer. Many firms prefer to avoid prosecution in order to avoid the unfavorable publicity that might result from the disclosure of security breaches. This reasoning does not justify intermediate responses in these cases.

the public in the form of lost jobs. The use of invasive tracebacks by a private firm in response to an attack staged from machines used by state officials of another nation could result in an international incident that damages the relationship between those nations.

Again, the point here is not that we have reason to think that these worst-case scenarios are very likely; rather the point is that a victim contemplating an intermediate response cannot reliably estimate the probabilities of such scenarios in the short time available to her. Because she cannot reliably assess these probabilities, she lacks adequate reason to think that the application conditions of the necessity principle are satisfied.

Together with the evidentiary principle, this seems to imply that, other things being equal, the victim of a digital attack cannot permissibly adopt intermediate responses under the necessity principle. Unless she has some special reason to think that the attack is being staged directly from the hacker's own machines without the use of intermediate agent machines or networks, she does not have adequate reason to think that intermediate measures will succeed in identifying the culpable parties.

This is, of course, not to deny that it is sometimes true that the victim has some special reason to think that the attack is being directly staged from the culpable party's own machines; however, such cases are the exception and not the rule. As hacking technologies and methods progress, it is reasonable to hypothesize that even younger attackers will adopt more sophisticated tactics to conceal their identities.

Accordingly, it is reasonable to assume at this juncture that, in most cases, the use of intermediate responses is not likely to succeed in identifying the culpable attackers. In such cases, then, the victim lacks adequate reason to think that the moral disvalue associated with trespassing against the innocent agent machines is outweighed by the significantly greater moral value of bringing the wrongdoer to justice and hence lacks adequate reason to think that the application conditions of the necessity principle are satisfied. If this is correct, then victims are usually barred by the evidentiary principle from adopting intermediate responses under the necessity principle.

Nevertheless, it is important to emphasize that the analysis here is limited to current traceback technologies with their limitations. Many researchers are making considerable progress in improving the reliability and efficacy of traceback technologies.[11] Indeed, one might reasonably expect researchers to eventually improve these technologies to the point where they are sufficiently efficacious in identifying culpable parties that they can generally be justified under the necessity principle as bringing about the greater moral good of identifying culpable parties to an attack. Thus, although presumptively unjustified under the necessity principle at this juncture, this may not be the case for long.

6.5.3. Benign Measures

As defined herein, *benign active defense measures* do not have any causal effects on systems that are external to the victim's network. Such measures include moni-

---

[11]See, for example, http://footfall.csc.ncsu.edu, which documents some intriguing advancements in these technologies.

toring traffic on the victim's own networks (sniffing); restructuring the victim's network to confuse the attacker who relies on previous reconnaissance about the network's structure; employing decoy networks or systems (honeypots) as a means of steering attacks away from the networks of genuine concern; and scanning the victim's own system to attempt to identify the vulnerabilities that the attack is exploiting.

Aggressive and intermediate responses are ethically problematic precisely because of their causal impacts on other agents; intermediate responses typically involve a physical trespass onto the property of other persons, and aggressive responses typically inflict harms on other persons. Acts that cause harm to innocent third persons or causally impact the property of innocent third persons are problematic from a moral standpoint because innocent persons enjoy a presumptive immunity from unwanted intrusions of these kinds.

One might think that benign responses do not present such problems because the only causal effects that they have are on the victim's own property. On this line of argument, a person has a moral liberty to do with her property as she sees fit. Other things being equal, the property owner has a liberty to make physical alterations in her property; thus, for example, I have a liberty to make my home safer by installing a new lock in my door. Although a person's financial responsibilities to her family may preclude damaging her own property if doing so precludes satisfying those responsibilities, these constraints are exceptional. Persons are at considerable liberty to use or modify their property as they see fit. Thus, this argument concludes that if a benign response affects only the victim's own property, it is ethically permissible.

Nevertheless, this argument is problematic in a couple of ways. First, the party implementing a benign measure may be a nonowner who has authorized control over the owner's resources. The scope of the owner's liberty to dispose of her property does not extend unrestricted to agents of the owner. What the agent may permissibly do depends on other factors, including the terms of the agreement she has with the owner.

Second, and more important, the scope of a person's moral liberty to do with her property as she sees fit is limited by the rights of other persons. For example, the fact that the owner of a company owns the workplace does not imply that she has a right to install cameras in the bathroom to monitor employees. In this case, the owner's liberty to do with her property as she sees fit is outweighed by the right of her employees to privacy.

Accordingly, the mere fact that benign measures impact only the property of the victim is not by itself sufficient to imply that they are ethically justified; if there are other persons, for example, who have privacy rights (such as might be true of an Internet service provider) that might be violated by benign measures, then such measures are not clearly permissible. Indeed, users of a system might have a reasonable expectation of privacy in the contents of their files or communications that give rise to privacy rights that would be violated even by benign measures. Such expectations might arise, for example, among users of a university or corporate network.

For this reason, it is not possible to draw any general conclusions about the permissibility of benign responses to digital attacks. Because they are impermissible in cases where they violate the rights of third parties, it is necessary in any given instance to determine whether there are third parties who have rights that might be violated by the adoption of even benign responses.

6.6. The Relevance of Consent

The foregoing analysis presupposes that the victim of a digital attack does not have express or implied permission to causally impact the machines of innocent owners. Recourse to the defense and necessity principles is necessary to justify impacts on innocent parties only insofar as those parties cannot reasonably be presumed to have consented to such impacts. As a general matter, parties have the ability to change the structure of their moral relations with other persons either by freely waiving any moral claims they might have to constrain the behavior of others or by doing something that justifies an inference that they have waived such claims. Simply by inviting another person into my home, for example, I explicitly waive my claim against her that she not enter my home. In effect, my consent transforms an act that would otherwise be wrongful into an act that is permissible: My consent suffices to create a moral liberty in another person to enter my home.

As this discussion suggests, consent may be either explicit in the sense that it is intentionally and expressly given or tacit (or implied) in the sense that it is imputed to the agent on the basis of behaviors not intended to express consent. Attributions of tacit consent are usually grounded in considerations of fairness.

6.6.1. Explicit Consent

There are both formal and substantive limits on the efficacy of explicit consent. First, consent must be fully informed and freely given by a person of appropriate maturity and reasonable intelligence; the consent of a 13-year-old child alone is insufficient in many contexts to waive claims against the behavior of other persons. Second, it must be reasonable for other persons to believe that the claimant has effectively waived the relevant claim by consent. Third, there are some claims that simply cannot be waived by consent. Although it might be true that one can waive one's right to life by consenting to assisted suicide in cases where one has a painful, terminal illness of short duration, it is reasonable to think that one cannot give effective consent to being killed in just any set of circumstances (e.g., to end the pain of a stubbed toe). Likewise, it is reasonable to think that one cannot effectively consent to a life of slavery.

Although one might think that consent issues do not arise in the case of benign responses because these are limited to the victim's own property, this is mistaken. The fact that the victim of a digital attack owns the physical structures and connections making up a network does not imply that there are no other stakeholders who have rights. If, for example, innocent third parties are contractually permitted to use the networks and have a reasonable expectation of privacy in their activities, benign measures that impact these activities might very well infringe the privacy rights of these third parties. Of course, it might be that the parties have consented to waive their privacy rights in such circumstances, but this is something that must be investigated. Consent simply cannot be assumed.

Consent issues arise more conspicuously in connection with aggressive and intermediate responses to attacks staged from innocent agent machines.[12] If, for example, the victim has the permission of a network owner to enter onto the network to gather information and has permission of all the relevant users, it is arguably permissible for her to perform such activities. Of course, it will frequently be difficult—especially in the short time available to the victim of a digital attack—to identify all affected parties and to obtain permissions from such parties. But, as an ethical (as opposed to legal) matter, intermediate responses that would otherwise be wrongful are permissible with the consent of all affected parties.

As a general matter, however, victims have no reason to think that owners of agent machines have explicitly consented to either having their machines used for an attack or being targeted by aggressive countermeasures. In the absence of any other reason to think aggressive countermeasures against these machines are permissible, victims would be committing a wrong against the owners under the evidentiary principle should they direct aggressive countermeasures at these machines.

6.6.2. Tacit Consent

In some rare instances, persons can be presumed to have tacitly or impliedly waived a right on the basis of some nonexpressive behavior not intended to effect a waiver. Indeed, in some instances, a person's failure to object to some act can be treated as tacit consent to that act. For example, there is little disagreement about the justice of the legal rule that treats an attorney's failure to object to something opposing counsel has done as having waived the objection.

Accordingly, one might, for example, argue that it is reasonable to infer that owners of agent machines used in a digital attack have consented to being targeted by active response.[13] On this line of analysis, the failure of such owners to protect a network or machine against unauthorized entry with a firewall is reasonably construed as consent to entry in cases where it is needed to investigate or defend against a digital attack staged from their machines. On this line of reasoning, someone who fails to take such precautions is reasonably thought to be sufficiently indifferent about the prospects of intrusions that she may be presumed to consent to them.

There are a couple of problems with this line of reasoning. First, it not only implies consent to the victim's intrusion, but also implies consent to the attacker's intrusion. If sound, such reasoning effectively waives any complaints that someone whose machine has been used by the attacker as a staging ground for the attack otherwise has against the attacker—a result that is sufficiently implausible to warrant rejecting any claims that imply it.

Second, failure to implement a firewall is no more reasonably construed as consent to entry than failure to lock the door to one's car is reasonably construed as consent to enter one's car. One might forget to take such precautions for any

---

[12] If the victim knows that the culpable party is staging the attack directly from her own machines, then she is justified in inferring that the culpable party has at least partly waived her immunity to aggression.

[13] Again, attacks that are known to be staged directly from the culpable party's machines raise a different set of issues. See Section 6.3.3.2 and footnote 5.

number of reasons without being indifferent about unwanted entries. Moreover, in the case of computer intrusions, one might simply not know about the available security options.

A somewhat more plausible argument for treating failure to take adequate security precautions is grounded in ethical principles that impute a duty of reasonable care to protect others from foreseeable harm. In cases where one person's negligence potentially puts another person at risk, considerations of fairness require imputing some responsibility or disadvantage to the former person that must ordinarily be voluntarily accepted. If, for example, you negligently disclose my whereabouts to someone who wants to harm me, you might thereby obligate yourself to do something for me that you ordinarily would not be obligated to do—perhaps hide me in your home.

One might, then, argue that persons who fail to take reasonable precautions to prevent unwanted computer intrusions and whose computers are used to stage an attack have tacitly consented to aggressive and intermediate active defense measures directed at their computers by the victims of those attacks. Because their negligence has wrongfully put innocent persons at risk, they have released the victims of the attacks from any duties they otherwise might have had to refrain from intermediate or aggressive active defense.

If ordinary intuitions and practices are correct, this line of reasoning does not justify directing aggressive measures at owners of compromised machines. Ethical principles of negligence are not generally thought to justify aggression against negligent parties; they do not, for example, justify me in attacking a person who has negligently injured me or in damaging her property. Rather, they are thought to require a person to compensate parties for injuries proximately caused by her failure to take reasonable precautions to protect such parties from injury; this, of course, is how such principles are interpreted and applied by the courts under tort law.

Whether ethical principles regarding negligence might justify intermediate responses is a much more difficult issue that cannot be addressed here. Admittedly, there is little in ordinary practices to justify an inference that these principles allow intermediate responses. There are simply no obvious analogies in ordinary practices to digital attacks staged from innocent machines.

Even so, the idea that the owner of a compromised agent machine might have waived any immunity she otherwise would have had to intermediate responses is not obviously unreasonable. If, for example, it is reasonable to think that such persons have a duty, at the very least, to contribute to compensating the victim of a digital attack for injuries sustained during the attack, it also seems reasonable to think that such persons have a duty to permit victims to commit a trespass for the purpose of tracing the attack back to its source. If, during the course of an attack, the victim had adequate reason to think that (1) intermediate responses would successfully identify the attacking party and (2) owners of compromised machines negligently failed to take reasonable precautions to prevent their machines from being used in a digital attack, they might very well be justified in directing intermediate responses against those machines.

For all practical purposes, the argument is moot. Because victims rarely are able to gather during the course of a digital attack adequate evidence for thinking either that intermediate responses would be successful or that owners of compromised machines have failed to take reasonable precautions, they are unable to justify adopting these responses under ethical principles of negligence. For this reason, the evidentiary principle seems to preclude adopting intermediate responses on the strength of ethical principles of negligence—assuming, of course, that these principles are even applicable.

6.7. The Inadequacy of Law Enforcement Efforts

There is, however, one powerful argument that can be made in defense of the idea that it is permissible for private individuals to undertake various active defense measures. The argument rests on the idea that the state may legitimately prohibit recourse to self-help measures in dealing with a class of wrongful intrusions or attacks only insofar as the state is providing minimally adequate protection against such attacks. If (1) digital intrusions are resulting in significant harm or injury of a kind that the state ought to protect against and (2) the state's protective efforts are inadequate, then private individuals, on this line of reasoning, are entitled to adopt active defense measures that conduce to their own protection.

Both antecedent clauses appear to be satisfied. Depending on the target and sophistication of the attack, an unauthorized digital intrusion can result in significant financial losses to companies. For example, an extended DDoS attack that effectively takes Amazon.com offline for several hours might result in hundreds of thousands of dollars of business going to one of its on-line rivals. In the worst-case scenario, these financial losses can result in loss of value to shareholders and ultimately loss of jobs. It seems clear that the harms potentially resulting from digital intrusions fall within a class that the state ought to protect against.

Further, there is good reason to think that the state's protective efforts are inadequate. At this point in time, law enforcement agencies lack adequate resources to pursue investigations in the vast majority of computer intrusions. But even when resources allow investigation, the response might come after the damage is done. Law enforcement simply has not been able to keep pace with the rapidly growing problems posed by digital attackers.

There are a variety of reasons for this. Most obviously, the availability of resources for combating cybercrime is constrained by political realities; if the public is vehemently opposed to tax increases to increase the resources for investigating cybercrime, then those resources will not keep pace with an increasing rate of intrusions. But, equally importantly, there are special complexities involved in investigating and prosecuting digital intrusions. First, according to Mitchell and Banker (1998), investigation of digital intrusions is resource-intensive "[w]hereas a typical (non 'high-tech') state or local law enforcement officer may carry between forty and fifty cases at a time, a high-tech investigator has a full-time handling three or four cases a month" (p. 710). Second, most sophisticated attacks pose jurisdictional complexities that increase the expense of law enforcement efforts because such attacks frequently involve crossing jurisdictional lines. For example, an attacker in one country might compromise machines in another country to stage an attack on a network in yet a third country.

Although such considerations show that the growing problem associated with digital intrusions demands an effective response of some kind, they fall well short of showing that it is permissible, as a general matter, for private parties to undertake intermediate or aggressive active defense measures. The underlying assumption is that private individuals can adequately do what the state cannot—namely, protect themselves from the threats posed by digital intrusion.

At this time, however, there is very little reason to think that this underlying assumption is correct. For starters, invasive intermediate measures intended to collect information are likely to succeed in identifying culpable parties in only direct attacks staged from the attacker's own computer; such measures are not likely to succeed in identifying parties culpable for intrusions that are staged from innocent machines. Because an attacker sophisticated enough to stage an attack likely to result in significant damage is also likely to be sophisticated enough to interpose at least one layer of innocent machines between her and her target, there is little reason to think that invasive investigatory measures are likely to achieve their objectives in precisely those attacks that are likely to result in the sort of damage that the state is obligated to protect against.

Moreover, aggressive measures are not likely to conduce to the protection of the victim in any reasonably sophisticated attack. As noted, aggressive countermeasures are not usually calculated to result in the cessation of the attack and can frequently result in escalating the attack; for this reason, such countermeasures are not likely to succeed in purely defensive objectives. Unfortunately, they cannot succeed in achieving legitimate punitive objectives in attacks staged from innocent machines. Punitive measures directed at the innocent agents do nothing by way of either punishing the ultimate source of the attack or deterring future attacks. A reasonably sophisticated attacker who knows that her target will respond with aggressively punitive measures will simply evade the effects of those measures by interposing an additional layer of innocent machines between her and her target.

But if this argument fails to justify active defense by private victims, it succeeds in showing that the problem of digital intrusions needs an effective coordinated solution of some kind. One notable proposal deserves mention here. Mitchell and Banker (1998) suggest a private–public solution that involves state licensing of security professionals trained in responding to digital intrusions and authorized to do so subject to certain constraints. It is reasonable to hypothesize that an evaluation of such proposals will become the focus of normative research on active defense in the near future.

Acknowledgments

This is a greatly expanded version of an analysis that appears in an essay entitled "Active Response," which was cowritten with David Dittrich. The essay appears in Hossein Bidgoli (ed.), *The Handbook of Information Security*, John Wiley & Sons, Inc., 2005. I am grateful to Wiley and David Dittrich for permission to reprint portions of that essay in this one.

References

Mitchell, Stevan D., and Elizabeth A. Banker. (1998, Summer). "Private Intrusion Response," *Harvard Journal of Law & Technology*, Vol. 11, No. 3, pp. 699–732.

Radcliff, Deborah. (2000, November 13). "Should You Strike Back?" *Computer World.* Available at www.computerworld.com/governmenttopics/government/legalissues/story/0,10801,53869,00.html. Accessed 5/7/06.

Chapter 7: A View of Cyberterrorism 5 Years Later

Dorothy E. Denning

A few weeks after the September 11 terrorist attacks, the Pakistani Muslim hacking group GForce Pakistan announced the formation of the "Al-Qaeda Alliance Online" on a U.S. government Web site it had just defaced. Declaring that "Osama bin Laden is a holy fighter, and whatever he says makes sense," the group posted a list of demands and warned that it planned to hit major U.S. military and British Web sites (McWilliams, 2001a). Another GForce defacement contained similar messages along with heart-wrenching images of badly mutilated children said to have been killed by Israeli soldiers. A subsequent message from the group announced that two other Pakistani hacking groups had joined the alliance: the Pakistan Hackerz Club and Anti India Crew. Collectively, the groups defaced hundreds of Web sites, often with political messages.

Was this a sign that al Qa'ida had acquired a hacking unit bent on causing cyberterror, or just another group of hackers expressing themselves on public Web sites while trying to impress their peers? In this case, it looked more like the latter. On October 27, GForce wrote on a defaced U.S. military Web site that it was "not a group of cyber terrorists." Condemning the attacks of September 11 and calling themselves "cyber crusaders," they wrote, "ALL we ask for is PEACE for everyone." This was among their last recorded defacements. GForce Pakistan and all mention of the Al-Qaeda Alliance Online disappeared.

The possibility of cyberterrorism, however, remains a concern, as al Qa'ida and other terrorist groups have become increasingly aware of the value of cyberspace to their objectives. They have become adept at using the Internet to distribute propaganda and other information, collect data about potential targets and weapons, communicate with cohorts and supporters, recruit, raise money, and generally facilitate their operations. They have advocated conducting cyberattacks and engaged in some hacking. New hacking groups have emerged with apparent ties to terrorists. Even if the Al-Qaeda Alliance Online does not pose a threat of cyberterror, others might.

This chapter assesses the cyberterror threat, particularly from al Qa'ida and the global jihadists who are part of the broader social movement associated with al Qa'ida. As such, the view offered here supersedes that which I presented about 5 years ago, first to the Special Oversight Panel on Terrorism of the Committee on Armed Services in the U.S. House of Representatives in May 2000 (Denning, 2000) and then in an article written shortly after the September 11 attacks in 2001

(Denning, 2001b). This assessment was based primarily on speculation of what terrorists would likely be interested in and capable of achieving. My overall conclusion was that, at least for the time being, bombs posed a much greater threat than bytes, but we should not shrug off the threat of cyberterrorism.

The assessment offered herein is based less on speculation and more on indicators of cyberterror. These are pieces of evidence that demonstrate a capability or intent to conduct cyberterror. The ones I have found so far range from the actual conduct of cyberattacks to other types of activities that show at least some capability or intent. The indicators are grouped into five categories, and each category is examined in terms of the evidence found so far.

Although this chapter evaluates the threat of cyberterror, it does not attempt to evaluate its risk. To assess the cyberterror risk, one must consider not only the capabilities and motives of terrorists (the threat), but also the vulnerability of critical information systems to attack. Without such vulnerabilities, there is no risk. This paper does not address the vulnerability side of risk, and hence does not evaluate the likelihood of cyberterror operations succeeding. Hence, it only addresses half of the risk equation.

Before offering my current assessment, I discuss what cyberterror is and is not. I also review two studies of cyberterror conducted by the Center on Terrorism and Irregular Warfare at the Naval Postgraduate School in 1999 and 2000, before my arrival in late 2002. Although the studies are now over 5 years old and summarized in my earlier writings, my goal for the current paper is to provide a fairly complete assessment of the threat side of cyberterror.

7.1. What Is Cyberterrorism?

Cyberterrorism is generally understood to refer to highly damaging computer-based attacks or threats of attack by non-state actors against information systems when conducted to intimidate or coerce governments or societies in pursuit of goals that are political or social. It is the convergence of terrorism with cyberspace, where cyberspace becomes the means of conducting the terrorist act. Rather than committing acts of violence against persons or physical property, the cyberterrorist commits acts of destruction and disruption against digital property.

Cyberterrorism is distinguished from *cyberwar* in that the former comprises acts performed by non-state actors, whereas the latter consists of government activity. With cyberwar, a state's military engages in cyberattacks against an adversary within the context of a declared war.

Although cyberspace is constantly under assault by non-state actors, the attacks so far are generally not considered to be acts of cyberterrorism. They fall short for two reasons. First, the attacks that are the most destructive and generate the most fear are conducted for goals that are neither political nor social. For example, the worst denial of service (DoS) attacks have generally been conducted to extort money from victims, put competitors out of business, and satisfy the egos and curiosity of young hackers. Second, the attacks that have been linked to political and social goals generally have not been intimidating. Most have been simple Web deface-ments that, although annoying and disruptive, do not have much impact. They cor-respond more to the activity one might expect to see from protestors, not terrorists. For this reason, such cyberattacks are often referred to as "hacktivism," reflecting the convergence of hacking with activism rather than terrorism.

To fall in the domain of cyberterror, a cyberattack should be sufficiently destruc-tive or disruptive to generate fear comparable to that from physical acts of terror-ism, and it must be conducted for political and social reasons. Critical infrastructures, which include telecommunications, electric power, oil and gas, water supply, trans-portation, banking and finance, emergency services, and essential government services, are likely targets. Attacks against these infrastructures that lead to death or bodily injury, extended power outages, plane crashes, water contamination, or billion dollar banking losses are examples.

To date, the most serious reported attack against a critical infrastructure took place in Australia in early 2000. A 49-year-old Brisbane man penetrated the Maroochy Shire Council's waste management system and used radio transmissions to alter pump station operations. A million liters of raw sewage spilled into public parks and creeks on Queensland's Sunshine Coast, killing marine life, turning the water black, and creating an unbearable stench. However, the man's goals were neither political nor social. He was a former employee of the company that had installed the system, and was angry about being rejected for a council job ("Sewage Hacker Jailed," 2001).

Several computer viruses and worms have affected critical infrastructures. For example, the Slammer worm shut down emergency 911 systems, ATMs, and at least one airline booking system. It disabled the safety monitoring system at a nuclear power plant for nearly 5 hours and affected several electrical and water utilities. Although the source of the worm was not confirmed, it did not appear to be tied to any terrorists or terrorist motives. The worm's code contained a reference to the Honkers Union of China, a major Chinese hacking group.

There have been numerous attacks against financial systems, including bank and credit card fraud. However, such attacks have been conducted for money, not to coerce governments and societies. A terrorist group could attempt to steal bil-lions through a cyberattack, with the dual goals of getting money to fund their organization and of coercing a target government. So far, however, this has not happened.

Because there have been no incidents that are generally regarded as cyberter-rorism, the term itself has come to raise eyebrows. Skeptics wonder if it is all hype, used mainly to justify spending on new programs and increased government sur-veillance of the Internet.

Beside bearing little relation to any actual cyber incidents, the term also fails to capture the bulk of what terrorists are doing in cyberspace. Terrorists are making extensive use of cyberspace to facilitate their objectives, and it is important to understand, exploit, and counter this use. Too much emphasis on cyberterror, espe-cially if it is not a serious threat, could detract from other counterterrorist efforts in the cyber domain.

7.2. NPS/CTIW Studies

The first comprehensive treatment of the cyberterrorism threat was performed by the Center on Terrorism and Irregular Warfare (CTIW) at the Naval Postgraduate School (NPS) in Monterey, California. In August 1999, they issued a report on the prospects of terrorist organizations pursuing cyberterrorism (Nelson et al., 1999). They concluded that the barrier to entry for anything beyond annoying hacks is quite high, and that terrorists generally lack the wherewithal and human capital needed to mount a meaningful operation. Cyberterrorism, they argued, was a thing of the future, although it might be pursued as an ancillary tool. The NPS study defined three levels of cyberterror capability:

- *Simple unstructured:* The capability to conduct basic hacks against individual systems using tools created by someone else. The organization possesses little target analysis, command and control, or learning capability.
- *Advanced structured:* The capability to conduct more sophisticated attacks against multiple systems or networks and possibly to modify or create basic hacking tools. The organization possesses an elementary target analysis, command and control, and learning capability.
- *Complex coordinated:* The capability for coordinated attacks capable of causing mass disruption against integrated, heterogeneous defenses (including cryptography). Ability to create sophisticated hacking tools. Highly capable target analysis, command and control, and organization learning capability.

They estimated that it would take a group starting from scratch 2 to 4 years to reach the advanced structured level and 6 to 10 years to reach the complex coordinated level, although some groups might get there in just a few years or turn to outsourcing or sponsorship to extend their capability.

The study examined five terrorist group types: religious, New Age, ethno-nationalist separatist, revolutionary, and far-right extremists. They determined that only religious groups are likely to seek the most damaging capability level, because it is consistent with their indiscriminate application of violence. New Age, or single issue terrorists, such as the Animal Liberation Front, pose the most immediate threat; however, such groups are likely to accept disruption as a substitute for destruction. Both the revolutionary and ethnonationalist separatists are likely to seek an advanced structured capability. The far-right extremists are likely to settle for a simple unstructured capability; cyberterror offers neither the intimacy nor the cathartic effects that are central to the psychology of far-right terror. The study also determined that hacker groups are psychologically and organizationally ill-suited to cyberterrorism, and that it would be against their interests to cause mass disruption of the information infrastructure.

In October 2000, the CTIW at NPS issued a second report following a conference aimed at examining the decision making process that leads substate groups engaged in armed resistance to develop new operational methods (Tucker, 2000). They were particularly interested in learning whether such groups would engage in cyberterrorism. In addition to academics and a member of the United Nations, the participants included a hacker and five practitioners with experience in violent substate groups. The latter included the PLO, the Liberation Tigers of Tamil Eelan (LTTE), the Basque Fatherland and Liberty-Political/Military, and the Revolutionary Armed Forces of Colombia. The participants engaged in a simulation exercise based on the situation in Chechnya.

The "terrorist" team authorized only one cyberattack during the game, and that was against the Russian Stock Exchange. The attack was justified on the grounds that the exchange was an elite activity and thus disrupting it would not affect most Russians. Indeed, it might appeal to the average Russian. The group ruled out mass disruptions impacting e-commerce as being too indiscriminate and risking a backlash.

The findings from the meeting were generally consistent with the earlier study. Recognizing that their conclusions were based on a small sample, they concluded that terrorists have not yet integrated information technology into their strategy and tactics; that substate groups may find cyberterror attractive as a nonlethal weapon; that significant barriers between hackers and terrorists may prevent their integration into one group; and that politically motivated terrorists had reasons to target selectively and limit the effects of their operations, although they might find themselves in a situation where a mass casualty attack was a rational choice.

7.3. Cyberterror Indicators

The NPS researchers applied their general knowledge of terrorists and cyberweapons to evaluate the threat of cyberterrorism. By contrast, my recent work is based on identifying indicators of cyberterrorism. These are pieces of evidence that demonstrate a capability or intent to conduct acts of cyberterror. The ones I have identified so far fall into five categories:

- *Execution of cyberattacks:* This covers all types of computer network attack, not just acts of cyberterror.
- *Cyberweapons acquisition, development, and training:* This includes acquisition and distribution of cyberweapons, research and development in cyberweapons, and training in the use of cyberweapons. Activities can take place on-line or in special facilities.
- *Statements about cyberattacks:* This covers all types of statements relating to cyberattacks, including discussions, declarations of intent, and calls for performing cyberattacks.
- *Formal education in information technology:* This includes all areas of IT education, but especially studies in network and information security.
- *General experience with cyberspace:* This covers cyber activities that do not fall within the first four categories, including general use of the Internet for communications and distribution of news and propaganda.

The categories are listed in order of generally decreasing significance; that is, the actual execution of cyberattacks carries more weight than acquisition and development of cyberattack tools, which in turn carries more weight than simply making statements about cyberattacks, and so on. However, the ordering is not strict, as the nature of the evidence also matters. Evidence of a cybertraining camp that has been instructing scores of cyber-jihadists in attacks against the Supervisory Control and Data Acquisition (SCADA) is a stronger indicator of cyberterrorism than evidence of a successful Web defacement. SCADA and other types of digital control systems are used to monitor and control critical infrastructures such as those for electricity, oil and gas, water, dams, and sewage, and are considered likely candidates for cyberterrorist attacks.

The last two categories—formal education in information technology (IT) and general experience in cyberspace—are not indicators of cyberterrorism so much as enablers. A terrorist could study computer science, for example, to manage information resources such as Web sites for an organization. Even a focus on network security could be for the purpose of defending terrorist systems and information rather than launching cyberattacks. Still, terrorists with formal education in IT and experience using the technology are in a better position to develop a cyberterror capability than those without this background, so evidence in these categories is relevant to assessing the cyberterror threat.

In seeking evidence relating to these indicators, I considered activities attributable not only to terrorist groups, but also to hackers expressing an alliance or sympathies with such groups. Although the latter may not be willing to engage in physical acts of violence, they may be amenable to causing extensive damage to information resources. Also, it can be difficult to know the exact relationship between a terrorist group and hackers claiming some sort of affiliation. The Al-Qaeda Alliance Online, for example, appeared to have no formal ties to the terrorist organization, but it might be considered part of the broader jihadi movement associated with it.

The following subsections discuss each of the five indicator categories and the evidence I have found so far.

7.3.1. Execution of Cyberattacks

Evidence of successful or even attempted computer network attacks is generally the strongest indicator of a cyberterrorism threat. However, as suggested, the specifics involved in such attacks also matter, including the objectives, targets, results, methods, and overall prevalence. Attacks that seek to cause harm and generate fear are a stronger indicator of cyberterrorism than ones that seek only other types of objectives such as money. Even if terrorists fund their operations by hacking Web servers and stealing credit card numbers, for example, such attacks fall more in the domain of terrorist support operations than acts of terrorism.

In addition, attacks against critical infrastructures are a stronger indicator than those against Web sites and nonessential services. Whether an attack is successful and the level of damage it causes also matters. Even so, a failed attack against the power grid is more indicative of a cyberterror threat than a successful Web defacement. The level of skill involved in an attack, as displayed through the methods used, is another important factor in judging an attack's significance. Finally, a single, isolated attack bears less significance than a demonstrated capability manifest in multiple attacks.

Over the years, numerous cyberattacks have been attributed to hackers affiliated with terrorist organizations or sympathetic to terrorist causes. Although none of these attacks has caused sufficient damage to be labeled an act of cyberterror, they have demonstrated a capability to disrupt e-mail and Web services, and to use cyberattacks to raise money.

The first reported incident of this nature took place in 1997 when an offshoot of the LTTE claimed responsibility for "suicide e-mail bombings" against Sri Lankan embassies over a 2-week period. Calling themselves the Internet Black Tigers, the group swamped Sri Lankan embassies with about 800 e-mails a day. The messages read, "We are the Internet Black Tigers and we're doing this to disrupt your communications" ("Email Attack," 1998, p. 8). The Tamil Tigers are also credited with using a cyber attack to raise money. After compromising a computer system at Sheffield University in England in 1997 and capturing the user IDs and passwords of respected faculty, they used the e-mail accounts to send out messages asking donors to send money to a charity in Sri Lanka (Vatis, 2001).

The Kosovo conflict in 1999 inspired numerous hackers to join the conflict on one side or the other, or to protest the whole thing. Most of their cyberattacks took the form of Web defacements, but there were also a few DoS attacks. Of particular interest here are the activities of the Serb Black Hand (Crna Ruka) group, because of the radical nature of Crna Ruka. According to reports, they crashed a Kosovo Albanian Web site, justifying their actions with the statement "We shall continue to remove ethnic Albanian lies from the Internet." They also planned daily actions against NATO computers and deleted data on a Navy computer (Denning, 2001a, p. 273).

Several years ago, the Animal Liberation Front took responsibility for a few cyberattacks. These included Web defacements and virtual sit-ins (modest DoS attacks against Web sites). They threatened additional cyberattacks, but I have not seen evidence of such.

The Israeli–Palestinian conflict has provoked numerous cyberattacks from hackers on both sides of the conflict. This was especially intense during the Second Intifada, which erupted in late September 2000. According to the security firm iDefense (2000), at least two of the pro-Palestinian groups involved in the parallel cyber intifada had terrorist connections. One of these was UNITY, a Muslim extremist group with ties to Hizballah. After pro-Israeli hackers attacked Hizballah's Web site, the hackers launched a coordinated, multiphased DoS attack, first against official Israeli government sites, second against Israeli financial sites, third against Israeli ISPs, and fourth against "Zionist E-Commerce" sites. The other group, al-Muhajiroun, has ties to a number of Muslim terrorist organizations as well as to Osama bin Laden. The London-based group directed their members to a Web page, where at the click of a mouse members could join an automated flooding attack against Israeli sites that were attacking Moqawama (Islamic Resistance) sites. iDefense also noted that UNITY recruited and organized a third group, Iron Guard, which conducted more technically sophisticated attacks. According to a Canadian government report, the group's call for cyber jihad was supported and promoted by al-Muhajiroun (Office of Critical Infrastructure Protection and Emergency Preparedness, Government of Canada, 2001).

The opening paragraph of this paper mentions the cyberattacks by GForce Pakistan and the formation of the Al-Qaeda Alliance Online in the wake of the September 11 attacks. Muslim hackers associated with one of the other Alliance members, the Pakistan Hackerz Club (PHC), had already defaced numerous Web sites with messages supporting Kashmir independence and the Palestinians. During the cyber-intifada in November 2000, Doctor Nuker, a founder of PHC, posted 700 credit card numbers and 3,500 e-mail addresses on the Web site of the American Israel Public Affairs Committee. He acquired the data from the Web server when he broke into it.

In 2003, a call for cyberattacks against Israeli computers appeared on a Web site affiliated with Al-Qassam Brigades, the military wing of Hamas. Under the heading "the electronic jihad," someone opened a discussion about using computer viruses to inflict harm on Israel. The idea was to load a virus-infected page onto a Web site and then take steps to attract as many Israeli visitors as possible to the site (Reynalds, 2002).

In early 2004, Internet Haganah, a Web site devoted to confronting Islamic terrorists on the Internet and stopping their use of the net as a communications and propagation tool, reported that the Al Aqsa Martyrs Brigade was planning a cyberattack against the El Al Web site (Internet Haganah, 2004). Internet Haganah also reported that its own Web site, which is part of the Israeli domain ".il," was the target of jihadists. A message posted to a Yahoo! group attempted to recruit 600 Muslims for jihad cyberattacks against Internet Haganah. The motive was retaliation against Internet Haganah's efforts to close down terrorist-related Web sites. Muslim hackers were asked to register to a Yahoo! group called Jehad-Op (Reynalds, 2004).

According to the Anti-Terrorism Coalition (ATC), the jihad was organized by a group named Osama Bin Laden (OBL) Crew, which also threatened attacks against the ATC Web site ("ATC's OBL Crew," 2004).[1] Founded in 2000 by an al Qa'ida member living in Holland, since 2002 OBL Crew has been under the leadership of a San Diego man calling himself Ibn Shahbaz. Although the promised attacks against ATC either failed or never materialized, OBL Crew hackers did take over the Asian Hangout forum on June 26, 2004, which they used for recruiting.

As I complete this chapter in February 2006, Zone-h has recorded over 2,000 Web defacements, many in Denmark, protesting the 12 cartoons satirizing the Prophet Mohammad that were first published in the Danish newspaper *Jyllands-Posten*. Although many of the attacks were conducted "just for fun," "as a challenge," and "to be the best defacer," the substantial number performed for "political reasons," "patriotism," and "revenge" might be indicative of a growing cadre of cyber-jihadists. According to Zone-h, one of the defacers, the Internet Islamic Brigades, had also posted warnings of suicide bombings on a Danish forum, suggesting the group was interested in more than just relatively minor cyberattacks (Preatoni, 2006).

According to the Jamestown Foundation, the radical jihadist al-Ghorabaa Web site coordinated a 24-hour cyberattack against *Jyllands-Posten* and other newspapers' sites. Participants in the al-Ghorabaa forum also discussed broadening their

---

[1]The ATC's Intelligence Department became an independent organization, called Anti-Terrorism Intelligence, in March 2005.

campaign. Following the burning of the Danish and Norwegian embassies in Damascus and Beirut, they purportedly called for a global "embassy-burning day" against Danish embassies all over the world (Ulph, 2006). Internet Haganah also reported that a group (perhaps the same?) claiming credit for attacking *Jyllands-Posten*'s Web site had released a video purporting to document the attack. The video was in the style of jihadi videos coming out of Iraq, showing that the hackers were emulating the tactics of violent jihadists (Internet Haganah, 2006). These activities show an association between hacking and more violent forms of jihad, which could be precursors to cyberterrorism.

Cyber-jihadists have also conducted cyberattacks in support of other objectives, including intelligence collection and information sharing. In an article on the challenges of terrorism in the information age, Magnus Ranstorp reports that al Qa'ida broke into the e-mail account of a U.S. diplomat in the Arab world. The terrorists used simple password cracking tools, freely available on the Internet, to gain access to the account. They retrieved his bank statements, which revealed information about his location and movement (Ranstorp, 2004).

Terrorists or their sympathizers have reportedly hijacked Internet servers to share documents. Although this might not be considered an "attack," it nonetheless represents unauthorized use of computers. In one such case, 70 files were uploaded to an unprotected file transfer protocol site run by the Arkansas government for its contractors. A person calling himself Irhabi 007, or Terrorist 007, put links to the files on a message board belonging to al Ansar (McGuire, 2004). The motivations for using hijacked sites could include access to free storage and avoidance of detection by authorities.

7.3.2. Cyberweapons Acquisition, Development, and Training

Terrorist groups typically supply their members with weapons, acquired on black markets or developed in house. They also provide training in the use of these weapons. Al Qa'ida, for example, operated training camps in Afghanistan and Sudan for thousands of jihadists. Some of these facilities are also used for weapons research and development. In addition, terrorists provide training materials in the form of written documents and videos, which are distributed to members. One video even shows how to build a suicide belt.

If terrorists are to conduct highly damaging cyber attacks, I would expect to see similar activities in the cyber domain, including acquisition, research, development, distribution, and training in cyberweapons. So far, there have been a few such indicators. According to Magnus Ranstorp (2004), an al Qa'ida safe house in Pakistan was used to train operational members in computer hacking and to conduct cyber reconnaissance against infrastructure and SCADA systems, probing the control mechanisms of electrical power grids and dam structures. Although this could be a strong indicator of an attempt to develop a cyberterror capability, I could not find any other information about it or information suggesting that al Qa'ida had developed or acquired cybertools for attacking these systems.

In January 2002, the National Infrastructure Protection Center (NIPC) also reported that al Qa'ida members had "sought information on SCADA systems available on multiple SCADA-related websites. They specifically sought information on water supply and wastewater management practices in the U.S. and abroad." The NIPC bulletin also noted that the Federal Bureau of Investigation had found structural architecture software (CATIGE, BEAM, AUTOCAD 2000, and MICROSTRAN) on the computer of a person with indirect ties to bin Laden. The software suggested the individual was interested in structural engineering as it relates to dams and other water-retaining structures (NIPC, 2002). However, the software could be useful in planning either physical or cyberattacks against these structures, so the research is not necessarily related to cyberterror.

Other indicators point to on-line training in cyberattacks. In late 2003, an affiliate of al Qa'ida announced the opening of Al-Qa'ida University for Jihad Sciences on the Internet, with a college on electronic jihad. The announcement was circulated by the Islamic Information Center, which in the past had disseminated statements by bin Laden on the Internet. The other colleges include the technology of explosive devices, booby-trapped cars and vehicles, and media jihad. The announcement noted that there were already specialists in electronic jihad (al-Shafi, 2003).

In August 2005, the Jamestown Foundation reported that the jihadist al-Farouq Web forum contained postings calling for heightened electronic attacks against U.S. and allied government Web sites, and information for mujahid hackers. The Web site included a hacker library with information for disrupting and destroying enemy electronic resources. The library held keylogging software for capturing keystrokes and acquiring passwords on compromised computers, software tools for hiding or misrepresenting the hacker's Internet address, and disk and system utilities for erasing hard disks and incapacitating Windows-based systems (Pool, 2005a).

Two months later, Jamestown reported that a manual on hacking was posted on another Internet forum frequented by jihadists, Minbar ahl al-Sunna wal-Jama'a (The Pulpit of the People of the Sunna). The document was said to be written in a pedagogical style and discuss motives and incentives for computer-based attacks, including political, strategic, economic, and individual. It was also said to discuss three types of attack: direct intrusions into corporate and government networks, infiltration of personal computers to steal personal information, and interception of sensitive information such as credit card numbers in transit (Pool, 2005b).

In February 2006, Jamestown noted that "Most radical jihadi forums devote an entire section to [hacker warfare]." They said that the al-Ghorabaa site, which had coordinated an attack against *Jyllands-Posten*, contained information on penetrating computer devices and intranet servers, stealing passwords, and security. It also contained an encyclopedia on hacking sites and a 344-page book on hacking techniques, including a step-by-step guide for "terminating pornographic sites and those intended for the Jews and their supporters" (Ulph, 2006).

Imam Samudra, one of the terrorists convicted in the October 12, 2002, Bali bombings, offers rudimentary information on hacking, particularly as it applies to credit card fraud ("carding") in a chapter titled "Hacking: Why Not?" of his autobiography *Me Against the Terrorist!* Sumadra advocates the use of computer attacks to raise funds for terrorist activities. Evidence found on his seized computer showed he at least had made an attempt at carding (Sipress, 2004).

Hacking groups provide a forum for exchanging cyberattack tools and methods, and learning how to use them. Although much of the activity takes place on-line, in some cases, members meet in person and learn from each other. In 1998, for example, the Muslim Hackers Club (MHC) sent an e-mail announcing that their president, brother Ibrahim, would be visiting Pakistan and offering local MHC chapters classes in hacking Internet service providers and network protocols. The classes would also teach how to set up Windows-NT–based servers. The message went on to say that "MHC's main orientation will be to setup a nonstate capability in information warfare, err, research, if that makes you feel better." The MHC also operated a Web site with hacking information, tutorials, and software tools ("Computer Lessons for Terrorists," 2002).

There are thousands of hacking groups worldwide. A group could align itself with terrorists at any time, adding to the skill base that can be applied to cyberterrorism. Even though the overwhelming majority would never support terrorism, evidence has shown that at least some have hacked in support of the same objectives.

7.3.3. Statements About Cyberattacks

Statements by terrorists pertaining to the use of cyberattacks can indicate an interest in or intent to carry out cyberterrorism. Such statements can take the form of exploratory discussions, forecasts, threats, advocacy, calls to action, and claims relating to capability or responsibility for attacks.

In some cases, statements about cyberterrorism have been issued in conjunction with lesser attacks. For example, not long after September 11, an anti-U.S. defacement carried the message: "IN NEXT DAYS YOU'LL LOOK THE GREATEST CYBERTERRORIST ATTACK AGAINST AMERICAN GOVERNMENT COMPUTERS." The threatened cyberterrorism, however, never materialized.

Various statements from al Qa'ida and its supporters have shown that the possibilities of cyberterrorism are at least on the terrorist network's radar screen. For example, following the September 11 attacks, Osama bin Laden allegedly told Hadmid Mir, editor of the *Ausaf* newspaper, that "hundreds of Muslim scientists were with him and who would use their knowledge in chemistry, biology and (sic) ranging from computers to electronics against the infidels" (Office of Critical Infrastructure Protection and Emergency Preparedness, Government of Canada, 2001).

In December 2001, *Newsbytes* reported that a suspected member of al Qa'ida said that members of the terrorist network had infiltrated Microsoft and attempted to plant Trojan horses and bugs in the Windows XP operating system (McWilliams, 2001b). According to the report, Mohammad Afroze Abdul Razzak told Indian police that the terrorists had gained employment at Microsoft by posing as computer programmers. Microsoft responded by saying the claims were "bizarre and unsubstantiated and should be treated skeptically."

Although the claims are almost certainly false, the story is troubling for the simple reason that it shows that at least some terrorists are fully cognizant of the potential of cyberattacks and how such attacks can be launched with the aid of Trojan horses and insider access into the world's dominant software producer.

National Review reported that a Syrian cyberterrorist whose day job was running a car dealership invited potential Islamic hackers to join the Arab Electronic Jihad Team (AEJT). Announced in 2002, the goals of AEJT were to bring down all Web sites in the United States and Israel. The group sought members who were "advanced in the art of hacking" (Robbins, 2002). As 2002 drew to a close, U.S. and Israeli Web sites remained standing.

Sheikh Omar Bakri Muhammad, the London-based Islamic cleric who heads al-Muhajiroun and has ties to bin Laden, told *Computer World* in November 2002 that al Qa'ida and other radical Muslim groups were actively planning to use the Internet as a weapon in their holy war against the West. He noted that the military wings of al Qa'ida and other radical Islamic groups were using and studying the Internet for their own operations. He said that "in a matter of time, you will see attacks on the stock market," and that he "would not be surprised if tomorrow I hear of a big economic collapse because of somebody attacking the main technical systems in big companies" (Verton, 2002a, 2002b).

As noted, postings on the al-Farouq Web site in 2005 called for cyberattacks against the U.S. and allied governments. One participant, who identified himself as "archrafe," proposed forming an operations unit within the Islamic Hacker Army (*Jaish al-Hacker al-Islami*). He offered advantages to organizing the electronic jihad community, including the ability to launch simultaneous DoS attacks (Pool, 2005a).

Two years earlier, a book advocating cyberattacks against infidel Web sites was posted on al-Farouq's Web site. Titled *The 39 Principles of Jihad*, the book calls on every Muslim to "obey the Jihad against the infidels." The principles suggest different ways of doing so, including participating in martyrdom and other operations, supplying money and equipment to fighters, and so forth. Principle 34 specifically directs computer experts to "use their skills and experience in destroying American, Jewish and secular websites as well as morally corrupt websites" (Halevi, 2003).

According to Fouad Husseing, cyberterrorism is part of al Qa'ida's long-term war against the United States. In his book, *al-Zarqawi-al-Qaeda's Second Generation*, Husseing describes al Qa'ida's seven-phase war as revealed through interviews of the organization's top lieutenants. Phase 4, which is scheduled for 2010 to 2013, includes conducting cyberterrorism against the U.S. economy (Hall, 2005). Given other evidence, this is conceivable.

7.3.4. Formal Education in Information Technology

Although it is not hard to carry out relatively simple cyberattacks using readily available hacking tools, considerably greater skill would be required to develop software to perform original and highly damaging attacks against critical infrastructures. For such attacks, formal education in a field such as computer science or computer engineering would be helpful, especially if the program of study included digital controls systems and network security. Although courses in information and network security emphasize how to defend against cyberattacks, they inevitably teach something about attacks: It is not possible to build adequate defenses without a solid understanding of the threat.

A few people with formal education in these areas have been associated with terrorist groups. Sami Al-Arian, the professor at the University of South Florida charged with raising money for Palestinian Islamic Jihad, was in the department of Computer Science and Engineering. Although Al-Arian's area of specialty did not appear to be network security, Sami Omar Al-Hussayen, the Saudi graduate student at the University of Idaho charged with operating Web sites used to recruit terrorists, raise money to support terrorism, and disseminate inflammatory rhetoric, was studying computer security in the Computer Science Department. However, neither Al-Arian or Al-Hussayen was convicted of any crimes.

In *Black Ice*, Dan Verton describes how a computer science major at Columbia College in Missouri became al Qa'ida's procurement officer in the United States for computers, satellite telephones, and sophisticated surveillance technologies. Along the way, Ziyad Khalil, using the pseudoname Ziyad Sadaqa, registered as the operator of Hamas's Web site, www.palestine-info.net. From there, he eventually came to the attention of al Qa'ida (Verton, 2003, pp. 88–91).

In perhaps the most significant case of all, a computer science graduate student at Bradley University was allegedly assigned by al Qa'ida to explore ways of hacking into the computer systems of U.S. banks and to help settle al Qa'ida members entering the United States for attacks. According to reports, Ali S. Marri had been trained in computer hacking and the use of poisons, and had met Osama bin Laden at the al Farooq camp in Afghanistan. Marri was designated an enemy combatant by President Bush in 2003 (Schmidt, 2003). This is the only case where the subject's activities and educational program were tied to an objective of conducting cyberattacks. Those of Al-Arian, Al-Hussayen, and Khalil did not appear to involve cyberattacks.

7.3.5. General Experience with Cyberspace

Although most people who use computers and the Internet never conduct any cyberattack, it is also true that experience with the technology is a prerequisite for conducting destructive cyberattacks. Terrorist groups that make extensive use of cyberspace are better equipped to move in the direction of employing cyberterrorism than those that do not.

In this regard, numerous terrorist groups, and especially those affiliated with al Qa'ida and the global jihad, have made extensive use of cyberspace to distribute documents, videos, audio recordings, and other materials; and to communicate with cohorts, recruit, raise money, gather intelligence about targets and weapons, discuss options, and generally facilitate their organizations and operations. They have operated Web sites with password-protected areas and used e-mail, Web forums and discussion groups, instant messaging and chat, and encryption (Denning, 2001a/2006; Weimann, 2004). Jihadists are even said to have developed a Web browser that filters out all Web sites except for that of the preeminent Salafist ideologue Abu Muhammad al-Maqdisi ("Jihadist Web Browser," 2006). However, none of these activities requires the skills needed to carry out cyberattacks, so they are not strong indicators of cyberterror.

7.4. Conclusions

The foregoing evidence shows that terrorist groups and jihadists have an interest in conducting cyberattacks and at least some capability to do so. Further, they are attempting to develop and deploy this capability through on-line training and calls for action. The evidence does not, however, support an imminent threat of cyberterrorism. Any cyberattacks originating with terrorists or cyber jihadists in the near future are likely to be conducted either to raise money (e.g., via credit card theft) or to cause damage comparable to that which takes place daily from Web deface-ments, viruses and worms, and DoS attacks. Although the impact of those attacks can be serious, they are generally not regarded as acts of terrorism. Terrorists have not yet demonstrated that they have the knowledge and skills to conduct highly damaging attacks against critical infrastructures (e.g., causing power outages), although there are a few indicators showing at least some interest. Using the ter-minology from the 1999 NPS study, their capability is at the lowest level, namely that required to carry out simple unstructured attacks.

A disclaimer, however, is in order. This assessment is based entirely on open sources. Intelligence agencies may have additional information that would suggest a higher level of threat. Further, terrorists could be engaging in cyberactivities that have not even made the radar screens of the intelligence agencies.

Looking further into the future, it is difficult to know where terrorism might lead. It is conceivable that cyberweapons will never draw the appeal of bombs and oth-er physical weapons. However, I can suggest a few indicators that would likely pre-cede a successful incident of cyberterror:

- Failed cyberattacks against critical infrastructures, particularly the SCADA and other digital systems that are used to monitor and control these infrastructures. It seems unlikely that a first attempt would succeed with the desired effect, given the novelty of such an attack and uncertainty about how it would play out.
- Research and training labs, where terrorists simulate the effects of cyberat-tacks against critical infrastructures, develop methods and tools of attack against those infrastructures, and train people on how to conduct such attacks. Although hackers use the Internet itself as their research and training lab, trying out var-ious attacks on live systems, it is hard to perform controlled experiments and analyze the consequences without a lab. Absent special facilities, I would expect to at least see training materials showing terrorists how to conduct damaging attacks against critical infrastructures and software tools designed to facilitate such attacks.
- Extensive discussions and planning relating to acts of cyberterror against crit-ical infrastructures, not just attacks against Web sites and attacks aimed at making money.

Many authors have suggested that terrorists may be more inclined to use cybert-error as an ancillary tool to amplify the effects of a physical attack. For example, they might launch a cyberattack against the 911 system while blowing up a hotel, the goal being to impede response to the incident and increase fear. However, ter-rorists do not normally integrate multiple modes of attack. Although there have been numerous incidents involving coordinated attacks—including the September 11 hijackings, the London subway bombings, the Madrid train bombings, and the East African Embassy bombings—these have always involved multiple occurrences of pretty much the same thing (e.g., four hijacked planes turned into missiles in the September 11 attacks). It seems unlikely that terrorists would suddenly suc-ceed with an attack requiring coordination across the cyber and physical domains.

Even if this becomes their goal, I would expect to see evidence of failed attempts, cross-domain training and simulation, and discussions and planning relating to such attacks before a successful incident. Given terrorists' capabilities today in the cyber domain, this seems no more imminent than other acts of cyberterror.

In summary, my overall assessment of the cyberterror threat is much the same as 5 years ago. At least in the near future, bombs remain a much larger threat than bytes. However, we cannot ignore the potential of cyberterror. During the past 5 years, terrorists and jihadists have shown a stronger interest in and capability to conduct cyberattacks, and they have successfully conducted numerous attacks against Web sites.

Moreover, even if our critical infrastructures are not under imminent threat by terrorists seeking political and social objectives, they must be protected from harmful attacks conducted for other reasons such as money, revenge, youthful curiosity, and war. The owners of these infrastructures and their governments must defend against cyberattacks regardless of who may perpetrate them.

References

al-Shafi, Muhammad. (2003, November 20). "Al-Qa'ida Reportedly Establishing Open 'Internet University' to Recruit Terrorists" [OSAC Foreign Press Report]. *Al-Sharq al-Aswat* (London).

"ATC's OBL Crew Investigation." (2004, July 1). Available at http://atdatabase.r8.org/. Accessed 2/10/06.

"Computer Lessons for Terrorists." (2002, May 20). *Newsweek.*

Denning, Dorothy A. (2000, May 23). "Cyberterrorism." Special Oversight Panel on Terrorism, Committee on Armed Services. Presented to the U.S. House of Representatives.

Denning, Dorothy A. (2001a). "Activism, Hacktivism, and Cyberterrorism." In John Arquilla and David Ronfelt, eds. *Networks and Netwars.* Santa Monica, CA: RAND.

Denning, Dorothy A. (2001b, November). "Is Cyber Terror Next?" In Craig Calhoun, Paul Price, and Ashley Trimmer, eds. *Understanding September.* New York: The New Press.

Denning, Dorothy A. (2006). "Information Operations and Terrorism." In Lars Nicander and Magnus Ranstorp, eds. *Terrorism in the Information Age.* Swedish National Defence College, Stockholm. 2006.

"Email Attack on Sri Lanka Computer." (1998, June). *Computer Security Alert,* No. 183, p. 8.

Halevi, Jonathan D. (2003, September). "39 Principles of Jihad." Center for Special Studies, Intelligence and Terrorism Information Center. Available at www.intelligence.org.il/eng/var/39p_e.htm. Accessed 6/12/06.

Hall, Allan. (2005, August 24). "Al-Qaeda Chiefs Reveal World Domination Design." *The Age.*

iDefense. (2000, January 3). *Israeli-Palestinian Cyber Conflict.* Dulles, VA.

Internet Haganah. (2004). Available at http://haganah.org.il/haganah/index.html. Accessed 3/24/04.

Internet Haganah. (2006, February 7). "How the Brothers Attacked the Website of Jylland-Posten." Available at http://haganah.org.il/harchives/005456.html. Accessed 6/12/06.

"Jihadist Web Browser." (2006, February 8). Available at www.fbis.gov. Accessed 6/12/06.

McGuire, David. (2004, July 13). "Al Qaeda Messages Posted on U.S. Server." *The Washington Post.*

McWilliams, Brian. (2001a, October 17). "Pakistani Hackers Deface U.S. Site With Ultimatum." *Newsbytes.*

McWilliams, Brian. (2001b, December 17). "Suspect Claims Al Qaeda Hacked Microsoft." *Newsbytes.*

National Infrastructure Protection Center (NIPC). (2002, January 30). "Terrorist Interest in Water Supply and SCADA Systems" [Information Bulletin 01-001]. Washington, D.C.

Nelson, Bill, Rodney Choi, Michael Iacobucci, Mark Mitchell, and Greg Gagnon. (1999, August). *Cyberterror: Prospects and Implications.* Monterey, CA: Center for the Study of Terrorism and Irregular Warfare.

Office of Critical Infrastructure Protection and Emergency Preparedness, Government of Canada. (2001). "Al-Qaida Cyber Capability." Available at www.epc-pcc.gc.ca/emergencies/other/TA01-001_E.html. Accessed 6/12/06.

Pool, Jeffrey. (2005a, August 23). *New Web Forum Postings Call for Intensified Electronic Jihad Against Government Websites.* Washington, D.C.: Jamestown Foundation.

Pool, Jeffrey. (2005b, October 11). *Technology and Security Discussions on the Jihadist Forums.* Washington, D.C.: Jamestown Foundation.

Preatoni, Roberto. (2006, February 7). "Prophet Mohammed Protest Spreads on the Digital Ground." *Zone-h.* Available at www.zone-h.org/en/news/read/id=205987/. Accessed 6/12/06.

Ranstorp, Magnus. (2004). "Al-Qaida in Cyberspace: Future Challenges of Terrorism in an Information Age." In Lars Nicander and Magnus Ranstorp, eds. *Terrorism in the Information Age–New Frontiers?* Stockholm: Swedish National Defence College.

Reynalds, Jeremy. (2002, September 29). "Hamas Sympathizers Have a Plan for Computers–Maybe Yours!" Available at www.joyjunction.org/bulletin/forums/showthread.php?t=226. Accessed 4/24/04.

Reynalds, Jeremy. (2004, February 28). "Internet 'Terrorist' Using Yahoo to Recruit 600 Muslims for Hack Attack." Available at http://209.157.64.201/focus/f-news/1089396/posts. Accessed 6/12/06.

Robbins, James S. (2002, July 30). "The Jihad Online." *National Review Online.* Available at http://nationalreview.com/robbins/robbins073002.asp. Accessed 6/12/06.

Schmidt, Susan. (2003, June 24). "Qatari Man Designated an Enemy Combatant." *Washington Post*, p. A01.

Sipress, Alan. (2004, December 14). "An Indonesian's Prison Memoir Takes Holy War Into Cyberspace." *The Washington Post*, p. A19.

"Sewage Hacker Jailed." (2001, October 31). *Herald Sun.*

Tucker, David. (2000, October). "The Future of Armed Resistance: Cyberterror? Mass Destruction?" Conference Report and Proceedings. Monterey, CA: Center for the Study of Terrorism and Irregular Warfare.

Ulph, Stephen. (2006, February 7). "Internet Mujahideen Refine Electronic Warfare Tactics." *Terrorism Focus*, Vol. III, No. 5.

Vatis, Michael. (2001). "Cyber Terrorism and Information Warfare: Government Perspectives." In Yonah Alexander and Michael S. Swetnam, eds. *Cyber Terrorism and Information Warfare.* Ardsley, NY: Transnational Publishers.

Verton, Dan. (2002a, November 18). "Bin Laden Cohort Warns of Cyberattacks." *Computerworld.*

Verton, Dan. (2002b, November 25). "Al-Qaeda Poses Threat to Net." *Computerworld.*

Verton, Dan. (2003). *Black Ice.* New York: McGraw-Hill.

Weimann, Gabriel. (2004, March). "United States Institute of Peace: Special Report 116." Available at www.terror.net. Accessed 6/12/06.

Part 3: Ethical Issues in Professionalism and Design

The threat of security breaches and unauthorized intrusions involves ethical issues with many dimensions. Most obviously, some of these issues concern the behavior of persons committing such breaches or intrusions. Is a particular breach morally justified and should it be punished by the state? But, equally important, some ethical issues concern the behavior of those professionals who develop the technologies that may be compromised. Given that, for example, the relation between buyers and sellers is shaped by market forces, what obligations does a software developer have to consumers to produce code without vulnerabilities? This section addresses questions of professionalism as it concerns Internet security.

The first chapter in the section is Donald Gotterbarn's and David Tarnoff's "Internet Development: Professionalism, Profits, Ethics, or Sleaze?" Gotterbarn is one of the most distinguished information ethicists working today and is widely recognized as one of the founding parents of this burgeoning field. He and Tarnoff argue that focusing on the deviant behavior of hackers is of limited utility to developers. In particular, it cannot help them to make software or the Web better and safer. They argue for the importance of codes of professionalism intended to guide developers far more constructively than negative standards focusing on other people. To this end, they present an "Internet-appropriate" model of professionalism.

Batya Friedman, Daniel Howe, and Edward Felten apply the concept of value-sensitive design (VSD) to the problem of informed consent in browser-to-Web transactions involving the creation of cookies. The authors explain the concept of VSD and give an ethical analysis of informed consent. They go on to show how the principles of VSD can be utilized to produce a browser mechanism that satisfies the ethical principles governing informed consent. This paper provides an outstanding model of how to approach some of the relevant issues of professionalism that arise in connection with developing software.

The last chapter is Richard Epstein's "The Impact of Computer Security Concerns Upon Software Development." Epstein's essay focuses on developing a comprehensive set of principles that can guide developers in writing software. Epstein addresses a number of important questions in this essay, including: (1) What should be the basic security and project goals for developing secure software? (2) What properties distinguish a good software development process from one likely to produce software with security flaws? (3) What team culture issues are relevant? (4) What legal, professional, and ethical issues are relevant to security concerns in the software development process? Epstein's analysis will be invaluable to developers who want practical guidance in developing software.

Chapter 8: Internet Development: Professionalism, Profits, Ethics, or Sleaze?

Don Gotterbarn and David Tarnoff

8.1. Introduction

It is incredible to watch the phenomenal growth of the Internet. Loosely managed as it is, it is still the catalyst for the rapid development of new technologies and capabilities. It is much like pioneering efforts in America's westward expansion. It attracts practitioners of varying skill, degree of dedication, and understanding of the impact of their work. One consequence of this diversity is seen in the unsettling emphasis on issues like cyberstalking, cyber-rape, Internet pornography, and numerous other significant negative ethical problems. Some have argued (Gates, 1995) that industries, such as pornography, with their willingness quickly to adopt new technologies, have served to finance the Internet infrastructure as they did print media in the past. This simplistic analogy of the Internet to print media serves only to diminish the significant impact that the Internet has in all areas.

Today, 10 years into Web development, an emerging industry called *cyberethics* has actually contributed to a significant problem in Web development. Cyberethics focuses on "dysfunctional human behavior" on the Web that includes flaming, hacking, harassment, misinformation, obscenity, plagiarism, and viruses and worms (Clarke, 1995). This focus is reinforced by the mistaken equating of legal and ethical issues; by equating cyberethics with cybercrime (Computer Crime and Intellectual Property Section, 2005; National Cyber Security Alliance, N.D.). This focus on the behavior of the malcontents and dishonest developers distracts the honest Internet developer who is led to believe that they do a good job if they are not like those people. This focus on deviant behavior does not help professional Internet developers to address potential negative impacts of the software, nor does it help them to address ways in which to make the Web better.

Web development, like other software development, has significant social and ethical impacts that the developer must consider. The Web is run by software we develop, and just as avionics software developers have responsibilities to those who ride in the airplane, so developers have responsibilities to Web users and those impacted by the Web.

8.1.1. Transition to Professionalism

Look at a simple, non-headline–grabbing example of how poorly Internet developers are addressing issues of professional responsibility. A user of AOL Instant Messenger (AIM) had just undergone a series of eye surgeries and was visually challenged for a few months. Several accessibility functions facilitated his continued laptop use. Unfortunately, the AIM News Ticker could not be enlarged. Believing the claim on AOL's Web site that they pride themselves on accessibility, the user contacted AOL's technical support asking that something be done to make the news readable to the visually challenged. The AOL technician told the user to simply select the "large text option," not realizing that AOL had not only set, but also locked the text size, so it shows at 800 × 600. Rather than admit that this limited the visually challenged user, the technician ended the discussion saying the only thing they could do was suggest that this user (and all visually challenged users) change the resolution on his screen to 800 × 600. Enforcing a specific monitor resolution on a whole class of users would be considered a "bug" in any other software (Gotterbarn, 2004).

This developer was not a malcontent nor was he intentionally engaged in unethical behavior. There was a lack of understanding of the developer's responsibility to the user. I am not faulting the technician here. This is just a simple example of the harm caused by the absence of a professional responsibility in Internet development. The AOL technician presumed his responsibility ends at the illumination of the computer screen (Gotterbarn, 2004). There are several different types of responsibility including legal, causal, and role responsibility. The technician may have felt free to not address the problem because he was not the developer and did not cause the problem; he had no direct causal responsibility. Nevertheless, the technician did not fulfill his role responsibility as technical support (Nissenbaum, 1994). To understand the type of responsibility now required of Internet developers, we need to look at what it means to be a professional. Although Internet development is not a formal profession, we can use the concept of a profession and professionalism to clarify the responsibilities of Internet developers.

8.2. The Concept of a Profession

"Profession" is often used as an empty synonym for "occupation." Sometimes, "profession" is used as an emotive term recommending that a particular occupation be accorded prestige and high pay. Several authors (Bayles, 1981; Johnson, 1995) have specified hallmarks of a professional. Generally, they include being a person of above average income because of monopolistic practices by the profession, doing white-collar work, having a code of ethics expressing ideals of service, licensing procedures, and a representative professional association.

A *profession* requires monopolistic knowledge that circumscribes a clearly defined territory. The traditional model is based on the interaction between an individual professional and a recipient of the benefit of the professional's skill. The recipient may be an individual, an organization, or the public at large. Medicine and law are paradigm professions in this sense. Professionals frequently set their own tasks and are not closely supervised. There are two reasons they are allowed to be self-regulating. First, they have mastered a specialized knowledge which is useful to society and not easily mastered by the nonprofessional. Second, they set higher standards for themselves than society requires of its citizens. Therefore, only they are able to recognize and censure those members who do not live up to these standards. Society in turn generally requires proof of such competence before giving someone license to enter the profession. Entrance to the profession and its standards are generally managed by a single organization. Membership in that organization is necessary for membership in the profession.

Internet development does not seem to fit into this formal model of a profession. Although there are standards for Web development such as those developed by W3C (www.w3.org), the apparent ease of Internet coding using software tools leads many people to develop Web pages and Internet systems with no formal credentials. There are no mandatory or legislated development requirements for them to follow, nor is membership required in an association that promotes those standards. Underwriters Laboratory ensures the safety of electrical equipment that carries their seal. There is no equivalent to this assurance for Internet development. At most, there are aids such as validators for coding style (http://validator.w3.org).

The number of self-taught programmers contributes to the concept of "if it's easy to do, then there can't be anything wrong with it" (for two examples of self-taught programmers, see Bigelow [2003] and Youngblood [1998]). For many, this concept mistakenly places software development outside the concept of the special skills and responsibilities of the professional. "Programming knowledge is becoming relatively common knowledge, no longer restricted to an engineering elite, but widely distributed throughout society" (Stadler, 2003). The people who claim software development is easy would much rather cheer on the self-taught person who's working out of their garage. Potential Web designers do not even need a garage; they work from the public computers in the public library.

Even though Internet developers are not formally professionals, we argue that some elements of professionalism and an understanding of professional responsibility are critical for good Internet development. These elements become clearer if we look at the types of professional interaction with clients.

8.2.1. Models of a Professional's Relation to Their Clients
Bayles (1981) characterizes several models of a professional–client relationship. In the traditional "paternalistic" model, the professional assumes much of the decision-making power, making decisions believed to be in the best interest of the client. The professional's concern for the well-being of the client is the assumed basis for these decisions.

Internet developers, however, have sometimes operated with a different model, namely, an agency model. Here the practitioner merely acts as the agent of the client, doing whatever the client requests. The practitioner's special knowledge is not used to help decide what the client should request. The practitioner is merely a "hired gun," doing whatever is necessary to accomplish the client's request.

Questions about how the request is satisfied or the quality of the system which satisfies the requests are not relevant (Gotterbarn, 1996).

The first standard of professionalism, mastering a specialized knowledge that is useful to society and not easily mastered by the nonprofessional, is denied by many vendors. FrontPage was always touted as being the logical step from Word to the Web. It was suggested that with Microsoft's tools, one can easily step into the role of Web designer. This made it easy for businesses to simply find an office manager or marketing employee to become the company's Web master. Some of this language still exists on the Microsoft Web site. For example, on the Web site promoting FrontPage, there is a section describing the ease of their coding tools which says, "And, because the coding tools are easy to work with, you can even use them to start learning HTML" (Microsoft Corporation, 2003). The introductory page for Adobe's Web publishing tools says, "Whether you're new to Web publishing or a seasoned pro, move rapidly from information architecture to interactive graphics to the implementation and management of dynamic, data-driven sites" (Adobe, 2006). This implies that novices could even create database-driven Web sites and implicitly removes any special professional responsibility due to special skills. It does not matter how the system is designed or what it does as long as it satisfies the customer.

8.2.2. Ethical Obligations of Professionals

The professionalization of any discipline involves the realization that being a professional involves more than the rigid application of formal principles to the artifacts of that discipline. The practice of medicine is more than the application of drugs to the human body. Physicians are concerned with the well-being of their patients. The professional architect does not merely apply principles of structural stress when designing a building. She is also concerned with the effect of the design on the people who will be using the building.

Take, for example, a Web site for a company offering replacement sterling and silver-plated eating utensils [http://www.nancysilver.com/]. The site is quite easy to navigate: The user simply scrolls through an alphabetical list of the silver pattern names, and upon finding the pattern of interest, clicks on the name. This takes the user to a screen with a picture of the handle of the utensil allowing the user to verify the correct selection. They can then place an order through a standard shopping cart form.

What if, however, the user is holding a fork in his hand, but has no idea what the name of the pattern is. There are no pictures on the screen listing the silver pattern names. To see a picture of the available utensils, the user must click on each individual pattern name to see its picture. This may require as many as 248 clicks before finding the pattern in which the user is interested.

In the professionalization of a discipline, there is a realization of the impact on society of the application of the special skills and knowledge of the practitioner of that profession. There is also an acceptance of the responsibility that comes with the privilege of being allowed to apply those principles. The traditional concept of a profession dictates that professionals go beyond minimal morality, offering legal counsel to the indigent and providing medical service even if the patient cannot pay.

Some of the onus for pushing novices into the role of Web designer resides with the business that does not consider the broader impacts of the Web, but is looking to get a good economic deal on Web design. Businesses see clear advantages in trying to develop their own Web pages. First, they perceive that hiring someone to develop their company Web presence is going to cost them more money than developing it from within. As with any form of advertising, however, it is impossible to measure how much revenue is lost through bad design. It is similar to thinking that because of the advent of self-publishing, anyone can write a best-selling novel.

In a profession, however, singular focus on economic factors leads to disaster. The literature is rife with examples of the consequences of taking financial shortcuts. Unfortunately, many Internet developers are led to believe that the major problems with Internet development are primarily the result of dysfunctional developers. An Internet developer who does not see himself as "dysfunctional" easily lets economic factors distract him from his professional responsibilities.

Professions are a distinctive subclass of occupations and significant ethical problems arise in connection with this subclass that do not arise with occupations. The professional's unique understanding of professional situations and how to deal with them places an extra set of ethical obligations on the professional. These obligations constitute *professional ethics*. One does not have to participate in a formally recognized profession to have the obligations of a professional. Assuming the role of a professional carries with it the acceptance of these professional ethics. The agency model of professionalism presumes a primary focus on economic factors by the developer.

8.2.3. The Need to Professionalize Internet Development?

Emerging professions or groups trying to take a professional approach to their work include people with significant differences in educational background and commitments to the service orientation of a profession. Currently, one can be an Internet developer without any formal training; those who teach Internet development tend to be highly trained and recognizable as professionals. This distinction of type and degree of training within emerging professions sometimes leads to a two-tier structure as it did in nursing in the United States. In nursing, there is a distinction between professional and technical nurses. This has led to a heterogeneous model (Barber, 1963). One could argue that engineering in the United States has made a similar distinction in that one can practice engineering without being a licensed professional engineer. Internet development is at that point where it can decide to model professional development, decide to remain merely a profitable occupation, or follow nursing's model and take a multitiered approach. The most obvious question is why developers should adopt a professional approach.

8.2.4. A Professional Approach Addresses Broad Impact

There is another argument for professionalization of Internet development. This argument is based on the belief that a set of ethical obligations, called *professional ethics*, is due to the societal impact of the occupation. Because of the nature and impact of the Internet on all areas of society, a higher level of care is required. Other arguments for the professionalization of Internet development are sometimes motivated by concerns with impeding risks. Approaching professionalization from these two directions requires a different model of the professional–client relation than the traditional paternalistic or agency model.

8.2.5. An Internet-Appropriate Model of Professionalism

In contrast to the traditional paternalistic model of professionalism and the agency model, there is another model of professionalism called the *fiduciary model*. This is a model in which the professional's superior technical knowledge is recognized, but the client retains a significant authority and responsibility in decision making.

> In such a relationship both parties are responsible and their judgments given consideration, but because one party is in a more advantageous position, he has special obligations to the other. The weaker party depends on the stronger and in ways in which the other does not and so must trust the stronger party. In this model the client has more authority and responsibility in decision making than in the paternalistic model, but the client depends on the professional for much of the information on which he [the client] gives or withholds consent. (Bayles, 1981)

8.3. From Internet Development to Internet Professional Ethics

Using the fiduciary model of professionalism, we can talk of a positive sense of Internet professional ethics, which is relevant and avoids the harms evident in the early stages of Internet development. Ignoring positive professional responsibilities will lead to significant negative social consequences. Internet developers are often mainly focused on the newest and the best ways to technically develop and manage Internet applications, but they have missed a lesson learned in other disciplines, namely that it is just as important for a professional to address the question of whether this is the best system to develop because of its social and ethical impacts. The Internet professional has a responsibility to the broader society.

Lawrence Lessig (1999, 2004), Harvard cyberlaw professor, talks of four legs to the Internet. In addition to the social and political legs, he talks of code as one of the most critical legs. This is a significant change in focus when talking about the various types of responsibility we have when dealing with the Internet. Internet developers have responsibilities when it comes to the design of sites. They also have responsibilities to those who are harmed by the impact of what the developers make possible.

What sort of impacts do the choices of the Internet professional have? The professional is supposed to follow ethical practices such as "cause no harm." Many developers merely focus on the technology and ignore the impact of their work. Many Internet designers are not aware that there are interface design templates to help them make good choices in interface design. In many courses, the only interface responsibility is, "Don't make it ugly." The AOL story above illustrates how making inflexible interfaces disenfranchises certain users. It is amazing that this problem of the visually challenged has been addressed by so few developers of voting machine interfaces. But this does not seem to cause real harm. The designers assume that their only responsibility is to convey the information. But interfaces can do real harm. The developers do not address the ethical responsibility to their users who may be dyslexic and will be harmed by Web pages that have a bright white background and use fonts with excessive serifs. They do not think of the need for text-only versions of the site (Davis Dyslexia Association International, 2006, U.S. Department of Justice, 2003). It is the responsibility of Internet professionals to motivate them to think of these issues while they are developing. In the world of Web design, the customer can and does change brands with far more ease than with houses or cars. It is even easier to change Web-based support than to change your long distance telephone provider. Given that there are also significant economic motivators, it is surprising that so little attention is paid to the impact of the Web sites that are developed.

The emphasis on the latest technology sometimes blinds us to particular ethical issues. Some design changes impede the ability of the disadvantaged to use computers. Shortly after blind users could access the keyboard with Braille, keyboard independent Windows-Icon-Menus-Pointers were introduced (Farlex, 2005). These visually challenged users were no longer able to use this interface because the only way to click on an icon is to see it first. We need to be aware of subtle decisions that would make use more difficult for people with physical and mental difficulties and those from different cultures (see Cooper, 2004).

8.4. Internet Professionalism

8.4.1. What Is It?

Internet professional ethics consists of two major elements. One element, called *technical ethics*, consists of doing a technically competent job at all phases of the software development process. The other, *professional ethics*, uses a set of moral values to guide the technical decisions.

In general, all professional ethics—engineering ethics, legal ethics, and medical ethics—are only distinguished by the context to which they apply moral rules. We are familiar with these rules and do not have to learn a unique set of ethical rules to follow Internet professional ethics. But we do need to think about applying these principles in our development process. We need practice at seeing how these rules fit Internet development. There are, of course, differences in how these rules apply in different contexts. The contexts bring out different ethical problems. Because different contexts raise different ethical concerns, the order in which the moral rules are applied varies depending on where we are in the development process or application domain we are working in. We make a mistake when we teach that one technical solution fits all.

Consider the different ways informed consent is applied in different contexts. This rule seems to have different priorities in different stages of development. During the requirements phase of a system to manage life—critical software, informed consent—understanding agreement from the customer—is an important rule.

During testing, principles about not deceiving and not cheating are very important, but informed consent is less significant. Internet professional ethics not only consist of the context, but also the order in which the moral rules are consulted. The professional side of Internet ethics is the application of moral rules in Internet development and management.

Professionalism maintains a proactive posture rather than the merely reactive, "Oh my!!" of Internet development. We expect software professionals to anticipate and plan for risks. It is hoped that because of the professional's special knowledge that they will avoid many of the risks and continue their education to learn how to avoid other risks. The anticipatory approach produces better software more efficiently; the same is true in the ethical, social, cultural, political domains. By adopting this attitude of the professional, one learns to consider issues related to the impact of their software on others and avoids many of the ethical problems that develop in the process of building software artifacts. When properly understood, Internet professional ethics do not consist of a litany of mistakes that can be made or a collection of stories about immoral developers; rather, Internet professional ethics is a positive guide to behavior. With this understanding of the way a professional functions, we can see that our current Internet development education is incomplete and that we need to include material on professional ethics.

8.5. Conclusion

Internet professional ethics require a double-edged sense of positive responsibility, both technically and values based. Both are necessary for a concept of professional responsibility. Positive responsibility points both backward and forward. It points backward when it identifies unmet obligations and what people ought to have done. This sense of responsibility goes beyond the malpractice model. Responsibility is more than just blame; there should also be some lessons learned from failures of responsibility. The knowledge of this kind of failure and its consequences also places responsibility on other computer practitioners and places responsibilities on the profession of computing. For example, the activity of establishing Internet standards of practice is justified by the forward-looking sense of positive responsibility of the professional Internet developer.

Frequently, developers have a dedication to a craftsman-like application of their technical skills. This is only one element of the professional approach. This kind of technical knowledge and skill does not distinguish a technician from a professional. To make this distinction, one must go beyond mere technical responsibility.

In a profession, the professionals pledge to use their skills for the good of society and not merely to act as agents for the client, doing whatever a client asks. To be a professional, one assumes another layer of responsibility beyond what has been described in positive responsibility. The professional commits to a "higher degree of care" for those affected by the computing product. Most occupations have a principle of "due care" as a standard. For example, a plumber is responsible that the results of his work do not injure his customers or users of the plumbing system. But the plumber does not bear the responsibility to advise the customer of potential negative impacts a new system may have on the customer's business, the customer's quality of life, or the environment. The concern to maximize the positive effects for those affected by Internet artifacts goes beyond mere "due care," or mere avoidance of direct harm. The addition of this layer of responsibility to technical responsibility is what is necessary to change an Internet practitioner into an Internet professional.

References

Adobe. (2006). "Web Publishing." Available at www.adobe.com/web/main.html. Accessed 11/18/05.

Barber, Bernard. (1963, Fall). "Some Problems in the Sociology of Professions." *Daedalus*, Vol. 92, pp. 669–688.

Bayles, M. (1981). *Professional Ethics.* Belmont, CA: Wadsworth, pp. 71-72.

Bigelow, Bruce B. (2003, October 12). "Software Entrepreneur Prevails Against Ex-Client." *Union-Tribune* (San Diego). Available at www.signonsandiego.com/news/business/20031012-9999_1b12verdict.html. Accessed 11/18/05.

Clarke, Roger. (1995). "Net-Etiquette: Mini Cases of Dysfunctional Human Behaviour on the Net." Available at www.anu.edu.au/people.Roger.Clarke/II/Netethiquettecases/html. Accessed 11/19/05.

Computer Crime and Intellectual Property Section. (2005, February 7). "Cyberethics Web Sites." Available at www.cybercrime.gov/links1.htm. Accessed 11/19/05.

Cooper, D. (2004). *Ethics for Professionals in a Multicultural World*. Upper Saddle River, NJ: Prentice Hall, p. 72.

Davis Dyslexia Association International. (2006, March 20). "Internet Circle of Friends." Available at www.dyslexia.com/links.htm. Accessed 11/19/05.

Farlex. (2005). "WIMP." Available at http://computing-dictionary.thefreedictionary.com/WIMP. Accessed 11/18/05.

Gates, Bill. (1995). *The Road Ahead.* New York: Penguin Books.

Gotterbarn, D. (1996). "Software Engineering: The New Professionalism." In Colin Myer, ed. *The Responsible Software Engineer.* New York: Springer.

Gotterbarn, D. (2004). "Cyber-Ethics Considered Harmful." *Proceedings of the Internet@10 Conference.* Terre Haute, IN: Rose-Hulman University.

Johnson, Deborah. (1995). *Computer Ethics*, 2nd ed. Englewood Cliffs, NJ: Prentice-Hall.

Lessig, Lawrence. (1999, December 3). "The Law of the Horse: What Cyberlaw Might Teach." Available at www.lessig.org/content/articles.works.finalhls.pdf. Accessed 11/18/05.

Lessig, Lawrence. (2004). *Code and Other Laws of Cyberspace.* Boston: Beacon Press.

Microsoft Corporation. (2003, March 10). "FrontPage 2003 Product Overview." Available at www.microsoft.com/office/frontpage/prodinfo/overview.mspx. Accessed 11/18/05.

National Cyber Security Alliance. (N.D.). "Computer Crime and Intellectual Property." Available at www.staysafeonline.info. Accessed 11/18/05.

Nissenbaum, H. (1994, January). "Computing and Accountability," *Communications of the ACM*, Vol. 27, No. 1, pp. 72-80.

Stadler, Felix. (2003, September 11). "One Size Doesn't Fit All." *Make World Newspaper*, No. 3. Available at http://felix.openflows.org/html.one-size.html. Accessed 11/21/05.

U.S. Department of Justice, Civil Rights Division, Disability Rights Section. (2003, June 19). "Accessibility of State and Local Government Websites to People With Disabilities." Available at www.ada.gov/websites2.htm. Accessed 11/18/05.

Youngblood, Dick. (1998, June 15). "Self-Taught Whiz Is Writing Software for Wall Street; Programmer's Entrepreneurial Ways Began at Young Age." *Star Tribune* (Minneapolis). Available at www.highbeam.com/library/doc0.asp?docid=1G1:62581005&refid+ink_tptd_np&skeyword=&teaster=. Accessed 11/18/05.

Chapter 9: Informed Consent in the Mozilla Browser: Implementing Value-Sensitive Design

Batya Friedman, Daniel C. Howe, and Edward Felten

This chapter reports on one of the first efforts to apply value-sensitive design (VSD) to a large-scale, real-world software system. We sought to improve informed consent in Web-based interactions through the development of new technical mechanisms for cookie management. We describe our VSD methodology, explicate criteria for informed consent in on-line interactions, and summarize how current browsers fall short with respect to those criteria. Next we identify four goals for the redesign and methodology, wherein we move among the design and implementation of new technical mechanisms, formative evaluation, and the design goals coupled with the criteria for informed consent on-line. Key mechanisms include peripheral awareness of cookies and just-in-time interventions. At various phases in the design process, we implement our design improvements in the Mozilla browser (the open source for Netscape Navigator).

9.1. Introduction

Informed consent provides a critical protection for privacy, and supports other human values such as autonomy and trust. Yet currently there is a mismatch between industry practice and the public's interest. According to a recent report from the Federal Trade Commission (2000), for example, 59% of Web sites that collect personal identifying information neither inform Internet users that they are collecting such information nor seek the user's consent. Yet, according to a Harris poll (2000), 88% of users want sites to garner their consent in such situations. The Federal Trade Commission (2000, p. iv) hopes that industry will continue to make progress on this problem, in conjunction with its proposed legislation. Toward such progress, however, we in the computing community should be helping to shape the dialogue by providing technical means to realize informed consent in on-line interactions.

This paper reports on our effort to improve support for informed consent in Web-based interactions, particularly through the development of new technical mechanisms for cookie management in the Web browser. We chose to focus on the browser because browsers play a critical role in informing the user about a Web site's desire to set a cookie and in determining how the cookie will be handled on the user's machine. Drawing on our prior work, we first describe criteria for informed consent in on-line interactions (Friedman, Millet, and Felten, 2000) and, in light of those criteria, summarize how current browsers fall short (Millet, Friedman, and Felten, 2001). Next we identify four goals for the redesign of current browsers to improve support for informed consent. These four goals, in turn, initiate an iterative design process that lies at the heart of the VSD methodology—wherein we move among the design and implementation of new technical mechanisms, formative evaluation, and the four design goals coupled with the criteria for informed consent on-line. At various phases in the design process, we implement our design improvements in the large-scale, real-world open-source browser Mozilla (the open source for Netscape Navigator). Thus, our end product is integrated into an existing browser and can be made available to the public.

In addition to the new technical mechanisms we report here, this work represents one of the first efforts to apply a VSD approach to a large-scale, real-world software system. In brief, *value-sensitive design* is an approach to the design and implementation of systems that systematically and comprehensively accounts for human values throughout the design and implementation processes (Friedman, 1997, 1999; Friedman and Kahn, in press-a; Friedman, Kahn, and Howe, 2000). In VSD, conceptual, technical, and empirical investigations are employed iteratively throughout the design and implementation process. Conceptual investigations provide philosophically informed analyses of the central constructs and issues relevant to the system under development. Technical investigations identify how existing technical designs and mechanisms engender value suitabilities and, conversely, how the identification of specific values can lead to new technical designs and mechanisms to better support those values. Empirical investigations draw on social science methodologies to understand the value-oriented perceptions and experiences of the direct and indirect stakeholders of a given system. The VSD investigations are employed in consort with other already successful technical methods (Ackerman and Cranor, 1999; Cranor and Resnick, 2000; Friedman, Kahn, and Howe, 2000; Introna and Nissenbaum, 2000).

In addition to VSD, four other central approaches to human values, ethics, and design can be identified (Friedman and Kahn, in press-b). These approaches include computer ethics that has focused on how to utilize existing moral theory to bring clarity to ethical issues involving computer technology and, conversely, on how such technological innovations extend the boundaries of traditional ethical concepts (Johnson and Miller, 1997; Moor, 1985; Rogerson and Bynum, 1999). The second approach is *social informatics*, which emphasizes sociotechnical analyses of deployed technologies that take into account their interaction with institutional and cultural contexts (Borgman, 2000; Iacono and Kling, 1987; Kling, Rosenbaum, and Hert, 1998; Orlikowski, 1993). The third approach is computer-supported cooperative work (CSCW), which focuses on the design of new technologies to help people collaborate effectively in the workplace. The values considered in CSCW designs have been closely tied to group activities and workplace issues (Fuchs, 1999; Hudson and

Smith, 1996; Isaacs, Tang, and Morris, 1996; Olson and Teasley, 1996). The fourth approach is *participatory design*, which fundamentally seeks to integrate a worker's knowledge and a sense of work practice into the system design process. Traditionally, participatory design has embedded within it a commitment to democratization of the workplace and human welfare (Bjerknes, Ehn, and Kyng, 1987; Greenbaum and Kyng, 1991; Kyng and Mathiassen, 1997).

Researchers are just now beginning to apply VSD methodologies proactively in the design process. Thus, this work contributes not only to specific knowledge on how to support informed consent in Web browser design and the redesign of the open source Mozilla browser, but explicates and extends the systematic use of VSD methodologies in the context of large-scale, real-world software systems.

9.2. Criteria for Informed Consent On-line

Before we can design cookie and Web browser technologies to support informed consent, we need a robust conceptual understanding of what exactly informed consent entails. Both "informed" and "consent" carry import ("The Belmont Report," 1978; Faden and Beauchamp, 1986; Friedman, Millet, et al., 2000).

The idea of "informed" encompasses disclosure and comprehension. *Disclosure* refers to providing accurate information about the benefits and harms that might reasonably be expected from the action under consideration. *Comprehension* refers to the individual's accurate interpretation of what is being disclosed. In turn, the idea of "consent" encompasses voluntariness, comprehension, and agreement. *Voluntariness* refers to ensuring that the action is not controlled or coerced. *Competence* refers to possessing the mental, emotional, and physical capabilities needed to be capable of giving informed consent. *Agreement* refers to a reasonably clear opportunity to accept or decline to participate. Moreover, the component of agreement is ongoing. See Friedman, Millet, et al. (2000) for an expanded discussion of these five criteria.

In addition, the empirical investigations conducted as a part of this research yielded a sixth criterion, that of *minimal distraction*, which refers to meeting the above criteria without unduly diverting the individual from the task at hand. Minimizing distraction is an inherent challenge for any implementation of informed consent as the very process of informing users and obtaining their consent necessarily diverts users form their primary task. Two sorts of situations are of concern here. First, if users are overwhelmed with queries to consent to participate in events with minor benefits and risks, they may become numbed to the informed consent process by the time participation in an event with significant benefits and risks is at hand. Thus, the user's participation in that event may not receive the careful attention that is warranted. Alternatively, if the overall distraction to obtain informed consent becomes so great as to be perceived to be an intolerable nuisance, users are likely to disengage from the informed consent process in its entirety and accept or decline participation by rote. Thus undue distraction can single-handedly undermine informed consent.

9.3. Retrospective Analysis of Cookies, Browsers, and Informed Consent

With criteria for assessing informed consent in hand, we next conducted a retrospective analysis of existing browser technologies to identify where they fall short with respect to informed consent (Millet et al., 2001). Specifically, we documented how design changes in Netscape Navigator and Internet Explorer from 1995 to 1999 responded to concerns about informed consent. From the perspective of VSD methodology, the retrospective analysis represents a technical investigation that is informed by the results of a prior conceptual investigation.

In brief, through the retrospective analysis we found that although cookie technology has improved over time regarding informed consent (e.g., increased visibility of cookies, increased options for accepting or declining cookies, access to information about cookie content), some startling problems remain. For purposes of this paper, we summarize key results here:

- Although browsers now disclose to users some information about cookies, they do not disclose the right sort of information—that is, information about the potential harms and benefits from setting a particular cookie.
- Through preference settings, browsers now offer users many more options for managing cookies. However, these preference settings are typically located in obscure menu hierarchies and pose challenges for opportunities to accept or decline participation.
- In Internet Explorer, the burden to accept or decline all third-party cookies still falls to the user, placing undue burden on the user to decline each third-party cookie one at a time.
- As of 1999, browsers provided users with no means to control how long a cookie would remain on the user's machine. (Note: In January 2000, Netscape Navigator added the feature to delete a cookie, which partially remedies this situation.)
- Users' out-of-the-box experiences of cookies (the default setting) is no different in 1999 than it was in 1995: to accept all cookies. That is, the novice user installs a browser that accepts all cookies and discloses nothing about that activity to the user.
- No browser alerts a user to when a site wishes to use a cookie and for what purposes, as opposed to when a site wishes to store a cookie.

9.4. Four Overarching Design Goals

From our retrospective analysis of cookies, current browsers, and criteria for informed consent, four primary goals emerged as central to our redesign effort. We discuss each goal in turn.

9.4.1. Design Goal 1: Enhance Users' Local Understanding of Discrete Cookie Events as the Events Occur with Minimal Distraction to the User

Current browsers require users to select a present agreement policy that applies to all cookies of a specified type (e.g., accept all cookies; decline all third-party cookies) or to explicitly accept or decline each cookie one at a time. The former mechanism—presetting a general policy—minimizes user distraction at the expense of rote decision making, disclosure, and comprehension. With this type of mechanism, the user is never notified that a cookie meeting the policy has been accepted and placed on the user's machine; nor does the user have an opportunity to examine the cookie. In contrast, the latter mechanism—to explicitly accept or decline each cookie—supports the criterion of disclosure but at the expense of extreme distraction. A middle ground is warranted here—one that provides users with some awareness of a cookie when it is set followed by the opportunity to make a decision about that cookie based on this newly acquired information, but without undue distraction.

9.4.2. Design Goal 2: Enhance Users' Global Understanding of the Common Uses of Cookie Technology Including Potential Benefits and Risks Associated with Those Uses

The potential benefits and risks from accepting or declining an individual cookie is part of a larger sociotechnical practice wherein cookies are used to create profiles of users over time and across sites. For users to be able to make informed choices about individual cookies, they must also possess some understanding of how an individual cookie fits into this larger sociotechnical practice, including commonly employed uses of cookie technology as well as potential benefits and risks associated with such uses. For example, if a user does not understand the common practices of sites that employ cookie technologies and the implications of these technologies, then disclosing the data associated with individual cookies (e.g., domain, expiration, name, value, path) is of limited use in fostering comprehension, without which there cannot be genuine informed consent. In this way, global understanding of cookie technology is a necessary piece of disclosure and comprehension.

9.4.3. Design Goal 3: Enhance Users' Ability to Manage Cookies

Our retrospective browser analysis also revealed inadequate mechanisms for effective cookie management, particularly with respect to the easy viewing of cookie information and ongoing control over the lifetime and removal of cookies. Specifically, with browser technology as of December 1999, users were unable to easily give and later revoke agreement for a cookie.[1] To highlight the importance of this functionality for informed consent, consider the following scenario in which a user, after reading a Web site's privacy policy, has agreed to allow a number of cookies from that site that persist between visits to be set on the user's machine. However, before the user's next visit, new owners purchase the Web site and substantively modify the site's stated privacy policies. With the 1999 browser technology, the user has no easy means to remove the previously set cookies and thereby revoke consent. Recall that in our model for informed consent, agreement is ongoing—that is, users must be able to give their consent not only at the start

---

[1]Technically skilled users could delete cookies directly from their cookie files. However, such activity required significant technical knowledge and diverted users from their primary Web-based tasks. Thus, this option was not available to users with typical skill levels and violated the criterion of minimal distraction for highly skilled users.

of the interaction (as current browsers with this preference provide), but to revoke that consent at any point later in the interaction. Thus, the cookie management of 1999 technology violates the informed consent criterion of agreement.

9.4.4. Design Goal 4: Achieve Design Goals 1, 2 and 3 While Minimizing Distraction for the User

As noted, the very process of informing a user and obtaining consent diverts the user from the primary task at hand. Moreover, functionality that overwhelms the user with interruptions or consumes excessive user resources will not be utilized and might as well not exist. Thus, effective informed consent requires supporting mechanisms with minimal overhead for the user.

9.5. Prototype One: The Gedanken Prototype

9.5.1. Description

After articulating our primary design goals of enhanced local understanding, global understanding, and cookie management with minimal distraction for the user, we began our development work with what we refer to as a *Gedanken* prototype: an initial, "imagined" design with which to begin the iterative design process. A Gedanken or thought prototype has the advantage (along with traditional cardboard mock-ups [Ehn and Kyng, 1991]) of allowing for initial design work without devoting costly resources to rapidly developing "throw-away" user interfaces (UIs) with RAD tools like Director or Visual Basic. The starting point for our Gedanken prototype was Mozilla version 0.8 (Figure 9.1).

Our first step involved the identification of concrete mechanisms that could potentially further the four design goals. Two key insights emerged. One entailed the potential use of *peripheral awareness* (c.f. Weiser and Brown [1996]) as a strategy to increase users' awareness of cookie events as they occur without requiring direct attention from the user. Traditionally, peripheral awareness mechanisms have been used successfully to provide users with ongoing information about machine state through non–attention-grabbing visual or auditory cues that users may or may not choose to attend to. The second insight entailed the potential use of *just-in-time interventions* as a strategy to provide users with access to information and cookie management facilities for cookie events as they occur, while allowing for but not requiring an intervention from the user. Again, traditionally, just-in-time interventions have been used successfully to present users only with relevant information and facilities, and only at the moment when such information or facilities are necessary for the completion of a task or the making of a decision. Taken together, these two strategies address both the criterion of minimal distraction and the problem of information overload experienced by many users. In the context of the Gedanken prototype, we used the insights of peripheral awareness and just-in-time interventions to envision features (new technical mechanisms) that would:

- Make users aware of discrete cookie events as they occur, perhaps through visual or auditory peripheral cues.

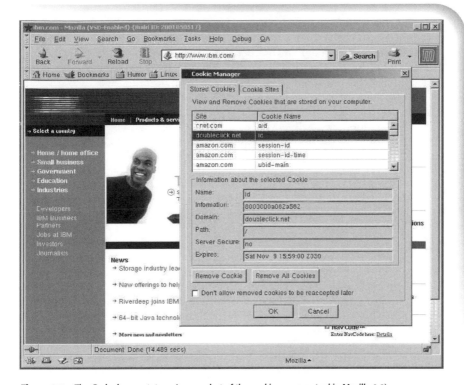

Figure 9.1   The Gedanken prototype (screen shot of the cookie manager tool in Mozilla 0.8).

- Make users aware of different types of cookie events (e.g., third-party cookie, duration of cookie) as they occur, perhaps through additional visual or auditory peripheral cues.
- Allow users to obtain detailed information about the most recently set cookie, perhaps with a just-in-time intervention that provides the user with access to the cookie's data fields and the existing Mozilla cookie manager tool.
- Allow users to edit the expiration date or delete cookies separately or in groups with a just-in-time intervention that provides the user with access to the Mozilla cookie manager tool.

9.5.2. Formative Evaluation
To identify the strengths and weakness of the Gedanken prototype at this preliminary stage, we employed a modified informal heuristic evaluation (Nielson, 1993) that coupled traditional usability concerns (e.g., of consistency, ease of use) with value-oriented concerns (e.g., disclosure, comprehension, minimal distraction, enhanced local discrete understanding of cookies, enhanced global understanding of cookies). Five graduate students in The Information School at the University

of Washington were invited to conduct the informal heuristic evaluations. Each evaluator was shown a color mockup of Mozilla version 0.8 with the Mozilla cookie manager window open (similar to Figure 9.1). In addition to the color mockup, we described the use of visual and auditory cues to notify users of cookie events as they occurred, as well as mechanisms for allowing users to view relevant data fields of the most recently set cookie in the Mozilla cookie manager by activating a button or key combination. With each evaluator, we solicited spontaneous comments on the interface itself as well as the elements of peripheral functionality not easily viewed via the paper mockup. If evaluators did not spontaneously comment on the cookie manager, we explicitly solicited feedback on the tool's functionality and interface. We attended to comments on traditional usability as well as value-oriented aspects of the prototype.

The informal heuristic evaluations yielded a good deal of valuable information about our specific design goals and the interface as a whole. Feedback from evaluators specifically identified the need for:

- An easy means to learn more about discrete cookie events as they occurred.
- A more intuitive representation for our cookie classification scheme.
- A mechanism to permanently block a site from setting cookies, once a user had manually removed a cookie from that site (e.g., a third-party ad service).
- A mechanism to link a discrete cookie event (as indicated peripherally) with cookies identified in the cookie manager.

In addition to feedback from the evaluators, our design team recognized that although our prototype presented a wide range of information about each discrete cookie stored on a user's machine in an intuitive and easy-to-manage fashion, there was still no way for users to conceptually link these discrete cookies with a global understanding of common practices, usage patterns, benefits, and risks associated with individual cookies.

9.6. Prototype Two: The Mozilla Cookie Watcher

9.6.1. Description

In conjunction with our criteria for informed consent on-line, the formative evaluation of the Gedanken prototype provided us with new data with which to return to our overarching design goals of enhanced local understanding, global understanding, and cookie management with minimal distraction for the user. How best can we make discrete cookie event information available to users in a consistent fashion that would divert users' attention only at appropriate times?

We approached this question first in terms of a peripheral awareness mechanism. A robust peripheral awareness mechanism needs to notify users not only about the occurrence of a cookie event, but also about the type of cookie being set. We next considered several venues of notification: static visual notifications, flashing animation notifications, and audio notifications. Based on the heuristic evaluations and further discussion among the design team, we settled on a primarily visual notification venue—one that would take up a small but persistent area of the screen. Key justifications for this decision included the ability to link visual cues for discrete cookie events with the existing cookie management tool kit, the opportunity to present persistent data about recently set cookies, and the ease with which a focused user could ignore a small visual representation on the screen. In addition, we suspected a visually based notification system would provide far greater flexibility and expandability for representing the cookie classification scheme as it evolved, as well as custom display cues should they be desired.

With these and other design imperatives in mind, we implemented a small application—the cookie watcher tool–docked in Mozilla's sidebar window (Figure 9.2). In the cookie watcher, cookies appear in real time as they are delivered to the machine. In addition, the cookie watcher provides classification information for each cookie according to domain and expiration that was keyed to the background color for each cookie as follows: third-party cookies (those set by other sites than the one being visited) were displayed with a red background; cookies with expirations set more than 1 year in the future were displayed with a yellow background; and all other cookies were displayed with a green background.

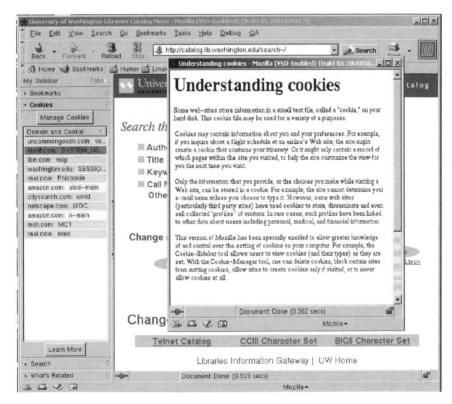

Figure 9.2   The Mozilla cookie watcher prototype implemented in Mozilla showing the cookie watcher tool (at the left) and the cookie information dialog box (in the center).

Having designed a peripheral awareness mechanism, we next considered mechanisms to support just-in-time interventions. Two sorts of just-in-time interventions at the time of decision making seemed needed: one to provide general information about cookies—the cookie information dialog box (see Figure 9.2), and one to provide access to the existing cookie manager tool. Less clear was when to provide each type of just-in-time mechanism. We faced a common problem: It is difficult, if not impossible, to know when a particular decision is in fact important to a given user in a given context. Traditionally, strategies that attempt to infer this information from users' behavior have failed; interpretation of human behavior eludes our current knowledge and the capacity of today's computational systems. In our design, we took a somewhat different approach: We assumed that only the users themselves are able to properly discern when their present task is one that may be disturbed and would constitute a valid disturbance of that task. In this way, the application need only make the user peripherally aware of a potential task-disrupting decision, at which time the user (perhaps even subconsciously) may opt to engage in a task-disrupting decision or to continue with the primary task.

Having determined how users would access the just-in-time interventions, we next turned to defining each mechanism. To obtain just-in-time information about cookies in general, users could click on a button labeled "Learn More" at the bottom of the cookie watcher window. At that time, the cookie information dialog box would appear containing a text description of the nature and implications of cookies in the larger context of day-to-day usage. In our first version of the text, the discussion was brief (limited to four short paragraphs): a one-sentence definition of a cookie, a paragraph mentioning the benefits of cookies for personalization, a paragraph mentioning potential limitations and risks from cookie use, and a paragraph highlighting our modifications to the Mozilla browser. No information was provided about the color coding in the cookie watcher and no discussion was provided of the importance of domain and expiration of cookies for assessing their potential benefits or risks. The second just-in-time intervention provided a mechanism for moving smoothly from awareness of a cookie event to proactive cookie management. As identified in the formative evaluation, users felt the need to move from their awareness of a cookie event directly and efficiently to more in-depth information about the particular cookie if they felt inclined to act upon it. To satisfy this requirement, we activated each line in the cookie watcher so that a mouse click would bring up the cookie manager tool with the selected cookie highlighted and its data fields visible. This design change served not only to allow users to move quickly and easily from observation to management, but also helped users to construct at least some of the global understanding we had identified as an overarching design goal.

9.6.2. Formative Evaluation

As with our earlier formative evaluation of the Gedanken prototype, the usability studies we conducted with the Mozilla cookie watcher prototype were two pronged. One dimension focused on those aspects of the prototype that directly impacted the values targeted by our design efforts—in this case, informed consent. In this context, we were specifically interested in assessing how well the prototype met our theory-driven goals to enhance local understanding, global understanding, and cookie management with minimal distraction for the user. The second dimension focused on how well the interface met traditional human computer interaction criteria, such as intuitiveness, consistency, and ease of use (cf. Johnson [2000], Nielson [1993]).

9.6.2.1. Participants

A formal usability study of the prototype was conducted with eight individuals (three men and five women) between the ages of 20 and 30. Participants were undergraduate students, graduate students, or postgraduate student employees at the University of Washington. All participants were experienced Web users (ranging from 3 to 8 years of Web use) and regularly used one of the two most popular browsers, Internet Explorer 5.x or Netscape Navigator/Communicator 4.x. In presession interviews, two participants (25%) were significantly confused about the nature of cookies.

9.6.2.2. Methods

The usability study began with a presession semistructured interview about participants' prior Web experience and knowledge of cookies. The presession interview was followed by a 30-minute hands-on session during which participants interacted with the Mozilla cookie watcher prototype and completed a set of directed and nondirected Web-based browsing. During the hands-on session, participants were asked to talk aloud and machine-recorded interaction data were collected. The direct browsing ensured that all participants would encounter a wide variety of cookie interactions, including sites that used cookies for state management, internal profiling, anonymous recommendation systems, and featured banner ads in which third-party servers set cookies on the user's machine. The nondirected Web browsing allowed us to observe participants' use of the cookie watcher in the context of their more typical browsing behavior. The hands-on session concluded with a semistructured interview about participants' reactions to the Mozilla cookie watcher prototype including their assessment of the cookie watcher, increased awareness of information for individual cookies, increased awareness of patterns of cookie behavior, and level of distraction to attend to the cookie features. Finally, following the postsession interview and if the participant had not spontaneously interacted with the cookie management tool during the directed and nondirected Web browsing, the participant was asked to perform an additional task that explicitly used the cookie manager tool and to evaluate that tool.

9.6.2.3. Results and Discussion

The majority of participants used the cookie watcher spontaneously. Based on the machine collected interaction data, five participants (63%) explored the cookie watcher tool on their own. Of the three participants who did not explore the cookie watcher, two stated a desire to close the tool at some point during the session to free up screen space on the 19-inch high-resolution monitor. Interestingly, these two participants were the same individuals who possessed limited or mistaken understanding of cookies in the presession interview.

Participants appeared to increase their awareness and understanding of cookies in a local context. In both solicited and unsolicited comments, users commented on their ability to easily recognize individual cookie events as they occurred in real time. Moreover, observation of participant behavior (e.g., surprise at seeing a cookie event recorded in the cookie watcher) confirmed participants' recognition of cookie events as they occurred.[2]

Participants also appeared to increase their awareness and understanding of cookies in a global context. In contrast to participants' self-assessment that their global understanding of cookies remained unchanged after the hands-on session, it was evident from participants' talk-aloud and unsolicited comments during the hands-on session that this was not always the case.

Although the cookie watcher appeared to contribute to the participants' global understanding, the cookie information tool appeared less successful. Some participants failed to notice the cookie information tool in its entirety. Of those who accessed the cookie information tool, some did not read the text even though it was only four short paragraphs. Participants who did read the text found the language too technical for novice users, that the text did not adequately tie in with information presented elsewhere in the cookie tools, and that the text did not adequately convey a sense of the benefits and risks of cookie use.

Participants also found the cookie watcher, easy access to the cookie management tools, and just-in-time information presentation to be a significant improvement over prior browsers for managing both individual and groups of cookies as they arrived. Observations of participant behavior and participant comments suggested that direct access to information on individual cookies from mouse events triggered in the cookie watcher helped to reduce learning time as well as eased cookie management. Participants almost always examined and/or removed cookies as they arrived and were far less likely to return to a cookie from a previous site visit, even if that cookie was classified and displayed in a manner intended to attract the users' attention (e.g., third-party cookies). Participants also commented favorably on the option to ban sites from resetting cookies and one participant suggested an additional option to ban a site by manually entering its domain. In general, the cookie management mechanisms present in this prototype were perceived to be far more efficient, effective, and intuitive than those found in other current browsers, where one typically has to locate and hand edit cookie files stored on the local machine.

In terms of traditional HCI measures for interface design, the cookie toolset interface was largely successful. Based on observation of participant behavior and participants' comments, participants were able to intuitively and readily use the new cookie tools with minimal effort and reasonable success. We also note some use-

---

[2]As noted in the retrospective analysis of browsers, users can obtain a comparable awareness of cookie events as they occur if users enable a preference setting that queries the user about each individual cookie event. However, with this type of implementation, the browser interrupts the user from the primary task with a modal dialog box each time a new cookie arrives and requires the user to explicitly accept or decline the cookie. Moreover, the dialog box does not present enough information about the incoming cookie to allow the user to make an informed decision. This interruption occurs for every cookie, even though sites typically set more than five cookies on a given page.

ful suggestions that arose from both the observations and the interviews, including better separation of classification and cookie data; a reexamination of color and text choices in the representation of cookie events; use of icons and color gradients for redundancy of classification information; 'real estate' issues associated with the cookie watcher; as noted, the addition of an "add domain" function for the cookie watcher's "banned" site panel; and a way to view the number of cookies set per domain.

As an overall measure of the success of the Mozilla cookie watcher prototype in the postsession interview, seven of the participants (88%) stated that if such a toolset were available as an add-on to their browser of choice they would use it. One participant stated reservations about the use of the cookie toolset without a greater global understanding of cookies—a comment with which the design team concurred.

9.7. Prototype Three: The Mozilla Cookie Watcher Revisited

9.7.1. Description
Following the VSD iterative methodology, we again revisited our design in light of our criteria for informed consent on-line, our design goals, and the results from the usability study. Based on these, we implemented several refinements to the cookie watcher and cookie information dialog box (Figure 9.3) as follows:

- The cookie watcher no longer uses background color to represent both cookie domain and expiration information. Background color (green for same domain and red for third-party cookies) is now used to represent cookie domain information. Font style (italics for within-session duration; plain text for up to 1 year duration; and bold for more than 1 year duration) is now used to represent cookie duration.
- The cookie information dialog box now contains a key to the color and font style representations of cookie information for domain and duration, respectively.
- The cookie information dialog box now contains information about the potential benefits and risks associated with a cookie by type of domain and duration. For example, a cookie from the Web site the user is currently visiting that lasts only for the current session allows for personalization during this one visit, but poses no risks for tracking within or across sites.

9.7.2. Formative Evaluation
We are currently conducting usability tests with prototype three. Preliminary results are positive. Shortly, we intend to install this version on several individuals' machines to be used as the primary browser. In addition to attending to traditional usability concerns, the evaluation will focus on prototype three's impact on the user's global understanding of cookies, including common patterns for cookie deployment and potential benefits and risks associated with different types of cookies.

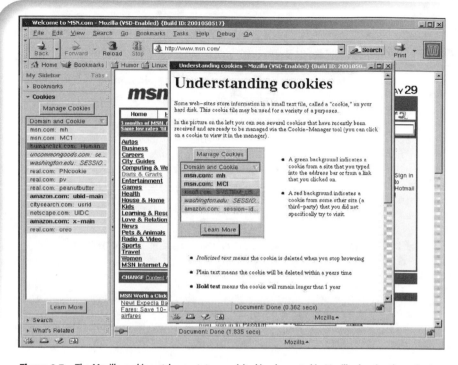

Figure 9.3   The Mozilla cookie watcher prototype revisited implemented in Mozilla showing the revised cookie watcher tool (at the left) and the revised cookie information dialog box (in the center).

9.8. Conclusions

Informed consent is an important human value to integrate into our on-line inter-actions. However, doing so depends on the existence of underlying technical mech-anisms to support the activities of informing and obtaining consent. In this research, we demonstrate with an implementation in the Mozilla browser how specific tech-nical mechanisms of peripheral awareness and just-in-time interventions can be employed to support informed consent for cookies in the context of individuals' Web browsing. These mechanisms follow from our design goals to enhance users' local understanding of cookies, global understanding of cookies, and cookie man-agement, all with minimal distraction from the task at hand. In turn, these design goals follow from our criteria for informed consent in on-line interactions as devel-oped in prior work. Our formal evaluation efforts—particularly the usability study conducted with prototype two—suggest we have been largely successful in meet-ing these goals.

Our work is ongoing. In the near term, we anticipate conducting longer term evaluation studies of the currently modified Mozilla browser in labs, offices, and participants' homes and with individuals who possess a wider range of experience, backgrounds, and technical skills. In later stages, we will solicit feedback from the open source community. An additional goal of the project is the potential integration of the cookie watcher and cookie information dialog box into the official Mozilla browser release.

In addition to providing an improved solution for cookies, browsers, and informed consent, our work also demonstrates the viability of the VSD methodology in the context of a real-world, large-scale software system, a methodology in which, as designers, we move from conceptual investigations of relevant values, to the development of new technical mechanisms to support those values, to empirical validation of our technical work in light of the conceptual investigations, and back again to the refinement of our technical mechanisms. It is our hope that in providing a large-scale, real-world example of the VSD methodology in action—from theory through implementation and formative evaluation, and back again—other researchers, designers, and engineers may more easily adopt aspects of VSD methodologies and apply these to a wide range of problem domains.

Acknowledgments

Austin Henderson, Lynne Henderson, David Hurley, and Valerie Wonder contributed to early discussions related to this work. This research was funded in part by National Science Foundation Awards IIS-9911185 and SES-0096131.

References

Ackerman, M., and L. Cranor. (1999). "Privacy Critics: UI Components to Safeguard Users' Privacy," *CHI99 Extended Abstracts.* New York: ACM Press, pp. 258–259.

The Belmont Report: Ethical Principles and Guidelines for the Protection of Human Subjects of Research. (1978). The National Commission for the Protection of Human Subjects of Biomedical and Behavioral Research. Washington, D.C.: U.S. Department of Health and Human Services.

Bjerknes, G., P. Ehn, and M. Kyng, eds. (1987). *Computers and Democracy: A Scandinavian Challenge.* Aldershot, England: Avebury.

Borgman, C. L. (2000). *From Gutenberg to the Global Information Infrastructure: Access to Information in the Networked World.* Cambridge, MA: MIT Press.

Cranor, L., and P. Resnick. (2000). "Protocols for Automated Negotiations With Buyer Anonymity and Seller Reputations." *Netnomics*, Vol. 2, No. 1, pp. 1–23.

Ehn, P., and M. Kyng. (1991). "Cardboard Computers: Mocking-It-Up or Hands-On the Future." In J. Greenbaum and M. Kyng, eds. *Design at Work: Cooperative Design of Computer Systems.* Hillsdale, NJ: Lawrence Erlbaum Associates, pp. 169–195.

Faden, R., and Beauchamp, T. (1986). *A History and Theory of Informed Consent.* New York: Oxford University Press.

Federal Trade Commission. (2000, May). *Privacy Online: Fair Information Practices in the Electronic Marketplace* [A Report to Congress]. Washington, D.C.

Friedman, B., ed. (1997). *Human Values and the Design of Computer Technology.* New York: Cambridge University Press and Stanford, CA: CSLI, Stanford University.

Friedman, B. (1999). *Value-Sensitive Design: A Research Agenda for Information Technology* [Contract No: SBR-9729633]. Arlington, VA: National Science Foundation.

Friedman, B., and P. H. Kahn, Jr. (in press-a). "A Value-Sensitive Design Approach to Augmented Reality." In W. Mackay, ed., Conference Proceedings of DARE 2000: Design of Augmented Reality Environments (163–164). New York: Association for Computing Machinery.

Friedman, B., and P. H. Kahn, Jr. (in press-b). "Human Values and Ethics, and Design." In J. Jacko and A. Sears, eds. *Handbook in Human–Computer Interaction.* Mahwah, NJ: Lawrence Erlbaum Press.

Friedman, B., P. H. Kahn Jr., and D. C. Howe. (2000). "Trust Online." *Communications of the ACM,* Vol. 43, No. 12, pp. 34–40.

Friedman, B., Millet, L., and Felten, E. (2000). *Informed Consent Online: A Conceptual Model and Design Principles.* Seattle, WA: University of Washington Dept. of Computer Science Engineering. [UW-CSE Technical Report 00-12-2].

Friedman, B., and H. Nissenbaum. (1999). "Bias in Computer Systems." *ACM Transactions on Information Systems*, Vol. 14, No. 3, pp. 330–347.

Fuchs, L. (1999). "AREA: A Cross-Application Notification Service for Groupware." In *6th ECSCW Proceedings.* Dordrecht: Kluwer, pp. 61–81.

Greenbaum, J., and Kyng, M., eds. (1991). *Design at Work: Cooperative Design of Computer Systems.* Hillsdale, NJ: Lawrence Erlbaum Associates.

Harris Poll/Business Week. (2000). "A Growing Threat." Available at http://www.businessweek.com/2000/00_12/b3673010.htm. Accessed in 2001.

Hudson, S. E., and I. Smith. (1996). "Techniques for Addressing Fundamental Privacy and Disruption Tradeoffs in Awareness Support Systems." In *CSCW '96 Proceedings.* New York: ACM Press, pp. 248–257.

Iacono, S., and R. Kling. (1987). "Changing Office Technologies and the Transformation of Clerical Jobs." In R. Kraut, ed. *Technology and the Transformation of White Collar Work.* Hillsdale, NJ: Lawrence Erlbaum Associates.

Introna, L. D., and H. Nissenbaum. (2000). "Shaping the Web: Why the Politics of Search Engines Matters." *The Information Society,* Vol. 16, pp. 169–185.

Isaacs, E. A., J. C. Tang, and T. Morris. (1996). "Piazza: A Desktop Environment Supporting Impromptu and Planned Interactions." In *CSCW '96 Proceedings.* New York: ACM Press, pp. 315–324.

Johnson, D. G., and K. Miller. (1997). "Ethical Issues for Computer Scientists and Engineers." In A. B. Tucker, Jr., ed-in-chief. *The Computer Science and Engineering Handbook.* Boca Raton, FL: CRC Press, pp. 16–26.

Johnson, J. (2000). *GUI Bloopers: Don't and Do's for Software Developers and Web Designers.* San Francisco, CA: Morgan Kaufman Publishers.

Kling, R., H. Rosenbaum, and C. Hert. (1998). "Social Informatics in Information Science: An Introduction." *Journal of the American Society for Information Science,* Vol. 49, No. 12, pp. 1047–1052.

Kyng, M., and Mathiassen, L., eds. (1997). *Computers and Design in Context.* Cambridge, MA: MIT Press.

Millet, L., B. Friedman, and E. Felten. (2001). "Cookies and Web Browser Design: Toward Realizing Informed Consent Online." In *CHI 2001 Proceedings.* New York: ACM Press, pp. 46–52.

Moor, J. H. (1985). "What Is Computer Ethics?" *Metaphilosophy,* Vol. 16, No. 4, pp. 266–275.

Nielson, J. (1993). *Usability Engineering.* Boston: Academic Press.

Olson, J. S., and S. Teasley. (1996). "Groupware in the Wild: Lessons Learned From a Year of Virtual Collaboration." In *CSCW '96 Proceedings.* New York: ACM Press, pp. 419–427.

Orlikowski, W. J. (1993). "Learning From Notes: Organizational Issues in Groupware Implementation." *The Information Society,* Vol. 9, No. 3, pp. 237–250.

Rogerson, S., and Bynum, T. W., eds. (1999). *Information Ethics: A Reader.* Cambridge, MA: Blackwell.

Weiser, M., and J. S. Brown. (1996). "Designing Calm Technology." *PowerGrid Journal,* Vol. 1, No. 1. Available at http://powergrid.electriciti.com/1.01. Accessed in 2001.

Chapter 10: The Impact of Computer Security Concerns on Software Development

Richard G. Epstein

10.1. Introduction

Developing a software product is not just about computer programming. In fact, the time spent writing the code (coding) is usually just a small fraction of the total amount of time spent on developing the product. An often-cited software metric states that coding represents a mere 7% of the total effort in a software project. In other words, writing the code is just one factor among many that help to determine the quality, reliability, and security of a software product. Some of the other important factors are (1) the software process (methodology) used to develop the product, (2) the work environment (work culture) that drives the manner in which developers, managers, and stakeholders interact and share knowledge, and (3) the professional and ethical obligations and awareness of the developers, managers, and stakeholders. This chapter explores these factors from a security perspective. We address the following fundamental question: How has the growing concern about security influenced the manner in which software professionals go about developing their products? We focus primarily on the software professionals involved in the creation of these products. These professionals include those who are involved in collecting the requirements, designing the systems, and coding and testing those systems. We use "software developers" and "software engineers" to refer to these professionals in general.

Things have changed dramatically since Robert Morris launched the Morris worm back in 1988 (Spafford, 1989). In many ways, Robert Morris (a graduate student at Cornell at the time) not only launched a worm that attacked the fledgling Internet, he also launched the modern era of interest in and focus on issues in computer security. Although some computer security topics were being researched before the Morris worm, it was the Morris worm that represented a kind of "wake-up call" to the computer science community. That wake-up call was about acknowledging that the emerging world of the Internet would have major security problems and concerns. Nonetheless, it has taken the software engineering community quite a long time to fully acknowledge and respond to that wake-up call.

If one were to pick up a popular book (or even a technical book) on software engineering from 1990 or 1995, one would most likely not see a detailed treatment of security issues as an intrinsic and fundamental aspect of the software development process. Security issues were at best implicit in terms such as "reliability" and "safety". For example, the first edition of Steve McConnell's influential book, *Code Complete* (1993), does not discuss security; "security" is not even in the index!

However, during the last several years, more and more books have been written that focus on the problem of creating secure software. This fact can be attributed to quite a few more recent wake-up calls. The first of these took place in March 1999 with David Smith's release of the Melissa virus. The Melissa virus was a shock wave for the security community. It spread over the Web with amazing efficacy using newly available technologies (Garber, 1999) that Microsoft incorporated into some of its Windows applications. Other wake-up calls soon followed, including the Code Red worm (Berghel, 2001b) in July 2001 and dozens of other worm epidemics that have done many billions of dollars in damages (including time wasted trying to clean up the mess left by these ever more prolific Internet worms). The September 11 terrorist attacks were another wake-up call for the security community. At issue was whether a terrorist organization could use worms and other malicious devices to disrupt the national economy.

The software engineering community came to recognize the bottom line: These worms exploit flaws in the software that underlies the technology of the Web. One of the first books on the topic of creating secure software was Viega and McGraw's *Building Secure Software* (2002). Another book on this topic is Howard and LeBlanc's *Writing Secure Code* (2003). These excellent books and others now available place more emphasis on incorporating security considerations into the software development process right from the start.

This chapter explores the impact of security concerns on the software development process. We examine several different ways in which these concerns manifest during project development. In particular, we explore the following issues that relate to developing secure software:

- What should be the basic security goals and the basic software project goals for developing secure software? These questions are discussed in Section 10.2.
- What properties characterize a good software development process as opposed to one likely to produce software with security flaws? This question is discussed in Section 10.3.
- What team culture issues are relevant to developing secure software? In particular, we need to look at the tensions between developers, testers, and security experts. This issue is addressed in Section 10.4.
- What legal, professional, and ethical issues are relevant to discussions of security in the software development process? These issues are discussed in Section 10.5.

Section 10.6 summarizes what we have learned from our consideration of these and other questions. The references provide the reader with a substantial list of resources that can be used to explore many of the topics discussed in this chapter more deeply.

10.2. Tensions Between Security Goals and Project Goals

Before discussing the impact of security issues on the software development process (Section 10.3), let us now consider basic security goals and how they might conflict with basic software project goals. The distinction between security goals and software project goals made in this section is somewhat of a historical accident. After all, it seems that all of the security goals should be software project goals. However, we are making this distinction to point out the difficulties that some organizations might face in developing secure software if they do not explicitly include security goals as fundamental goals for their software projects. By making this distinction, we draw attention to the security goals in light of the fact that these goals might have been short changed or ignored in many software projects over the years. Security goals need to be seen as worthwhile, as important and worthy of consideration as the traditional software project goals, and the tensions between these two types of goals need to be acknowledged and examined.

Those involved in a software development project (including analysts, designers, developers, and testers) must consider these conflicts in a risk management framework. That is, if a particular security goal is in conflict with a software project goal, the project team must analyze the situation carefully. In fact, it is desirable to have someone on the project team who is knowledgeable in the area of security, and understands the security goals and also the tradeoffs that may need to be made between security goals and software project goals.

The software team needs to ask some deep questions about the tensions between the various goals. These questions include: (1) What would be the consequences of compromising on a particular security goal to satisfy a particular software project goal? and (2) Would a particular compromise make the application vulnerable to exploits that are just not acceptable? A *vulnerability* is a flaw or weakness in the software and an *exploit* is some activity conducted by someone with malicious intent that takes advantage of the vulnerability. If we might use building a house as an analogy, then building a house without a lock on the front door is analogous to creating software with a vulnerability. Entering the house through the unlocked door and stealing money and jewelry is an exploit. A more detailed account of how the intruder entered the house and moved through the home to find the money and the jewelry would be called an "attack vector" by the computer security experts.

In examining a particular software vulnerability, we need to consider the likely adversaries that might want to exploit the vulnerability. Do the likely adversaries have the financial resources and technical knowledge that might be required to perform a successful exploit? If, in fact, an attack of this nature is both likely and unacceptable, what would be the cost of securing the system against such an attack? What would be the cost both in terms of development time (which relates to the software project goal of timeliness) and other software project goals such as efficiency and usability?

These are the kinds of questions that must be raised in considering the security goals and their relationship to the software project goals. In the following paragraphs, we consider a list of security goals inspired by two separate lists in Viega and McGraw's (2002) book on building secure software. Their lists differentiate between goals and principles, and we have combined these concepts somewhat. For each security goal, we explore the implications for one or more of the following commonly acknowledged software project goals:

- Timeliness
- Functionality
- Usability
- Efficiency
- Simplicity
- Reliability
- Maintainability
- Reusability

Timeliness refers to the project's being completed in a timely manner in the light of market conditions. *Functionality* refers to the behaviors that the system supports. From the user's perspective, *functionality* refers to the capabilities that the system has which enable the user to perform tasks that the user needs to accomplish. Developers, especially talented ones, are often eager to provide many features, just to show their enthusiasm by exploring the capabilities inherent in the underlying technology. It is sometimes a challenge to rein in this kind of creativity to achieve other project goals, such as timeliness. *Usability* refers to the degree to which the system is user friendly. The goal is to allow users to accomplish their tasks in a straightforward manner. The difficulty of accomplishing a specific task should not be disproportionate to the importance of the task. *Efficiency* refers to the system's response time. Users might be turned off by a slow response time. In certain real-time applications, slow response times might be unacceptable or even dangerous. *Simplicity* refers to the structure and size of the software product. Simplicity tends to correlate with reliability, maintainability, and reusability. Complexity can diminish the reliability, maintainability, and reusability of a system. Complexity can also have a cost in terms of efficiency and timeliness. Reliability is clearly related to security. However, we are distinguishing between *reliability*, which we characterize as having nothing to do with malicious attackers (or, the offense in Dorothy Denning's theory [1999] of information warfare) and *security*, which we characterize as relating to defensive postures taken against potential adversaries. *Maintainability* refers to the ease with which a system can be modified, either because of defects found in the design or in the code, or because the specifications have changed owing to an evolving operating environment. *Reusability* refers to the ease with which components within the software can be reused in subsequent projects.

Let us now look at the basic security goals and give examples of how they might be in conflict with these software project goals:

- Prevent vulnerabilities that can lead to exploits.

- Implement auditing and/or monitoring.
- Ensure confidentiality, integrity, and accessibility.
- Provide multilevel security.
- Provide trustworthy authentication processes.
- Follow the principle of least privilege.
- Fail securely.
- Be reluctant to trust.
- Use community resources.

10.2.1. Prevent Vulnerabilities That Can Lead to Exploits

The basic security goal is to avoid introducing "holes" or vulnerabilities into the system that might lead to exploits. This requires an understanding of the most common attack vectors and the most common kinds of attacks, whether they are attacks against the network or attacks against particular components in the system. Achieving this goal also requires understanding the physical and social environment under which the software will be operating so that the risk of social engineering attacks (as chillingly described by Kevin Mitnick [2002]) can be avoided. Preventing vulnerabilities that can lead to exploits may be in conflict with many of the software project goals. Preventing such vulnerabilities may require that the product spend more time under development. Achieving this goal may require security training for the designers and developers, so that they understand what the issues are. These considerations may be at odds with the software project goal of timeliness.

Preventing vulnerabilities that can lead to exploits may require simplifying the functionality of the system, which may make developers unhappy because they do not get to engage in the creativity that gives them so much satisfaction. Preventing vulnerabilities may also make the product less fun to use and, thus, this goal may be in conflict with the goal of usability. Consider a situation in which a software product might be made more fun to use if it incorporated available software that includes state-of-the-art graphics and animation. However, it turns out that the available off-the-shelf graphics software has known vulnerabilities and security flaws. Thus, the decision might be made to do without the graphics features in favor of protecting the security of the product. Adding functionality without careful analysis may introduce new vulnerabilities into the software. Preventing exploits may make a system less user friendly, as users are required to take additional steps to authenticate who they are. Preventing vulnerabilities may also have some costs in terms of the efficiency and the simplicity of a system. This additional complexity may make the work of maintenance more difficult. In addition, component reusability may become more difficult because it is important to analyze the component being reused in its new environment. If the new environment exposes the reused component to new situations that it might not have been coded to deal with, the component may prove to be insecure in that new environment.

Preventing vulnerabilities that can lead to exploits is a very general goal. Many of the other goals that we discuss have something to do with this general goal of preventing attacks against the system. Thus, many of the tensions that we mentioned between the goal of preventing vulnerabilities and the software project goals also apply between the more specific security goals (which follow) and the software project goals.

10.2.2. Implement Auditing and/or Monitoring

Auditing relates to keeping track of what is going on within the system. Auditing requires software to record events in a log file (or files). If an exploit occurs, the auditing information can be used to recreate the sequence of events that led to the malicious attack. Events might include requests being made to enter a network or the execution of specific processes by the operating system. Events might include specific interactions between an application and a database or specific communications between system components over a network. Auditing serves several purposes that relate to security. First, auditing can help a recovery effort when a system fails (e.g., rolling back a database to where it was before it was subject to a malicious attack). Auditing is also essential for forensic work. One argument for auditing is that criminals and malicious attackers might avoid a system that is known to have effective auditing capabilities.

Monitoring refers to real-time auditing. This technology is usually associated with intrusion detection systems (IDSs) (see McHugh, Christia, and Allen [2000]). An intrusion detection system looks at network activity or activity at a particular desktop to look for suspicious patterns. When a suspicious pattern is detected, the IDS might alert the system administrator or invoke specific protective measures. IDS technology is related to the research by Forrest, Hofmeyr, and Somayaji (1997) on computer immunology. Intrusion detection systems are a relatively new technology with a reputation for creating false positives.

Implementing auditing and/or monitoring tools for a given application can be at odds with many of the software project goals, including timeliness, efficiency, simplicity, maintainability, and reusability. For example, auditing and/or monitoring tools clearly can have a cost in terms of system efficiency. The system might become less efficient in terms of response time because of the resident auditing and/or monitoring components. Perhaps even more disruptive are the false positives created by an IDS. The administrative actions that result from these false positives can delay the successful completion of valid transactions.

10.2.3. Ensure Confidentiality, Integrity, and Accessibility

Confidentiality, integrity, and accessibility are sometimes called the "big three" in computer security. This goal is related to the goal of preventing vulnerabilities that can lead to exploits in that protecting the confidentiality, integrity, and/or accessibility of information is often a matter of protecting that information from a malicious intruder who might want to use that information to achieve malevolent ends. In particular, *confidentiality* is about preventing unauthorized persons from gaining access to private information. *Integrity* is about preventing an attacker from modifying data. *Accessibility* is about making sure that resources are available for authorized users. Accessibility is a special concern in this world of distributed denial-of-service (DoS) attacks, as exemplified by so many recent Internet "worms" (like the Blaster [Bailey et al., 2005] and Slammer [Moore et al., 2003] worms).

Protecting confidentiality and integrity is not only about protecting systems from people with criminal intent (malicious parties); it is also about protecting information from unauthorized access or modification by parties who may not have malicious intent, but who might still cause inadvertent harm.

Ensuring confidentiality, integrity, and accessibility may have a cost in terms of the timeliness, functionality, usability, efficiency, simplicity, maintainability, and reusability of the project. For example, protecting confidentiality (or privacy) may have implications for the system architecture, requiring one or perhaps two firewalls (one to protect a network and the second to protect a desktop on the network) plus the use of encryption between system components that must communicate over a network. This added complexity might result in a system that takes longer to develop, may be less simple and less efficient, and may be more difficult to maintain. The use of encryption technology may have an impact on the usability of the system.

Protecting privacy in the world of the Internet is increasingly difficult. For example, Hal Berghel (2001a) wrote about the risk to privacy posed by cookies.[1] So, an application that supports and uses cookies (to achieve greater functionality and usability) may be less secure in terms of privacy.

A fundamental security concern is posed by extensible software. The major software vendors have made an effort to make their software *extensible*, which means that new components (often developed by other vendors) can be added to their software and can interact with the original software in useful ways. Often, users download software extensions from the Web to gain new capabilities not present in the original software. Martin et al. (2001) investigated the privacy practices of Web browser extensions and found them severely lacking. The extensions that they studied were often marketed as tools to make Web interactions more user friendly. So again, the security goal of protecting confidentiality (privacy) conflicts with software project goals such as usability and reusability.

10.2.4. Provide Multilevel Security

Software designers and developers are advised to practice "defense in depth." If an intruder can get through a firewall and eavesdrops on traffic over a network, he or she is less likely to do harm to that system if that traffic is encrypted. The presence of encrypted data may dissuade the attacker from attempting to exploit that particular system. Encryption, then, represents a second layer of defense behind the first layer, the firewall.

There is clearly a tension between providing multilevel security and software project goals such as simplicity and efficiency. Providing multilevel security makes the system architecture more complex. This may make for a system that takes more

---

[1]When a person visits a Web site, that person is called the *client* and the Web site is referred to as the *server*. A *cookie* is information that the server might store on the client's computer so that the next time that client visits the same Web site, the Web site recognizes the client as a particular individual, someone who as visited the Web site on at least one previous occasion. Cookies can improve the user friendliness of client interactions with a Web site (e.g., the Web site may remember some of the interests and preferences of the client), but they also pose serious security concerns.

time to get out to market and is more difficult to maintain. The extra levels of security may be at odds with usability if users are required to authenticate themselves at various doorways into the system.

10.2.5. Provide Trustworthy Authentication Processes

The problem of identifying authorized users (authentication) is difficult in computer security. There is much research being done on the subject of authentication, including the use of digital signatures (Dowd and McHenry, 1998), the memorability of passwords (Yan et al., 2004), and the use of challenge question systems (Just, 2004). Let us consider the use of a challenge question system as an example of how security can be at odds with certain software project goals.

Mike Just describes how he helped to design a challenge question system for the Canadian government. A basic purpose of a challenge question system is to protect a system against a common kind of social engineering attack. In this kind of attack, the social engineer calls the help desk, speaks with an angry voice, and claims to be the CEO's favorite nephew (or something like that). The attacker claims that he has lost his password and demands that the help desk give him the password over the phone. A challenge question system is a strategy designed to force the person who has forgotten his or her password to answer specific, personal questions on-line, questions that the person answered when his or her account was created. An important goal of Mike Just's challenge question project was to determine the characteristics of a good challenge questions system, a system that would be both secure and reasonably acceptable to users.

Implementing an effective and secure challenge question system is difficult. From the perspective of system usability and simplicity, it is a lot easier to just have the folks who cannot remember their passwords call the help desk, but the cost is that a malicious party could obtain the password using the social engineering attack as described. So, we add complexity and perhaps detract somewhat from the usability of the system when we implement a challenge question system as part of the software.

10.2.6. Follow the Principle of Least Privilege

The principle of least privilege is a fundamental goal for the design of a secure system. It is an important principle for protecting the confidentiality and integrity of information in a system. The principle of least privilege states that only the minimum privileges necessary to perform an operation should be granted. Furthermore, those privileges should be granted only for the amount of time necessary to perform that operation and no longer. Thus, for example, if an authorized user needs to read items in a database, that user should be granted that privilege to perform the necessary read operations. That user should not be granted a write privilege with respect to that database, nor should that user have access to the database information for a longer time than necessary to obtain the required information.

Granting privileges with excessive generosity can also have implications for accessibility. An attacker may be able to exploit a granted privilege to perform a DoS type of attack (e.g., by causing the system to crash).

Implementing the principle of least privilege requires development time. It may have costs in terms of usability because users are required to provide authentication information to perform certain operations. It may also have implications for system simplicity, efficiency, and maintainability.

10.2.7. Fail Securely

Systems should be designed to fail securely, whether the failure is due to a software defect, a hardware failure, or the malicious action of an attacker. Designing a system to fail securely requires various strategies. One of those strategies is to compartmentalize, so that, for example, if one part of a database is damaged, other parts of the database remain functional while the damaged portion of the database undergoes a recovery process. Jajodia, Ammann, and McCollum (1999) discussed designing systems to fail securely in information warfare environment. Designing systems to fail securely means the systems might be more complex, requiring more development time and making maintenance more difficult. There might also be costs in terms of usability.

10.2.8. Be Reluctant to Trust

This is a basic security goal (or principle). Suppose a software component has been developed with the utmost care and after much attention and the appropriate quality assurance and testing procedures, is deemed to be reasonably secure. (We know from some results in theoretical computer science that we dare not say that the system is provably secure; making such a claim could bring the wrath of twentieth-century logician Kurt Gödel down upon our heads.) However, if the secure component, X, communicates with an insecure component, Y, then what does it mean to say that X is secure? Y might be providing X with invalid data, causing X to update a database in violation of the goal of data integrity. Perhaps Y is susceptible to DoS attacks. If X depends on Y to function properly, the DoS attack against Y also affects X. If X protects the confidentiality of data, but Y does not, then any data that X sends to Y are no longer adequately protected against unauthorized access.

The issue of trust is a topic of great interest in the computer security community. Viega, Kohno, and Potter (2001) discuss this issue in an interesting manner in their paper "Trust (and Mistrust) in Secure Applications." A more theoretical treatment of this issue is found in an article by Turing Award winner Butler Lampson (2004).

Being reluctant to trust has implications for system design. The result may be a system that is more complex, takes more time to develop, and is less user friendly. The issue of trust must be considered when a trustworthy component is reused in a new environment.

10.2.9. Use Community Resources

The final security goal (or principle) is to take advantage of community resources. This especially applies to systems for encryption and authentication. For example, many authors recommend use of Kerebos (Tung, 1999) to implement authentication processes for systems. Using community resources may be less in conflict with software project goals than some of the other security goals. Using community resources may save time and support reliability and functionality. The community resources may be highly reliable, usable, and efficient.

Perhaps the greatest danger involved in using community resources is the possibility that a particular resource (such as a commercially available firewall product) is not as secure as the vendor claims. Before commercial off-the-shelf components are incorporated into a project, the security properties of that product must be carefully investigated. Lindqvist and Jonsson (1998) have researched the security vulnerabilities of commercial off-the-shelf software.

The conflicts alluded to in this section may manifest in the work environment. Thus, they have implications for the work culture and the relationships between various team members, including analysts, designers, developers, testers, and security personnel. We return to a discussion of work culture issues in Section 10.4. Before discussing the work culture issues, let us now turn our attention to the issue of how to create a good software process for building secure software.

10.3. Computer Security and Software Processes

Imagine a team of software developers working on creating a new software product. For many projects, the Internet infrastructure and the nature of attacks in the world of the ubiquitous Web have enormous implications for the development of this product. The kinds of risks that the development team has to consider during the software development process depends on the nature of the development environment (the environment in which the developers are working and communicating) and the real-time environment in which their product (or system) will eventually operate.

Even if the proposed system were to operate in a closed environment, not exposed to Internet traffic during its operation, security issues would arise during the development of the software. In particular, how might an attacker (the *offense* in information warfare terminology) attempt to subvert the code that would eventually be used in the system? Possibilities include an insider attack, in which a disgruntled employee tries to subvert the project for malicious purposes, or a social engineering attack, in which a malicious hacker (perhaps with a personal, commercial, or political agenda) gains access to the development environment by stealing a password. There is also the possibility of a network intrusion by a malicious hacker who wants to insert a Trojan horse into the development code so that he or she can claim "bragging rights" among his or her "black hat" colleagues.

The same kinds of problems, but magnified manyfold, might occur if the system under development is to be connected to the Internet during operation. For example, the system under development might need to communicate with a trusted database (one that must be secure and trustworthy), and the attacker could perform a network attack against the communications channel between the system and that database. One possible attack of this nature would be a "man-in-the-middle attack." In a man-in-the-middle attack, the system thinks it is communicating with the trusted database server, but is in fact communicating with the attacker, who, in turn, is communicating with the trusted server. ("Man in the middle" attacks are described in Viega and McGraw [2002, pp. 454–456].) Another possibility is that the attacker is capturing encrypted network packets and manipulating them to destroy the integrity of the communications between the system and the database. The attacker might give the database incorrect data that the database thinks is coming from the system (going in one direction) or the attacker might give the system incorrect data that the system thinks is coming from the database (going in the other direction). It might be that it is critical that the system receive responses from the database within a certain time frame (maybe measured in seconds), but a DoS attack is taking place, making it impossible for the system to get information from the database or vice versa.

Some of the possible exploits might relate to vulnerabilities within the code created by the software development team. For example, the determined attacker might discover a buffer overflow[2] problem in the code, allowing him or her to send long input strings to the system, strings that include malicious executable code. This does not require that the attacker have access to the code. Rather, the attacker could send experimental inputs into the system (perhaps by *network spoofing*, pretending to be sending information from a trusted IP address). Getting strange responses back from the system might indicate that there is a buffer overflow problem.

Other exploits might relate more to the networking architecture surrounding the system, including the firewall products (whether in-house or bought from a perhaps unreliable vendor) and commercial off the shelf components that the system might be using. (Again the reader is referred to the research of Lindqvist and Jonsson [1998]).

Whatever the nature of the attacks the software system is eventually subject to, the software process used to design the architecture of the system and to generate the system's code is critical to the security of that system. The software process must examine the possible threats and use "risk management" to decide whether an individual threat needs to be addressed. Experts agree that the software process for such a system needs to include security considerations right from the start. These experts include folks like Viega and McGraw (2002), Howard and LeBlanc (2003), and a panel of experts gathered together by experts in academia, the software industry and the Department of Homeland Security (2004). This panel emphasized the need to use well-documented software processes that have been shown to produce code that is nearly defect free. Such processes are more likely to yield secure systems. Furthermore, they emphasize the need to incorporate security considerations into these good software processes. The panel mentions several software processes that have been used successfully in industry to produce secure code. These processes include the Team Software Process (Davis and Mullaney, 2003), Cleanroom Software Engineering (Mills and Linger, 2002), and an enhancement to the Capability Maturity Model called Systems Security Engineering (SSE-CMM) (2003).

The heart of the matter is that security needs to be figured into the software development process from the start. The following paragraphs summarize the

---

[2]A large percentage of software vulnerabilities are due to the buffer overflow problem. This is a technical concept that relates to how some programming languages (like C and C++) handle the computer's memory. If there is a buffer overflow problem in the software, an attacker is able to flood the application with information that overflows the intended memory area, overwriting information stored in adjacent memory areas. The result might be that the attacker is able to insert malicious code into the computer's memory, code that, when executed, can cause considerable harm.

basic considerations in doing this, based largely on the discussions in Viega and McGraw (2002) and Howard and LeBlanc (2003) and report by the panel of experts (Davis et al., 2004). After we discuss these basic guidelines, we turn our attention to two common software processes: open source software development and eXtreme programming (XP). XP is the most prevalent example of what are called *agile process-es*. The emphasis in an agile process is on intense interaction between the customer and the developers and among the developers themselves. This intense interaction has many positive implications in terms of producing usable products for customers in very short time frames, in a highly iterative fashion, and with a minimal number of defects. Rather than have customers wait until the entire product is finished, an agile process delivers the product in stages. The customer receives a subset of the final functionality in short order and receives expanded versions of the product in *releases* every few weeks or so. We consider whether open source and XP provide good frameworks for building secure software. There are many sources of information on these topics, but the reader is referred to Raymond (2001) for open source and Neill and Laplante (2003) for XP.

Empirical studies have shown that an iterative waterfall (or lifecycle) process is still common in the software development industry (see Neill and Laplante [2003]). The waterfall process takes the project through sequential phases (stages) of requirements analysis, design, coding, and testing. After the product gets out to the customer, the product enters an additional phase, maintenance, which, based on empirical data, is usually the most costly. When the development process is made iterative, the process iterates over these phases. The iteration may run through analysis, design, coding, and testing over and over again, until a stable product is developed. (An iterative process of this nature is sometimes called a "spiral process.") An iterative process emphasizes customer interaction and satisfaction. In fact, Neill and Laplante report in their empirical study that there can be a lot of iteration in the first phase (requirements gathering) and maybe less iteration during the latter phases in a software process that developers characterize as being a waterfall process. The idea is to use prototyping during the requirements gathering (analysis) phase and once the requirements are agreed on, to proceed into the later phases of the project. Requirements gathering using prototyping is highly iterative. The basic principles for incorporating security considerations into a waterfall or an iterative software process are as follows:

1. Consider security policy from the start.
2. Perform a risk assessment.
3. Incorporate security policies into the requirements document.
4. Perform architectural design consistent with the requirements.
5. Perform lower level design consistent with the requirements.
6. Perform coding consistent with the requirements and consistent with "safe" coding practices.
7. Make security a consideration in all quality assurance practices.
8. The testing phase specifically needs to include security testing.

9. Maintenance should not be done using a "penetrate and patch" mentality.

We now discuss each of these principles briefly.

10.3.1. Consider Security Policy from the Start

The first principle is to consider security policy from the start of the software process, during the requirements analysis process. The goal of the requirements analysis process is to create both functional and nonfunctional requirements for the system, requirements that are agreeable both to the customer (the party who needs the software, sometimes called the *client*) and to the developers (or, more broadly, the organization that is agreeing to create the software). The nonfunctional requirements describe the constraints under which the system will be operating, and these should include a statement of security policies. *Security policies* are security-related constraints and rules that must be enforced throughout system development, by the system architecture, by the system code, and so forth. Functional requirements describe the specific, observable behaviors of the system. The functional requirements can also reflect security issues. For example, a functional requirement developed as a use case scenario (a scenario detailing how a user will perform a specific task using the system) might show that a user trying to gain access to a system component must enter a password as part of that scenario.

"Considering security policy from the start" implies the existence of security-knowledgeable personnel on the development team. In addition to the security personnel, the development team includes analysts, designers, coders, and testers. In some contexts, those who will eventually be responsible for maintaining the code (*maintainers*) may also be on the team. Stating a security policy, performing risk management tasks, and designing and coding for security all require knowledge of the security issues. There needs to be a presence on the team of one or more persons who have expertise in the area of security. This question of "security-knowledgeable personnel" is discussed at more length in Section 10.4.

10.3.2. Perform a Risk Assessment

Before the requirements are agreed upon, a formal risk assessment process must be undertaken. Risk assessment is an important activity that falls under the more general rubric of risk management. Risk management includes all of the activities and decision-making processes that relate to risk identification, evaluation, and prevention during the software development process. Risk assessment is a specific aspect of risk management. *Risk assessment* requires gathering a list of all possible types of attacks that might be perpetrated against the system and prioritizing those types of attacks according to their severity and according to the likelihood of their occurrence. For example, if an encrypted database is attacked and the encryption broken, that could be disastrous for the organization. However, analysis will show that if the encryption information (e.g., the cryptographic key) is properly handled, then a successful attack is highly unlikely because only an organization with tremendous financial resources (like a foreign intelligence agency) could possibly launch a successful attack of this nature. If a list of possible adversaries does not include a foreign intelligence agency, then this particular issue might be given a low priority during the risk assessment process. The cost of protecting against this specific type of attack might be too great given the low risk of such an attack actually occurring. For each type of attack that is either likely or possible (given the nature of the proposed system, the identity of one's potential adversaries, and the reality of life on the Internet), preventive measures must be discussed and their costs analyzed. If the cost of a particular preventive measure is consistent with the magnitude of the perceived risk, then that preventive measure should be included in the requirements for the proposed system. Good sources of information on risk management (in general) and risk assessment (in particular) include Viega and McGraw (2002) and Whitman and Mattord (2003).

10.3.3. Incorporate Security Policies into the Requirements Document

The risk management processes (including risk assessment) lead to a requirements document that reflects both the security policies and the preventive measures that were agreed on during the requirements gathering and risk assessment processes. The security policies define what security means for this particular system. The discussion of preventive measures might lead to some decisions about how those policies will be enforced, but many of those specific decisions are made during the design process that follows. For example, a security policy might state that customer credit card numbers stored in the organization's database must be protected. The security policy briefly explains why that information requires protection. The specific implementation details—relating to the required encryption components and processes—emerge in detail during the design process. The same is true for deciding how the system will be protected using firewalls and other security components.

10.3.4. Perform Architectural Design Consistent with the Requirements

The design of the top-level system architecture is now performed with the security policies and relevant security risks in mind. Depending on the nature of the system, the architectural design might include strategies for encrypting data in a secure manner, protecting system components from intrusion, and making decisions about the trustworthiness of components and the communications channels between them. The architectural design reflects the basic security goals discussed in Section 10.2.

10.3.5. Perform Lower Level Design Consistent with the Requirements

As the design process goes into lower level components (like classes and methods implemented in a specific programming language), the design of these components must be consistent with the security policies. For example, the system might include a specific process for writing data to a database. The lower level design must include considerations such as who has the right to write to the database and how those privileges will be enforced so that they cannot be violated.

10.3.6. Perform Coding Consistent with the Requirements and "Safe" Coding Practices

One of the basic messages in Viega and McGraw's book (2002) is "It's the code, stupid!" Many security vulnerabilities arise due to poor coding practices. One can certainly argue that all security vulnerabilities are due to coding errors or misjudg-ments at some level in a system or the infrastructure that supports the system. Howard and LeBlanc (2003) are both important members of the major security push at Microsoft. All four of these authors (Viega, McGraw, Howard, and LeBlanc) agree that developers need to be aware of specific coding practices that make soft-ware vulnerable to attacks, including the preeminent buffer overflow kind of attack. Achieving "safe" coding may not be easy. Microsoft is forcing its developers to undergo training in secure coding. Viega and McGraw emphasize the need for secu-rity expertise somewhere in the development team. These security experts can review the code to make sure that it will not be subject to known kinds of exploits.

10.3.7. Make Security a Consideration in All Quality Assurance Practices

Project deliverables, whether the requirements document, an architectural design document, or the code itself, must all be subject to quality assurance measures. They must be reviewed for correctness and completeness in terms of the security policy that was developed as part of the analysis process. And, of course, the very process of developing a security policy must be subject to some kind of quality assur-ance process. One possibility is to bring in an outside consultant to review the secu-rity decisions that have been made. The most important practice for quality assurance for the code itself is code inspection (Glass, 1999). Every line of code that is to be in the delivered product needs to be reviewed by peers, including peers who are knowledgeable in the area of secure coding. Some tools are available for scan-ning the software for known vulnerabilities. An example of such a tool for C, C++, Python, PHP, and Perl is Rough Auditing Tool for Security (RATS) (Secure Software, 2006). However, knowledgeable security personnel are required to understand the output from a system like RATS.

10.3.8. The Testing Phase Specifically Needs to Include Security Testing

Cynthia Cohen and her colleagues (2004) found that there can be a lot of tension between testers and developers on software projects. We explore the security impli-cations of this issue (the tension between testers and developers) in more detail in Section 10.4, but suffice it to say that the implications of their research for secu-rity are profound. The software testers that Cohen and her colleagues interviewed often felt that testing was not given sufficient "respect" in the software process. (Perhaps we should call this the "Rodney Dangerfield Effect" in the software devel-opment culture.) Developers were often given to the very last minute to finish a project and testers found themselves testing systems under great pressure and with-in very limited time frames. When developers fell behind schedule relative to the project plan, the amount of time devoted to the testing phase was often sacrificed to allow for more development time. Inevitably, this has a negative impact in terms of product quality.

Secure software requires good testing. Even good, standard testing procedures make the software more secure. However, security testing is different from the usu-al forms of testing. Security testing must be done specifically as security testing, probing the system as a malicious attacker might probe it, rather than just look-ing at the system from the perspective of a naïve or careless user. The software process must include both good testing practices for "normal" situations and security testing practices that try to break the system in creative and unusual ways.

10.3.9. Maintenance Should Not Be Done Using a "Penetrate and Patch" Mentality

Shari Pfleeger (2001) points out that maintenance includes many of the issues that preceded it in the software lifecycle. These might include requirements issues, design issues, coding, and testing issues. Thus, maintenance for security must reexamine some of the policy, design, and coding decisions that were made in creating the system that is undergoing maintenance. If new functionality must be added to the system, a risk management approach must be used to evaluate that new functionality and its implications. Security experts must review any modified code and any code that might be impacted by the code that has been modified. The modified system must undergo rigorous security testing.

The "penetrate and patch" mentality has played a big role in creating an insecure environment in the world of the Web. This mentality precludes good security practices from the start and instead allows the users of the system to do the security testing. When a user or community of users finds a vulnerability (sometimes at great personal expense), the vendor creates a patch and the patch is made available to the public. Arbaugh, Fithen, and McHugh (2000) wrote an important paper that showed how reckless this approach to security really is. Using data obtained from CERT at Carnegie Mellon University, they showed that most of the intrusions into systems occur after the patch is released. They describe the lifecycle of a vulnerability as consisting of the following stages:

- Vulnerability found
- Patch released
- Script written and published on the Web
- The number of intrusions using the vulnerability increases dramatically

When a vulnerability is found and publicized, that gives the script writers an opportunity to write a script that exploits that vulnerability. Writing these scripts requires some level of technical expertise. The scripts are then used by hundreds or thousands of "script kiddies," young folks (mostly teenagers, but sometimes younger) who have little technical knowledge. They just like to use the scripts to see the kind of damage they can do so that they can earn bragging rights with their colleagues in the hacking community. The number of intrusions that use a particular script explodes once the script has been published in part because system administrators do not patch the systems with the published patch. Note that the patch is usually released before the scripts are published during the vulnerability lifecycle. The system administrators may not install a patch either because they are overworked or because they are concerned about the risk of patching a system that works. They adhere to the maxim, "If it ain't broke, don't fix it." The only problem is, in many cases, it is "broke". The Code Red worm is a dramatic example of the vulnerability lifecycle in action (Berghel, 2001b). One month after Microsoft made available a patch for a MS IIS buffer overflow vulnerability, the Code Red worm was launched with dramatic consequences.

Security issues, as we have seen, have many implications for the software process, but there are many software processes that are used in the software community. Let us now consider briefly the security implications of two of these processes: the open source process and XP.

The open source process involves allowing developers from all over the world to contribute to open source projects. Eric Raymond describes this process in his book, *The Cathedral and the Bazaar* (2001). However, some critics of open source have claimed that it is not really a defined software process (e.g., see McConnell [1999]). We focus on just one issue in open source development, the "many eyeballs" approach to software development and its implications for quality assurance and security.

Imagine a software project whose code is available over the Web. Usually, the project starts with a prototype, which represents a point of departure for the evolution of the software. If the prototype is of sufficient interest to a community of developers, the software evolves over time as developers from all over the globe contribute to the project. A project leader and associated colleagues are in charge of managing the project as modifications, changes, and additions come in from the community of developers. This community of developers is responsible for designing and implementing the system. There is no formal design document. There are no formal processes or standards. Instead, one has the enthusiasm and expertise of a group of people who love to program and want to share their knowledge and expertise with a larger community.

According to Eric Raymond, "Given enough eyeballs all bugs are shallow." The point is that having so many eyeballs reviewing the code means that the code has fewer defects. However, the historical data do not support this assertion in terms of security vulnerabilities. The consensus in the software development community is that open source is neither more nor less secure than closed source. For example, the Linux operating system has had over 1,000 security vulnerabilities exposed (according to CERT), and therefore claiming that open source is more secure than closed source is just not true. This seems to be the consensus of many experts, including Spafford and Wilson (2004), George Lawton (2002), and Viega and McGraw (2002).

What is the problem? The problem seems to be that the eyeballs looking at the code may not have the security expertise that is required to create secure software. If you have 1,000 eyeballs looking at some ftp[3] source code, and if none of those eyeballs are really knowledgeable in security issues, then the ftp source code might contain security defects that are either never found or remain in the product for a long time. In fact, Viega and McGraw mention six serious security defects in an important open source ftp utility, wu-ftpd. Some of these defects lay undetected in the code for over 10 years. Perhaps open source security will improve as more eyeballs become more aware of secure coding practices.

There is another (rather obvious and dark) side to the open source "many eyeballs" phenomenon and that is that the openness of the code exposes it to some

---

[3]ftp stands for file transfer protocol; it is a popular protocol for communications over the Internet.

eyeballs that might have malicious intent. If these mean-spirited eyeballs discover-er a vulnerability, they do not share their discovery with the larger community. Instead, they find ways to exploit those vulnerabilities to their own advantage. So, when a vulnerability is made public, that does not imply that the vulnerability was not known for a period of time (perhaps years) to one or more "black hat" hackers.

Another software process that has received a lot of attention in recent years is XP, a collection of over a dozen specific development practices that constitute a high-ly iterative approach to software development. Unlike open source, XP is definite-ly a defined process, even though it may come across as being radical upon first exposure. XP has been characterized as a software process that took some good development practices to the extreme. A good introduction to XP and an evalua-tion of XP in terms of the SEI's Capability Maturity Model (CMM) is found in an arti-cle by Mark Paulk (2001). In Paulk's opinion, XP has many strengths as a development process. He concludes that XP is not inconsistent with the CMM up to a certain lev-el of maturity in the CMM model[4] (basically satisfying almost all of the key process areas that define CMM level 2 and a few of the key process areas at higher matu-rity levels).

XP is perhaps oriented toward developing Web applications in relatively short time frames. XP is, after all, an agile process. The emphasis is on continuous cus-tomer involvement, intense interaction among developers, and getting a usable prod-uct out to the customer as soon as possible. The fact that the customer does not have to wait for many months, perhaps years, to get a usable product is one of the great advantages of XP. The product is developed iteratively. Each iteration provides a more complete version of the eventual finished product. An iteration typically takes about 2 weeks. The usable product that is given to the customer after an iter-ation is called a "release." (Not every iteration produces a release, but the goal is to give the customer a usable product as quickly as possible.) Giving the customer a usable product in a short time frame is one of the great advantages of XP in terms of customer satisfaction. The product undergoes continuous refinement during the development process, with each new release of the product including new features that the customer needs. Features are prioritized according to customer needs and the highest priority features are developed first. XP includes the following extreme practices:

- *Customer on-site at all times.* The customer interacts with the developers and plays an important role in determining the functionality of the system being developed.
- *Customer requirements gathered using "user stories," which are written on index cards.* A *user story* is a brief description of product functionality. For example, a user story might assert: "The user of the system will be asked to enter an account number to receive account information."

---

[4]The Capability Maturity Model (CMM) from the Software Engineering Institute (SEI) provides guidelines to help organizations achieve software process improvement. The CMM assessment process characterizes an organization as being at one of five levels of "maturity." The higher the level of maturity, the more likely it is that the organization will produce high-quality products on time.

- *Project planning (called release planning) based on prioritizing the user stories.* Each release is the result of implementing a collection of user stories. The first release implements the highest priority user stories. Each subsequent release implements the user stories which follow given their ranked priorities.
- *Release planning leads to iterations of approximately two weeks in length.* The project plan consists of a sequence of such iterations.
- *No big up-front design.* In "big up-front design," the functionality is determined "up front" before the customer gets a chance to interact with any piece of working software. The customer may have to wait months or years for a working product.
- *All delivered code developed using pair programming.* Two programmers work at one computer. This has been shown to lead to fewer defects in the delivered product.
- *Unit tests written before the actual code.* Each system component (unit) has test code written to test its functionality even before the code for the unit itself is coded.
- *Acceptance testing guided by the customer.* Each release goes through acceptance testing by the customer to ensure that the relevant user stories have been implemented successfully and in an acceptable manner.
- *Frequent integration of new components into the code repository.* This allows for defects and problems to be discovered earlier rather than later. The code repository contains the absolute latest version of the software being developed.
- *No overtime! Forty-hour work week.* Software developers who work overtime tend to introduce more defects into the software they produce than those who do not work overtime.
- *Daily stand-up meetings to assess project progress.* The emphasis is on standing up as opposed to sitting down because this helps to keep the meetings short.
- *Do not add functionality the customer does not want.* The emphasis is on what the customer wants and only on what the customer wants.
- *Redesign code to keep it simple and correct.* XP calls this process "refactoring."

There is a growing interest in XP (and the more general class of similar processes, called "agile processes") in the software engineering community, but the issue for us is whether XP is consistent with creating secure software. Many security experts (including Viega and McGraw [2002], Howard and LeBlanc [2003], and Spafford [2003]) have expressed negative opinions with regard to XP in terms of creating secure software.

The big downside to XP for creating secure software may be its attitude toward gathering requirements and doing system design. One way of expressing this attitude is that XP is opposed to "big up-front design," the sort of design process that we described as a requirement for producing secure software. The requirements for an XP system are captured in terms of user stories written on index cards. Each user story is one to three sentences long. There are no formal design documents in XP except for class responsibility and collaboration (CRC) cards. Each such card shows a class, its public functions, and the classes that collaborate with that class by sending messages to that class—not an appropriate tool for recording decisions about high-level security decisions.[5] Annie Anton and Don Wells (2003) debate the advantages and disadvantages of how XP handles requirements engineering in an IEEE *Software* Point/Counterpoint feature. Although their discussion does not focus on security, the issues that the authors raise clearly have implications for whether or not XP is appropriate for creating secure software.

Pair programming has been shown to improve software quality (e.g., Williams et al. [2000]). Pair programming requires that every line of code in the delivered product be developed by two developers working side by side at one computer. One developer is the driver, who does the typing, and the other developer can be described as the "back seat driver." The back seat driver continuously offers advice and examines the code for flaws. Pair programming is a difficult practice for many organizations to implement. Williams et al. (2000) report some impressive results in terms of software quality from pair programming projects. However, their research was not about security issues per se and was conducted using software engineering students in a university environment. Pair programming probably does improve quality (it is a manifestation of the "many eyeballs" principle), but for security purposes, you would want every line of code to be reviewed by at least a few eyeballs that are well-versed in secure coding practices.

Can XP be redeemed for creating secure code? One possibility is to add a security expert to the development team, just as there is a customer on site at all times. If a security expert is on site at all times, that would certainly help in terms of creating secure code, but one wonders whether the security expert would be successful without some kind of formal risk management process. Exploring how XP can be modified to create a secure process would certainly be an interesting line of research.

This completes our overview of what is a huge and an interesting topic. The interested reader is encouraged to consider the references that specifically deal with the relationship between computer security and software processes (Davis et al., 2004; Howard and LeBlanc, 2003; Viega and McGraw, 2002).

10.4. Team Culture Issues

We now turn our attention to team culture issues. These include matters like clashing personalities on a development team, the lack of appreciation for good software development practices among high-level managers, and problems with knowledge sharing and communication during team meetings.

Earlier, we mentioned research relating to the relationship between developers and testers (Cohen et al., 2004). Their research showed that testers have a user-oriented perspective on the systems they are testing. The developers of those same systems are more likely to be focused on the underlying technology and the technical issues. They are also likely to want to try out new things regardless of the impact

---

[5]The terminology associated with CRC cards derives from an approach to writing programs that is called *object-oriented programming*. The basic design component in object-oriented programming is called a *class*. An *object* is a specific instance of a class (like a carrot is a specific instance of a vegetable). Classes provide designs for objects. Objects contain data and functions can be applied to objects to change their state or obtain information from the objects.

on issues such as usability and portability (e.g., whether a particular new techno-logical feature will port to other Web browsers). An important problem in system development, when there is an especially talented group of developers, is to rein in this passion for creativity and novelty on the part of developers to make sure software project goals are satisfied (e.g., timeliness, simplicity, portability, and user friendliness). Although we did not list portability in our list of software project goals, it is an important software project goal in some contexts. Portability is related to reusability. However, reusability is commonly used to refer to the reusability of com-ponents in a new system. Portability usually refers to the porting of an entire sys-tem to a new operating environment (like a new operating system). Incorporating a new technology into an application just for the fun of it may make the applica-tion less portable. That new technology may have implications for the reliability and/or security of the software in new operating environments.

Cohen et al. (2004) report that testers often felt that they were unappreciated by management. They often saw themselves as being lower on the organizational totem pole than the developers. One manager described the situation in this way: "If you had an diagram with God at the top, the engineers [developers] would put themselves above that" (Cohen et al., 2004, p. 79).

The same kinds of tensions in the workplace that have been observed between testers and developers have also been observed between the security experts and what Viega and McGraw (2002) refer to as "roving bands of developers." Again, the language implies developers who just want to do their thing, and do not want to be reined in by concerns that are not central to their view of coding reality. Just as testers bring a user-oriented perspective to the process, security experts bring a security-oriented perspective, and the security-oriented perspective may be of no more interest to the developers than the user-oriented perspective.

What is required is team training and efforts to identify the specialized groups (e.g., developers, testers, security personnel) and to find ways to improve the relationships and communications between these groups. For example, if a security expert criti-cizes the code that a developer writes because it might lead to a buffer overflow exploit, the manner in which the security expert communicates this information to the developer is important. It is important to avoid the use of personal terms: Rather than saying, "How could you be so stupid as to call this strncpy[6] function in this man-ner?" The security expert must be factual and impersonal: "This call to strncpy would create a buffer overflow situation, and here's a safer way to accomplish the same ends."

Creating good relationships and objective, useful communications is difficult. It certainly seems advisable to have the security personnel involved in the devel-opment process all along, so that they do not come in at the end of the project. If they come in at the end of the project, they are likely to end up tearing the code apart, creating a lot of conflict and resentment. Furthermore, it is well known in the software engineering community that correcting a defect is much more expen-sive (in terms of necessary time) later in the lifecycle than earlier. The sooner a defect

---

[6]strncpy is a function in the C language that, if used incorrectly, can create a buffer overflow vulnerability.

is found, the less costly it is to fix it. Somehow, a team orientation needs to be created that acknowledges the various perspectives. Of course, there could be tensions between the security personnel and the testers if the latter are not trained to do security testing. Creating a team spirit and teaching the entire team basic security principles and issues right from the start would certainly be helpful.

McLendon and Weinberg (1996) wrote about the concept of congruence in software development. They define *congruence* as an alignment between what is felt and thought and what is said. Incongruence is just the opposite. In an incongruent organization, people do not say what they think or feel. Thus, communications cannot be trusted. One symptom of an incongruent organization is blaming. Rather than focusing on solving a problem, the focus is on trying to blame someone, whether a programmer, manager, or tester, for the problem. McLendon and Weinberg call blaming the dark secret behind many software project failures. Their experience as industry consultants has convinced them that a blaming culture has many negative consequences for a software project. These include the time wasted because people cannot trust the information that they receive from their colleagues as well as the time wasted because developers find themselves devoting a considerable amount of time to planning how to defend themselves when the "day of reckoning" arrives.

When people with different perspectives work on a software project, there is likely to be conflict. If this conflict leads to blaming, the results can be disastrous. The software team must view conflict as a potentially positive thing, leading to deeper insight into the issues that the team faces. Software project managers must have good conflict management skills. Because security issues create new avenues for disagreement and conflict, good conflict management skills become even more important as one incorporates security issues into the software development process. Walz, Elam, and Curtis (1993) discuss the role of conflict and the options for creative conflict management in their study of knowledge acquisition and sharing in software development.

We next explore some basic principles for creating a good team culture, a team culture that is consistent with effective handling of security issues during the software process. These include:

- Creating an effective and sensible software process;
- Team ownership of the process;
- Team ownership of the product;
- Creating a congruent culture without blaming; and
- Managing workplace demons.

We discuss each of these items briefly in the following paragraphs.

10.4.1. Creating an Effective and Sensible Software Process

One cannot have a good team culture if the software process that is imposed on the project team does not make sense; is not well-documented, understood, and adhered to; and if the software process is overridden with bureaucratic record keeping that no one takes seriously. So, the first prerequisite for a good team culture is to create an effective process, a process that handles security issues in an effective manner, a process that is rooted in common sense. This normally requires appropriate training for all team members with respect to the security issues relevant to their roles (e.g., as designers, coders, and testers) in product development.

10.4.2. Team Ownership of the Process

Bill Pitterman (2000), in his account of how Telcordia achieved the highest CMM maturity level (level 5), emphasizes the need not only for a common-sense process, but team ownership of the process. Analysts, designers, developers, testers, and security personnel all need to have some say in the definition of the process and in the continuous improvement of the process. They must feel a sense of ownership for the process, as opposed to feeling that the process is being imposed on them by managers who do not understand the nuances of software construction. Feedback from analysts, designers, developers, testers, and security personnel should help the organization to continuously improve their secure software process.

10.4.3. Team Ownership of the Product

All team members must feel that the product that they are working on is theirs, that they have a stake in the quality of the product that eventually goes out the door. If team members become alienated (e.g., by insensitive and insulting communications), then they are less likely to create a quality product, a product that is secure and reliable.

10.4.4. Creating a Congruent Culture without Blaming

McLendon and Weinberg (1996) discuss how a congruent culture can be created by a five-step process. The process they describe starts with the individual team member's awareness of the incongruence in his or her own being. The awareness leads to inner exploration and eventually honest communication with one's colleagues. The goal is to have the entire team see the importance of honest and trustworthy communication, and to understand the consequences of blaming and incongruence on the quality of the products that the team is producing.

10.4.5. Managing Workplace Demons

The author has expanded on McLendon and Weinberg's idea of a blaming culture by creating a list of over 40 workplace demons that can impair progress on a software project (Epstein, 2004). For example, these demons include arrogance, perfectionism, sexism, fear, and inflexibility. All of these demons need to be managed intelligently, because all can disrupt the work culture, which can have implications for the quality of the product the team is trying to produce.

Part of building secure software is building security into the culture, not just into the process. Howard and LeBlanc (2003) describe how this is being done at Microsoft. Analysts, developers, testers, and maintainers—all need to have an awareness of security issues and the importance of creating a secure product. It is interesting to read what Howard and LeBlanc are saying about how security concerns are being integrated into the software development process at Microsoft and to compare this with what Cusumano and Selby (1997) reported. Cusumano and Selby studied software development at Microsoft during the mid-1990s. Security was clearly not a major emphasis in the software development process at Microsoft as reported by these authors. Instead, the emphasis was managing the tension between timeliness and the extraordinary enthusiasm and creativity of the Microsoft developers.

10.5. Professional and Ethical Issues

In this section, we explore some of the professional and ethical issues relevant to the production of secure software. We devote considerable attention to the Software Engineering Code of Ethics (Gotterbarn, Miller, and Rogerson, 1997), which clearly states that it is the responsibility of software developers to produce reliable and safe software. However, before discussing the Software Engineering Code of Ethics, let us briefly consider two important ethical issues that could potentially have an impact on software security. These issues are (1) intellectual property and (2) liability. We begin with a brief discussion of some of the security implications of intellectual property laws that relate to software patents and copyrights.

Let us first focus on patent law here in the United States (e.g., Nichols [1999] and Samuelson [2004]). It seems likely, unless the law is changed dramatically during the coming years, that patent law litigation will become more common. How might this legal environment impact the security of the systems being built?

Imagine a software application that absolutely requires real-time communications between the application and a database server in a local area network. Furthermore, imagine that this is a safety-critical application. For example, perhaps this is an application to be used by pharmaceutical companies as process control software. In other words, the software will play a major role in controlling the quality and safety of the drugs being produced at a drug manufacturing plant. Intrusions into this network would be intolerable and could have serious safety implications for the consumers who consume those pharmaceutical products. Let us suppose (for this hypothetical scenario) that the software developers work for a company called PharmASoft that develops process control software for pharmaceutical companies. Imagine that the developers of this safety-critical application created a new kind of intrusion detection technology that reacts to intrusions automatically, in real time. The PharmASoft developers conclude that an automated, real-time response (that does not require human intervention) is absolutely necessary for their application to run safely and reliably. One can even imagine that this new technology generates a lot of excitement and enthusiasm on the PharmASoft development team. (In fact, intrusion detection systems with automated responses to intrusions are often called *intrusion prevention systems*. Intrusion prevention systems are a topic of great interest in the security research community.)

Suppose, after the new PharmASoft application is released into the market and is being used by PharmASoft's clients (the pharmaceutical companies), another company, PatentHolder, Inc., claims that the intrusion detection process used in this application violates a patent that they hold. PatentHolder, Inc., bought the patent several years back from a technology company that folded. If the amount of money that PatentHolder, Inc., wants is too great, PharmASoft might decide to use a less secure intrusion detection process to protect their application from attackers. As a result, PharmASoft has to revise its product and the system that the pharmaceutical companies end up using is less secure than the original system that the developers had intended.

Copyright law can also have security implications. Suppose the developers of our hypothetical pharmaceutical process control software are aware of a new kind of attack that is out there in the wild (i.e., on the Internet). That attack has proven to be highly effective against firewalls like the MurkyMoat Firewall that the PharmASoft developers decided to use to protect communications between their application and the database server. The PharmASoft developers paid MurkyMoat big bucks for this firewall product, despite the fact that MurkyMoat has a somewhat questionable reputation in the security world. The MurkyMoat Firewall code is proprietary (or closed source). The only way the PharmASoft developers can protect their application against the new kind of attack and future possible attacks of a similar nature is to reverse engineer the MurkyMoat product they purchased and share the knowledge thus acquired with knowledgeable experts in the field of computer security. The PharmASoft developers are motivated, in part, by a desire to contribute to the ability of the computer security community to prevent these kinds of attacks in the future. The PharmASoft developers soon discover that they have to reverse engineering-specific aspects of the MurkyMoat Firewall code that MurkyMoat incorporated into their product for the sole purpose of protecting MurkyMoat's intellectual property rights. In particular, MurkyMoat used rather unproven code obfuscation techniques specifically for the purpose of making it difficult for their code to be reverse engineered. (Gleb Naumovich and Nasir Memon [2003] give an interesting introduction to code obfuscation techniques.) A PharmASoft lawyer points out to the developers that reverse engineering the MurkyMoat Firewall code, which includes these protective mechanisms, and sharing their discoveries with the larger community of computer security experts, would probably be in violation of the Digital Millennium Copyright Act (DMCA). Rather than risk criminal prosecution or a civil lawsuit, PharmASoft decides not to reverse engineer this potentially flawed firewall.

The author feels somewhat uncomfortable with these examples, because they may seem rather farfetched. However, many authors (including Andrew Grosso [2002]) have pointed out that the DMCA is already having a negative impact upon research in the field of computer security. Patent law is less commonly viewed in this context (as having an impact on computer security), but it seems only a matter of time before there is some kind of impact. For example, as of this writing, a company called Acacia claims to hold a patent on streaming video. This author feels that the process they patented does not meet the legal requirement of nonobviousness and should not have been granted a patent. The academic world is fearful that they will end up having to pay Acacia for the use of streaming video in distance-learning courses (Carlson, 2003). Isn't it only a matter of time before some company claims a patent on a basic security process, like intrusion detection?

Another important issue that software engineers have to deal with in the coming years is the issue of who is responsible for insecure software. There are precedents for the application of "strict liability" law in situations in which software has been deemed responsible for causing harm to innocent parties. There are also precedents for malpractice cases against those involved in software development, if their software does harm and if those developers did not follow established professional practices.

The legal environment in terms of legal responsibility for insecure code is likely to evolve over the next few years (e.g., Mead [2004]). One piece of legislation, called the Uniform Computer Information Transactions Act (UCITA), has been criticized by many as giving too much protection to software vendors in situations in which the software they created and sold causes harm. Whether or not UCITA becomes law throughout the United States (it is law in two states—Virginia and Maryland—as of this writing), new legal precedents and legislation are likely during the next few years relating to this issue. Software vendors are likely to become less and less cavalier about creating insecure software for their customers in light of the evolving legal environment.

Now, let us look at the Software Engineering (SE) Code of Ethics. It is interesting that the term "security" is not used in the code (as published in the *Communications of the ACM* [Gotterbarn et al., 1997]). This is not an oversight on the part of the authors, for the security issues are there beneath the surface (e.g., with their use of words that relate to the public safety). However, one might speculate that the wording of the document might more explicitly discuss security concerns if it were redone in this post 9/11 world.

The SE Code of Ethics describes three levels of ethical responsibility (or obligation). These relate to the ethical obligations that are incumbent upon the software engineer as a human being, the ethical obligations that are incumbent upon the software engineer because he or she is a professional, and the ethical obligations that are specifically related to the profession of software engineering. The SE Code of Ethics uses the following language to summarize these three levels of ethical obligation:

- Level 1: Aspire to be human.
- Level 2: Expect to be professional.
- Level 3: Demand to use good practices.

With respect to security, these fundamental obligations call upon the software engineer to recognize his or her responsibility to protect the safety of the public and to ensure that their software products do no harm. These obligations call upon the software engineer to be a responsible professional, both in terms of his or her interactions with colleagues and clients, and with the larger community of users. These obligations call upon the software engineer to be a responsible software engineer, which, in the context of this chapter, means that the software engineer is aware of security issues, and is using an effective process for ensuring security consistent with the associated risks and costs.

The code is organized around eight keyword principles. They are:

1. product;
2. public;

3. judgment;

4. client and employer;

5. management;

6. profession;

7. colleagues; and

8. self.

For each keyword principle, the code presents a basic statement of ethical obligations with respect to that keyword principle. Each of these statements is followed by a list of guidelines relating to that keyword principle.

In the following paragraphs we present the basic statements of ethical obligation for the keyword principles, followed by a brief discussion of the relevance of these principles for the problem of developing secure software. In particular, we relate these statements to the issues discussed earlier in this chapter.

10.5.1. Principle 1. Product

"Software engineers shall, insofar as possible, ensure that the software on which they work is useful and of acceptable quality to the public, the employer, the client, and the user; completed on time and at reasonable cost; and free of error" (Gotterbarn et al., 1997).

There is a consensus within the security community that creating absolutely secure software is not possible. New attack vectors and exploits are to be expected. The issue is to create software that is reasonably secure using effective and sensible risk management procedures as important aspects of the software process the engineer uses for a particular project. The public will eventually come to expect software products to be secure. Producing software with avoidable and serious vulnerabilities will have serious economic and perhaps legal consequences.

The possible economic consequences of an insecure software product vary greatly, depending on the nature of the product. Perhaps the most serious consequences would result from attacks perpetrated by cyberterrorists or by an enemy nation during a time of war. For example, the theory of information warfare includes the possibility of tremendous economic ruin brought about by an adversary (e.g., a foreign nation with enormous economic resources) attacking our communications infrastructure using malicious software. The result could be economic disaster on an unprecedented scale. Cyberterrorists are also capable of doing great damage according to some experts. One possibility would be a cyberterrorist attack against the power grid. Lesser economic consequences due to insecure software might result in economic ruin for a company that is the victim of an attack. For example, customers might lose their faith in a credit card company if that company's customer database is attacked, resulting in serious financial consequences for its customers (e.g., because of identity theft). The legal consequences for producing insecure software might also become severe as state legislatures and the federal government consider new liability laws (like UCITA, although UCITA is considered to be overly vendor friendly by some of its opponents) that will hold software vendors culpable for producing insecure software.

10.5.2. Principle 2. Public

"Software engineers shall act only in ways consistent with public safety, health, and welfare" (Gotterbarn et al., 1997).

The public safety, health, and welfare demand the production of secure software. To produce this kind of software, the software engineer must adhere to effective professional practices, including adherence to defined processes that effectively handle security concerns.

10.5.3. Principle 3. Judgment

"Software engineers must protect the independence of their own judgment and the reputation of the profession for sound judgment" (Gotterbarn et al., 1997).

Software engineers need to avoid becoming victims to false claims made by security software vendors. For example, some security vendors exaggerate the ability of their products to protect networks and applications. In fact, these same vendors may be aware of vulnerabilities in their own products, vulnerabilities that are never openly revealed to prospective customers. Such security tools may themselves introduce vulnerabilities into a customer's system that might not otherwise be there. Some writers have referred to these kinds of security tools as "security snake oil." Software engineers need to be as objective as possible in assessing the appropriateness of various security tools. Software engineers who do not make responsible decisions will harm the reputation of the profession.

10.5.4. Principle 4. Client and Employer

"Consistent with the public health, safety, and welfare, software engineers shall act as faithful agents and trustees of their client or employer" (Gotterbarn et al., 1997).

Software engineers must acknowledge their responsibilities to client and employer. Honest communication is essential and it is important to work in a congruent work culture. If one is in an incongruent work culture, one should work to improve that culture. Perhaps, if the culture cannot be fixed, then it is time for the software engineer to find employment elsewhere. Security issues must be discussed honestly with the client, both to determine the appropriate security policies and to inform the client of new and unexpected problems. Similarly, if there are security issues that are not being addressed properly in a project, the software engineer must communicate this to his or her manager, and if need be, to managers at a higher level.

10.5.5. Principle 5. Management

"Software engineers in leadership roles have specific obligations" (Gotterbarn et al., 1997).

Managers of software projects must help to create an effective software process for creating secure software. They must set specific and measurable goals for software quality. Guidelines for doing this were presented in Sections 10.3 and 10.4. Managers must strive to create a work culture in which the focus is on fixing problems rather than on casting blame for those problems. They must strive to create a work culture in which honest communication is encouraged and appreciated. They must work to encourage effective communication among security personnel, analysts, developers, testers, and maintainers.

10.5.6. Principle 6. Profession

"Software engineers shall advance both the integrity and the reputation of their profession" (Gotterbarn et al., 1997).

Creating secure software is a prerequisite for enhancing the integrity and reputation of the profession of software engineering. Creating insecure software does just the opposite.

10.5.7. Principle 7. Colleagues

"Software engineers shall treat those with whom they work fairly" (Gotterbarn et al., 1997).

Creating secure software requires effective and honest communication among the various groups working on the project, including the security personnel, developers, and testers. These groups must treat each other with mutual respect and understanding; otherwise, the security of the software product is likely to suffer.

10.5.8. Principle 8. Self

"Software engineers shall, throughout their careers, strive to enhance their own abilities to practice their profession as it should be practiced" (Gotterbarn et al., 1997).

Software engineers need to practice deep listening to learn from the perspectives of others. The developer can learn from the security expert and the security expert can learn from the tester, and so on. Also, training in the appropriate technologies and underlying principles is essential for all participants in a project dedicated to producing secure software.

Clearly, a software engineer who knowingly participates in the creation of insecure software is in violation of the code. One important professional responsibility of the software engineer is to appreciate the impact of security issues on the software development process.

10.6. Conclusions

Issues in computer security are having a major impact on software professionals. This chapter attempted to provide an overview of this impact in terms of the software processes that are used to build software, the work cultures in which software developers work, and the professional and ethical obligations that software developers have to produce secure software. This chapter ends with a list of references that the reader can use to pursue in greater depth those topics that the reader found especially interesting.

It is no exaggeration to say that every day the news is filled with interesting issues that relate to computer security. As the exploits become more and more imaginative, one is tempted to wonder what the issues in computer security will be like 10, 20, or 50 years from now. Given the "imagination for evil" possessed by many of the attackers, it would be dangerous to make a specific forecast. However, it seems safe to project that the future will be fascinating, filled with new challenges and discoveries. Maybe 50 years from now we will have an entirely new communications infrastructure based on new technologies that we can hardly imagine right now, technologies that will solve most, if not all, of the security problems we face today. Of course, it is also possible that a new technology (like quantum computing) might make contemporary security measures (like cryptography) completely obsolete without giving rise to appropriate replacement technologies. All that we can say for sure is that the future will be interesting. We need to welcome both the challenges and the blessings of life in this new century.

References

Anton, Annie I., and Don Wells. (2003, May/June). "Successful Software Projects Need Requirements Planning (Anton)," and "Don't Solve a Problem Until You Get to It (Wells)" [Point/counterpoint feature]. *IEEE Software*, pp. 44–47.

Arbaugh, William A., William L. Fithen, and John McHugh. (2000). "Windows of Vulnerability: A Case Study Analysis." *IEEE Computer*, pp. 52–59.

Bailey, Michael, Evan Cooke, Farnam Jahanian, and David Watson. (2005). "The Blaster Worm: Then and Now." *IEEE Security and Privacy*, pp. 26–31.

Berghel, Hal. (2001a, May). "Caustic Cookies." *Communications of the ACM*, pp. 19–22.

Berghel, Hal. (2001b, December). "The Code Red Worm." *Communications of the ACM*, pp. 15–19.

Carlson, Scott. (2003, November). "A Patent Claim that May Cost Millions." *Chronicles of Higher Education*.

Cohen, Cynthia F., Stanley J. Birkin, Monica J. Garfield, and Harold W. Webb. (2004, January). "Managing Conflict in Software Testing." *Communications of the ACM*, pp. 76–81.

Cusumano, Michael A., and Richard W. Selby. (1997, June). "How Microsoft Builds Software." *Communications of the ACM*, pp. 53–61.

Davis, Noopur, and Julia Mullaney. (2003, September). "The Team Software Process in Practice: A Summary of Recent Results" [technical report CMU/SEI-2003-TR-014]. Pittsburg, PA: Software Engineering Institute, Carnegie Mellon University.

Davis, Noopur, Watts Humphrey, Samuel T. Redwine, Jr., Gerlinde Zibulski, and Gary McGraw. (2004, May/June). "Processes for Producing Secure Software," *IEEE Security and Privacy*, pp. 18–25.

Denning, Dorothy E. (1999). *Information Warfare and Security*, Boston, MA: Addison-Wesley.

Dowd, Patrick W., and John T. McHenry. (1998, September). "Network Security: It's Time to Take It Seriously." *IEEE Computer*, pp. 24–28.

Epstein, Richard G. (2004, June). "Demons in the IT Workplace" [IEEE ISTAS 2004 Conference]. Worcester, MA: Worcester Polytechnic Institute.

Forrest, Stephanie, Steven A. Hofmeyr, and Anil Somayaji. (1997, October). "Computer Immunology." *Communications of the ACM*, pp. 88–96.

Garber, Lee. (1999, June). "Melissa Virus Creates a New Type of Threat." *IEEE Computer*, pp. 16–19.

Glass, Robert L. (1999, April). "Inspections–Some Surprising Findings." *Communications of the ACM*, pp. 17–19.

Gotterbarn, Don, Keith Miller, and Simon Rogerson. (1997, November). "Software Engineering Code of Ethics." *Communications of the ACM*, pp. 110–116. Also available at www.acm.org/constitution/code.html.

Grosso, Andrew. (2002, February). "Why the Digital Millennium Copyright Act is a Failure of Reason." *Communications of the ACM*, pp. 19–23.

Howard, Michael, and David LeBlanc. (2003). *Writing Secure Code*, 2nd ed. Redmond, WA: Microsoft Press.

Just, Mike. (2004, September/October). "Designing and Evaluating Challenge-Questions Systems." *IEEE Security and Privacy*, pp. 32–39.

Jajodia, Sushil, Paul Ammann, and Catherine D. McCollum. (1999, April). "Surviving Information Warfare Attacks." *IEEE Computer*, pp. 57–63.

Lampson, Butler W. (2004, June). "Computer Security in the Real World." *IEEE Computer*, pp. 37–46.

Lawton, George. (2002, March). "Open Source Security: Opportunity or Oxymoron?" *IEEE Computer*, pp. 18–21.

Lindqvist, Ulf, and Erland Jonsson. (1998, June). "A Map of Security Risks Associated with Using COTS." *IEEE Computer*, pp. 60–66.

Martin, David M., Jr., Richard M. Smith, Michael Brittain, Ivan Fetch, and Hailin Wu. (2001, February). "The Privacy Practices of Web Browser Extensions." *Communications of the ACM*, pp. 45–50.

McConnell, Steve. (1993). *Code Complete.* Redmond, WA: Microsoft Press, 1993.

McConnell, Steven. (1999, July/August). "Open-Source Methodology: Ready for Prime Time?" *IEEE Software*, pp. 6–11.

McHugh, John, Alan Christia, and Julia Allen. (2000, September/October). "Defending Yourself: The Role of Intrusion Detection Systems." *IEEE Software*, pp. 42–52.

McLendon, Jean, and Gerald M. Weinberg. (1996, July). "Beyond Blaming: Congruence in Large Systems Development Projects." *IEEE Software*, pp. 33–42.

Mead, Nancy R. (2004, July). "Who Is Liable for Insecure Systems?" *IEEE Computer*, pp. 27–34.

Mills, Harlan, and Richard C. Linger. (2002). "Cleanroom Software Engineering." In J. Marciniak, ed., *Encyclopedia of Software Engineering*, 2nd ed. New York: John Wiley and Sons.

Mitnick, Kevin D. (2002). *The Art of Deception*. New York: John Wiley and Sons.

Moore, David, Vern Paxson, Stefan Savage, Colleen Shannon, Stuart Staniford, and Nicholas Weaver. (2003, July/August). "Inside the Slammer Worm." *IEEE Security and Privacy*, pp. 33–39.

Naumovich, Gleb, and Nasir Memon. (2003, July). "Preventing Piracy, Reverse Engineering, and Tampering." *IEEE Computer*, pp. 64–71.

Neill, Colin J., and Phillip Laplante. (2003, November/December). "Requirements Engineering: The State of the Practice." *IEEE Software*, pp. 40–45.

Nichols, Kenneth. (1999, April). "The Age of Software Patents." *IEEE Computer*, pp. 25–31.

Paulk, Mark C. (2001, November/December). "Extreme Programming from a CMM Perspective." *IEEE Software*, pp. 19–26.

Pfleeger, Shari L. (2001). *Software Engineering: Theory and Practice*, 2nd ed. Upper Saddle River, NJ: Prentice Hall.

Pitterman, Bill. (2000, July/August). "Telcordia Technologies: The Journey to High Maturity." *IEEE Software*, pp. 89–96.

Raymond, Eric S. (2001). *The Cathedral and the Bazaar: Musings on Linux and Open Source by an Accidental Revolutionary*, 2nd ed. Cambridge, MA: O'Reilly and Associates, p. 241.

Samuelson, Pamela. (2004, June). "Why Reform the U. S. Patent System?" *Communications of the ACM*, pp. 19–23.

Secure Software. (2006). Rough Auditing Tool for Security (RATS). Available at www.securesw.com/rats/.

Spafford, Eugene H. (1989, June). "Crisis and Aftermath." *Communications of the ACM*, pp. 678–687.

Spafford, Eugene H. (2003, June). "Keynote Address." CEPE 2003 conference at Boston College, Boston, MA.

Spafford, Eugene H., and David L. Wilson. (2004, September 24). "No Software is Secure." *Chronicles of Higher Education*, special section on Information Technology.

Systems Security Engineering CMM. (2003, June 15). "Model Description Document, Version 3.0." Available at www.sse-cmm.org.

Tung, Brian. (1999). *Kerebos: A Network Authentication System*. Boston, MA: Addison-Wesley.

Viega, John, Tadayoshi Kohno, and Bruce Potter. (2001, February). "Trust (and Mistrust) in Secure Applications." *Communications of the ACM*, pp. 31–36.

Viega, John, and Gary McGraw. (2002). *Building Secure Software*. Boston, MA: Addison-Wesley.

Walz, Diane B., Joyce J. Elam, and Bill Curtis. (1993, October). "Inside a Software Design Team: Knowledge Acquisition, Sharing, and Integration." *Communications of the ACM*, pp. 63–76.

Whitman, Michael, E., and Herbert J. Mattord. (2003). *Principles of Information Security*. Boston, MA: Thomson Course Technology, p. 542.

Williams, Laurie, Robert R. Kessler, Ward Cunningham, and Ron Jeffries. (2000, July/August). "Strengthening the Case for Pair Programming." *IEEE Software*, pp. 19–25.

Yan, Jeff, Alan Blackwell, Ross Anderson, and Alasdair Grant. (2004, September/October). "Password Memorability and Security: Empirical Results." *IEEE Security and Privacy*, pp. 25–31.

Introduction to Part 4: Other Security Issues

There are a wide variety of ethical issues involving the security of the Internet and associated information technologies. While no single volume could comprehensively identify—much less evaluate—them all, this last section contains a selection of essays on problems that are perhaps less familiar to the public but that are equally important.

The first chapter is Frances Grodzinsky's, Keith Miller's, and Marty Wolf's "The Ethical Implications of the Messenger's Haircut: Steganography in the Digital Age." Steganography, like cryptography, is concerned with concealing content from persons who are not authorized to view it. While cryptography conceals content by encoding it, steganography conceals content by placing it within a seemingly unrelated artifact (e.g., one might send a message in a medium that is not usually used to send messages). This helpful essay explains some of the technical and ethical issues associated with the use of stegangography.

In the next chapter, Kai Kimppa, Andy Bissett, and N. Ben Fairweather explore ethical issues involving security in on-line games. Internet gaming is becoming increasingly popular among persons of all ages, but many of those who participate may be unaware of the security risks they face. The authors argue persuasively that these problems have been wrongly overlooked because of prejudices about the social utility of on-line games. After establishing the importance of these issues, they go on to discuss and evaluate some of the specific risks faced by gamers.

Adam Moore's contribution is concerned with the overlap between ethical issues involving hacking, privacy, and intellectual property. Moore begins his discussion by arguing for ethical principles that presumptively protect privacy and intellectual property. Because these principles provide "presumptive" protection, Moore acknowledges that they can be defeated by other ethically relevant considerations. He argues, however, that the free-access arguments frequently cited to justify hacker attacks are insufficient to defeat the presumptive protection of privacy and intellectual property.

This section and volume close with Maria Canellopoulou-Bottis's "Disclosing Software Vulnerabilities." Information is often thought to be utterly benign in character, but Canellopoulou-Bottis argues that this is not always true. In particular, information that discloses software vulnerabilities is often the first link in an all-too-predictable causal chain that results in a digital attack that inflicts harm on an innocent user. Canellopoulou-Bottis's essay provides an explanation of some of the legal and ethical issues that arise in connection with posting software vulnerabilities on Web sites.

Chapter 11: The Ethical Implications of the Messenger's Haircut: Steganography in the Digital Age

Frances S. Grodzinsky, Keith Miller, and Marty J. Wolf

Information hiding has been of interest since the time of the Greeks. Steganography is one technique to hide information. This chapter reviews the historical uses of steganography and the impact that advances in information and communication technology have had on steganographic techniques. We note that computing has made steganography accessible and convenient. This widespread availability raises ethical challenges. The first part of the paper examines the role of digital steganography in providing privacy and anonymity. The next part looks at security issues and the implications of strict government regulation. The third part examines the role of steganography in digital rights management and the implications for fair use. Finally, we conclude that steganography should neither be prohibited for individuals, nor be secretly imposed on equipment users without their consent.

11.1. Introduction

Steganography is the art and science of placing information within a seemingly unrelated artifact to hide the information. "Steganography" comes from the Greek meaning "covered writing." The Greeks etched messages in wooden tablets and covered them with wax. Another Greek technique was to tattoo a shaved messenger's head, let his hair grow back, and then shave it again after he had traveled to the recipient of the message.

Since that time, advances in technology have changed the way steganography is carried out, but it has continued to be an important tool in ensuring private and anonymous communication. In Section 11.2 we review steganography's role in private and anonymous communication, comparing and contrasting it to cryptography. We also describe how information technology has complicated the ethical issues surrounding steganography.

Computing has put steganography in the hands of just about everyone with a computer and an Internet connection. There are digital steganographic tools freely available on the Web. In particular, this puts steganography in the hands of terrorists and criminals as well as the legitimate user. In Section 11.3, we analyze the threat to security that comes with terrorists having this tool at their disposal. That analysis includes an examination of the tradeoffs of particular steps that governments have taken or might attempt to take to thwart the use of steganography.

Some governments have already taken action that has had an impact on the use of steganography, which, in turn, has had an impact on free speech. In Section 11.4, we examine the historical and current tension between government control and individual rights. These government regulations, both proposed and passed, seem to adversely impact what people do in their homes and on their computers and have threatened to stifle the information-hiding research community.

One area that has already derived some benefit from steganography is digital rights management (DRM). In Section 11.5, we briefly describe some of these techniques and how they might impact the relationship between copyright holders and users of copyrighted materials.

Although steganography is an effective technique for achieving private and anonymous communication, it can also be used to monitor communication, thus threatening civil liberties. In Section 11.6, we explore the implications of an application of steganography that is currently used by the manufactures of color laser printers and copiers and ensures that all documents printed by the device are traceable to the device.

11.2. The Role of Digital Steganography in Providing Privacy and Anonymity

Cryptography has important connections to steganography. However, the two techniques are distinct and are used under different assumptions. A user of cryptography often assumes that attackers are aware of the message being transmitted and seeks to make the message unintelligible to the attackers. A user of steganography is (typically) intent on hiding even the existence of the intended message. Steganographic strategies usually place one message within another communication medium, called the *carrier*. In digital steganography, the carrier medium could be text, an image, sound, or video. For example, there is a program that takes a short text message and embeds it in the bits of an ASCII text message designed to appear to be a commercial spam message. (For details on this and several other examples, see Kessler [2004].)

As an additional security measure, the steganographer can encrypt a message first and then hide it using steganography to further thwart an attacker; similarly, a message can be embedded using steganography and the resulting media can itself be encrypted. Thus, both techniques can facilitate private and potentially anonymous communication.

Steganography can give anonymity to the sender of a message or to the receiver, or to both. A message successfully "camouflaged" by steganography could be put in a public space where only those who were told how to extract the message would realize its presence. (If the scheme is detected, of course, the audience widens.) This kind of secrecy could be used in several different ways to enhance privacy and anonymity. For example, two people wanting to communicate incognito could agree on a steganographic technique, and pass messages using carriers that would, if successful, not be perceived by others as communication between the two parties—think of a newspaper classified ad in which every 10th character in the description of a yard sale spelled out a hidden address. In this case, the sender and receiver of the messages could, conceivably, be anonymous to each other. Alternatively, the carrier could be within a message passed explicitly between the two parties—a picture file that appeared to be a digitized photo of a pastoral scene, into which was embedded a hexadecimal encoded formula. Here the hidden communication is kept private from outsiders but the identity of the two communicating parties is known to each other. A newspaper columnist (the sender is not anonymous) could put hidden messages in published articles that could be discovered by anyone reading the column that knew the technique (the recipients could be anonymous).

When it comes to digital steganography, it is important to note that even though current steganographic techniques are good, they are not perfect. *Steganalysis*, the detection of steganographic messages in electronic media, can often identify the presence of steganographic messages (Wang and Wang, 2004). For example, one technique analyzes the noise in an image; an unusual amount of noise in an image that does not appear degraded can be an indication that the image is carrying a hidden message. As another example, if an image suspected as including a hidden message is similar (or seemingly identical) to a known image such as a famous painting, then the suspect image and the well-known image can be compared. That comparison may uncover patterns that will reveal the hidden message (Johnson and Jajodia, 1998).

Thus, it is possible for outside parties (such as governments)—with effort—to detect and possibly track down both the sender and receiver of steganographic messages. Some contend that restricting steganography will improve security (both cybersecurity and physical security); however, restricting the private use of steganography also restricts free speech. We argue that there is an important benefit to society when there is a balance between regulation and individual rights. Steganalysis detection techniques, if used fairly, would give law enforcement and security officials the means to fulfill their responsibilities under the watchful eye of the courts, and allow citizens, as a rule, to communicate freely. Despite the strong public benefit of unfettered communication, there may be risks associated with an inability to detect such messages in the case of "bad actors" such as criminals or terrorists.

11.2.1. Ethical Challenges

Because steganographic techniques have been used for centuries, why is digital steganography a particular ethical challenge? First, computing has made it easier to hide messages, especially for nonspecialists. There are many Internet sites where you can download free software that embeds and extracts text messages into and out of picture files, sound files, and text files. It takes less time, fewer resources, and less skill to accomplish sophisticated steganography with computers than without them. This lowers the threshold of effort and expense necessary to hide a message, and that can change the consequentialist costs and benefits of allowing or prohibiting the practice. A computer user can hide a relatively complex message in a picture or a music file in less than a minute. Contrast that with the elaborate and time-consuming technique of hiding a message on a messenger's scalp!

Second, the message hiding that is so easily accomplished using digital means is highly effective. Unless someone suspects that a message is hidden in digitized images, sounds, or text, what little degradation occurs in the carrier signal is rarely discernable to the casual or even careful human viewer. There are some algorithmic techniques that will uncover some digital hidden messages when they are applied to the proper object. But that's partly why digital steganography is so effective—there are far too many digital text, image, and sound files for anyone to examine, even automatically, to find out which few include steganographic messages. The messenger hiding information on his scalp might be disguised, but still might be recognized as an agent of the message's sender. Digital carriers have a far greater variability than people.

A third difference between digital steganography and previous steganographic methods is that once a message is hidden by digital steganography, it can be disseminated worldwide in minutes with minimal effort and cost. Digital steganography increases the scale and power of steganography (Johnson, 2001). The message on the scalp of our long-suffering messenger was far slower and would be seen by far fewer people than a digitally hidden message e-mailed or posted on the Web.

For these three reasons—the low cost to hide a message, the effectiveness of the hiding, and the scale and power of dissemination—digital steganography is distinct from other methods of steganography. These differences lead to changes in how steganography can and should be used. The "ethical calculus" of costs, benefits, duties, and tradeoffs is altered.

Another reason to look carefully at the ethics of digital steganography is its relation to digital cryptography, as the social and ethical implications are similar. Some think steganography is a type of cryptography, and others think they should be in separate categories. Either way, steganography can be used either alone or in conjunction with other cryptographic techniques to accomplish the same goals of privacy and anonymity that are sought using nonsteganographic cryptographic techniques. Even though steganography is often functionally interchangeable with other encoding techniques, there is a distinct difference in U.S. law: There are legal restrictions on the dissemination of cryptographic techniques, and far fewer restrictions (at least so far) on steganographic techniques.

For example, the U.S. International Traffic in Arms Regulations restricts export of controlled munitions from the United States, and cryptographic software has been identified as munitions with respect to that act. For many years, the dissemination of the Pretty Good Privacy (PGP) encryption algorithm was (and in some cases, still is) opposed by U.S. government agencies on the basis of that act (Back, N.D.). Phil Zimmerman, the author of PGP, was investigated for 3 years, with the case finally dropped in 1996. The Bureau of Industry and Security (BIS) in the U.S. Department of Commerce now controls the export of cryptography (BIS, 2005). The restrictions in place when PGP was first posted on the Internet have been somewhat relaxed, but there are still regulations against exporting cryptography software to certain states and organizations. Such regulations are not unique to the United States. The *Wassenaar Arrangement* is an agreement among 30 countries (including the United States) that encourages restrictions on encryption similar to the U.S. regulations [Wassenaar Arrangement, 2005].

Attempted restrictions on PGP and other strong encryption techniques were aimed at limiting encryption. Another set of restrictions is aimed at *enforcing* encryption when encryption is used commercially. Examples of this kind of restriction are laws against the dissemination or implementation of algorithms to decrypt DVD movies. The Digital Millenium Copyright Act (DMCA) includes such restrictions. (For an example of a recent case, see Lambers [2005].) Some research scientists have been threatened with legal action for the presentation of scholarly papers on decryption algorithms (Gross, 2001), and in 2001 a Russian programmer was arrested for trafficking in software that could decrypt Adobe's eBook Reader files. The programmer was eventually released and charges dropped; the government pursued the case against his employer, the company that published the decryption software. However, the government lost that case (Electronic Frontier Foundation [EFF], 2002).

More recently, some U.S. states have passed measures similar to the DMCA, nicknamed "super-DMCA". At least some believe these new state measures are more restrictive than the federal DMCA, and one researcher in steganographic algorithms has taken steps to avoid prosecution under the Michigan super-DMCA law (Poulson, 2003). These super-DMCA state laws are discussed further in Section 11.4.

Regulations that seek to restrict dissemination of encryption and decryption algorithms and technologies are in place for commercial protections and to allow authorities to monitor communications more easily. In the case of monitoring, the perception is that public security is enhanced when private communication is restricted (by allowing government monitoring). Nonetheless, steganography has far fewer restrictions than cryptography and can be exported legally in some situations where encryption is prohibited, although the super-DMCA laws may be interpreted to restrict steganographic techniques as well. Because software that uses cryptographic techniques has legal restrictions that are not leveled against steganographic software, the ethics of using steganography is clearly an issue worthy of exploration.

11.3. Analysis of Steganography as a Security Threat: The Terrorist Example

One of the most compelling arguments for controlling the use of digital steganographic tools is the threat of terrorism. In early 2001, there were press reports that Osama bin Laden and others were using both encryption and steganography to hide maps, photographs of targets, and instructions in pictures and text on various Web sites and in various chat rooms. Even a spokesperson for the Hezbollah indicated that it was an ingenious way for militants to communicate (Kelley, 2001).

Conway (2003) provides a historical account of popular press articles concerning the use of steganography in 2001, both before and after the attacks on the United States on September 11. She gives evidence that the notion that the

September 11 attackers used steganography was largely fabricated by the press and was never publicly substantiated. She also argues that there are effective steganalysis techniques currently in place that have been used to catch suspects in crimes. Furthermore, more sophisticated steganalysis techniques are under development as the United States National Security Agency and the United States military are openly funding research in steganalysis. She also argues that steganography can be an unreliable means of communication as it is straightforward for a third party to introduce random noise into images, thereby defacing any steganographic message. Conway also gives evidence that the use of secret symbols and codes are at least as effective as steganography for coverting terrorist communication. Furthermore, captured terrorists have substantiated the use of this "secret codes and symbols" technique. Thus, Conway concludes that it is unlikely that terrorist organizations use steganography to pass messages (Conway, 2003).

As Conway suggests, by mandating that Internet service providers add enough noise to posted files with certain formats (pictures, sound, movies) to disrupt any steganographic communication without disrupting the apparent quality of the end product, it is possible to thwart the use of steganography by terrorists (and others). To ensure that the effects of random noise were undetectable at the human level in the final artifact, the noise would have to be placed into the carrier in the same places that are used in steganography. Such action would surely disrupt the bit pattern of the steganographic message, rendering it useless. This technique is quite effective at mitigating the threat caused by terrorists who might want to use steganography to pass information.

To illustrate some of the costs and benefits of possible legislation against the use of steganography, we focus on this particular proposal. We structure our analysis on Schneier's (2003) process for analyzing and evaluating security systems. The first step in Schneier's process is to be clear about the assets that the security measure is trying to protect. The second step is to understand what is being defended and the consequences of a successful attack. Schneier's next step is to assess the effectiveness of the security solution at mitigating the risks. In addition to determining the effectiveness of the security measure, Schneier calls for analysis to determine any unintended consequences of introducing a security solution. Schneier's final step involves analysis of the costs and tradeoffs imposed by the security solution.

The first two steps require little beyond stating them. In discussing terrorists' use of steganography, the assets under consideration are the lives of people in the affected country, and the potential consequences are grave when considering a terrorist attack. The analysis becomes more complicated with the third step; the particular method of attack that might be chosen by terrorists is open to speculation. Terrorist leaders could conceivably use steganographic techniques to communicate to operatives in the field information about targets, attack methodologies, and timings. As noted, there was speculation in early 2001 that terrorists were using steganography. However, by the end of August of that year, Provos and Honeyman (2001) had provided strong technical evidence that it was unlikely that terrorists (or anyone for that matter) were using eBay or Amazon.com for covert message passing. They developed or used tools that search the Web for images, download them, and analyze them for steganographic content placed there by certain open-source steganographic tools. If there was an indication that an image may contain steganographic content, the image was further analyzed by a network of computers to determine whether there was actually steganographic content. Of the more than two million images processed, they did not find any steganographic messages. Unfortunately, their research focused on detecting embeddings only of three widely available steganographic programs, rather than using a more general analysis that would be more likely to detect more types of steganography.

In addition to being of questionable utility, there is a chance that by spending money on disrupting steganography, there would be less money available for other security measures, and a likely target might be steganalysis research; there would be less urgency for steganalysis tools. Nonetheless, it is easy to imagine terrorists studying the filters and developing techniques to circumvent them. A public sense that digital noise is effectively disrupting all digital steganography would be unwarranted. The ease with which noise addition can be detected and circumvented suggests the futility of this method for eliminating hidden messages between determined bad actors.

In analyzing the costs of this security measure, it is clear that the biggest burden would fall upon those responsible for disrupting digital steganographic communication and those responsible for monitoring the Internet for possible violations of a prohibition of digital steganography. There is a financial burden to undertake either of these efforts. Another cost of implementing either of these tactics is the possibility of missing information about a potential attack. Even though terrorists do not seem to be currently using digital steganography to communicate, there is no reason to assume that they will not in the future, especially because steganographic techniques are regularly improving. Even though improvements in steganalysis necessarily lag behind improvements in using steganography, steganalysis does open the possibility of detecting hidden information, even though it may be after the fact. The ability to possibly intercept or later detect information that was passed provides some incentive to *allow* steganography to *enhance* security. After all, the level of sophistication of governmental steganalysis tools is not a matter of public knowledge. Another cost of introducing noise into files with certain formats is that the files lose some of their integrity immediately and will likely lose more and more integrity as they are reposted to the Web. Although this may also serve the desires of those seeking to preserve control over copyrighted material, it infringes on the rights of those sharing noncopyrighted materials, such as the family sharing a special photo. Finally, another significant cost imposed by either disrupting or making digital steganography illegal is the loss of the possibility of anonymous communication for ordinary people. Although it is likely true that most electronic communication is not monitored, the availability of steganography goes a long way to ensure that those wishing to communicate anonymously have that opportunity and enhances a general sense of a free and open society. Schneier (2003) argues that security is always about tradeoffs and our analysis raises the question of whether the additional security of these measures is worth the burdens imposed, or whether that money would be better spent on some other security measure.

11.4. Analysis of the Threat That Comes from Government Regulation of Steganography/Steganalysis

Over the last 30 years, there have been numerous attempts by the United States government to regulate individual rights to privacy in communication. From the Clipper Chip to limits on encryption, security concerns have prompted calls to curtail privacy. Soon after public key cryptography was discovered in 1976, the U.S. National Security Agency demanded that information about that algorithm not be published. Digital cryptography and its government regulation have been controversial at least since then (Back, 2005). The furor over PGP is another example of this issue. Because steganography might be loosely classified as a security threat, we might consider the repercussions of limiting the use of steganography by government regulation.

In some ways, the battle over government regulation as applied to steganography is a recapitulation of the earlier arguments over other digital encryption techniques. However, the steganography issue is distinct in that, unlike cryptography, steganography is being discussed most intently surrounding the September 11 attacks. The public fear of terrorist attacks provides an added motivation to trade an erosion of privacy and a reduction in the free flow of information for some supposed protection against terrorists. Our analysis in Section 11.3 casts doubt on the validity of this tradeoff, but the expanded availability of the Internet and the perceived threat of terrorism have pushed governments to once again take a more proactive approach to enact legislation to control such technology. Since 2001, nowhere has this been more evident than the implementation of state laws known as super-DMCA that grew out of the DMCA. These bills were modeled after legislation proposed by the Motion Picture Association of America (von Lohmann, 2003). The model language proposes four prohibited categories of activity. In the following excerpt from a 2003 version of the model language, the bold face language was added after complaints that earlier versions would have had the side effect of prohibiting many legitimate software applications such as virus protection and spam reduction software that included decryption algorithms (Beauchamp, 2003).

> (a) *Offense defined.*—Any person commits an offense if he knowingly **and with the intent to defraud a communication service provider**:
>
> (1) possesses, uses, manufactures, develops, assembles, distributes, transfers, imports into this state, licenses, leases, sells or offers, promotes or advertises for sale, use or distribution any communication device:
>
> (i) for the commission of a theft of a communication service or to receive, intercept, disrupt, transmit, re-transmit, decrypt, acquire or facilitate the receipt, interception, disruption, transmission, re-transmission, decryption or acquisition of any communication service without the express

consent or express authorization of the communication service provider; or

(ii) to conceal or to assist another to conceal from any communication service provider, or from any lawful authority, the existence or place of origin or destination of any communication, **provided that such concealment is for the purpose of committing a violation of subparagraph (i) above**; or

(2) modifies, alters, programs or reprograms a communication device for the purposes described in subparagraphs (a)(1)(i) and (ii) above; or

(3) possesses, uses, manufactures, develops, assembles, distributes, imports into this state, licenses, transfers, leases, sells, offers, promotes or advertises for sale, use or distribution any unlawful access device or

(4) possesses, uses, prepares, distributes, sells, gives, transfers or offers, promotes or advertises for sale, use or distribution any:

(i) plans or instructions for making, or assembling or developing any communication or unlawful access device, under circumstances evidencing an intent to use or employ such communication or unlawful access device, or to allow the same to be used or employed, for a purpose prohibited by this section, or knowing or having reason to believe that the same is intended to be so used, or that the aforesaid plans or instructions are intended to be used for manufacturing or assembling such communication or unlawful access device for a purpose prohibited by this section; or

(ii) material, including hardware, cables, tools, data, computer software or other information or equipment, knowing that the purchaser or a third person intends to use the material in the manufacture, assembly or development of a communication device for a purpose prohibited by this section, or for use in the manufacture, assembly or development of an unlawful access device; and

(5) Assist others in committing any of the acts prohibited by this section.

von Lohmann, a senior intellectual property attorney who writes for the Electronic Freedom Foundation Web site, maintains that section (a)1(i) of these proposals, which has been incorporated into legislation in six states, will give "communication service providers unilateral control over what you can connect to your home entertainment systems" (von Lohmann, 2003). Opponents of the bills worry about the impact on innovation and competition that currently benefit the consumer, if providers were empowered to decide what could or could not be attached to home systems. The language in section (a)(1)(ii) that places a ban on devices that "conceal ... the existence or place of origin or destination of any communication" can be interpreted broadly to include items such as network address translation software and hardware found in networking equipment and virtual private networks. Indirectly, the super-DMCAs seem to restrict the use of digital steganography, as steganography can be used to keep both the sender and the receiver of the message anonymous. It is also important to keep in mind that the perceived restrictions on steganography were "collateral damage" (seemingly an unintended side effect) of bills that were designed to target illegal copying of proprietary intellectual property. Such broad types of legislation leave us on a slippery slope concerning privacy (see Section 11.5). Curiously, since 2003 there has been little movement to pass super-DMCA bills in other states.

Since then, concern has shifted from terrorist threats via steganography to spam and phishing messages that use steganography to exploit vulnerabilities in e-mail clients and Web browsers. Commercial enterprises are developing tools like Zero Spam that block steganographic images associated with malicious e-mail and spam (Fisher, 2004). In response to these efforts, spammers have started randomizing bits in the image so that it will not match any known "bad image" and thus be filtered. Although we do not condone the action of spammers, the old adage prevails in the case of steganography: When privacy (i.e., anonymous private communication) is outlawed, only outlaws have privacy. Legitimate users of steganography for personal communication could be prevented from passing undetected e-mail messages.

Interestingly, compliance with recently passed laws such as the Health Insurance Portability and Accountability Act, which mandates the protection of personal health information, and the International Trade in Arms Regulation, which prevents companies that deal in defense products from sharing information with non-U.S. citizens, has created a market for steganographic techniques (Authentica, 2004). Correspondingly, it appears the U.S. government has backed off in its attempts to enact new legislation specifically targeting steganography.

Another serious consequence of the provisions of the super-DMCAs was increased fear about academic freedom and scholarly research, including open source software efforts. Most of the problems stem from the broad language associated with the second and fourth categories previously listed and attempts by the Recording Industry Association of America (RIAA) to stop publication of papers that discussed encryption and decryption algorithms. Section 11.4.1 examines the repercussions on scholarship associated with these acts.

11.4.1. Steganography and Scholarship

In 2001, the RIAA challenged the right of researchers to present a paper at the 4th International Information Hiding Workshop. Professor Felten and his co-authors had discovered some security vulnerabilities in the technology used to protect music, and the RIAA sent him a letter threatening possible legal action if he reported his findings at the conference. The EFF (2001), "together with USENIX, an association of over 10,000 technologists that publishes such scientific research, and Princeton Professor Edward Felten and his research team had asked the court to declare that they have a First Amendment right to discuss and publish their work, even if it may discuss weaknesses in the technological systems used to control digital music."

However, after receiving assurances from the government and the RIAA that the RIAA would not contest the rights of researchers to present their research, Judge Garrett Brown of the Federal District Court in Trenton, New Jersey, dismissed the case. The interference of the recording industry with academic research, and the intimidation and waste of time and money, was of particular concern to John McHugh, who chaired the conference. McHugh indicated that security research was seldom proprietary and that "the cycle of development followed by attack followed by redevelopment, etc. has played a major role in the strength of current systems. There is no reason to expect information hiding to be different in this respect" (McHugh, 2001). His fear was that this research might have to be presented outside the United States if this type of lawsuit becomes a regular occurrence.

Super-DMCA legislation has had a chilling effect on academic scholarship wherever it has been adopted. In 2001, Tom Liston pulled his open source LaBrea software off of his Web site in response to the first provision of the super DMCA that was passed in Illinois. His software had the capability of trapping hackers and preventing worms from continuing their attacks on networks (Hulme, 2003). In another case, Niels Provos (mentioned in Section 11.3), then a graduate student at the University of Michigan, moved his research to a site in The Netherlands, afraid of prosecution under the Michigan super-DMCA state law. He also denied access to his software to anyone in the United States. "Provos says the Michigan law also makes most of his academic career a crime" (Poulson, 2003).

We are confident that instilling fear in legitimate researchers was not the government's aim. However, by using the language suggested by commercial copyright holders without completely understanding the ramifications of this legislation on technological research, legislators have created unanticipated problems for scholars.

11.5. Steganography and Its Implications for Digital Rights Management

We have examined reasons why we should be suspicious of laws that try to regulate steganography. We contend that steganography should be available to those who wish to use it to preserve anonymous communication and privacy. Anonymity is a useful tool in preserving privacy—much like cash provides a way to make purchases so that others cannot collect information about us as individuals. We realize that although the absence of regulation might pose a problem for some, organizations can opt to use steganalysis to detect the use of steganography on their servers and networks. In this section, we examine the role of steganography in the domain of digital information and digital rights management, and its implications for fair use.

With the vast amounts of digital information on the Internet, another use of steganography that has attracted wide attention is the use of watermarks in digital rights management. *Watermarks* are hidden images that convey information that ascertains the legitimacy of the digital file and thus fall under the rubric of steganography. Usually, the watermark conveys copyright information and is robust enough to sustain normal changes to the file from compression (Webopedia, 2006). A study by Dhamija and Wallenberg (2003) examined, in part, digital information as a public good and the impact of digital rights management proposals that include steganography on fair use. The discussion of sharing digital information in the public domain goes beyond the scope of this paper. It is important to note, however, in the context of these watermark definitions, that some intellectual property proposals suggest using watermarking to make digital information excludable, that is, "to allow owners to monitor who is using the product in order to charge for use and pursue those who don't pay" (Dhamija and Wallenberg, 2003).

How would these techniques affect fair use? Fair use grants legal exemptions to U.S. copyright law, often without express permission of the copyright holder. If digital content were protected to the point of excluding access to anyone who could not read or decipher the steganographic markings, then fair use could become far more complex. When fair use is the default, as it is with printed documents, there is no need for explicit permission from the copyright holder (e.g., to copy a document for use in scholarly work). However, if digital documents were protected via encoding, explicit permissions would be required to "unlock" the digital content to allow fair use. There have been proposals to encode default exemptions into the DRM system or to allow licensing schemes between rights holders and users. These go beyond the scope of this paper (see Dhamija and Wallenberg for further discussion of these proposals). In using steganographic schemes, digital content may become less shared and nonexcludable, and less of a public good. These protection schemes would limit benefits to those who have paid for it, and impose limitations that are more stringent than current nondigital protections (Dhamija and Wallenberg, 2003).

11.6. Analysis of the Threat Steganography Has on Privacy and Anonymity

To this point, we have argued that steganography can facilitate private, anonymous communication. Curiously, steganographic techniques can pose a threat to private, anonymous communication even when both the sender and the receiver of the message are known. A surprising fact is that steganography has been in widespread use since at least 1985 by many well-known corporations. Xerox pioneered a technology that embeds the serial number of a color laser printer or photocopier in every document that it produces (Tuohey, 2004). The most common use of this technology is to track the origin of counterfeit documents including currency, passports, and travel documents. In fact, the Dutch police have recently been successful in using this technology in tracking down the source of counterfeit railway tickets (DeVries, 2004).

It is a widely held belief that businesses make decisions that will help improve their bottom line. Xerox developed the technology because governments expressed concern about allowing color laser printer technology into their countries without some mechanism to help curb their use in counterfeiting (Tuohey, 2004). The printer company Canon claims that they put the technology in place to "protect their customers" (De Vries, 2004). However, the customers that they appear to have in mind are business and government customers, not individuals.

This use of steganography has troubling implications for privacy and anonymity. At this point in time, there are no U.S. laws governing the use of embedded serial numbers. Manufactures are free to include them. Law enforcement is free to request the information—apparently without requiring a search warrant. Finally, there is no legal mechanism for citizens to request that the embedding mechanism be disabled, and there is apparently no mechanism for the consumer to disable this technology without destroying the printer (Tuohey, 2004). Thus, it is possible that a person using a color laser printer for legitimate purposes cannot protect his or her identity.

Consider a political activist who prints an anonymous newsletter with a color laser printer. Although such action is lawful and protected in the United States, the activist can be tracked using the steganographic serial number hidden in the printed pages. Law enforcement is capable of determining the purchaser of the printer that produced the newsletter and, quite likely, the identity of the activist. This opens the possibility of the activist being subject to harassment. In general, without stricter controls on the conditions under which law enforcement (or anyone) can obtain serial number information, the situation is ripe for abuse.

Another scenario is a whistleblower who prints copies of documents as evidence of an employer's wrongdoing. Anonymity may be essential for the whistleblower, at least for some amount of time. An employer that comes to possess the document could well have the ability to track down the printer that made it, especially given Canon's interest in protecting their customers. However, the real question raised in this scenario is whether printer manufacturers are as willing to share identifying information with businesses and private individuals as they are with law enforcement.

Restricting the practice of embedding a printer's serial number in documents would abate the threat to individuals, but it would also increase the difficulty for law enforcement officials of tracing documents. As in many ethically significant decisions, this decision embodies a tradeoff. In this case, individual privacy rights are pitted against the possibility of law enforcement tracking down bad actors.

However, law enforcement would not be powerless in tracing documents if the embedded serial numbers were not present. Researchers are discovering that there is enough variability in the components of color laser printers to allow them to distinguish brands from samples of printed documents (Chiang et al., 2004). They also believe that their techniques can be refined to allow them to distinguish among printers of the same brand due to individual nature of the mechanical devices in a printer. Thus, in the near future a law enforcement official with a counterfeit document and suspect printer can, with near certainty, identify whether the document was printed with the printer. This approach would make the police work more difficult than the embedded serial number approach; however, it represents a tradeoff position in which the values of privacy and anonymity are part of the equation.

If embedded serial numbers remain, another way to reduce the threat to personal privacy is to allow users to disable the steganographic embedding. People who want this feature could have it, and people who do not could avoid it. Again, the usefulness of the feature is diminished for law enforcement. Even if the embedded numbers could not be turned off, simply informing users of their presence would reduce the threat to privacy.

Notice that if customers want the embedded printing feature (e.g., to be able to track documents within a company), and if users are aware of the feature, there is little threat to privacy. The fact that the feature is hidden from customers and users is the crux of the problem. The people who buy the equipment may be, unknowingly and without consent, cooperating in their own potential future surveillance.

Perhaps the most troubling question that stems from the revelation that printer manufacturers have been embedding hidden serial numbers in printed documents is whether other hardware and software manufactures are doing the same thing. Because manufacturers are not required to notify customers of this embedding, it is quite possible that digital cameras could embed their serial number in every photo, hard drives could embed their serial number in every file written to disk, and that CD and DVD burners could put their mark on every disk burned. Software manufactures also have similar opportunities to put their imprint on documents created with their software. Two serious threats come from operating system software that would embed serial numbers in all files and compiler software that would embed serial number information in executable binaries. With such information, it would be possible to track a piece of software back to the compiler that created it. These types of tracking could be used to implement increasingly intrusive surveillance techniques that some fear are becoming pervasive. These techniques, it is argued, pose a significant threat to an open and free society.

11.7. Conclusion

With the advent of the digital age, steganography is a message passing technique that has become available to ordinary citizens. The ease of use has opened up the possibility that some will use steganography for nefarious purposes. This potential for abuse has led some to suggest that the use of steganography be regulated in some way. We have argued that there are strong reasons why such government regulation would not be consistent with a free and open society. However, we discovered that steganography is currently being used without users' consent by governments and businesses in ways that may create the potential for abuse by corporations and law enforcement. This kind of abuse is also inconsistent with a free and open society.

Based on our analysis, we conclude that individuals and organizations should be allowed to use steganography at their own discretion. When computer equipment manufactures develop and market devices with the capability of embedding serial numbers, they should either market an equivalent device without this capability or one where this capability can be turned off. We also contend that hidden, automatic implementations of steganography by manufacturers of computer equipment without the consent of their customers are not acceptable. Thus, a manufacturer who wishes to sell equipment that uses steganography to embed serial numbers in its output is free to do so, but only if customers and users are made aware of the feature. Our judgment is that steganography should be used to enhance privacy and anonymity in communications, not stifle it.

References

Authentica. (2004). "Authentica: Protect Your Information." Available at www.authentica.com. Accessed 6/5/05.

Back, A. (N.D.) "PGP Timeline." Available at www.cypherspace.org/adam/timeline. Accessed 5/17/05.

Beauchamp, Geofffrey. (2003). Draft Model Communications Security Legislation: Broadband and Internet Security Task Force." Available at www.eff.org/IP/DMCA/states/mpaa_3apr.pdf. Accessed 7/8/05.

Bureau of Industry and Security (BIS). (2005). "Commercial Encryption Export Controls." Available at www.bisa.doc.gov/encryption/default.htm. Accessed 7/7/05.

Chiang, P., G.N. Ali, A.K. Mikkilineni, E.J. Delp, J.P. Allebach, and G.T.-C Chiu. (2004). "Extrinsic Signatures Embedding Using Exposure Modulation for Information Hiding and Secure Printing in Electrophotography." IS&T's NIP20: International Conference on Digital Printing Technologies. Salt Lake City, UT, October 31–November 5.

Conway, M. (2003). "Code Wars: Steganography, Signals Intelligence, and Terrorism." *Knowledge, Technology & Policy*, Vol. 16, No. 2, pp. 45–62.

De Vries, Wilbert. (2004, October 26). "Dutch Track Counterfeits Via Printer Serial Numbers." *PC World.* Available at www.pcworld.idg.com.au/index.php/id;1002274598. Accessed 5/20/05.

Dhamija, R., and F. Wallenberg. (2003). "A Framework for Evaluating Digital Rights Management Proposals." In *Proceedings of the First International Mobile IPR Workshop: Rights Management of Information Products on the Mobile Internet.* Available at http://sims.berkeley.edu/~fredrik/research/papers/EvaluatingDRM.html. Accessed 5/20/05.

DRM Technologies. (N.D.). "DRM Technologies: The Foundations of Usable Content Control." Available at www.info-mech.com/drm_technology.html. Accessed 5/6/05.

Electronic Frontier Foundation (EFF). (2001, November 28). "Judge Denies Scientists Free Speech Rights." *EFFector*, Vol. 14, No. 37. Available at www.eff.org/effector/HTML/effect14.37.html#I. Accessed 5/6/05.

Electronic Frontier Foundation (EFF). (2002, December 17). "Jury Acquits Elcomsoft in eBook Copyright Case." Available at www.eff.org/IP/DMCA/US_v_Elcomsoft/20021217_eff_pr.html. Accessed 7/8/05.

Electronic Frontier Foundation (EFF). (2004). "State-Level 'Super DMCA' Initiatives Archive." Available at www.eff.org/IP/DMCA/states. Accessed 3/14/05.

Fisher, D. (2004, September 13). "New Scam Tactic Hits Online." *Eweek.* Available at www.eweek.com. Accessed 5/17/05.

Gross, Robin. (2001). "Digital Millennium Dark Ages." Available at www.virtualrecordings.com/dmda.html. Accessed 7/8/05.

Horvath, J. (2001). "The Internet: A Terrorist Network." Available at www.heise.de/tp/r4/artikel/9/9350/1.html. Accessed 3/18/05.

Hulme, G. V. (2003). "Update: Software Developer Fears Legal Tar Pit." *InformationWeek.* Available at www.informationweek.com/story/showArticle.jhtml?articleID=8800603. Accessed 3/18/05.

Johnson, D. (2001). *Computer Ethics*, 3rd ed. Upper Saddle River, NJ: Prentice Hall, pp. 15–16.

Johnson, N., and S. Jajodia. (1998). "Steganalysis of Images Created Using Current Steganography Software." In 2nd Information Hiding Workshop. Portland, Oregon, April 15–17.

Kelley, J. (2001, February). "Terror Groups Hide Behind Web Encryption." *USA Today*, Available at www.usatoday.com/life/cyber/tech/2001-02-05-binladen.htm. Accessed 3/14/05.

Kessler, G. C. (2004, July). "An Overview of Steganography for the Computer Forensics Examiner." *Forensic Science Communication*, Vol. 6, No. 3. Available at www.fbi.gov/hq/lab/fsc/backissu/july2004/research/2004_03_research01.htm. Accessed 3/17/05.

Lambers, R. (2005, June 15). "Macrovision DMCA Lawsuit Targets DVD Copying Products." Available at http://constitutionalcode.blogspot.com/2005/06/macrovision-dmca-lawsuit-targets-dvd.html. Accessed 7/8/05.

McHugh, John. (2001). "Declaration." Available at www.eff.org/IP/DMCA/Felten_v_RIAA/20010813_mchugh_decl.html. Accessed 3/18/05.

Poulsen, K. (2003, April 14). "'Super-DMCA' Fears Suppress Security Research." *The Register.* Available at www.theregister.co.uk/2003/04/14/superdmca_fears_suppress_security_research/. Accessed 3/17/05.

Provos, N., and P. Honeyman. (2001). "CITI Technical Report 01-11: Detecting Steganographic Content on the Internet." Ann Arbor: University of Michigan Center for Information Technology Integration. Available at www.citi.umich.edu/techreports/reports/citi-tr-01-11.pdf. Accessed 3/14/05.

Schneier, B. (2003). *Beyond Fear: Thinking Sensibly About Security in an Uncertain World.* New York: Copernicus Books.

ThinkQuest. (N.D.). "Cryptology: Classical Steganography." http://library.thinkquest.org/27993/crypto/steg/classic1.shtml?tqskip1=1. Accessed 1/7/05.

Tuohey, J. (2004, November 22). "Government Uses Color Laser Printer Technology to Track Documents." *PC World.* Available at www.pcworld.com/news/article/0,aid,118664,00.asp. Accessed 1/3/05.

von Lohmann, F. (2003). "State 'Super DMCA' Legislation: MPAA's Stealth Attack on Your Living Room." Available at www.eff.org/IP/DMCA/states/200304_sdmca_eff_analysis.php. Accessed 3/23/05.

Wang, H., and S. Wang. (2004, October). "Cyber Warfare: Steganography vs. Steganalysis." *Communications of the ACM*, Vol. 47, No. 10, pp. 76–82.

"Wassenaar Arrangement." (2005). Available at www.wassenaar.org/welcomepage.html. Accessed 7/7/05.

Webopedia. (2006). "Digital Watermark." Available at www.webopedia.com/TERM/D/digital_watermark.htm. Accessed 5/6/05.

Chapter 12: Security in On-Line Games

Kai K. Kimppa, Andy Bissett, and N. Ben Fairweather

The authors first establish the possibility of on-line computer games as being worth examining from a security perspective. Then, several potential Internet security problems that occur with on-line computer games are presented. For each of these, the way in which the vulnerability is exploited, why the vulnerability is exploited, and how the vulnerability might be remedied is studied.

12.1. Introduction

The authors find that the Internet security issue in on-line games is an often overlooked matter. This might have several reasons. On-line games might be considered to be "just entertainment" or "just for children." Alternatively, they might be considered nonproblematic in the sense that there would be no serious security issues. The authors believe that these reasons are not valid, and show why in the following section. Thereafter, the ways in which Internet security issues in on-line games present themselves are examined. For all the areas so considered, the security problems are divided into parts in which it is seen how the security problems emerge and what the potential breaches would be exploited for, and ideas on what should be done to remedy the issues are offered. First, we handle the information collected by the companies providing games and gaming possibilities. Second, so-called account scams are covered. Third, using third-party software in various ways to gain unauthorized entry to the game is discussed. Finally, potential problems with account sharing are looked at. Many of the security problems considered in this article are readily identified in Figure 12.1: account scams, third party software, and trading real money for valuables in the game.

12.2. Are On-Line Games Worth Consideration as a Potential Internet Security Threat?

The computer gaming industry alone is worth US$9.9 billion in the United States (CNN, 2005) and is within an entertainment software industry globally worth US$19 billion yearly (Bissett et al., 2004). Globally, the computer gaming industry is worth AUS$40.9 billion, compared to a movie industry worth AUS$39.6 billion, according

Account Security Alert!

4/10/2005

Recently we have witnessed a large number of World of Warcraft accounts that have been compromised. In order to protect your account from being compromised and possibly banned, please take the advice below to heart:

- Never give out your account name and password
- Only download add-ons from reputable sites
- Never download an add-on that requires you to run an executable (.exe) file
- Always keep your firewall up-to-date and running
- Always keep your anti-virus programs up-to-date and run them frequently
- Never use a power-leveling or gold buying service
- Frequently change your password and use both alphabetic and numeric characters

If you believe that your account has been compromised, please send all the details about the incident to WoWAccountReviewEU@blizzard.com.

Figure 12.1 An example of an actual on-line games–related security alert (Blizzard Entertainment®, Inc., 2005).

to PricewaterhouseCoopers' *Australian Entertainment and Media Outlook Report (2003)* (Computer Games, 2004). For companies such as Sony, it now represents a bigger market than their film or music recording activities. This widespread significance in today's world alone, in the view of the authors, makes it an area of life that should not be casually overlooked. Despite the huge "reach" of on-line computer games, for a number of reasons to be discussed, the phenomenon is commonly thought to be not worthy of serious consideration.

Multiplayer computer games can be played in various ways (for a more technical explanation, see e.g., Smed, Kaukoranta, and Hakonen, [2002]). Among common approaches are (1) using a split screen or "hot seat" play, where players alternate sitting in front of a single computer or console, (2) using peer-to-peer architecture, in which multiple computers form a web with no centralized server, or (3) client/server architecture (which can be one server–multiple clients or multiple servers–multiple clients in a web structure, but for our purposes this division is not relevant). This third situation, however, is typically such that the server can be kept by anyone such as a game hosting company, and the players do not know each other outside the game. This distances the players from each other, and creates a potential for hostile behavior, which results in some of the security threats presented.

12.2.1. Games Are for Kids

We often tend to think that children do not do anything "important." This is not a valid argument for obvious reasons: (1) children do worthwhile things at least for themselves; (2) in both a moral and a security sense, the playing person being a child is not a reason for having less concern for them; (3) considerable amounts (at least to the children) of children's money is spent on the games; and (4) the target age group for average computer game has in any case traditionally been 18 and 35—hardly children—although it is extending at both ends (Bissett et al., 2004). The average age of a computer and videogame player is 29 years (Entertainment Software Association [ESA], 2004).

It should also be remembered that, although the proportion of gamers who are children is often overemphasized, they do nevertheless constitute a significant proportion of the market, which makes the industry unusual among e-businesses, giving rise to security-related issues that do not arise in e-businesses where all (legitimate) customers are adults.

A typical example of a game in which children participate and that includes real money is Habbo Hotel (www.habbohotel.com/habbo/en). This is an on-line game, in which no money needs to be spent and the chat functions can be used for free; however, if the player wants to furnish his or her avatar's room in the hotel, they need to purchase virtual items through text messages on a mobile phone. If unauthorized access were gained, the "items" and a considerable amount of (real) money compared to the income of a child or a teenager could easily be lost.

When children and teenagers play games, their experiences while playing (and surrounding playing the game) may have an impact on forming attitudes, dispositions, and personality. *Ceteris paribus*, the younger the player and the more emotional investment they place in playing the game, the greater these influences are likely to be.

12.2.2. Games Are Low-Level Entertainment, Not Worth Worrying About

Computer games are considered to be only a pastime and thus something that, in themselves, are not very important. However, many players spend extensive amounts of their time playing, so computer games can reasonably be expected to have some importance to them. Indeed, there is evidence, particularly with role-playing games, that players can invest considerable emotional energy in the well-being of their character[1] within the game, and could be severely distressed by harm to that character as a result of security breaches (e.g., Dibbell, 1993; ABC News, 2005[2]). If we reject paternalist views of what is important and thus morally valuable to people, we cannot bypass the issue lightly.

It is now hard to accept that novels would be considered not to be important to people just because they are generally not read for the purposes of work, but yet computer game playing is often seen as something rather trivial and of little consequence. Such cultural assessments can change. Two hundred years ago, an English

---

[1] A *character* is an avatar within the game, which the player directs. The character can be a temporary one, as in the type of game known as "first-person shooters," or a continuing one, for example, in a role-playing game. In real-time strategy games, the characters vary from temporary ones (so-called cannon fodder) to role-playing kinds, which follow the player from one game to another.

[2] Neither the often cited LambdaMOO case or the case of murder because of a stolen virtual sword presented here are due to security breaches. It is, however, not difficult to see similar results due to issues brought forth by security breaches. In the LambdaMOO case, an avatar was "virtually raped"; in the case of the stolen virtual sword, another player was actually stabbed to death with a knife after selling a virtual sword in an auction for the worth of 3 months' average pay in China.

tailor deplored his fellow workers reading "the obscene trash raked up from the pest holes that are unfortunately to be found in every town" (James, 1974, p. 6). Yet the popular novels to which he refers, often published in serial form, helped to foster a genre in which novelists such as Charles Dickens and Henry James, who are now considered central to the Western literary canon, produced some of their best-known work (Kirby, 1991). Whatever one may feel about the relative cultural value of computer games, it would be a mistake to assume that an apparently small matter may not pose a potential security threat.

In more conventional security settings, the importance of a security risk can be, and probably usually should be, related to the amount spent in combating the threat. A consequence of the greater emotional than economic investment in gaming is that on-line games provide one arena where disproportionate emotional damage can result.

12.2.3. The General Threat

By definition, on-line games involve large amounts of shared data within the gaming "domain." The environment is highly interactive—potentially, any part of the data is susceptible to modification by another party; otherwise, the game would be static, unrealistic, and meaningless. Although the early self-contained computer games were satisfactory so far as they went, as massively multiplayer games (MMORPGs) have gone on-line, their players have come to expect ever-greater interactivity and "realism." Furthermore, this is all expected in a reasonable simulacrum of real time. Given all this, there is little time for checking of access and blocking of data modification.

Many of the potential security threats have emerged from, or are associated with, cheating methods, such as third-party applications. Such "cheats" are extensive and ubiquitous (Kimppa and Bissett, 2005), and may be linked to a culture among a significant proportion of game players that everything is permitted within the game except that which is technically prevented (Fairweather, 2000). With little modification, these factors provide the seed of the security threat. Thus, for example, Sony BMG Digital Rights Management software can be modified to allow players to cheat in the World of Warcraft MMORPG by bypassing the cheat-prevention program, "the Warden," installed with the game by sending sys commands to the server (SecurityFocus, 2005).

Some of the security problems are common to all Internet applications. Others are more specific to on-line games and have shared characteristics with the cheating methods that have emerged. Sometimes the security breaches are used to gain advantages in relation to the particular game played (such as being able to play without having to pay for the privilege); other times, the breaches may be used for more generic purposes, such as direct money making through selling items gained through the security breach in a network auction. These problems are discussed in the next sections.

These discussions go some way toward explaining why computer games are often seen as a trivial question, considered to be of slight interest to anyone beyond the, admittedly large, circle of people believed (in this view) to be the "nerds" and obsessives who make up on-line gaming communities. In the next sections, we begin to outline why this mistaken view can blind one to the security problems that can accompany these activities.

12.3. Information Given to the Game Hosting Company

MMORPGs or any other monthly billed games have similarities to other on-line services, be it music downloads, movie "screenings," or e-commerce. For the business to operate, billing information must be supplied by the customer (in this case a game player).

12.3.1. What Information Is Given to the Company, and Why?

A lot of information is typically requested to play or purchase a game on-line. Information such as credit card or billing information, e-mail, phone numbers, and especially (but not only) for purchasing games on-line, the postal address of the purchaser is requested. A lot of this information is of course necessary for the company, but companies may well ask for more information than is strictly necessary to operate the account,[3] so as to gather information and contact details useful for marketing. In a globalizing world, it is very difficult for a customer to know what exactly is done with the information he or she gives to the company.

Many on-line companies are well known and respected, but many are also small and unknown. The information can travel easily from one country to another, and even if we expect a citizen to be aware of the laws governing him or her in his or her own country, it would be too much to expect them to know what the laws of other countries may allow to be done with the information. A typical example of this is "spam" (unsolicited e-mail). In the European Union (EU, 2002) the opt-in system, in which the customer must request commercial messages through e-mail for them to be sent, is in place; however, in the United States (USC, 2004), for example, an opt-out system is in place, where the customer must specifically forbid such messages (or often cancel further messages after he or she has already received an unsolicited commercial message).

12.3.2. How Can the Information Given to the Company Produce an Internet Security Threat?

Information given to game hosting companies faces all the same security threats that information given to any company working through the Internet faces. However, because that is not the focus of this chapter and other chapters in this volume handle those issues more thoroughly, we concentrate on the issues specific to on-line gaming companies. Not all employees of these companies play games themselves. They may hold views introduced in the second section of the paper. It is difficult to see that a majority of a game hosting company's support personnel would be gamers themselves, and many could well share the commonly held view that the games are no more than low-level entertainment, affecting their view of the importance of their job.

For example, one of the authors of this article has been asked to provide an e-mail address to download a patch for a game already fully paid for. It is difficult to see what legitimate reason there could be for that.

If there is an ethos that the information held is not important or valuable except to the business and its competitors, there is a very real danger that a culture of lax security about individuals' data will prevail. This could be particularly worrying where players are children.[4] Morality suggests that the level of protection afforded personal data about children should be significantly greater than the level of protection for data about adults.

As with so many on-line phenomena, there are different laws in different places about how the information can be used, although the games are internationally played and the information typically (at least in Europe and the Americas) transmitted to another jurisdiction from that of the user (see, e.g., the spam laws previously mentioned). Thus, the user very rarely understands the ways in which they "agree" for their information to be used when they click the "I agree" button. The problem is particularly severe with children who may not have sufficient intellectual or linguistic ability and judgement to meaningfully enter such an agreement; and, as elsewhere, the vast bulk of users (including adults) are unlikely to read the end-user license "agreement" (EULA).[5]

12.3.3. Solutions

There is a need for technical action, managerial action, and changes to the law to improve the practical security with respect to the personal data of on-line game players. The technical measures needed include appropriate use of encryption, technical measures to ensure restricted access to personal data, and logging of accesses to personal data. Management of game hosting companies should, similarly, ensure adequate staff training.

To make the task of understanding agreements more practical, there is a need for consolidation of common clauses into statute law. There is also a need for more robust enforcement of existing protections, and we suspect that there is a need for particular regulation of data about children, who cannot reasonably be expected to take the levels of responsibility for their own data that competent adults can. In particular, there need to be measures to reduce the likelihood that children will use on-line facilities and games that they do not know are regulated by the laws of much less protective jurisdictions.

12.4. Account Scams

In addition to the ways usernames and passwords are illicitly acquired in other on-line contexts, on-line gaming allows spamming of official requests to chats within the game (and elsewhere). These official requests clearly originated as cheats within the game (Kimppa and Bissett, 2005), but have corresponding potential to be used to breach security. Because there is a growing opportunity for criminals to

---

[4]We know, for example, of children as young as 6 playing on-line games.

[5]Indeed, a significant proportion of adults would be unable to penetrate the highly complex legalistic language of EULAs anyway; moreover, we are aware of such an "agreement" of more than 4,500 words that requires users, as part of the "agreement," to review it "on at least a weekly basis" in a game directed specifically to children and teenagers (Sulake Labs, 2005).

convert on-line "goods" into hard currency,[6] e-mail contacts similar to bank spam mails may additionally become more important.

12.4.1. Why Are Usernames and Passwords Abused?

12.4.1.1. Access to the Game

Sometimes, but comparatively rarely, illicit access may be used simply to play the game. The limitation of this is that if the original user can see that someone else has used their account, they are likely to contact the server keeper or at least change their password. An example of how illicit access may be used quite successfully would be the game "World of Warcraft," in which there exist several servers in several different language areas. If the owner of the account uses only one server for playing, he or she practically never needs to look at the other servers and thus would not know that someone else has created characters there and is using his or her account as well. Also, one could create the characters on other language regions. If the player is not capable of speaking English, but instead only plays on German or French servers, he or she would not be aware of the other characters on the other language servers. Finally, if the player is a very infrequent player, the illicit access could go on for quite some time.

12.4.1.2. Access to Characters

Within games, it is normally possible to "move" characters from one account to another. Where this relates to a security breach, this typically will be to the adversary's own account, but it is also possible that they would be moved to the accounts of purchasers where the character is sold by the adversary. In such cases, the considerable amount of time spent developing the character is lost by the original player. It is, of course, technically possible to keep track of the movements of characters moved between accounts, but we have no knowledge of a game in which it is done (perhaps because to do so would increase the overheads of the hosting company). Also, there is a privacy issue, although a rather minor one, in extending the user's database to include this data. Other fixes to this have been recently attempted, such as restricting access to characters to those created by a client who has a certain code. It is likely, however, that there exists third-party software that can be used to fake the codes (as we have seen in the past with other games).

Players may also seek to gain access to characters for other purposes, which may be related to interpersonal relationships either within or outside the game. Thus, a character could be abused to gain revenge (whether for an on-line or offline act).[7] Players may also seek to gain access to other's characters simply out of malice.

---

[6]On the value of the items and characters see, for example, Castronova (2001): "the auction market puts the shadow price of an avatar level at about $13 per level, and data from the NES show that Norrath's avatars create about $15,000 in avatar capital in an hour. This makes the gross national product of Norrath about $135 million. Per capita, it comes to $2,266. According to GNP data from the World Bank, Norrath is the 77th richest country in the world, roughly equal to Russia."

[7]Such cases are more likely between people who are acquainted offline, where the offline acquaintance may provide opportunities to learn usernames and passwords.

12.4.1.3. Access to Items

Characters are not the only objects within games that can be moved from account to account. Within games, there are also representations of items which typically can comprise individual "possessions" of characters within the game. Much of the game play, for many players, revolves around acquiring and making use of these possessions, which thus become objects of desire. Because sometimes obtaining these objects requires considerable skill, effort, and/or luck within the game, players may try to find methods outside of the game to obtain coveted items. Short-term and comparatively minor abuse of someone else's character may be sufficient to expropriate from that character some of the items they "own,"[8] possibly unnoticed. Again, a considerable amount of time spent acquiring the item is typically lost; only valuable items (at least in the game currency, but also often in real currency) are considered worth stealing, and legitimately acquiring such items through game play typically requires countless hours of play.

Access to items can be sought for a variety of reasons: The adversary may seek the items because they directly want them for their own character(s) within the game. Alternatively, the adversary may seek the items to sell them within the game, thus making it easier to obtain other, coveted items. A third possible reason is so that the virtual items could be sold in auctions (such as eBay) outside the game using on-line theft of virtual items to generate offline income. Fourth, the items may be coveted so they can be duplicated with third-party software, which sends duplicating commands to the server. These illicit duplicates then are sold either in-game or in auctions. For example, in "Diablo II," there was for quite some time a possibility to send a certain code to the game to duplicate an item the character had in their possession.[9] This "inflated" the economy of the game where a certain "magic item," namely the Stone of Jordan Ring, was used as "currency" instead of the "official currency" of the game. These duplicated rings were even sold in on-line auctions before they became so common that their price was negligible.

Where on-line virtual "possessions" are traded for offline money, there is always a significant potential for there to be a "spillover" between on-line activity and offline consequences. We are aware of on-line activities being implicated in a murder, with one player murdering a competitor who had stolen and subsequently sold for cash a virtual sword (Krotoski, 2005). In another case, a player carried out a "virtual mugging spree" by using a game character controlled by an unbeatable software agent to beat up and rob characters in the on-line computer game "Lineage II" (Knight, 2005). The stolen virtual possessions were subsequently exchanged for real cash.

12.4.2. Solutions

Although in-game "crime" can be problematic, it does not appear to us to be necessary to use technical measures or policing to drive in-game crime out of exis-

---

[8]For a more thorough handling on who owns the items, see Reynolds (2002).

[9]This has happened accidentally to one of the authors—an item duplicated itself in the inventory of a character accidentally and was available to be given to other characters—through a glitch in the program that could be repeated on purpose. The author, of course, destroyed the accidentally received duplicate.

tence. The added realism or complexity of games in which such things may happen may add to user experience. Simulated worlds are not, after all, the real world, and it is not unreasonable for people to want to experience a simulation of life in lawless situations as a diversion from their real life.

We do, however, advocate monitoring and censoring of communications in in-game chats and so on, so that usernames and passwords are not phished within the game. It may be advisable to use technical means to restrict user access to characters created with a client which has a certain code. Where games simulate lawless situations or otherwise do not offer adequate policing of in-game crime, this must be made perfectly clear to those playing the game (using measures more obvious to the user than the EULA).

Law needs to be clarified to ensure that where a game offers in-game policing, there is no gap between in-game policing and real-world policing that can be exploited by adversaries. It may be appropriate to restrict access by children to on-line games to those where there is adequate in-game policing that marries up with real-world policing adequately. Also, the law should be clear on what can be considered to be owned by whom (Reynolds, 2002). If, as in the earlier example of a theft of a virtual sword, the auction value of the sword was in the level of 3 months' earnings in China, or if the worth of a character in an on-line game can be worth US$ 13 per level (presumably up to and beyond US$1300 for a level-100 character; Castranova, 2001), the issue seems to warrant consideration even in offline law.

12.5. Third-Party Software

As with other security-relevant situations, third-party software such as trojans can be problematic in on-line gaming. The problem, however, can be particularly bad because game developers may use third parties to distribute software patches, leaving users with additional uncertainties about the trustworthiness of the distributors. Moreover, there can be third-party enhancements (such as user interface enhancements) that may be positively authorized by the game developer; third-party enhancements that are permitted (but not encouraged) by the developer; enhancements that are formally discouraged, but not seen as a security breach (in themselves); and ones countered by the developer or distributor of the game using technical means so far as possible.

12.5.1. Why Is Third-Party Software a Security Threat?

To some extent, then, whether third-party software is used legitimately or itself abuses the game depends on the attitude of the developers. Third-party software, when it comes to on-line games, is typically abused to enable cheating in various ways (see Kimppa and Bissett, 2005). The abuse includes packet sniffing software, which then tries to send false data packets to the server (e.g., for item duplication purposes, to help aiming, or to enhance "damage"). Third-party software can also be included on top of the client in the player's end. Such software could be, for example, "wallhacks," which "sniff" the incoming data from the server and remove obstacles from the terrain while adding information that the player is not supposed to know. The player then is effectively able to see through the representations of walls in the game.

Beyond software that is nominally opposed by the game developers, third-party software causes problems with reliability of the game.[10] Further, it may try to exploit holes in server–client communication, either for the benefit of the user or, through trojan code, for the benefit of its authors or other parties.

A general problem with Web sites is the possibility of their being defaced for malicious purposes. A more subtle and dangerous case arises with the planting of "daemon"-like code that executes when a particular set of circumstances occurs. Given the openness and dynamic operation of multiuser game environments, the possibilities here for a wide range of malignant actions whose occurrence is unpredictable and difficult to replicate are considerable.

12.5.2. Solutions

12.5.2.1. Finishing Development

The logically simplest solution to this problem is for games to be produced that work properly, having good interfaces (without third-party enhancements) even when released. Unfortunately, the economics of game development (as with other software development) works against this (Williams, 2002).[11] However, it may be possible for legal systems and reviewers in the media, or the media in general, to increase the costs to the developers of releasing buggy and shoddy products, and thereby induce developers to spend more on finishing products before release. There may also be a role for professional societies in promoting good practice.

12.5.2.2. Games with Inbuilt Detection of Unauthorized Code

To some extent, it is possible for game developers to increase the security of their games by incorporating systems for the detection of unauthorized code or activity (Le Charlier, Mounji, and Swimmer, 1995). It is not entirely clear whether this would be a desirable development; the economics of game development suggests that unfinished games will continue to be released to answer to the competition in the field. Further, the creativity of players and developers can reasonably be expressed in the production of third-party enhancements.

12.5.2.3. User Education

Because unfinished games can be expected to continue to be released, and the production of third-party enhancements may be desirable, user education is a necessary part of the solution to the security problems of third-party software in gaming. The threshold of awareness that is required of users should, however, be lowered. Developers should have a role in the distribution of bug fixes and authorized and

---

[10]This is more of a problem with unauthorized third-party software, but it can also be a problem with some of the authorized software when not functioning correctly.

[11]Williams notes that, historically, personal computer (PC) games have been frequently released with bugs, whereas console games almost never had bugs. Williams explains the difference is that "PC games can be fixed retroactively with software 'patches'," whereas console games historically could not be. By definition, on-line games, whatever platform, have access to on-line patches.

tested enhancements through channels that even inexperienced players and Web users can recognize as being trustworthy.[12]

12.6. Sharing Accounts

Sharing of accounts has been a mainstream security problem for a long time, but one that has been of receding importance in societies that have been computerized for a long time as the resources accounts give access to have become cheaper. Increasing penetration of computing—and gaming—into less wealthy cultures where there is less of a culture of individualism, and a greater culture of sharing, is giving the problem new life.

12.6.1. Why Is Account Sharing a Security Threat?

Typically, many persons use one account to divide up the fee of using the game among the players, by leaving the account open, even when the individual player has finished their gameplaying session, or by using the same login details on the same or different computers.

There are two types of ways in which account sharing could be considered a security threat: First, the providers of games are likely to consider the very sharing of accounts as a security problem, in that it may reduce the revenue they collect. The issues here are in principle no different from the security issues of other on-line services.

Second, there is the issue of security between players of the game using a shared account. Although the situation may appear identical to the game suppliers (from the data exchanges at least), it differs from one player using many computers for several reasons. First, the person using the game from many computers is always the same person. Thus, all potential threats fall to the one person and his or her account, not to other people. When several people share an account, there is no guarantee that they all treat the account with same amount of care and can thus cause problems for the other players. Perhaps the clearest threat to the players in this kind of situation, especially in an open environment such as an Internet Café, would be leaving the account open and thus giving access to the account to an unknown third party who could then use the account as they please: send items to others, erase characters, and so forth. Typically, however, the user's financial information is safe because the account itself does not give access to banking information. Games that are billed monthly tend to use a separate interface that requires the password to be re-input before any information is accessible (or even use a separate password). In these situations, it is not so much the account sharing that is the problem, as the interaction between the players sharing an account that it enables.

In some countries, on-line games are played in Internet Cafés[13] from an "open account," from which time is sold to the users separately. In many of the cases, the

---

[12]To at least a reasonable extent.

[13]For example, China, India, South Korea—Internet cafés are common elsewhere too, but not so much for playing as in the East.

use is at least not in accordance with the license of use. Of course, in many countries the licenses that come with the games are not binding. There are various reasons for this—for example, local intellectual property law might not be in accordance with the law of the country in which the license is designed. Further, the applicability of contracts with parties in other countries may depend on treaties, and it may be that agreement by electronically ticking a check box does not fulfill the requirements under such treaties.

12.6.2. Solutions

The simplest, partial solution may be for game hosting companies to reduce charges in markets where account sharing is prevalent. This certainly will improve the situation for players. Because the marginal cost associated with running each account is minimal, this has a real prospect of being financially viable for the hosting companies. Access to on-line gaming from the point of view of infrastructure will remain a problem, however. Personal computers still tend to be expensive for many in these markets, as are the costs of personal Internet access.

12.7. Conclusions

There are various kinds of Internet security problems with on-line games. None of them are essentially unique, although when found elsewhere they may not be in the same format. Also, some issues are more significant in on-line games than anywhere else. What makes on-line games different? One difference is that the area is often overlooked.

A second difference is that many of these security problems might not seem as financially important as security problems in other fields, which explains some of the lack of interest in them. They are, however, often very important to the user of these services; the emotional investment may be greater. So, for example, an account scam can destroy a lot of effort from the person in question. This has particular consequences that are worthy of note. Another difference is that a higher proportion of those affected by security problems with on-line games may be children.

A further difference is that, for a significant proportion of users, on-line games are the most likely application in which account owner information will be delivered to a third country. The result might be to put the given information under a legislative system not familiar to the user and thus open possibilities for the use of the information of which the user was not aware.

References

ABC News Online. (2005, March 30). "Online Gamer Killed for Selling Cyber Sword." Available at www.abc.net.au/news/newsitems/200503/s1334618.htm. Accessed 10/31/05.

Bissett, A., P. Parry, I. Ritchie, B. Steele, and P. Vacher. (2004). "Addressing Ethics in Entertainment Software Development." In *Proceedings of Ethicomp 2004*. Syros, Greece: University of the Aegean, April 14–16, 2004, pp. 143–149.

Blizzard. (2005). "Account Security Alert." Available at www.wow-europe.com/en/news/wow-oldnews.html. Accessed 11/18/05.

Castronova, Edward. (2001, December). "Virtual Worlds: A First-Hand Account of Market and Society on the Cyberian Frontier [CESifo Working Paper No. 618]. Available at http://papers.ssrn.com/sol3/Delivery.cfm/SSRN_ID294828_code020114590.pdf?abstrac-tid=294828&mirid=3. Accessed 11/7/05.

CNN. (2005). "Video Game Sales Jump 8 Percent in 2004." Available at http://money.cnn.com/2005/01/18/technology/gamesales/. Accessed 7/7/06.

Computer Games. (2004). "Game Play: Australian Game Developers Are Finding a World Market, But They Want the Same Tax Concessions as Film Makers." Available at www.gdaa.asn.au/e3australia/brw_july_2004.pdf. Accessed 3/10/05.

Dibbell, J. A. (1993, December 23). "A Rape in Cyberspace: How an Evil Clown, a Haitian Trickster Spirit, Two Wizards, and a Cast of Dozens Turned a Database into a Society." *The Village Voice*, pp. 36–42. Also available at www.juliandibbell.com/texts/bungle_vv.html. Accessed 9/30/05.

Entertainment Software Association (ESA). (2004). "Essential Facts About the Computer and Video Game Industry: 2004 Sales, Demographics and Usage Data." Available at www.theesa.com/files/EFBrochure.pdf. Accessed 4/26/05.

European Union (EU). (2002). "The European Directive 2002/58/EC." Available at http://europa.eu.int/eur-lex/pri/en/oj/dat/2002/l_201/l_20120020731en00370047.pdf. Accessed 11/18/05.

Fairweather, N. Ben. (2000). "Cool New Cheats: Cheating and the Computer Games Industry, 2000." Conference on Sports Ethics, St. Martin's College, Lancaster, England.

James, L. (1974). *Fiction for the Working Man 1830–50: A Study of the Literature Produced for the Working Classes in Early Victorian Urban England*. New York: Penguin.

Kimppa, Kai K., and Andrew Bissett. (2005, July 17–19). "Is Cheating in Network Computer Games a Question Worth Raising?" In *Sixth International Conference of Computer Ethics: Philosophical Enquiry (CEPE2005)*. Enschede, The Netherlands, pp. 259–267.

Kirby, D. (1991). *The Portrait of a Lady and The Turn of the Screw: Henry James and Melodrama*. New York: Macmillan.

Knight, W. (2005). "Computer Characters Mugged in Virtual Crime Spree." Available at www.newscientist.com/article.ns?id=dn7865&feedId=online-news_rss2. Accessed 11/18/05.

Krotoski, A. (2005, March 30). Virtual Sword Theft Results in Real-Life Retribution." Available at http://blogs.guardian.co.uk/games/archives/2005/03/30/virtual_sword_theft_results_in_real-life_retribution.html. Accessed 11/18/05.

Le Charlier, B., A. Mounji, and M. Swimmer. (1995, September 20–22). "Dynamic Detection and Classification of Computer Viruses Using General Behaviour Patterns." In *Proceedings of Fifth International Virus Bulletin Conference*. Boston.

Reynolds, Ren. (2002). "Intellectual Property Rights in Community Based Video Games." In *Proceedings of Ethicomp 2002*. Universidade Lusíada, Lisbon, Portugal, pp. 455–470.

SecurityFocus. (2005, March 11). "World of Warcraft Hackers Using Sony BMG Rootkit." Available at http://online.securityfocus.com/brief/34. Accessed 11/7/05.

Smed, J., T. Kaukoranta, and H. Hakonen. (2002). "Aspects of Networking in Multiplayer Computer Games." *The Electronic Library*, Vol. 20, No. 2, pp. 87–97.

Sulake Labs. (2005). "Terms of Use." Available at www.habbo.com/footer_pages/terms_and_conditions.html. Accessed 11/7/05.

United States Congress. (2004). "The CAN-SPAM Act of 2003 [Public Law 108-187] of January 1, 2004." Available at www.spamlaws.com/pdf/pl108-187.pdf. Accessed 11/7/05.

Williams, D. (2002). "Structure and Competition in the U.S. HomeVideo Game Industry." *International Journal on Media Management*. Vol. 4, No. I, pp. 41–54.

Chapter 13: Privacy, Intellectual Property, and Hacking: Evaluating Free Access Arguments

Adam Moore

Advancements in computer networks, communication pipelines, and information tech-nologies of all sorts are radically changing the human experience—as life-altering as the changes that flowed from the introduction of Gutenberg's press, Darwin's theory of evolution, or Pasteur's germ theory of disease. Our money is stored and transmit-ted digitally. We listen to music files on small, handheld devices—files of songs that, in many cases, were originally recorded with analog technology, converted to digital format, and are now floating around computer networks. Spyware, video monitoring, and data surveillance are opening up private lives to those who are connected and know how to manipulate these technologies.

In modern times, the debate over access to information and intellectual prop-erty has been waged by two factions. Standing in the way of the cyberpunks, hack-ers, and Net surfers who claim that "information wants to be free" are the defenders of Anglo-American copyright, patent, trade secret, and privacy law. Those who defend a model of restricted access to information argue that authors and inven-tors have rights to control the intellectual works that they produce and individu-als have privacy rights that shield private information from public consumption. In both cases, accessing, trading, or manipulating the information in question is seen as a kind of trespass—a zone of control has been violated without justifica-tion.

Those who champion free access argue that an "author-centered" paradigm gives undue credit to innovators. If we view authors, inventors, and most importantly, information, as a social product, then it is not clear why individuals and corpora-tions should be allowed to hoard and control content at the expense of society. Hackers have held that information belongs to everyone and that access to com-puter systems should be unlimited and unrestricted. Support for this view is found in current attitudes related to file sharing. It is estimated that for every legitimate copy of software there are between 2 and 10 illegal copies costing software pro-ducers over $10 billion in lost revenue annually (Business Software Alliance, Software & Information Industry Association, 1999; see also James, 2002). The justification typically given for such pirating is that "owners still have their copy."

Hacking networks rather than software is also a common occurrence. Automated attack tools have progressed so that meaningful analysis of network hacking attempts is impossible. Computers and networks of all sorts are being probed nearly around the clock (Carnegie Mellon Software Engineering Institute, N.D.). Many of those who engage in these activities argue that they are performing a public service by finding security flaws.

Before considering the hacking and "free-access" position, I present several arguments in support of privacy and intellectual property. If these arguments are compelling, then a moral presumption in favor of controlling personal information and intangible works is established. Next, three arguments typically given by hackers and those who champion the "free-access" view are considered. After a presentation and analysis, I argue that the hacker position about information access and control is not strong enough to override the moral presumptions in favor of intellectual property and privacy—"information should not be free."

13.1. Establishing a Presumption in Favor of Privacy[1]

I favor what has been called a "control" based definition of privacy. That is, privacy has to do with control over access to oneself and to information about oneself (Allen, 2003; Fried, 1970; Gavison, 1983; Gross, 1971; Parker, 1974; Van Den Haag, 1971; Wasserstrom, 1979). Privacy may be understood as a right to control both tokens and types. In terms of tokens, privacy yields control over access to one's body, capacities, and powers. A privacy right in this sense is a right to control access to a specific token or object. But we may also control access to sensitive personal information about ourselves. In this sense, a privacy right affords control over types or ideas. For example, when a rape victim suppresses the dissemination of sensitive personal information about herself, she is exercising a right to control a set of ideas no matter what form they take. It does not matter if the information in question is written, recorded, spoken, or fixed in some other fashion.

To gain a sense of the importance of privacy and separation, it is helpful to consider similar interests shared by many nonhuman animals. Although privacy rights may entail obligations and claims against others—obligations and claims that are beyond the capacities of most nonhuman animals—a case can still be offered in support of the claim that separation is valuable for animals. Even though privacy may be linked to free will, the need for separation provides an evolutionary first step. Perhaps it is the capacity of free will that changes mere separation into privacy. Alan Westin, in *Privacy and Freedom*, notes,

---

[1]Part of this section on privacy was originally published in "Privacy: Its Meaning and Value," (2003).

One basic finding of animal studies is that virtually all animals seek periods of individual seclusion of small-group intimacy. This is usually described as the tendency toward territoriality, in which an organism lays private claim to an area of land, water, or air and defends it against intrusion by members of its own species. (1968, p. 8)

More important for our purposes are the ecological studies demonstrating that a lack of private space, due to overpopulation and the like, threatens survival. Under such conditions, animals may kill each other or engage in suicidal reductions of the population. Lemmings may march into the sea or there may be what is called a "biochemical die-off."

Given that humans evolved from nonhuman animals, it is plausible to think that we retain many of the same traits. For example, Lewis Mumford notes similarities between rat overcrowding and human overcrowding. "No small part of this ugly urban barbarization has been due to sheer physical congestion: a diagnosis now partly confirmed by scientific experiments with rats—for when they are placed in equally congested quarters, they exhibit the same symptoms of stress, alienation, hostility, sexual perversion, parental incompetence, and rabid violence that we now find in Megapolis" (1961, p. 210).[2] These results are supported by numerous more recent studies (Baum and Koman, 1976; Clauson-Kaas, et al., 1996; Edwards and Both, 1977; Farrington and Nuttal, 1980; Fuller et al., 1996; Morgan, 1972; Paulus, Cox, and McCain, 1978; Ruback and Carr, 1984). Overcrowding in prisons has been linked to violence (Megargee, 1977; Porporino and Dudley, 1984), depression (Cox, Paulus, and McCain, 1984), suicide (McCain, Cox, and Paulus, 1980), psychological disorders (Paulus et al., 1978), and recidivism (Farrington and Nuttal, 1980). If so, like other basic requirements for living, we may plausibly conclude that privacy is valuable.

Having said something about what a right to privacy is and why it is valuable, we may ask how privacy rights are justified. A promising line of argument combines notions of autonomy and respect for persons. A central and guiding principle of Western liberal democracies is that individuals, within certain limits, may set and pursue their own life goals and projects. Rights to privacy erect a moral boundary that allows individuals the moral space to order their lives as they see fit. Clinton Rossiter puts the point succinctly:

Privacy is a special kind of independence, which can be understood as an attempt to secure autonomy in at least a few personal and spiritual concerns, if necessary in defiance of all the pressures of the modern society. . . . It seeks to erect an unbreachable wall of dignity

---

[2]This view is echoed by Desmond Morris who writes, "Each kind of animal has evolved to exist in a certain amount of living space. In both the animal zoo and the human zoo [when] this space is severely curtailed . . . the consequences can be serious" (1969, p. 39).

and reserve against the entire world. The free man is the private man, the man who still keeps some of his thoughts and judgments entirely to himself, who feels no over-riding compulsion to share everything of value with others, not even those he loves and trusts. (1985, p. 188)

Privacy protects us from the prying eyes and ears of governments, corporations, and neighbors. Within the walls of privacy, we may experiment with new ways of living that may not be accepted by the majority. Privacy, autonomy, and sovereignty, it seems, come bundled together.

A second but related line of argument rests on the claim that privacy rights stand as a bulwark against governmental oppression and totalitarian regimes. If individuals have rights to control personal information and to limit access to themselves within certain constraints, then the kinds of oppression that we have witnessed in the 20th century would be nearly impossible. Put another way, if oppressive regimes are to consolidate and maintain power, then privacy rights, broadly defined, must be eliminated or severely restricted. If correct, privacy rights would be a core value that limits the forces of oppression (see DeCew, 1997; Frankel et al., 2000; Fried, 1968; Rachels, 1975; Schoeman, 1992).

Arguably any plausible account of human well being or flourishing will have as a component a strong right to privacy. Controlling who has access to ourselves is an essential part of being a happy and free person. This may be why "peeping Toms" and rapists are held up as moral monsters—they cross a boundary that should never be crossed without consent.

Surely each of us has the right to control our own thoughts, hopes, feelings, and plans, as well as a right to restrict access to information about our lives, family, and friends. I would argue that what grounds these sentiments is a right to privacy—a right to maintain a certain level of control over personal information. Although complete control of all our personal information is a pipe dream for many of us, simply because the information is already out there and most likely cannot or will not be destroyed, this does not detract from the view of personal information ownership. Through our daily activities, we each create and leave digital footprints that others may follow and exploit—and that we do these things does not obviously sanction the gathering and subsequent disclosure of such information by others.

Whatever kind of information we are considering, there is a gathering point that individuals have control over. For example, in purchasing a new car and filling out the car loan application, no one would deny we each have the right to demand that such information not be sold to other companies. I argue that this is true for any disclosed personal information, whether it be patient questionnaire information, video rental records, voting information, or credit applications. In agreeing with this view, one first has to agree that individuals have the right to control their own personal information, that is, binding agreements about controlling information presuppose that one of the parties has the right to control this information.

If all of this is correct, then we have a fairly compelling case in support of the view that individuals have moral claims to control access to specific places and things and also to certain kinds of information; we have established a presumption in favor of privacy.

13.2. Establishing a Presumption in Favor of Intellectual Property[3]

Anglo-American systems of intellectual property are typically justified on utilitarian grounds.[4] The United States' Constitution grants limited rights to authors and inventors of intellectual property "to promote the progress of science and the useful arts" (§ 8, cl. 8). Beginning with the first Patent Act of 1790 and continuing through the adoption of Berne Convention Standards in 1989, the basis given for Anglo-American systems of intellectual property is utilitarian in nature, and not grounded in the natural rights of the author or inventor.[5] Thomas Jefferson, a central figure in the formation of American systems of intellectual property, expressly rejected any natural rights foundation for granting control to authors and inventors over their intellectual work. "The patent monopoly was not designed to secure the inventor his natural right in his discoveries. Rather, it was a reward, and inducement, to bring forth new knowledge" (Francis and Collins, 1995, p. 92). Society seeks to maximize utility in the form of scientific and cultural progress by granting rights to authors and inventors as an incentive toward such progress. In general, patents, copyrights, and trade secrets are devices, created by statute, to prevent the diffusion of information before the author or inventor has recovered profit adequate to induce such investment. The justification typically given for Anglo-American systems of intellectual property "is that by slowing down the diffusion of information . . . it ensures that there will be more information to diffuse" (Nelkin, 1984, p. 15). Moreover, utilitarian based justifications of intellectual property are elegantly simple. Control is granted to authors and inventors of intellectual property because granting such control provides incentives necessary for social progress.

---

[3]For an in-depth analysis of the utilitarian incentives-based argument for intellectual property, see Moore (2003) and *Intellectual Property and Information Control* (2004).

[4]*See* United States Congress (1909). The courts have also reflected this theme: "The copyright law . . . . makes reward to the owner a secondary consideration" (*United States v. Paramount Pictures*, 1948). "The limited scope of the copyright holder's statutory monopoly, like the limited copyright duration required by the Constitution, reflects a balance of competing claims on the public interest: Creative work is to be encouraged and rewarded, but private motivation must ultimately serve the cause of promoting broad public availability of literature, music, and other arts" (*Twentieth Century Music Corp. v. Aiken*, 1974).

[5]This view is echoed in the following denials of a common law right to intellectual property. "Wheaton established as a bedrock principle of American copyright law that copyright, with respect to a published work, is a creature of statute and not the product of the common law" (Halpern, Shipley, and Abrams, 1992, p. 6). The General Court of Massachusetts (1641) adopted the following provision: "There shall be no monopolies granted or allowed among us, but of such new inventions as are profitable to the country, and that for a short time" (Deller, 1964). "The monopoly did not exist at common law, and the rights, therefore, which may be exercised under it cannot be regulated by the rule of common law. It is created by the act of Congress; and no rights can be acquired in it unless authorized by statute, and in the manner the statute prescribes" (*Gayler et al. v. Wilder*, 1850). See also, *Sony Corp. of America v. Universal Studios Inc.* (1984), *Weaton v. Peters* (1834), and *Graham v. John Deere Co.*, 383 US 1, 9 (1966).

Coupled with the theoretical claim that society ought to maximize social utility, we arrive at a simple yet powerful argument.[6]

13.2.1. A Second Argument in Favor of the Intellectual Property Presumption[7]

Independent of social progress or utility maximization arguments, John Locke offered what has become known as the *labor theory of acquisition*. Locke claimed "[f]or this labor being the unquestionable property of the laborer, no man but he can have a right to what that is once joined to, at least where there is *enough and as good left for others*" (Locke, 1698, §27; italics added). As long as the proviso that "enough and as good" is satisfied, an acquisition is of prejudice to no one. Locke argues that "[n]obody could think himself injured by the drinking of another man, though he took a good draught, who had a whole river of the same left him to quench his thirst . . ." (Locke, 1698, §33).

Suppose that mixing one's labor with an unowned object creates a prima facie claim against others not to interfere that can only be overridden by a comparable claim. The role of the proviso is to provide one possible set of conditions where the prima facie claim remains undefeated (see Wolf [1995] for a good summary of this view). Another way of stating this position is that the proviso in addition to X, where X is labor or first occupancy or some other weak claim generating activity, provides a sufficient condition for original appropriation.

Justification for the view that labor or possession may generate prima facie claims against others could proceed along several lines. First, labor, intellectual effort, and creation are generally voluntary activities that can be unpleasant, exhilarating, and everything in between.[8] That we voluntarily do these things as sovereign moral agents may be enough to warrant noninterference claims against others. A second, and possibly related justification, is based on merit. Sometimes individuals who voluntarily do or fail to do certain things deserve some outcome or other. Thus, students may deserve high honor grades and criminals may deserve punishment. When notions of desert are evoked, claims and obligations are made against others—these nonabsolute claims and obligations are generated by what individuals do or fail to do. Thus, in fairly uncontroversial cases of desert, we are willing to acknowledge that weak claims are generated, and if desert can properly attach to labor or creation, then claims may be generated in these cases as well.

---

[6]Please note that both of the arguments offered in support of intellectual property may not end up sanctioning particular rules or practices found in current Anglo-American institutions of copyright, patent, and trade secret. For example, the incentives-based social utility argument would not likely support the current term limits on copyrights and patents; there is no reason to think that incentives and utility have been maximized by insisting on copyrights that last the lifetime of the author plus 70 years (20 years for patents). See Moore (2003) and *Intellectual Property and Information Control* (2004). Also, the Lockean/Pareto argument would not support exclusive patent rights—those who independently invent an already patented intellectual work would be worsened.

[7]A more lengthy analysis of intangible property rights appears in *Intellectual Property and Information Control* (2004), "Intangible Property" (1998), Moore (1997). For other justifications of intellectual property see Himma (forthcoming), Hughes (1997), and Palmer (2005).

[8]Ken Himma notes that "content creation involves the expenditure of moments of our lives, something that we all tend to value intrinsically. Intellectual property protection might be justified as a matter of respect for this precious and limited resource" (Himma, forthcoming).

Finally, a justification for the view that labor or possession may generate prima facie claims against others could be grounded in respect for individual autonomy and sovereignty. As sovereign and autonomous agents, especially within the liberal tradition, we are afforded the moral and legal space to order our lives as we see fit. As long as respect for others is maintained, we are each free to set the course and direction of our own lives, to choose between various lifelong goals and projects, and to develop our capacities and talents accordingly. Simple respect for individuals prohibits wresting from their hands an unowned object that they acquired or produced. I hasten to add that at this point we are trying to justify weak, noninterference claims, not full-blown property rights. Other things being equal, when an individual labors to create an intangible work, then weak presumptive claims of noninterference have been generated on grounds of labor, desert, or autonomy.

The underlying rationale of Locke's proviso is that if no one's situation is worsened, then no one can complain about another individual appropriating part of the commons. If no one is harmed by an acquisition and one person is bettered, then the acquisition ought to be permitted. In fact, it is precisely because no one is harmed that it seems unreasonable to object to what is known as a *Pareto-superior move*.[9] Thus, the proviso can be understood as a version of a "no harm, no foul" principle.

13.2.2. Bettering, Worsening, and the Baseline Problem

Assuming a just initial position and that Pareto superior moves are legitimate, there are two questions to consider when examining a Pareto-based proviso. First, what are the terms of being worsened? This is a question of scale, measurement, or value. An individual could be worsened in terms of subjective preference satisfaction, wealth, happiness, freedoms, opportunities, and so on. Which of these count in determining moral bettering and worsening? Second, once the terms of being worsened have been resolved, which two situations are we going to compare to determine whether someone has been worsened? In any question of harm we are comparing two states—for example, "now" after an acquisition compared to "then" before an acquisition. This is known as the *baseline problem*.

In principle, the Lockean theory of intangible property being developed is consistent with a wide range of value theories. So long as the preferred value theory has the resources to determine bettering and worsening with reference to acquisitions, then Pareto-superior moves can be made and acquisitions justified on Lockean grounds. For now, assume an Aristotelian Eudaimonist account of value exhibited by the following theses is correct (for similar views, see Rawls, 1971;

---

[9]One state of the world, S_1, is Pareto superior to another, S_2, if and only if no one is worse off in S_1 than in S_2, and at least one person is better off in S_1 than in S_2. S_1 is strongly Pareto superior to S_2 if everyone is better off in S_1 than in S_2, and weakly Pareto superior if at least one person is better off and no one is worse off. State S_1 is Pareto optimal if no state is Pareto superior to S_1: It is strongly Pareto optimal if no state is weakly Pareto superior to it, and weakly Pareto optimal if no state is strongly Pareto superior to it. Throughout this essay, I use *Pareto superiority* to stand for *weak Pareto superiority* (adapted from Cohen, 1995). "Pareto Argument For Inequality" in *Social Philosophy & Policy* 12 (Winter 1995): 160.

Aristotle, 350 BCE, books I and X; Kant, 1785; Sidgwick, 1907; Perry, 1926; and Lomasky, 1987).

1. Human well-being or flourishing is the sole standard of intrinsic value.

2. Human persons are rational project pursuers, and well-being or flourishing is attained through the setting, pursuing, and completion of life goals and projects.

3. The control of physical and intangible objects is valuable. At a specific time, each individual has a certain set of things she can freely use and other things she owns, but she also has certain opportunities, to use and appropriate things. This complex set of opportunities, along with what she can now freely use or has rights over, constitutes her position materially—this set constitutes her level of material well-being.

Although it is certainly the case that there is more to bettering and worsening than an individual's level of material well-being, including opportunity costs, I do not pursue this matter further at present. Needless to say, a full-blown account of value explicates all the ways in which individuals can be bettered and worsened with reference to acquisition. Moreover, as noted, it is not crucial to the Lockean model being presented to defend some preferred theory of value against all comers. Whatever value theory is ultimately correct, if it has the ability to determine bettering and worsening with reference to acquisitions, then Pareto-superior moves can be made and acquisitions justified on Lockean grounds.

Lockeans as well as others who seek to ground rights to property in the proviso generally set the baseline of comparison as the state of nature. The commons, or the state of nature, is characterized as that state where the moral landscape has yet to be changed by formal property relations. For now, assume a state of nature situation where no injustice has occurred and where there are no property relations in terms of use, possession, or rights. All anyone has in this initial state are opportunities to increase her material standing. Suppose Fred creates an intangible work (perhaps a new gathering technique) and does not worsen his fellows— alas, all they had were contingent opportunities and Fred's creation and exclusion adequately benefits them in other ways. After the acquisition, Fred's level of material well-being has changed. Now he has a possession that he holds legitimately, as well as all of his previous opportunities. Along comes Ginger, who creates her own intangible work and considers whether her exclusion of it will worsen Fred. But what two situations should Ginger compare? Should the effects of Ginger's acquisition be compared to Fred's initial state, where he had not yet legitimately acquired anything, or to his situation immediately before Ginger's taking? If bettering and worsening are to be cashed out in terms of an individual's level of well-being with opportunity costs and this measure changes over time, then the baseline of comparison must also change. In the current case, we compare Fred's level of material well-being when Ginger possesses and excludes an intangible work to his level of well-being immediately before Ginger's acquisition.

At this point, I would like to clear up a common confusion surrounding the baseline of comparison. What if a perverse inventor creates a genetic enhancement technique that will save lives but decides to keep the technique secret or charge excessive prices for access? Those individuals who had, before the creation, no chance to survive now have a chance and are worsened because of the perverse inventor's refusal to let others use the machine.[10]

The baseline this case implies cannot be correct. On this view, to determine bettering and worsening, we are to compare how individuals are before the creation of some value (in this case the genetic enhancement technique) to how they would be if they possessed or consumed that value. But we are all worsened in this respect by any value that is created and held exclusively. I am worsened by your exclusive possession of your car because I would be better off if I exclusively controlled the car—even if I already owned hundreds of cars. Any individual, especially those who have faulty hearts, would be better off if they held title to my heart compared to anyone else's holding the title. I am also worsened when you create a new philosophical theory and claim authorship—I would have been better off (suppose it is a valuable theory) if I had authored the theory, so you have worsened me. Clearly this account of the baseline makes the notions of bettering and worsening too broad.[11]

A slightly different way to put the Lockean argument for intellectual property rights is:

- Step one: *The Generation of Prima Facie Claims to Control*—Suppose Ginger creates a new intangible work—creation, effort, and so on, yield her prima facie claims to control (similar to student desert for a grade).
- Step two: *Locke's Proviso*—If the acquisition of an intangible object makes no one (else) worse off in terms of their level of well-being compared to how they were immediately before the acquisition, then the taking is permitted.
- Step three: *From Prima Facie Claims to Property Rights*—When are prima facie claims to control an intangible work undefeated? Answer: when the proviso is satisfied. Alas, no one else has been worsened—who could complain?
- *Conclusion:* So long as no harm is done—the proviso is satisfied—the prima facie claims that labor and effort may generate turn into property claims.[12]

If correct, this account justifies moral claims to control intangible property like genetic enhancement techniques, movies, novels, or information. When an individual creates an intangible work and fixes it in some fashion, then labor and possession

---

[10]We also have to suppose that the system of intellectual property protection in this case allows multiple patents, assuming independent creation or discovery. If the perverse inventor's intellectual property excluded others from independent creation or discovery then worsening has occurred—the chance or opportunity that someone would find cure and help is eliminated.

[11]This sort of baseline confusion infects Farrelly (2002). For a similar, yet still mistaken, view of the baseline see Waldron (1993).

[12]Ken Himma in correspondence has suggested that this argument could succeed without defending initial prima facie claims to control. "Suppose I have no prima facie claim to X, but my taking X leaves no one worse off in any respect. Since they have no grounds to complain, what could be wrong with my taking it? If, however, there is a prima facie claim on my part, much more would be needed to defeat it than just pointing out that someone is made worse off by it. That's how [moral] claims work, it seems to me—and why they're needed: to justify making others worse off." My worry, though, is that without establishing initial prima facie claims to control, there would be no moral aspect to strengthen into rights by application of the proviso. In any case, this is an interesting line of inquiry.

create a prima facie claim to the work. Moreover, if the proviso is satisfied, the prima facie claim remains undefeated and moral claims or rights are generated.

13.3. Overriding the Privacy and Intellectual Property Presumptions: Arguments in Favor of Hacking

If the argument so far has been compelling, then moral presumptions in favor of intellectual property and privacy have been established. I now consider three arguments offered by hackers and the "free access" community that purport to override these presumptions.

13.3.1. The Social Nature of Information Argument[13]

As noted in the introduction, many hackers have held that information belongs to everyone and that access to computer systems should be unlimited and unrestricted. According to this view, information is a social product and enforcing access restrictions unduly benefits authors and inventors.[14] Individuals are raised in societies that endow them with knowledge which these individuals then use to create intellectual works of all kinds. On this view, the building blocks of intellectual works—knowledge—is a social product. Individuals should not have exclusive and perpetual ownership of the works that they create because these works are built on the shared knowledge of society. Allowing rights to intellectual works would be similar to granting ownership to the individual who placed the last brick in a public works dam. The dam is a social product, built up by the efforts of hundreds, and knowledge, upon which all intellectual works are built, is built up in a similar fashion.

Similarly, the benefits of market interaction are social products. It is not clear that the individual who discovers crude oil in their backyard should obtain the full market value of their find. And why should the inventor who produces the next technology breakthrough be allowed to harvest full market value when such value is actually created through the interactions of individuals within a society? Simply put, the value produced by markets and the building blocks of intellectual works are social products. This would undermine any claims to clear title.[15] A. John Simmons writes,

> Locke himself uses examples that point to the social nature of production (The Second Treatise of Government, II 43). But if the skills, tools, or invention that are used in laboring are not simply the product of the individual's effort, but are instead the product of a culture

---

[13]Often this argument is linked to the claim that "information should be free." For an in depth analysis of the "information should be free" argument, see Himma (2005b). Parts of this section draw from material published in *Intellectual Property and Information Control* (Transaction Pub. 2004), Chap. 7.

[14]John Perry Barlow (1997, p. 359) of the Electronic Frontier Foundation goes so far as to claim that information is a life form.

[15]Grant (1987) and Shapiro (1991), as well as others, have argued along these lines. For earlier and more general defenses of this sentiment see Marx and Engels (1848) and Proudhon (1994).

or a society, should not the group have some claim on what individual laborers produce? For the labor that the individual invests includes the prior labor of many others. (1992, p. 269)

A mild form of this argument may yield a justification for limiting the ownership rights of authors and inventors—alas, these individuals do not deserve the full value of what they produce given what they produce is, in part, a social product. A more radical form of this argument may lead to the elimination of intellectual property rights. If individuals are, in a deep way, social products and market value and knowledge are as well, then the creator-centered paradigm that grounds Anglo-American systems of intellectual property would be undermined.

The social nature of information argument, in either version, is suspect for several reasons. First, it is doubtful that the notion of "society" employed in this view is clear enough to carry the weight that the argument demands. In some vague sense, we may know what it means to say that Lincoln was a member of American society or that Aristotle's political views were influenced by ancient Greek society. Nevertheless, the notion of *society* is conceptually imprecise—one that it would be dubious to attach ownership or obligation claims to. Those who would defend this view would have to clarify the notions of *society* and *social product* before the argument could be fully analyzed.

But suppose for the sake of argument that supporters of this view come up with a concise notion of *society* and *social product*. We may ask further, why think that societies can be owed something or that they can own or deserve something?[16] Surely, it does not follow from the claim that X is a social product that society owns X. Likewise, it does not follow merely from the claim that X is produced by Ginger, that Ginger owns X. It is true that interactions between individuals may produce increased market values or add to the common stock of knowledge. What may be denied is that these byproducts of interaction, market value and shared information, are in some sense owned by society or that society is owed for their use. This should not be assumed without argument. It is one thing to claim that information and knowledge is a social product—something built up by thousands of individual contributions—but quite another to claim that this knowledge is owned by society or that individuals who use this information owe society something in return.[17]

Suppose that Fred and Ginger, along with numerous others, interact and benefit me in the following way. Their interaction produces knowledge that is then freely shared, and allows me to create some new value, V. Upon creation of V, Fred and Ginger demand that they are owed something for their part. But what is the argument from third-party benefits to demands of compensation for these benefits?

---

[16]Do notions of *ownership, owing,* or *deserving* even make sense when attached to the concept of society? If so, and if different societies can own knowledge, do they not have the problem of original acquisition? See Nozick (1974, p. 178).

[17]Spooner (1971, p. 58) argued that one's culture or society plays almost no role in the production of ideas. "Nothing is, by its own essence and nature, more perfectly susceptible of exclusive appropriation, that a thought. It originates in the mind of a single individual. It can leave his mind only in obedience to his will. It dies with him, if he so elect."

Why think that there are "strings" attached to freely shared information? And if such an argument can be made, it would seem that burdens create reverse demands. Suppose that the interaction of Fred and Ginger produces false information that is freely shared. Suppose further that I waste 10 years trying to produce some value based, in part, on this false information. Would Fred and Ginger, would society, owe me compensation? The position that "strings" are attached in this case runs parallel to Robert Nozick's benefit "foisting" example. In Nozick's case, a benefit is foisted on someone and then payment is demanded. This seems an accurate account of what is going on in this case as well.

> One cannot, whatever one's purposes, just act so as to give people benefits and then demand (or seize) payment. Nor can a group of persons do this. If you may not charge and collect for benefits you bestow without prior agreement, you certainly may not do so for benefits whose bestowal costs you nothing, and most certainly people need not repay you for costless-to-provide benefits which yet others provided them. So the fact that we partially are "social products" in that we benefit from current patterns and forms created by the multitudinous actions of a long string of long-forgotten people, forms which include institutions, ways of doing things, and language, does not create in us a general free floating debt which the current society can collect and use as it will. (1974, p. 95)

Arguably this is also true of market value. Given our crude oil example, the market value of the oil is the synergistic effect of individuals freely interacting. Moreover, there is no question of desert here—if the acquisition does not worsen, then "no harm, no foul." Surely the individual who discovers the oil does not deserve full market value any more than the lottery winner deserves her winnings.

On my view, common knowledge, market value, and the like are the synergistic effects of individuals freely interacting. If a thousand of us freely give our new and original ideas to all of humankind it would be illicit for us to demand compensation, after the fact, from individuals who have used our ideas to create things of value. It would even be more questionable for individuals 10 generations later to demand compensation for the current use of, the now very old, ideas that we freely gave. Lysander Spooner puts the point succinctly.

> What rights society have, in ideas, which they did not produce, and have never purchased, it would probably be very difficult to define; and equally difficult to explain how society became possessed of those rights. It certainly requires something more than assertion, to prove that by simply coming to a knowledge of certain ideas—the products of individual labor—society acquires any valid title to them, or, consequently, any rights in them. (1971, p. 103)

But, once again, suppose for the sake of argument that the defender of this view can justify societal ownership of general pools of knowledge and information. Nevertheless, it could be argued that we have already paid for the use of this collective wisdom when we pay for education and the like. When a parent pays, through fees or taxation, for a child's education, it would seem that the information—part of society's common pool of knowledge—has been fairly purchased. And this extends through all levels of education and even to individuals who no longer attend school.

Finally, in many contexts where privacy interests are at stake, an appeal to the social nature of intellectual property and information seems unconvincing—assuming that this view can be saved from the points already discussed. The fact that sensitive personal information about an individual's medical history is a social product may have little force when it comes to questions of access and control. This is also true of information related to national security and financial information.

13.3.2. But They Still Have Their Copy![18]

A common argument given by hackers and others who defend "free access" is that making a copy does not deprive anyone of their possessions. Intangible works are nonrivalrous, meaning that they can be used and consumed by many individuals concurrently. Edwin Hettinger argues,

> The possession or use of an intellectual object by one person does not preclude others from possessing or using it as well. If someone borrows your lawn mower, you cannot use it, nor can anyone else. But if someone borrows your recipe for guacamole, that in no way precludes you, or anyone else, from using it. This feature is shared by all sorts of intellectual objects. . . .
>
> This characteristic of intellectual objects grounds a strong prima facie case against the wisdom of private and exclusive intellectual property rights. Why should one person have the exclusive right to possess and use something that all people could possess and use concurrently? . . . [T]he unauthorized taking of an intellectual object does not feel like theft. (1997, p. 20)

Consider a more formal version of this argument.

P1.   If a tangible or intangible work can be used and consumed by many individuals concurrently (nonrivalrous), then maximal access and use should be permitted.

P2.   Intellectual works falling under the domains of copyright, patent, and trade secret protection are nonrivalrous.

---

[18]For an interesting analysis of this argument see Himma (2005a).

P3.   So it follows that there is an immediate prima facie case against intellectual property rights or for allowing access to intellectual works.

The weak point in this argument is the first premise—especially given that the second premise is generally true.[19] Again, consider sensitive personal information. It seems patently false to claim that just because this information can be used and consumed by many individuals concurrently that there is a prima facie moral claim that this be so. Snuff films, obscene pornography, information related to national security, personal financial information, and private thoughts are each non-rivalrous. Nevertheless, this fact does not, by itself, generate prima facie moral claims for maximal access and use.

Hettinger would likely reply that these sorts of examples would violate a "no harm, no foul" rule that underlies this argument. Taking personal information from someone harms them in a way that copying intellectual works does not. This view lies at the heart of the second argument establishing a presumption in favor of intellectual property rights. But consider a case provided by Mark Lambeth and Don Hubin.

> Dr. Demento . . . has discovered a drug that will put people into a trance for eight hours and rejuvenate their bodies so that they need no sleep. The fiendish doctor realizes that he has a way to use the bodies of others without making them any worse off than they would have been in his absence. . . . In addition to making his temporary zombies work in his lab at night, he engages in vile and disgusting sex acts with them which he videotapes . . . [and] sells at great profit in foreign countries. (1988, p. 495)

Arguably, Dr. Demento's actions are immoral even though, *ex hypothesi*, no harm has been done to his subjects. Similarly, a peeping Tom may engage in immoral activity without harming his victims—perhaps there will be no consequences to the victims and they will never know of the peeping. More forcefully, however, if Dr. Demento's victims have moral claims to control their own bodies, then they will be worsened by his activity—a moral claim or obligation will have been violated and certain risks imposed without consent. Although there is much more to say regarding these issues, I postpone comment until after considering a last argument in favor of hacking and free access.

In summary, the claim that maximal access should be allowed and perhaps promoted for goods that are nonrivalrous is without merit. Intangible works of all sorts are nonrivalrous, including sensitive personal information, financial records, and information related to national security. It may even be the case that our bodies could be nonrivalrously used by others. Nevertheless, this feature of most intangible goods and some tangible goods does not obviously justify such use.

---

[19]Some kinds of information are rivalrously consumed, for example, stock tips.

13.3.3. The Security and Social Benefits Argument

According to this view, presumptions in favor of privacy and intellectual property are overridden because of the social benefits that occur when hackers crack software and networks. Dittrich and Himma note,

> ... by gaining insight into the operations of existing networks, hackers develop a base of knowledge that can be used to improve those networks ... [and] break-ins themselves call attention to security flaws that could be exploited by cracker or, worse, cyber-terrorists. (Dittrich and Himma, 2005)

In many cases, hackers who, without authorization, access systems do no damage to files or programs and simply look around as a matter of curiosity. Viewing a file and making copies does no obvious damage. Moreover, by hacking systems and software, hackers are able to alert administrators and owners of potential security flaws. Nonmalicious hacking of this sort provides social benefits by strengthening computer networks and software packages against cyberterrorists.

Such behavior is often likened to neighborhood "crime watch" programs or innocently walking on someone else's property. In an interview with a hacker, Richard Spinello (1997, p. 182) asks about trespass. An unnamed hacker replied ". . . I don't see the problem here. What's wrong with snooping around especially if I do not alter any data or screw up some commands or programs . . . [w]here is the damage? It is the same as walking across Farmer Brown's field—as long as I leave the animals and crops alone what harm have I done?" In many of these cases a "no harm, no foul" sentiment is included within a social benefits or security argument.

But consider the following case. Suppose Ginger comes home to find that Fred, someone she has never met, is in her house looking around. Before Ginger can scream or call for help, Fred exclaims "Hey now, I have done no damage, I am only looking, and moreover, I have found several security flaws with your doors and windows." My guess is that few of us would find Fred's position tenable—but why? Arguably, Fred has harmed Ginger by foisting certain risks upon her. She cannot be sure of his intentions, goals, or ambitions. Without being able to trust Fred, Ginger's security is profoundly threatened. Fred could attack her directly or take away information that could be used as the basis for a later attack. For example, Fred could "innocently" note that Ginger is Muslim—information that if generally known may cause Ginger a host of problems.

Similar considerations apply to hacking software. When Crusoe cracks Friday's software program or simply obtains a copy he would not have otherwise purchased, he opens Friday up to unforeseen and unconsented to risks. A "black hat" hacker may crack Crusoe's machine, obtain a copy of Friday's program, and market a pirated copy at a lower price. When Crusoe legitimately buys a copy, Friday consents to certain risks—alas someone may break in to Crusoe's computer. But this is not the case when unauthorized copies are made or when security protections are cracked.

Moreover, the very existence of walls, doors, fences, firewalls, and passwords makes a difference. All of these are basically "keep out" signs erected, more often than not, by those who have legitimate moral claims to control access. Farmer Brown may put up fences to keep his animals in but also to keep others out. Window blinds, firewalls, and passwords serve a similar function.

13.4. Conclusion

It has been argued that a moral presumption in favor of privacy is justified by appeal to the value of privacy, autonomy, and respect for persons, and a general right to make contracts related to personal information. Individuals who do not have control over access to their own bodies or personal information exhibit increased stress levels, violent behavior, and other psychological and physiologic disorders. Allowing individuals to control access affords them the moral space to pursue their own experiments in living—social orders that recognize such control exhibit respect for persons.

A moral presumption in favor of intellectual property has been grounded in incentives to innovate or via a Lockean model. According to the former, control is granted to authors and inventors of intellectual property because granting such control provides incentives necessary for social progress. On the Lockean view, moral claims to intellectual works are grounded in desert or merit along with a "no harm, no foul" rule.

Finally, three prominent hacker or "free access" arguments have been discussed and dismissed as being forceful enough to override the presumptions in favor of privacy and intellectual property. The social nature of information argument trades on an imprecise notion of "society" or that society can own or deserve something. Even if society had some claim on certain pools of knowledge, individuals have fairly purchased such information through education fees and the like. Moreover, where privacy interests are at stake, an appeal to the social nature of intellectual property and information seems unconvincing.

The nonrivalrousness of information argument fails because, among other things, it is not at all apparent that just because something can be used and consumed by numerous individuals concurrently that it should be. Private sensitive information and violent pornography are two obvious examples.

The security and social benefits argument is problematic because it does not consider the hidden costs of foisting risks on others. When hackers break into systems or software they impose morally relevant risks on others without consent. As with the peeping Tom or the home intruder, we cannot be sure of the intentions of unauthorized hackers. Moreover, we must bear the costs of reestablishing the security and trustworthiness of our systems.

Acknowledgments
I am indebted to Bill Kline, Ken Himma, and Judith Wagner DeCew for commenting on earlier versions of this article.

References

Allen, Anita. (2003). *Why Privacy Isn't Everything: Feminist Reflections on Personal Accountability*. Lanham, MD: Rowan & Littlefield.

Aristotle. (350 BCE). Nicomachean Ethics. Trans by W.D. Ross. Princeton, New Jersey: Princeton University Press.

Barlow, John Perry. (1997). "The Economy of Ideas: Everything You Know About Intellectual Property Is Wrong." In A. Moore, ed. *Intellectual Property: Moral, Legal, and International Dilemmas*. New York: Rowman & Littlefield.

Baum, A. and S. Koman (1976). "Differential Response to Anticipated Crowding: Psychological Effects of Social and Spatial Density." *Journal of Personality and Social Psychology*. Vol. 34, pp. 562–536.

Business Software Alliance, Software & Information Industry Association. (1999, August). "Pirates Raid World Businesses." *Mobile Computing & Communications*. p. 24.

Carnegie Mellon Software Engineering Institute. (N.D.). "CERT/CC Statistics 1998–2006." Available at www.cert.org/stats/cert_stats.html. Accessed 1/2/06.

Clauson-Kaas, Jes, A. Dzikus, C. Stephens, N. Hojlyng, and P. Aaby. (1996). "Urban Health: Human Settlement Indicators of Crowding." *Third World Planning Review*. Vol. 18, pp. 349–363.

Cohen, G.A. (1995, Winter). "The Pareto Argument for Inequality." *Social Philosophy & Policy*. Vol. 12, p. 160.

Cox, C., P. Paulus, and G. McCain. (1984). "Prison Crowding Research: The Relevance of Prison Housing Standards and a General Approach Regarding Crowding Phenomena." *American Psychologist*. Vol. 389, pp. 1148–1160.

DeCew, Judith Wagner. (1997). *In Pursuit of Privacy: Law, Ethics, and the Rise of Technology*. Ithaca, NY: Cornell University Press.

Deller, A., ed. (1964). "Walker on Patents." In *Early American Patents*. Mount Kisco, NY: Voorhis Publishers.

Dittrich, David, and Ken Himma. (2005). "Hackers, Crackers, and Computer Criminals." In H. Bidgoli, ed. *The Handbook of Information Security*. Hoboken, NJ: John Wiley & Sons.

Edwards, J.N., and A. Both. (1977). "Crowding and Human Sexual Behavior." *Social Forces*. Vol. 55, pp. 791–808.

Farrelly, Colin. (2002). "Genes and Social Justice: A Reply to Moore." *Bioethics*. Col. 16, p. 75.

Farrington, D., and C. Nuttal. (1980). "Prison Size, Overcrowding, Prison Violence and Recidivism." *Journal of Criminal Justice*. Vol. 8, pp. 221–231.

Francis, W., and R. Collins. (1995). *Cases and Materials on Patent Law: Including Trade Secrets, Copyrights, Trademarks*. 4th ed. St. Paul, MN: West Publishing Company.

Frankel, Ellen, Paul Frankel, Fred Miller, Jr., and Jeffrey Paul, eds. (2000). *The Right to Privacy*. Cambridge: Cambridge University Press.

Fried, Charles. (1968). "Privacy." *Yale Law Journal*. Vol. 77, p. 477.

Fried, Charles. (1970). *An Anatomy of Values*. Cambridge, MA: Harvard University Press.

Fuller, Theodore D., J.N. Edwards, S. Vorakitphokatorn, and S. Sermsri. (1996). "Chronic Stress and Psychological Well-Being: Evidence from Thailand on Household Crowding." *Social Science and Medicine*. Vol. 42, No. 2, pp. 265–280.

Gavison, Ruth (1983). "Information Control: Availability and Control." In Stanley Benn and G. Gaus, eds. *Public and Private in Social Life*. New York: St. Martin's Press, pp. 113–134.

Gayler et al. v. Wilder. (1850). Chief Justice Taney.

Graham v. John Deere Co. (1966). 383 US 1, 9.

Grant, Ruth. (1987). *John Locke's Liberalism*. Chicago: University of Chicago Press.

Gross, Hyman. (1971). "Privacy and Autonomy." *Privacy: Nomos XIII*. p. 170.

Halpern, S., D. Shipley, and H. Abrams. (1992). *Copyright: Cases and Materials*. St. Paul, MN: West Publishing Company.

Hettinger, Edwin. (1997). "Justifying Intellectual Property." In A. Moore, ed. *Intellectual Property: Moral, Legal, and International Dilemmas*. Lanham, MD: Rowman & Littlefield.

Himma, Ken. (2005a, May 1). "Abundance, Rights, and Interests: Thinking About the Legitimacy of Intellectual Property." In Philip Brey, Francis Grodzinsky, and Lucas Introna, eds. *Proceedings of the 2005 International Conference of Computer Ethics—Philosophical Enquiry (CEPE 2005)*. Available at http://ssrn.com/author=328842. Accessed 1/6/06.

Himma, Ken. (2005b). "Information and Intellectual Property Protection: Evaluating the Claim That Information Should Be Free." *Law and Technical Scholarship*. Available at http://repositories.cdlib.org/cgi/viewcontent.cgi?article=1013&context=bclt. Accessed 1/2/06. Also appears in *APA Newsletter on Philosophy and Law* (2005, Spring). Vol. 4, No. 2.

Himma, Ken. (Forthcoming). "Justifying Intellectual Property Protection: Why the Interests of Content-Creators Usually Wins Over Everyone Else's." *Information Technology and Social Justice*. Hershey, PA: Idea Group.

Hughes, Justin. (1997). "The Philosophy of Intellectual Property." Chapter 6 in A. Moore, ed. *Intellectual Property: Moral, Legal, and International Dilemmas*. Lanham, MD: Rowman & Littlefield.

James, G. (2002, January). "Organized Crime and the Software Biz." MC *Technology*. Cited in Seale, Darryl. (2002). "Why Do We Do It If We Know It's Wrong?" In A. Salehnia, ed. *Ethical Issues of Information Systems*. London: IRM Press, p. 120.

Kant, Immanuel. (1785). *The Fundamental Principles of the Metaphysics of Morals*, Academy ed. Cambridge, NY: Cambridge University Press.

Lambeth, Mark, and Don Hubin. (1988). "Providing for Rights." *Dialogue*, Vol. 27, p. 495.

Locke, John. (1698). *The Second Treatise of Government*. London: Awnsham and Churchill.

Lomasky, Loren. (1987). *Persons, Rights, and the Moral Community*. New York: Oxford University Press.

Marx, Karl, and Friedrich Engels. (1848). *The Communist Manifesto*. New York, NY: New American Library.

McCain, G., V. Cox, and P. Paulus. (1980). *The Effect of Prison Crowding on Inmate Behavior*. Washington, D.C.: U.S. Department of Justice.

Megargee, E.I. (1977). "The Association of Population Density Reduced Space and Uncomfortable Temperatures with Misconduct in a Prison Community." *The American Journal of Community Psychology*, Vol. 5, pp. 289–298.

Moore, A. (1997). "Toward a Lockean Theory of Intellectual Property." Chapter 5 in A. Moore, ed. *Intellectual Property: Moral, Legal, and International Dilemmas*. Lanham, MD: Rowman & Littlefield.

Moore, A. (2003). "Intellectual Property, Innovation, and Social Progress: The Case Against Incentives Based Arguments." *The Hamline Law Review*, Vol. 26.

Moore, Adam. (1998, October). "Intangible Property: Privacy, Power, and Information Control." *American Philosophical Quarterly*, Vol. 35.

Moore, Adam. (2004). *Intellectual Property and Information Control: Philosophical Foundations and Contemporary Issues*. Piscataway, NJ: Transaction Publishing/Rutgers University Press.

Morris, Desmond. (1969). *The Human Zoo*. New York: McGraw-Hill.

Morgan, Griscom. (1972). "Mental and Social Health and Population Density." *Journal of Human Relations*, Vol. 20, pp. 196–204.

Mumford, Lewis. (1961). *The City in History*. New York: Harcourt Brace. Cited in Theodore D. Fuller, J.N. Edwards, S. Vorakitphokatorn, and S. Sermsri. (1996). "Chronic Stress and Psychological Well-Being: Evidence from Thailand on Household Crowding." *Social Science and Medicine*, Vol. 42, No. 2, pp. 265–280.

Nelkin, Dorothy. (1984). *Science as Intellectual Property*. New York: MacMillan.

Nozick, Robert. (1974). *Anarchy, State, and Utopia*. New York: Basic Books.

Palmer, Tom. (2005). "Are Patents and Copyrights Morally Justified." In A. Moore, ed. *Information Ethics: Property and Power*. Seattle: University of Washington Press, p. 123.

Parker, Richard. (1974). "A Definition of Privacy." *Rutgers Law Review*, Vol. 27, p. 280.

Paulus, P., V. Cox, and G. McCain. (1978). "Death Rates, Psychiatric Commitments, Blood Pressure, and Perceived Crowding as a Function of Institutional Crowding." *Environmental Psychology and Nonverbal Behavior*, Vol. 3, pp. 107–116.

Perry, R.B. (1926). *General Theory of Value*. New York: Longmans, Green.

Porporino, F., and K. Dudley. (1984). *An Analysis of the Effects of Overcrowding in Canadian Penitentiaries*. Ottawa, Ontario: Research Division, Programs Branch, Solicitor General of Canada.

"Privacy: Its Meaning and Value." (2003). *American Philosophical Quarterly*, Vol. 40, pp. 215–227.

Proudhon, P.J. (1994). *What s Property? An Inquiry Into the Principles of Right and of Government*, trans. By D. Kelly and B. Smith. New York: Cambridge University Press.

Rachels, J. (1975, Summer). "Why Privacy Is Important." *Philosophy and Public Affairs*, Vol. 4, pp. 323–333.

Rawls, John. (1971). *A Theory of Justice*. Cambridge, MA: Harvard University Press.

Rossiter, Clinton. (1958). *Aspects of Liberty*. Ithaca, NY: Cornell University Press. Quoted in Westin, Alan. (1985). "Privacy in the Modern Democratic State." In D. Johnson and J. Snapper, eds. *Ethical Issues in the Use of Computers*. Bellmont, CA: Wadsworth.

Ruback, B., and T. Carr. (1984). "Crowding in a Woman's Prison." *Journal of Applied Psychology*, Vol. 14, pp. 57–68.

Schoeman, Ferdinand. (1992). *Privacy and Social Freedom*. New York: Cambridge University Press.

Shapiro, Ian. (1991, February). "Resources, Capacities, and Ownership: The Workmanship Ideal and Distributive Justice." *Political Theory*.

Sidgwick, Henry. (1907). *Methods of Ethics*, 7th ed. London: Macmillan.

Simmons, A. John. (1992). *The Lockean Theory of Rights*. Princeton, NJ: Princeton University Press.

Sony Corp. of America v. Universal Studios Inc. (1984). 464 US 417, 78, ED 2d. 574.

Spinello, Richard. (1997). "Interview with a Hacker." In Richard Spinello, ed. *Case Studies in Information and Computer Ethics*. Upper Saddle River, NJ: Prentice Hall.

Spooner, Lysander. (1971). "The Law of Intellectual Property in Their Ideas: Or an Essay on the Rights of Authors and Inventors to a Perpetual Property in Their Ideas." In C. Shively, ed. *The Collected Works of Lysander Spooner*. Weston, MA: M&S Press.

Twentieth Century Music Corp. v. Aiken. (1974). 422 U.S. 151, 95 S. Ct. 2040 45 L.Ed.2d.

United States Congress. (1909). Copyright Act of 1909. H.R. Rep. No. 2222 60th Cong., 2nd Sess.

United States v. Paramount Pictures. (1948). 334 U.S. 131, 158.

Van Den Haag, Ernest. (1971). "On Privacy." *Privacy: Nomos XIII*, p. 147.

Waldron, Jeremy. (1993). "From Authors to Copiers: Individual Rights and Social Values in Intellectual Property." *Chicago Kent Law Review*, Vol. 68, p. 866.

Wasserstrom, Richard. (1979). "Privacy: Some Assumptions and Arguments." In R. Bronaugh, ed. *Philosophical Law*. Westport, CT: Greenwood Press, p. 148.

Weaton v. Peters. (1834). 33 US (8 Pet.) 591, 660–1.

Westin, Alan. (1968). *Privacy and Freedom*. New York: Antheneum.

Wolf, Clark. (1995, July). "Contemporary Property Rights, Lockean Provisos, and the Interests of Future Generations." *Ethics,* Vol. 105, pp. 791–818.

Chapter 14: Disclosing Software Vulnerabilities

Maria Canellopoulou-Bottis

Information can cause harm. A person may defame or defraud another. A person may use information offered to her by another on how to kill a person and kill, in fact, a person (Rice v. Paladin, 1997; for an extensive analysis of harms and liability because of the transfer of information in films or books see Kunich, 2000). A person may kill herself upon learning that she has a terrible cancer.[1] A kid may be exposed to illegal pornographic material.[2] A textbook may contain dangerously inaccurate technical instructions or allegations.[3] A label on a T-shirt should have said "flammable," but did not. A computer virus may cause millions of dollars in damage. This is a very short list of examples; information, which has so many facets, transmission channels and meanings, has an equally diverse potential of causing very different kinds of damage.

Information may be speech, artistic expression, tool, product, good, code, image, signal, power, capital, service, and so on. When information is seen as speech, freedom of speech in principle safeguards the free dissemination of information (Myers, 1992). Information as an intangible is characterized as a *nonrival good*,[4] because no one possesses less information because another possesses the same information. Therefore, information as a good is quite different from, say, television sets—if I give you my television set, I do not have it any more, which is not true when I give

---

[1]This is the reason offered in support of the so-called physician's therapeutic privilege (not to disclose the truth about a patient's condition to her, etc). See relevant analysis and criticism in Katz (1983).

[2]See discussion in *Reno, Attorney-General of the US v. American Civil Liberties Union* (1997) and *ALA v. US* (2000). On the question of harm by pornography see McKinnon (1983) and Becker, Bowman, and Torrey (1994, pp. 313–352).

[3]An aeronautical chart may have missed a geographical feature (Brocklesby v. US, 1985); a mushroom may be inaccurately described as harmless (*Winter v. G.P. Putnam's sons*, 1991; case of the mushroom *Amanita phalloeidcs*'s picture, which was negligently put next to another harmless mushroom's description, readers picked up the mushrooms, ate them, and needed liver transplants).

[4]"…commercial compilers of data have long suffered from a risk of market failure owing to the intangible, ubiquitous and, above all, indivisible nature of information goods…Information goods have the properties of so-called public goods: they are ubiquitous, inexhaustible, indivisible and nondepletable. A second comer's use of a new information good does not diminish or exhaust it. Once disclosed to the world, anyone can use an information good without the originator's permission…." (Samuelson and Reichman, 1997).

you information. Information is therefore by nature[5] very different from a product[6] (e.g., a car[7]); no product liability for information (as a product, which has caused damage) has been sustained as yet,[8] because product liability presupposes a product. Information's intangibility, the lack's of a publisher's control over its content, and the possible chilling effect strict product liability would have over free speech has sustained until today the courts' position that information is not a product, with the (criticized) exception of information published in maps and navigational and aeronautical charts (see Leadstrom, 2001). Apart from tortious product liability, in the special case of software, contractual clauses such as disclaimers of liability for damage have an excellent chance of being upheld by the courts.[9]

But even if information has a nature "pushing" it to freedom and even if the general idea is that this freedom is essential to a democracy, it is also generally accepted, again in principle, that information can cause harm and therefore, its transfer may be subject to certain legal limitations.

Information published on the Internet has a distinct ability to cause enormous harm. This is because the recipients may form a very big and perhaps unknown number; also, information may be multiplied and transferred automatically to them. A classic example is the transmission of a computer virus. By its very nature, the virus multiplies by itself[10] and causes damage to the property of the recipients. Code Red I and II are examples of how information published on the Web may cause harm. Code Red I was a computer virus that infected over 12,000 computers by July 18, 2001; a different version of Code Red I infected an estimated 359,000 computers within 14 hours of its release. Code Red II, a new and entirely different version, was more dangerous because it allowed the external unauthorized control of a com-

---

[5]See the oft-quoted eloquent statement by Thomas Jefferson in a letter to Isaac McPherson (1813): "… that ideas should freely spread from one to another over the globe, for the moral and mutual instruction of man, and improvement of this condition, seems to have been peculiarly and benevolently designed by nature, when she made them, like fire, expansible all over space."

[6]A *product*, in the sense of what item may trigger strict product liability, as a rule must have a physical existence, but intangibles such as gas, naturals (pets), and writings (only navigational charts, though) are included in the relevant definition (see Legal Information Institute, N.D.).

[7]On this particular comparison, see Druey (2004), "…a car can be seen as a car by anybody, and therefore respect for another's property can be claimed from anybody. Transferred to information, this would mean that the title to information has to be respected by persons not knowing it. This cannot be just by referring to the recipient…a car remains the same car when moved to another garage. Information, on the other hand, very much depends on the persons and the context…"

[8]*Aetna Casualty v. Jeppesen* (1981); *Saloomey v. Jeppesen* (1983); Brocklesby v. US (1985) (an airplane crashed with six victims; the pilot used a defective but Federal Aviation Authority–approved flight procedure, represented graphically on a chart); and *Fluor Corp. v. Jeppesen & Co*, 1985). In these cases, charts for airplanes (with geographical features and other elements to guide the flights) were considered products and product liability for erroneous charts leading to severe damage was upheld. See also Schultz (1999). Although there are also comments against this kind of liability (see Phillips, 1999), others have urged exactly the opposite: the expansion of liability to other situations (see, e.g., Leadstrom, 2001).

[9]See *ProCD v. Zeidenberg*, which upheld a "shrink-wrap" clause dealing with permissions to use the software, sold off the shelf. The UCC also permits a seller to disclaim warranties otherwise provided for under the code; if the software seller does disclaim liability and states that the software is sold "as it is," this defeats the potential plaintiff's ability to sue for software failure. "In boilerplate license agreements, buyers accept that they are buying the product as is," (Haley, 2002).

[10]For example, if in the first hour the victims of the virus are four and the virus requires 1 hour to be received by the next wave of victims, after 10 hours these victims become 1,048,576 (*see* Stadler, 2002). Stadler also notes that in this example, after 24 hours, there would be 10^{14} new victims; there are only 10^6 people on earth!

puter. But other viruses have caused more damage than Code Red; ILOVEYOU virus is alleged to have caused losses up to $10 billion to deferral agencies and to major networks like Dow Jones ("Computer Virus," 2000; Preston and Lofton, 2002). It follows that, if censorship of information must adhere to some particular rules when information is transmitted, for example, through a book sold in the market, perhaps censorship of information transmitted over the Internet should adhere to different (more stringent) rules.

The case of disclosing information on security "holes" presents special characteristics, quite different from the disclosure of other "dangerous" information. I do not refer here to the obvious case of a hacker who "frees" a "malignant" virus on the Internet; this is a crime, dealt with in criminal statutes all over the world. I refer to the rather controversial[11] case (hereafter, "the great debate") where a person acting in good faith[12] discovers certain vulnerabilities in a system and discloses these vulnerabilities, so that other people may learn about it and hopefully, engage in research, with the objective to "patch" ("cure") these vulnerabilities. A *vulnerability* may be a lacking security requirement (e.g., lack of, or improper authentication, encryption) or a development error in the software (e.g., buffer overflow, race condition).[13] The motive is benign; but when the vulnerability is disclosed, hackers may use it to take advantage of this vulnerability and cause significant damage.

Publication, therefore, increases the likelihood of malicious forceful intrusions. This likelihood logically increases, depending on what kind of information is made public: only that a certain vulnerability exists or, the worst scenario, the code able to take full advantage of the vulnerability. In the Code Red events mentioned, a company named eBay announced on its Web page and to BugTraq, a highly esteemed e-mail journal on computer security, that it had discovered a vulnerability in Microsoft's Internet Information Server. Three days later, an independent entity, self-called "HighSpeed Junkie," released the actual buffer overflow (the code, Code Red) necessary to the exploitation of this vulnerability in a public Web site (Preston and Lofton, 2002, p. 73). In another case that attracted a lot of attention, within days of the publication of a bug in Netscape's Java implementation to a Web site that also contained the example code for how this bug operated, thousands of users' systems were reported as compromised (Ranum, 2000).

A first response to the problem could be, in these cases, to censor the publication of such information.[14] But publication of information in the vulnerability case

---

[11] I refer to this case as *controversial* because it has propelled a big debate among the security community; see, among many others, Arbaugh, Fitchen, and McHugh (2002).

[12] That the particular person acts in good faith may not always be the case or it may be difficult to ascertain. For the purposes of the discussion in this particular paper, though, good faith is a fact to be taken as such.

[13] See Takanen et al. (2004, note 2). Types of vulnerabilities include access control errors, authentication errors, boundary error, configuration errors, exception handing errors, input validation errors, randomization errors, resource errors, and state errors. On security in cyberspace, see generally Tavani (2004). For particular cases on computer security see Spinello (1997, p. 165).

[14] Actually, eBay was criticized by, among others, Richard Smith, the director of Privacy Foundation, who sustained that disclosure was causally connected with the damage Code Red did (Preston and Lofton, 2002, p. 76). But see also Schneier (N.D.), who supports, after explaining why, that "most criticisms of eEye are not based on fact, but are rooted in a dislike of their brash style, in-your-face advisories, and choice of hair coloring."

has a dual nature: it may be the only way this vulnerability may be cured and people may, therefore, enjoy a more secure system than before; it may also serve as a tool to great damage. It is true that a bomb maker reading about bombs is not also provided with an actual bomb to explode at will, whereas a hacker may be provided with dangerous exploit code, in full disclosure cases. Publishing how to make a bomb cannot, as a rule, help lessening the likelihood of damage by bombing. But disclosing information about a vulnerable system may lead to a quick resolution of this vulnerability and therefore, increase the security of this system. This particular "bug-bomb" will be forever extinguished in the virtual world; bombs in the real world simply are not subject to a total disappearance. The physical world cannot be made safer by disclosure—the virtual world can.

Software vendors are pushed, when their product's defect is publicly exposed, to issue a patch as fast as they can. But vendors are not the only ones to react; in fact, the more people learn about it, the higher the possibility is to end up quickly with an effective patch. It is this quality of the particular information that makes the regulation of its dissemination so hard. It is also this quality that has led to an ongoing debate about whether, when, how, and where a particular vulnerability could be safely disclosed.

It follows that the resolution of the disclosure problem is not as easy as it may appear. In this respect, the discussion joins other difficult ethical conflicts about disclosure.[15] In Section 14.1, I present the current debate on disclosure or nondisclosure of system vulnerabilities. In Section 14.2, I describe the clash of interests in this debate. In Section 14.3, I discuss the general idea of silence.

14.1. The Debate About Disclosure

To disclose a software vulnerability may mean, mainly, two things[16]:

1. the discoverer (the "benign identifier" [17]) elects to notify the software vendor, in secret, that her product suffers from a particular deficiency, so that the vendor issues, as quick as possible, a patch or

2. the discoverer opts to post the vulnerability in the Internet, in sites[18] usually constructed to deal with this and perhaps other, relevant, issues.

---

[15]Dealing with who has and why access to a particular kind of information (e.g., physician–patient informational conflicts).

[16]Apart from the following options (inform the vendor and/or inform the public in general, through Internet sites, etc.), another rather exceptional case has also been reported, where the identifier elected to inform only people affected by the particular vulnerability (a company's customers, where their e-mail accounts were at risk; see Rasch [2003]).

[17]As described by Ozment (2005, p. 2), meaning persons interested in computer security who decide to discover and report software vulnerabilities and who are not necessarily employed by or associated with a vendor and who are not attackers, with malicious intent to cause harm.

[18]"Bugtraq," operated by SecurityFocus (www.securityfocus.com), one of the most comprehensive and trusted sources of security information on the Internet, is one of these mailing lists, devoted to fulfilling the aims of a policy toward full instant disclosure. Another one is the Full Disclosure mailing list, see Ozment (2005).

Intermediate solutions exist, such as a policy where the vendor is entitled to be the first to know and, after some time, if no real measures to correct the problem are taken, then the discoverer reports the vulnerability publicly. A middle solution is defended by Computer Emergency Response Team Coordinating Center (CERT/CC), a federally funded organization established in 1988 that is very influential in disclosure vulnerabilities issues and publishes 3,500 to 4,000 new vulnerabilities every year (Hernan, 2002). The policy advanced by CERT is to allow the vendor a window of time of 45 days, so that a patch may be, during this time, made available (this policy is characterized as a de facto, but unofficial policy; see Arora, Telang, and Xu, 2004). After this time limit, though, all vulnerabilities reported to CERT will be disclosed to the public, regardless of the existence or availability of patches or workarounds from affected vendors (CERT, 2000). This is referred to as *responsible disclosure*; the first option is sometimes called *instantaneous disclosure* (Ozment, 2005). *Full disclosure* has been described as including exploit code, whereas *limited disclosure* omits details on exploits. Full disclosure sometimes includes the disclosure of viruses (and not exploits only) in mailing lists (Gordon and Ford, N.D.). Exact definitions of kinds of disclosure have not been commonly accepted.[19]

Any decision about when, how, and to whom a software vulnerability should be disclosed or not must take the following into account:

a. the interests of the software vendors of the defective product;

b. the public's right to know when a particular system is compromised and how; and

c. the public's interest against attacks made possible because the vulnerability (perhaps along with a very convenient for hackers exploit) was reported.

In this last respect (c), empirical evidence on, for example, whether it is a fact that the disclosure of an exploit inescapably leads to very harmful security attacks, is necessary, as part of the foundation of an efficient disclosure legal or ethical rule. The lack of appropriate, comprehensive empirical evidence on these issues has been reported as in fact, a major problem; it also seems that we do not have evidence on the severity of damages caused by attacks (Arora, Krishman, et al., 2004). Some commentators are careful to note that their data are noisy and problematic (Ozment, 2005; Rescorla, N.D.). One should also take into account that there is reason to believe that security incidents are massively underreported (Mitchell and Banker, 1998).[20] Still, the assumption that once a computer program capable of bypassing an access control system is disseminated via the Internet, it will be used (Universal City Studios v. Reimerdes, 2001) is truly reasonable, but it is equally truly, until more con-

---

[19]See Cooper (2002): "We do not have a common, accepted definition of full disclosure…the problem is, there's all these questions about full disclosure and yet no definition of what we are talking about."

[20]One in 10 violations is detected, 1 in 10 is reported to the police, etc.

crete data are available, an assumption. Last, arguments for or against disclosure reasonably carry different weight among their supporters, depending on who their evaluator is.[21]

Arguments for full or *responsible*[22] disclosure view include the following:

1. Early disclosure has been reported as having a significant positive impact on vendor patching speed. Vendors respond slower to vulnerabilities not disclosed by CERT/CC (Advisor, 2002)—they always choose to patch later than a socially optimal disclosure time (Arora, Telang, et al., 2004).[23] Open source vendors patch more quickly than closed source vendors and severe vulnerabilities are patched faster (Arora et al., 2005).

2. Responsible disclosure best safeguards the critical infrastructure of the Internet (Duncan, 2002), whereas full disclosure necessarily leaves a large number of users vulnerable;

3. The frequency of attacks after disclosure decreases over time (Arora et al., 2005, note 17).

4. Early and full dissemination of vulnerabilities allows for extensive research to correct them faster; apart from promoting academic freedom of information, disclosure offers as an end result more security, not less (Granick, N.D.; Schneier, 2000, 2004).[24]

5. Crackers already know the vulnerabilities; systems administrators do not (Arbaugh et al., 2002, p. 57; Levy, 2001).[25] Vulnerabilities are often rediscovered independently within a relatively short period of time; vulnerability hunting is therefore socially useful and full disclosure pressures vendors into more rapidly providing patches (Ozment, 2005, p. 1, note 10).

---

[21]See diverse opinions on disclosure in a survey (Goens, N.D.): "Perceptions of the degree of risk involved with full disclosure announcements vary by association with certain computer security groups. BugTraq (a Web mailing list for reporting vulnerabilities) subscribers do not feel full disclosure is as harmful as those in professional membership computer security groups, such as the ISSA." Not surprisingly, BugTraq subscribers feel the strongest that not releasing vulnerability information will cause a high degree of risk for those involved with computer security. These results show that there is no strong consensus regarding the possible effects of full disclosure across the various types of persons employed in computer security. It is also reported that in another survey by Hurwitz Group of more than 300 software security professionals, users (another interest group in this debate) strongly supported prompt notification of potential problems, 39% said immediately, another 29% within a week, whereas the industry standard is about a month (Haley, 2002). The respondents to the survey opted for disclosure even if their own companies would be endangered by it (Advisor, 2002).

[22]The exact meaning of *full* and *responsible* disclosure is not clarified in the relevant literature; generally, full disclosure may mean the immediate disclosure of all details about a vulnerability (also, e.g., an exploit), whereas responsible disclosure may mean the delayed (e.g., after 45 days under CERT rules) disclosure of some characteristics of a certain vulnerability (or only its existence).

[23]The writers support, however, that instant disclosure is equally suboptimal. It is reported that security vendors often ignore vulnerabilities and that network administrators do not bother to install patches (Schneier, N.D.).

[24]There does not seem to be, however, clear empirical evidence to support the end result of "more security."

[25]Levy (2001) notes that "The Code Red worm is based on an earlier worm that exploited another vulnerability in Microsoft's IIS server. The vulnerability was a buffer overflow in the ISAPI filter. No details about this vulnerability were public. Yet, someone wrote a worm to exploit the vulnerability anyway." See also Vidstrom (N.D.): "How could we keep vulnerabilities secret when so many people at so many different places and organizations have them? The vulnerability details may already be in circulation in the computer underground."

6. Secrecy leads to a market for early notification of vulnerabilities only to a small number of willing payers[26]; a black market for security information may also be the result of secrecy policies (Granick, N.D.).

7. Vulnerabilities are a demonstration of faulty products; producers should produce better code, as a first priority, and not care so intensively that the defect of their product is not publicly exposed (Edwards, 2001).

Arguments against disclosure include the following:

1. Immediate publication of a security advisory has been shown to cause an equally immediate exploitation, which reoccurs on a regular cycle because of poor maintenance—malware never truly goes away (Arbaugh et al., 2001). This effect is avoided with a responsible disclosure policy.

2. Even when a patch is available, disclosing a vulnerability increases the frequency of attacks—clearly, attackers believe that users will not patch in time (Arora et al., 2004, p. 19, note 16).

3. Vulnerability disclosure increases the frequency of attacks (Arora et al., 2004, note 16); users are defenseless against attackers (Farrow, 2000; Gordon and Ford, N.D.; Levy, 2001); hackers, when only given minor details about a bug, can produce a working exploit in a relatively short amount of time (Edwards, 2001). Therefore, one must be aware that throwing exploit information out freely in the Internet means information anarchy (Culp, N.D.).

4. The data on the effectiveness of disclosure, in terms of its effect on the software security defect rate, are not positive: The effort being spent on vulnerability finding has been documented as sustained by weak evidence (Rescorla, N.D.). Even when a vulnerability is reported, large sections of users either do not respond at all or respond only when an exploit is circulating. Therefore, it is never "safe" to release immediately all the details of vulnerability (Rescorla, 2003).

5. If vendors are pressed by public disclosure to release a patch, then they will release it before it is thoroughly researched and tested; the patch may not fix the problem completely or it may cause compatibility problems (Vidstrom, N.D.).

14.2. The Clash of Interests in the Disclosure Debate

Sellers sell; their interests lie in persuading that they sell the best products available at the best market price. Any negative publicity about their product causes them, as a rule, losses. Software has been marketed as an information product where defects will always be present, defects not due to any negligence by its producer, but inherent in the very nature of the product. This particularity has sustained so far the lack of legal liability of software producers for their products, a liability, which would have been logically strict (irrespective of the proof of the vendor's negligence) covering probably great customer's losses.

---

[26]Levy (2001) states that "for $2,500 a year any black hat with a business name, PO BOX, and a Web site can get advance notice of vulnerabilities before most of the general public—at least in theory."

Perhaps it would be reasonable to assume that a software company would immediately react to a private vulnerability disclosure: thank and/or reward the benign identifier,[27] instantly produce a proper patch, and then notify its customers. After all, one could think that a software company needs to produce as secure a product as possible, because otherwise the product will not sell. This argument may hold true in the case of other products (for whose failings, notably, sellers do bear product liability, such as, e.g., cars), but the evidence does not support it in the case of software. What computer security professionals have noted, and been frustrated by, was the vendors' lack of interest in the timely correction of their software, unless they were pressed by a public disclosure of the vulnerability.[28] Administrators do not always apply available patches.[29] Indeed, a more general comment is that software vendors systematically disregard consumers' safety and hide behind lax legal codes (Morgenstern et al., N.D.)—they are also reported as making, in software construction, "the same mistakes over and over again" (Hernan, 2002). The Hurwitz survey was indicative of users' frustration with unresponsive vendors (see Haley, 2002).[30] Software vendor unresponsiveness is commonly mentioned in the relevant literature.

Software vendors may suffer market losses when their stock falls. Research has shown that vulnerability disclosures lead to a negative and significant change in market value for a software vendor (Telang and Wattal, 2005). In this respect, software products fall into the same class as automobiles or drugs, when their vendors recall them. On average, a vendor loses around 0.6% value in stock price when a vulnerability is reported, a number which equals a loss of $0.86 billion per vulnerability announcement (Telang and Wattal, 2005, p. 1). Losses are greater when no patch is simultaneously announced.

Therefore, although a threat of a dangerous negligence or product liability lawsuit is not available, to urge sellers to correct product deficiencies, a threat by a vulnerability disclosure exists and has been reported as a real one. Powerful economic

---

[27]Companies are not always eager to truly thank the identifier or to compensate her: "Typically hackers do a lot of research to figure out all the details about a security risk they have discovered. When they hand that research over to a vendor they generally do not receive other compensation other than a simple written thanks from the vendor" (Edwards, 2001).

[28]Schneier (N.D.); see also Morgenstern, Parker, and Hardy (N.D.) who mention as an example the case of a vulnerability of Microsoft's Windows XP, which was reported to Microsoft but was kept secret for almost 2 months—Microsoft elected not to alert the general public, notwithstanding that tools to get around the problem were available the entire time. Another example is the case of Tornado Development, Inc., a company notified by an employee about a major flaw in their Web-mail but did nothing at all to correct the vulnerability for more than 6 months (when the then ex-employee sent an e-mail on the matter to all 5,600 of Tornado's customers; Tornado first attempted to delete the e-mails to the customers, so that they do not learn about the flaw and then, finally, fixed the vulnerability [Rasch, 2003]).

[29]"There are many reasons for an administrator not to apply all available patches. They include worries that the patches will introduce new errors into the system, a high work load, plain laziness, and that patches for example the OS are not fully supported by application program vendors. Knowledge about the fact that vulnerability details are in circulation out there also gives the administrator an argument against management/vendors for more resources in security issues" (Vidstrom, N.D.).

[30]On unresponsiveness see also, among others, Rasch (2002): "Fixing security vulnerabilities may not be the vendor's highest priority, particularly where the product involved is freeware or shareware, previously released and unsupported software, or otherwise unprofitable to support. The vendor may not feel it is a worthy use of limited engineering resources to fix a vulnerability that is theoretical, or represents only a minor threat."

interests are aligned on the side of (at least) limited disclosure (Granick, N.D., p. 1). Microsoft is one of the major companies pressing for limited disclosure (Culp, N.D.) and it has the government as an ally (Olavsrud, 2002); so do a number of other companies, allegedly pushed by Microsoft to join the "war" against disclosure.[31] But consumers are reported, however, to have contributed to the problems of software security, because they do not demand enough of it: "if the vendors do not supply security, it's not because they do not want to sell it; it is because it is not expected" (Cooper, 2002). Under this view, consumers care far more for functionality and features than security. A parallel view is expressed in connection to the average Internet user: "(users) do not want to worry about security. It is not interesting to them. They do not care particularly about security and have better things to do with their time than to constantly patch their system against security bugs. It's largely academic to them" (Ranum, 2000).

14.3. The Choice of Silence: Costs in Freedom of Choice, Costs in Free Speech

No matter how much or how little the public cares about security in their software, it is legitimate to argue that it has the right to know that their software is vulnerable (Granick, N.D.). People should, in principle, be offered the chance not only to know that a product they bought is compromised, but also the chance to repair it by themselves (see Levy in Olavsrud, 2002), to stop using it, to use it with caution, to engage in relevant research, and so on. As in other cases of "the right to know" problems,[32] improperly harming the interest in knowledge means harming the interest in freedom of choice. Ultimately, deprivation of choices means wrongful substitution in decision making: The wrong party (the vendor, the discoverer) makes a decision that legitimately and again, in principle, belongs to the individual citizen. The burden of proof that such deprivation is legitimate falls on the parties arguing for silence and the justification needs to be supported by clear empirical evidence of harms—in principle, again, actual harms and not only the increase of a chance to harm, from reporting.[33] Such clear empirical evidence, as mentioned, is at present lacking.

There is, however, some evidence that the evaluation of the general benefit from reporting (public benefit deriving, e.g., from a quicker patch and the public's

---

[31]"if SecurityCompany A does not support Microsoft in this initiative, then certain negative things will happen. This could be anything from not sharing security information, revoking 'partner' status or anything else that hurts the company. . . . It is clear that Microsoft's vulnerability disclosure initiative is nothing more than a PR stunt. They are trying to sidestep the onslaught of negative press surrounding their security practices. Negative press that originates because Microsoft's track record of releasing shoddy products that receive inadequate testing, no auditing and wide distribution" (Martin, 2001).

[32]Compare, for example, with deprivation of patient choices when the physician breaches the obligation to inform the patient, in detail in the seminal work of Katz (1983).

[33]In principle, the law forbids behavior that causes damage or is certain to cause damage, not behavior that increases the likelihood of damage (relevant crimes are the exception to the rule). Similarly, a statute or a tort that punishes speech that has the propensity to be misused by some unknown recipient would be problematic, from a constitutionally significant respect (see United States Department of Justice, 1997).

right to know) has been evaluated differently, depending on the status of the evaluator: those reporting vulnerabilities hold a higher esteem for these values (they see their work as useful for the whole society) than that granted by those who receive the reports. Receivers usually see the issue as most important to the company they work for, first and foremost, and they see the company's role as promoting the general benefit, not theirs (Havana, 2003). Opposite positions are also taken, as it seems, depending on whether the person expressing them is a member of the computer security or the anti-virus community.[34]

As the public must be able to know, professionals and researchers in particular (and not only) must also be able to speak. Computer security researchers and professionals should not be deprived from their constitutional right to free speech. The clash between the sellers' and the public's interest in freedom from hacker activity and scientific freedom under the First Amendment has also been exposed (Preston and Lofton, 2002).[35] Civil and criminal liability under the Digital Millennium Copyright Act (DMCA) and the Computer Fraud and Abuse Act (CFAA) has been a real threat against publishers of software vulnerabilities.[36] The law on liability for publications has not offered any clear solution yet, as there are instances where the First Amendment may not protect a certain publication (which is considered a "tool" for a criminal act and not free scientific speech). Intent to harm is a crucial part of these crimes; as a rule, it is lacking in scientific publications, but sometimes courts may infer intent. The current map of the relevant jurisprudence points to no safe direction.[37] Cases like *Reimerdes* (2001) and *Corley* (2000), where the DMCA was successfully used as a legal foundation to sustain an injunction against the

---

[34]"Influential members of the security world in a position to contain the dissemination of viral code believe that disclosure is a necessary evil; the anti-virus industry believes that publication is unethical and harmful" (Gordon and Ford, N.D.), noting the diametrically opposed positions regarding information sharing.

[35]Until today, the influential question whether software is more like a can opener (no First Amendment protection) or a recipe (First Amendment protection) has not been totally resolved (Kaplan, 1998).

[36]See, for example, the letter Hewlett Packard (HP) sent to SnoSoft when it published in securityfocus.com a buffer overflow exploit of Tru64 UNIX, threatening with federal criminal liability under both DMCA and CFAA, at http://politechbot.com.docs.hp.dmca.threat.073002 (accessed September 29, 2005). SnoSoft had, however, waited for 3 months for HP to issue a patch; this never happened, but HP did issue a patch within 48 hours after publication by SnoSoft (Preston and Lofton, 2002, p. 139).

[37]See *Rice v. Paladin* (1997), where the publisher (Paladin) of a book called *Hit Man: A Technical Manual for Independent Contractors* was held civilly liable for the tort of aiding and abetting in the wrongful death of three persons killed after an independent contractor followed the book's instructions. In this case, Paladin, who relied unsuccessfully on a First Amendment defense, had impressively stipulated intent. Compare to *Brandenburg v. Ohio* (1969), the "classic" case attempting to set a line between abstract "dangerous" advocacy (speech) and a crime (act), where abstract advocacy was held protected speech. In *US v. Freeman* (1985), the 9th Circuit Court stated that, if the intent of the actor and the objective meaning of the words used are so close in time and purpose to a substantive evil as to become part of the ultimate crime itself, *the actor's intent is irrelevant* (italics mine) and she is liable (this was a case about tax evasion counseling at seminars held in protest of tax laws). There are many other relevant, but not on-the-point cases (see in detail Preston and Lofton, 2002). A researcher who publishes details of a system's vulnerability may really want to press the vendor to issue a patch; she may also know, though, that the publication may be used by "the bad" guys, hackers who will immediately take advantage of the new knowledge. In this case, the question of liability remains mainly open ("if Rice is correct, the intent to inform legitimate users as well as computer criminals is no barrier to liability," Preston and Lofton, 2002, p. 109). Until the lawmaker or the common law deal explicitly with a case like this one, there is no absolutely safe answer to the question of liability, and this vagueness reasonably leads to fewer publications and fewer publications have been reported as a factor for less security (not more).

publishing of the computer program DeCSS (code permitting access to data from DVDs on unlicensed platforms) show us that a First Amendment defense is not always available, when the governmental interests, here in protecting legal copyrights, are opposed to it; perhaps, the governmental interest in public safety from hacking would be held equally superior.

Rules suppressing the free dissemination of information have not always been successful; after all, information has a natural tendency to flow. Perhaps it is true that strategies enforcing secrecy are just doomed (Schneier, N.D.). Full disclosure is reported as akin, in many ways, to the open source movement; like open source, full disclosure allows for peer review, learning and collaboration that leads to making better software (Rauch, 1999).

The answer to the question "to tell or not to tell" is not an easy one and the parties to this conflict are not two; very diverse interests, too many different representatives of different communities, interplay in this discussion. But when companies, not bearing liability for their products, urge for silence and when this silence has to do with concealing their deficiencies, one ought to be very careful before siding with them. Physicians have for centuries argued for silence, only to cover up for their sometimes fatal mistakes (Katz, 1983); scientific research too, has its own very dark pages of immense harms covered by silence (Jordan, 2003). It is history itself, which gives us a perspective of suspicion before a mandate for concealment.

References

Advisor. (2002). "Security Vulnerabilities." Available at http://advisorevents.com/doc/10190. Accessed 10/5/05.

Aetna Casualty v. Jeppesen. (1981). 642 F. 2d 339, 9th Cir.

ALA v. US. (2000). 529 US 803.

Arbaugh, W., Fitchen, L., and McHugh, J. (2002, December). "Windows of Vulnerability: A Case Study Analysis." *Computer,* pp. 52–58.

Arora, A., R. Krishnan, A. Nandkumar, T. Telang, and Y. Yang. (2004, April). "Impact of Vulnerability Disclosure and Patch Availability–An Empirical Analysis." Available at http://www.dtc.umn.edu/weis2004/telang.pdf. Accessed 9/27/05.

Arora, A., R. Krishnan, R. Telang, and Y. Yang. (2005, March 4). "An Empirical Analysis of Vendor Response to Disclosure Policy. Available at www.osvdb.org/blog/?p=22. Accessed 9/27/05.

Arora, A., R. Telang, and Hao Xu. (2004). "Optimal Policy for Software Vulnerability Disclosure." Available at www.dtc.umn.edu/weis2004/xu.pdf. Accessed 5/14/05.

Becker, A., C. Bowman, and M. Torrey. (1994). *Cases and Materials on Feminist Jurisprudence: Taking Women Seriously.* St. Paul, MN: West.

Brandenburg v. Ohio. (1969). 395 US 444.

Brocklesby v. US. (1985). 767 F 2d. 1288, 9th Cir.; *Cert. denied* (1986). 474 US 1101.

CERT/CC. (2000). "CERT/C vulnerability disclosure Policy." Available at http://www.cert.org/kb/vul_disclosure.html. Accessed 7/10/06.

"Computer Virus Hits 14 Agencies." (2000, May 10). *Chicago Tribune,* p. C1.

Cooper, Russ. (2002, July). "The Disclosure Debate" [Roundtable]. Available at http://infosecuritymag.techtarget.com. Accessed 10/5/05.

Corley. (2000). 111 F. Suppl. 2d. 294. S.D.N.Y.

Culp, S. (N.D.). "It's Time to End the Information Anarchy." Available at www.microsoft.com.technet/treeview/default.asp?url=/technet/columns/security/noarch.asp. Accessed 9/29/05.

Druey, Jean Nicholas. (2004, March 9). "Information Cannot Be Owned: There Is More of a Difference Than Many Think." Presented at the Berkman Luncheon. Available at http://cyber.law.harvard.edu/home/uploads/339/Druey.pdf. Accessed 7/10/06.

Duncan, J. (2002). "Responsible Vulnerability Disclosure: Challenges for Vendors Whose Products are Infrastructural," Secure Businesses Quarterly. No. 3: Defining the Value of Strategic Security. Available at www.sbq.com. Accessed 9/27/05.

Edwards, Mark. (2001, June 27). "The Disclose or Not to Disclose, That Is the Question." Available at www.windowsitpro.com/Articles/Print.cfm?ArticleID=21618. Accessed 9/27/05.

Farrow, R. (2000). "The Pros and Cons of Posting Vulnerability." The Network Magazine. Available at www.networkmagazine.com/shared.article. Accessed 9/27/05.

Fluor Corp. v. Jeppesen & Co. (1985). 216 Cal. App.

Goens, T. (N.D.). "The Full Disclosure of Computer Security Vulnerabilities—An Examination of the Debate." Available at http://fisher.osu.edu/people/goens_1/results.htm. Accessed 10/5/05.

Gordon, S., and R. Ford. (N.D.). "When Worlds Collide: Information Sharing for the Security and the Anti-virus Communities." Available at http://vx.netlux.org/lib/asg06.html. Accessed 10/5/05.

Granick, J. (N.D.). "Untitled" [Working Paper]. Available at islandia.law.yale.edu/isp/digital%20cops/papers/granick_newcrimescen2.pdf. Accessed 9/29/05.

Haley, Colin C. (2002, June 28). "Users Urge Disclosure of Security Flaws." Available at http://boston.internet.com/news/print.php/1378631. Accessed 10/5/05.

Havana, T. (2003, April). "Communication in the Software Vulnerability Reporting Process." Available at www.oulou.fi/research/ouspg/protos/sota/reporting/gradu.pdf. Accessed 9/29/05.

Hernan, Shawn. (2002, July). "The Disclosure Debate" [Roundtable]. Available at http://infosecuritymag.techtarget.com. Accessed 10/5/05.

Jefferson, Thomas. (1813). Letter to Isaac McPherson. Available at www.temple.edu/lawschool/dpst/mcphersonletter.html. Accessed 5/10/05.

Jordan, N. (2003). HUSH, HUSH, The Dark Secrets of Scientific Research. London: Quintet.

Kaplan, C. (1998). "Is Software Like a Can Opener or a Recipe?" Cyberlaw Journal. Available at www.nytimes.com/library/tech/98/07/cyberlaw/17law.htm. Accessed 9/29/05.

Katz, Jay. (1983). The Silent World of Doctor and Patient. Baltimore, MD: The Johns Hopkins University Press.

Kunich, J. (2000). "Natural Born Killers and the Law of Shock Torts." Washington Law Quarterly, Vol. 78, p. 1157.

Leadstrom, N. D. (2001). "Internet Web Sites as Products Under Strict Products Liability: A Call for an Expanded Definition of a Product." Washburn Law Journal, Vol. 40, pp. 532–560.

Legal Information Institute. (N.D.). "Products Liability." Available at www.law.cornll.edu/topics/products_liability.html. Accessed 5/10/05.

Levy, E. (2001, August 16). "Full Disclosure Is a Necessary Evil." Available at http://securityfocus.com/news.238. Accessed 9/28/05.

Martin, Brian. (2001, November 10). "Microsoft's Responsible Vulnerability Disclosure, The New Non-Issue." Available at http://attrition.org/security/rant/z/ms-disclose.html. Accessed 9/29/05.

McKinnon, K. (1983). *Only Words.* Cambridge, MA: Harvard University Press.

Mitchell, D., and E. Banker. (1998). "Private Intrusion Response." *Harvard Journal of Law and Technology,* Vol. 699, No. 10, p. 704.

Morgenstern, M., Parker, T., and Hardy, S. (N.D.). "It's Time To Be Responsible." Available at http://securityfocus.com,/guest/10711. Accessed 10/5/05.

Myers, B. L. (1992). "Read at Your Own Risk: Publisher Liability for Defective How-To Books." *Arkansas Law Review,* Vol. 45, p. 699.

Olavsrud, Thor. (2002, August 1). "Government Against Full Disclosure of Vulnerabilities." Available at http://internetnews.com/dev-news/print.php/1437841. Accessed 9/29/05.

Ozment, Andy. (2005, June). "The Likelihood of Vulnerability Rediscovery and the Social Utility of Vulnerability Hunting" [Working Paper]. Available at http://infosecon.net/workshop/pdf/10.pdf. Accessed 5/14/05.

Phillips, J. (1999). "Information Liability: The Possible Chilling Effect of Tort Claims Against Producers of Geographic Information System Data." *Florida State University Law Review,* Vol. 26, p. 743.

Preston, E., and J. Lofton. (2002). "Computer Security Publications: Information Economics, Shifting Liability and the First Amendment." *Whittier Law Review,* Vol. 71, pp. 72–74.

ProCD v. Zeidenberg. (1996). US Court of Appeals, 7th Cir. 96 F. 3d 1447.

Ranum, H. (2000). "Have a Cocktail: Computer Security Today." Available at http://www.ranum.com/security/computer_security/archives/ranum_elx_cocktail. pdf. Accessed 10/5/05.

Rasch, Mark. (2002, March 11). "'Responsible Disclosure' Draft Could Have Legal Muscle." Available at http://www.securityfocus.com/columnists/66. Accessed 10/5/05.

Rasch, Mark. (2003, August 18). "The Sad Tale of a Security Whistleblower." Available at www.securityfocus.com/columnists/179. Accessed 10/5/05.

Rauch, Jeremy. (1999, December 8). "The Future of Vulnerability Disclosure." Available at http://usenix.org/publicatons/login/1999-11/features/disclosure.html. Accessed 7/10/06.

Reimerdes. (2001). 273 F. 3d 429, 2nd Cir.

Reno, Attorney General of the US v. American Civil Liberties Union. (1997). 521 US 844.

Rescorla, E. (2003). "Security Holes . . . Who Cares?" Available at http://www.rtfm.com/Upgrade-usenix.pdf. Accessed 9/27/05.

Rescorla, E. (N.D.). "Is Finding Security Holes a Good Idea?" Available at www.rtfm.com/burgate.pdf. Accessed 9/27/05.

Rice v. Paladin. (1997). 128 F. 3d 233 (4th Cir.).

Saloomey v. Jeppesen. (1983). 707 F. 2d 671, 2nd Cir.

Samuelson, P., and J. Reichman. (1997). "Intellectual Property Rights to Data?" *Vanderbilt Law Review,* Vol. 50, p. 51.

Schneier, B. (2000, September 15). "Full Disclosure and the Window of Exposure." Available at http://www.schneier.com/crypto-gram-0009.html. Accessed 9/29/05.

Schneier, B. (2004). "Secret Lies—Digital Security in a Networked World." New York: Wiley.

Schneier, B. (N.D.). "Crypto-Gram Newsletter: Full Disclosure." Available at http://www.schneier.com/crypto-gram-0111.html#/. Accessed 7/10/06.

Schultz, R. (1999). "Application of Strict Product Liability to Aeronautical Chartpublishers." *Journal of Air Law and Commerce,* Vol. 64, pp. 431–458.

Spinello, Richard. (1997). *Case Studies in Information and Computer Ethics.* Englewood Cliffs, NJ: Prentice Hall.

Stadler, Ronald B. (2002). "Examples of Malicious Computer Programs." Available at www.rbs2.com/cvirus.htm. Accessed 5/20/05.

Takanen, A., P. Raasakka, M. Laakso, and J. Roning. (2004, June). "Agents of Responsibility in Software Vulnerability Processes." *Ethics and Information Technology,* Vol. 6, No. 2.

Tavani, H. (2004). "Ethics and Technology." In *Ethical Issues in an Age of Information and Communication Technology*. New York: Wiley.

Talang, R., and S. Wattal. (2005, February). "Impact of Software Vulnerability Announcements on the Market Value of Software Vendors—An Empirical Investigation" [Working Paper]. Pittsburgh, PA: Carnegie Mellon University.

Vidstrom, A. (N.D.). "Full vulnerabilities—Pros and Cons and Fake Arguments." Available at http://www.net-security.org/article.php?id=86. Accessed 10/5/05.

United States Department of Justice. (1997, April). "Report on the Availability of Bombmaking Information, the Extent to Which Such Dissemination Is Controlled by Federal Law and the Extent to Which Its Dissemination May Be Subject to Regulation Consistent With the First Amendment to the US Constitution." Available at www.derechos.org.human-rights/speech/bomb.html. Accessed 10/5/05.

Universal City Studios v. Reimerdes. (2001). 111 F. Suppl. 2d 294, 331, S.D.N.Y.

US v. Freeman. (1985). 761 F. 2d 549, 5529th Cir.

Winter v. G. Putnam's Sons. (1991). 1033 F 2d 928, 1033, 9th Cir.

Index

Figures are noted with f; footnotes are noted with n

A

Abortion rights
  epistemic issues in justifying civil disobedience and, 82–83
  evidentiary principle and, 111
Acacia, 195
Academic freedom, super-DMCAs and, 214–215
Accessibility, ensuring, 176–177
Account scams, on-line games, 226–229
  access to characters, 227
  access to items, 228
  reasons for abuse of usernames and passwords, 227–228
  solutions related to, 228–229
Account sharing, on-line games, 231–232
  as security threat, 231–232
  solutions to problems around, 232
Acid Phreak, 14
Act Deontology theory, 41, 42
Active defense, 47–48
  evaluation of, under relevant ethical principles, 111–118

Active response, 99–100
  continuum, 100
  defense principle and, 105, 111
  evidentiary principle and, 110–111
  levels of, 102–103
    aggressive, 102–103
    benign, 102
    intermediate, 102
  punishment principle and, 107–109
  relevant ethical principles for, 101–110
  retaliation principle and, 106–107, 108
  spectrum of, 100–101
Adleman, Len, 18
Administrators, disclosure debate and, 262
Adobe's Web publishing tools, 146
Advanced structured cyberterror capability, 126
AEJT. See Arab Electronic Jihad Team
Aetna Casualty v. Jeppesen, 256n
Affirmative action, 81
Afghanistan, women in, 94
Aggressive active defense responses, 112–114
  defense principle and, 112–113
  necessity principle and, 113–114

Aggressive level of active response, 102–103
Agile processes, 182, 189
Agreement, informed consent and, 155
AIM. *See* AOL Instant Messenger
Air traffic control systems, virus attacks and, 22
al Ansar, 131
Al Aqsa Martyrs Brigade, 130
Al-Arian, Sami, 134, 135
Aldus, 20
al-Farouq Web site, 132, 134
al-Ghorabaa Web site, 130, 132
Al-Hussayen, Sami Omar, 134, 135
al-Maqdisi, Abu Muhammad, 135
al-Muhajiroun, 129, 134
al Qaeda, 91, 97, 130, 131, 132, 133, 134, 135
Al-Qaeda Alliance Online, 123, 130
Al-Qaida University for Jihad Sciences, 132
Al-Qassam Brigades, 130
al-Zarqawi-al-Qaeda's Second Generation (Husseing), 134
Amazon.com, 93, 121, 210
    hacker attack of, 61, 63
American Israel Public Affairs Committee, 130
Ames Research Center (NASA), 20
Ammann, Paul, 179
Analysts, 173, 180, 183
    SE Code of Ethics and, 198
    security concerns and, 193
    team ownership of process and, 193
Anarchists, 85
Animal Liberation Front, 97, 126, 129
Anonymity
    analysis of threat steganography has on, 216–218
    role of steganography and, 206–209
    tools, 39
Anonymous hactivist attacks, costs related to, 92
Anti India Crew, 123
Anti-Terrorism Coalition, 130

Antiviral protection, 21
Anton, Annie, 190
AOL Instant Messenger, 144
Apply Yourself software program, 35
Aquinas, Thomas, 43
Arab Electronic Jihad Team, 133
Arbaugh, William A., 186
Architectural design, security goals and, 184
Aristotle, 245
ARPANET, 6
Asian Hangout forum, 130
Astray Lumberjacks, 65, 96
ATC. *See* Anti-Terrorism Coalition
Attack vectors, 173
    SE Code of Ethics and, 197
Auditing, implementing, 176
Ausaf newspaper, 133
Australia, attack against critical infrastructure in, 125
Australian Entertainment and Media Outlook Report, 222
Authentication
    community resources and, 179
    trustworthy processes for, 178
AUTOCAD 2000, 132
Availability, computer security and, 30
Avatars, in on-line games, 223n

B
Bacteria, 32
Banker, Elizabeth A., 109, 121, 122
Bank fraud, cyberattacks and, 125
Bank of America, 14
Barry Manilow virus, 20
Baseline problem, bettering, worsening and, 241–242
Basque Fatherland, 127
Bayles, M., 145
BEAM, 132
Bedworth, Paul, 14
Bell Tymenet computers, 14
Beneich, Denis, 21
Benign active defense measures, 116–118

Benign level of active response, 102
Berghel, Hal, 177
Berne Convention Standards, 239
Bhabba Atomic Research Centre (India)
    hacking into, 96
    hactivist groups and, 62, 64
"Big Brother," social protector argu-
    ment and, 56, 57
Bigelow, Bruce B., 145
Big Red, 22
Big up-front design, eXtreme pro-
    gramming and, 189
Billing information, game hosting
    companies and, 225
bin Laden, Osama, 123, 129, 132, 133,
    134, 135, 209
Biometric technologies, 40
BIS. *See* Bureau of Industry and
    Security
Bissett, Andy, 203
Black Hand (Crna Ruka) group, 129
"Black hat" hackers, 38, 180, 188, 249
Black Ice (Verton), 135
Blaming
    creating congruent culture with-
    out, 193
    team culture issues and, 192
Blaster worm, 176
Blueboxes, 5
BMG Digital Rights Management
    software (Sony), 224
Boston Tea Party, 70
"Bragging rights," 180, 186
Brain virus, 18
Brandeis, Justice Louis, 34
Branscomb, Anne W., 32
Breton, Thierry, 21
British Telecom, penetration of e-
    mail system at, 11
Britton, John Bayard, 82, 111
Brown, Garrett, 215
Browsers, retrospective analysis of, 156
Buffer overflow problems, 181
BugTraq, 257

Building Secure Software (Viega and
    McGraw), 172
Bureau of Industry and Security, 208
Bush, George W., 135
Buy.com, hacker attack of, 61

C
Canellopoulou-Bottis, Maria, 203
Cannon fodder, on-line games and,
    223n
Canon, 216, 217
Capability Maturity Model, 188
    Systems Security Engineering, 181
Capital, electronic opposition
    groups and, 63
Captain Crunch (John T. Draper), 5
Captain Midnight (John
    MacDougall), 3–4
"Carding," terrorist activities and, 132
Carnivore, 40
Carriers, steganography and, 206, 207
Cathedral and the Bazaar, The
    (Raymond), 187
CATIGE, 132
Center for Intrusion Control, 66
Center on Terrorism and Irregular
    Warfare, cyberterrorism
    threat studies by, 126
CERT (Carnegie Mellon University),
    186, 187
CERT/CC. *See* Computer Emergency
    Response Team
    Coordinating Center
CFAA. *See* Computer Fraud and
    Abuse Act
Challenge question systems, 178
Chaos Computer Club, 66
Characters
    in on-line games, 223n
    on-line games and access to, 227
Chats, in-game, 229
Cheating
    on-line games and, 224
    third-party software and, 229
Chernobyl disaster, 12

Children
    information given by, to game
        hosting company, 226
    on-line gaming market and,
        222–223
China, antidemocratic crackdowns,
    hactivism and, 62
Chinese government Web sites, hac-
    tivist attacks on, 65, 93
Christian Broadcasting Network, 4, 6
Civil disobedience
    defined, 62
    discussion about, 74–76
    electronic, 47, 62–63
    epistemic issue in justification
        of, 81–84
    framework for evaluating acts of,
        84–86
    hactivism's moral justification
        as, 88–96
    morality and, 74–86
    moral permissibleness and, 76–80
    new form of?, 61
    unjustified, punishment and, 80–81
Civil liberties
    security technologies and, 40
    steganography and threat to, 206
Civil Rights movement, 70, 85, 92
Class responsibility and collabora-
        tion (CRC) cards, eXtreme
        programming and, 189
Cleanroom Software Engineering, 181
Client and employer, SE Code of
        Ethics, principle 4, 197, 198
Clients, 177n, 183
    professional's relation to, 145–146
Client/server architecture, multi-
        player on-line games and, 222
Clipper Chip, 40, 212
CMM. See Capability Maturity Model
CNN.com, hacker attack of, 61, 65
Code Complete (McConnell), 172
Code inspection, 185
Code Red I virus, 256
Code Red II virus, 256
Code Red worm, 172, 186

Coders, 183
Coding, 182
    percentage of total effort in soft-
        ware project, 171
Cohen, Cynthia F., 185, 191
Cohen, Fred, 18
Colleagues, SE Code of Ethics, princi-
        ple 7, 197, 199
Color laser printer technology,
        steganography and, 216–217
Commercial entities, hactivism and
        harm caused to, 89–90
Commercial off-the-shelf compo-
        nents, security vulnerabilities
        with, 180
Communication, team culture issues
        and, 191–192
Communications of the ACM, 196
Community resources, using, 179–180
Competence, informed consent
        and, 155
Complex coordinated cyberterror
        capability, 126
Comprehension
    cookie management and, 157
    informed consent and, 155
Computer break-ins, justification of,
        on moral grounds?, 41–42
Computer crime
    computer security vs., 33–34
    hacking vs., 7
    legislation, 68
Computer Emergency Response
        Team Coordinating Center,
        259, 260
Computer ethics, 154
Computer Fraud and Abuse Act of
        1986, 20
    civil and criminal liability under, 264
Computer gaming industry, eco-
        nomic worth of, 221–222
Computer hacker break-ins
    ethics around, 49–58
    hacker ethic and, 52
    idle system argument, 55
    motivations behind, 51–57

security arguments, 53–55
social protector argument, 56–57
student hacker argument, 55–56
sum total of all future effects,
    morality of, 51
Computer immunology, 176
Computer intrusions, psychological
    costs of, 1
Computer memory, Core Wars pro-
    grams and, 17–18
Computer Misuse Act, 14
Computer nerd syndrome, 8
"Computer psychosis," 8
Computers, use of, as civil disobedi-
    ence tool, 62
Computer security. See also Security
    classic definition of, 30
    computer crime vs., 33–34
    data security and integrity of
        information, 30–31
    moral aspects of, 36–40, 43
    moral dilemmas around, 40–43
    network security and threat of
        cyberterrorism, 32–33
    system security and vulnerability
        of system resources, 31–32
Computer-supported cooperative
    work, 154
Computer Virus Eradication Act of
    1988, The, 55
Computer World, 134
Conceptual investigations, value-
    sensitive design and, 154
Confidentiality. See also Privacy
    computer security and, 30
    data security and, 31
    ensuring, 176–177
    least privilege principle and, 178
Conflict management skills, team
    culture issues and, 192
Congruence, in software develop-
    ment, 192
Congruent culture, creating without
    blaming, 193
Consent. See also Informed consent
    explicit, 118–119

relevance of, 118–122
    tacit, 119–121
Consequentialist theories, justifying
    punishment and, 108
Constitution (U.S.), 239
Consumer culture, hactivism and, 62
"Control" based definition, of pri-
    vacy, 236
Convictions, epistemic issues in jus-
    tifying civil disobedience
    and, 83
Conway, M., 209, 210
Conxion, 99, 112
Cookie management, 166
    informed consent and, 153–154
    overarching design goals for,
        156–158
Cookies, 141, 177n
    retrospective analysis of, 156
    risk to privacy posed by, 177
Cookie watcher, Mozilla, 160–165
Coopers & Lybrand, 22
Copyright, 239
    steganography and, 216
Copyright law, security implications
    and, 195
Core, 17
Core values, privacy as, 34
Core Wars (game program), 17–18
Corley case (2000), 264
Cornwall, Hugo, 10
Corrupt, 14
Counterfeit documents, steganogra-
    phy and tracking of, 216
Counterhacking, 40, 100
    justification of, on moral
        grounds?, 42–43
Crackers, 64, 79
    software vulnerabilities and, 260
Cracking, 7, 38
Credit card fraud
    cyberattacks and, 125
    phone hacking and, 6
    terrorist activities and, 132
Credit card information, game host-
    ing companies and, 225

Credit reporting services, hacking of, 14
Crime, in-game, 228
Critical Infrastructure Assurance Office, 66
Cryptographic key, 183
Cryptography, 126, 200, 203
  steganography and, 206, 208
CSCW. *See* Computer-supported cooperative work
CTIW. *See* Center on Terrorism and Irregular Warfare
Cuckoo's Egg, The (Stoll), 13
Cult of the Dead Cow, 62, 66
Curtis, Bill, 192
Customers, eXtreme programming and, 188–189
Cusumano, Michael A., 194
Cyberactivism, 62
Cyberattacks, 32
  execution of, 127, 128–131
  formal education in information technology and, 134–135
  general experience with cyberspace and, 135
  statements about, 127, 133–134
Cybercrime, 121
Cyberethics, 143
Cyber-intifada, 130
Cyber jihad, 129
Cyber-jihadists, 131
Cyberpunks, 235
Cyber-rape, 143
Cyberspace
  general experience with, 127, 128, 135
  privacy in, 31
Cyberstalking, 33n, 143
Cyberterror indicators, 127–135
  cyberweapons acquisition, development, and training, 131–133
  execution of cyberattacks, 128–131
  formal education in information technology and, 134–135
  general experience with cyberspace, 135

kinds of, 127
  statements about cyberattacks, 133–134
Cyberterrorism, 30, 48, 62, 123
  defined, 32
  discussion about, 124–125
  electronic civil disobedience *vs.*, 79
  hactivism and, 65–68, 70
  hactivism *vs.*, 87
  indicators preceding successful incidents of, 136
  network security and threat of, 32–33
  NPS/CTIW studies, 126–127
Cyberterrorists, 64, 79, 197
Cybervandalism, 33
Cyberwar, 66
  cyberterrorism *vs.*, 124
Cyberweapons acquisition, development, and training, 127

D
"Daemon"-like code, on-line games and, 230
Damages, student hacker argument and, 56
Darwin, Charles, 235
Data security, 43
  integrity of information and, 30–31
Data surveillance, 235
Dataveillance, hactivism and, 62
DDOS attacks. *See* Distributed denial of service attacks
Decryption algorithms, software trafficking and, 209
DeCSS, 265
Defacement, of Web sites, 123, 125, 136
Defects, fixing, 191–192
"Defense in depth," 177
Defense principle, 105, 111, 118
  aggressive active defense responses and, 112–113
  justified use of force and, 103–104
Defensive measures, 101
Democracy

civil disobedience and citizens living in, 78, 85
hacking and, 12–13
Denial of service attacks, 99, 124
as aggressive responses, 102–103, 112
character of the hack and, 90, 91
cyberattacks and, 129
global commerce and, 61
granting privileges and, 178
Denmark, Web defacements in, 130
Denning, Dorothy E., 32, 48, 123, 174
Denning, Peter, 25
Deontologists, computer break-ins and views of, 41
Department of Defense, 66
Department of Homeland Security, 181
Design, 182
Designers, 173, 180, 183
team ownership of process and, 193
Design goals
achieving design goals 1, 2, and 3 while minimizing distraction to user (Design Goal 4), 158
enhancing users' ability to manage cookies (Design Goal 3), 157–158
enhancing users' global understanding of common uses of cookie technology (Design Goal 2), 157
enhancing users' local understanding of discrete cookie events (Design Goal 1), 156–157
Developers, 173, 180, 190
SE Code of Ethics and, 198
security concerns and, 193
team culture issues and, 191
team ownership of process and, 193
tension between testers and, 185
Dhamija, R., 216
Diablo II, 228
Dickens, Charles, 224
Digital activism, 62
hactivism vs., 87
Digital intrusions

hacker viewpoints on, 73
hactivism and, 88
law enforcement efforts and, 101, 121–122
Digital Millennium Copyright Act, 195, 209, 212
civil and criminal liability under, 264
Digital rights management, steganography and, 215–216
Digital signatures, 178
Digital steganography, 206
previous steganographic methods vs., 207–208
Director, 158
Disclosure of software vulnerability arguments against, 261
clash of interests in disclosure debate, 261–263
cookie management and, 157
debate about, 258–261
informed consent and, 155
Discrimination, hactivism and, 64
Disease theory (Pasteur), 235
Disinfectants, defined, 16
Distributed denial of service attacks, 8, 42, 93
accessibility and, 176
aggressive responses and, 112
character of the hack and, 90, 91
Dittrich, David, 249
DMCA. See Digital Millennium Copyright Act
Doctor Nuker, 130
Doucette, Lynne, 6
Dow Jones, 257
Draper, John T. (Captain Crunch), 5
DRM. See Digital rights management
"Due care" principle, 150, 151

E
Earth Liberation Front, 97
East African Embassy bombings, 136
East Timor, hactivism and occupation of, 62
eBay, 210, 228, 257
hacker attack of, 61

ECD. *See* Electronic civil disobedience

e-commerce, cyberterrorism and, 91

Economic inequality, hactivism and, 64

Effective, sensible software process, 192–193

Efficiency, 174

    auditing and/or monitoring and, 176

    ensuring confidentiality, integrity, and accessibility and, 177

    least privilege principle and, 179

    multilevel security and, 177

    using community resources and, 179

e-graffiti, 90

El Al Web site, 130

Elam, Joyce J., 192

Electrohippies, 92, 99, 112–113

Electronic activism, 63

Electronic civil disobedience, 47, 61, 62–63, 69, 96. *See also* Civil disobedience

    cyberterrorism *vs.*, 79

    digital activism *vs.*, 87

    hactivism and, 63–65

    political agendas: are they plausible and supported by adequate reasons?, 92–95

    purpose of, 63

    use of computers in support of *vs.* use of computers as act of, 63

Electronic Disturbance Theater, 62, 64, 92

Electronic Freedom Foundation Web site, 213

Electronic jihad, 132

Embedding technology, steganography and, 217

Emotions, 8

Empirical investigations, value-sensitive design and, 154

Encryption

    behind firewall, 177

    community resources and, 179

    risk assessment and, 183

Encryption technologies, 40

    restrictions on, 208–209

    usability and, 177

End-user license agreement, on-line games and, 226, 229

Entertainment software industry, economic worth of, 221–222

Environmental activism, 70

Epstein, Richard, 141

Ethical issues

    around hacking, 23–25

    production of secure software and, 194–199

Ethical obligations, of professionals, 146–147

Ethical principles, evidentiary restriction for justifiably acting under, 110–111

Ethics

    around electronic civil disobedience, 63–64

    defining, 50–51

    digital steganography and, 207–209

    distinction between morality and, 36

    moving towards hactivist ethic, 68–69

Ethno-nationalist separatist terrorist groups, cyberterror capability of, 126

EULA. *See* End-user license agreement

European Union, 225

Evidentiary principle, 110–111, 116

Evolution theory, 235

Explicit consent, 118–119

Exploits, 173, 181

    preventing vulnerabilities leading to, 175–176

    SE Code of Ethics and, 197

Extensible software, security and, 177

eXtreme programming, 182

    extreme practices and, 188–189

    security implications with, 187, 188–190

F

Failures, secure, 179
Fair use, steganography and, 216
Fairweather, N. Ben, 203
Far-right extremist terrorist groups,
    cyberterror capability of, 126
Federal Bureau of Investigation, 132
Federal Trade Commission, 153
Felten, Edward, 141, 214
Fiduciary model, 148
File sharing, 235
Financial records, data security and, 31
Financial systems, cyberattacks
    against, 125
Firewalls, 119, 177, 181, 195
    security policies and, 184
First Amendment defense, publish-
    ers of software vulnerabili-
    ties and, 264, 265
Fithen, William L., 186
Flag burning, 81
Flaming, 143
FloodNet, 63
Fluor Corp. v. Jeppesen & Co., 256n
Force, defense principle and justified
    use of, 103
Foreign intelligence agencies, 183
Forgery Act (Great Britain), 11
Forrest, Stephanie, 176
Forrester, Tom, 1
Forty-hour work week, eXtreme pro-
    gramming and, 189
Fourth Amendment, 34
Free access, champions of, 235
"Free access" defense, "they still
    have their copy" argument
    and, 247
Freedom of choice, silence about
    software vulnerability and
    costs in, 263–265
Freedom of information
    hackers and, 69
    hactivism and, 61
"Free" information, hacker ethic and,
    52
Free speech, 76, 77

silence about software vulnerabil-
    ity and costs in, 263–265
steganography and, 206
Friedman, Batya, 141
FrontPage, 146
Full disclosure, 259, 265
    arguments for, 260
Fully secure computing environ-
    ments, moral issues arising
    because of, 39
Functionality, 174
    ensuring confidentiality, integrity,
    and accessibility and, 177
    using community resources and,
    179
Functional requirements, 183

G

Game development, economics of, 230
Game hosting company
    information given to, 225–226
    information given to, and why?, 225
    information given to, as Internet
    security threat, 225–226
    practical security solutions and, 226
Gaming, security and, 203
Garfinkel, Simson, 30
Gedanken prototype, 158–160, 162
    description of, 158–159
    formative evaluation, 159–160
GForce Pakistan, 123, 130
Global commerce, denial of service
    attacks and, 61
GNU Manifesto, 52
Gödel, Kurt, 179
Goggerbarn, Donald, 141
Gold, Steven, 11
Goodrum, Abby, 47, 79, 91, 92, 96
Government regulation, of steganog-
    raphy/steganalysis, 212–214
Great hack, 6
Grodzinsky, Frances, 203
Gulf War, 21
Gutenberg's press, 235

H

Habbo hotel, 223
"Hacker ethic," 38, 52
   hactivism in support of, 94–95
Hackers, 38, 235
   cooperation among, 14
   crackdown on, 13–15
   criminals or modern Robin
      Hoods?, 11–13
   definitions of, 7
   reasons for hacking, 8–11
*Hackers: Heroes of the Computer
      Revolution* (Levy), 5, 68
Hacker's Dictionary, The (Raymond, et
      al.), 7, 86
Hacker's Handbook III (Cornwall), 10
Hacking, 143
   description of and meanings for, 5–7
   ethical issues arising from, 23–25
   hactivism vs., 87
   justifications for, 47
   moral issues around, 37–39
   overriding privacy and intellectual
      property presumptions: argu-
      ments in favor of, 244–250
   security and social benefits argu-
      ment in favor of, 249–250
   social nature of information argu-
      ment in favor of, 244–247, 250
   they still have their copy argu-
      ment in favor of, 235,
      247–248, 250
   viruses and, 3–25
Hacking back, 42, 100
   defense principle and, 105, 111
   evidentiary principle and, 110–111
   punishment principle and, 107–109
   retaliation principle and,
      106–107, 108
Hacking for fun, 38
Hacking for profit, 38
Hactivism, 33n, 47, 61
   amount of harm caused by, 89–91
      character of the hack, 90–91

      public, private, commercial, and
         noncommercial entities, 89–90
   cyberterrorism vs., 65–68, 70, 79, 87
   defining, 86–88
   description of, 62
   electronic civil disobedience and,
      63–65
   hacking vs., 87
   moral justification for, 73–98
   moral justification for, as civil dis-
      obedience, 88–96
   promise of, 69
   in support of "hacker ethic," 94–95
   in support of human rights, 93–94
   unjustified, punishment for, 97–98
Hactivist ethic, moving towards, 68–69
Hactivists, 61
   cognitive possession by, related to
      plausible justifications for
      positions motivating their
      acts, 95–96
   cyberwar condemned by, 66
   responsibility accepted by, 91–92
Hamas, 130
   Web site of, 135
Harassment, 143
Harvard Law Review, 34
Haynie, Thomas M., 4
HBO (Home Box Office), 3
Health information, steganographic
      techniques and, 214
Health Insurance Portability and
      Accountability Act, 214
Hebrew University, 19
Hettinger, Edwin, 247, 248
Hezbollah, 129, 209
"HighSpeed Junkie," 257
Hill, Paul, 81, 82, 111
Himma, Kenneth E., 42, 43, 47, 48, 249
!Hispahack, 66
*Hit Man: A Technical Manual for
      Independent Contractors,* 264n
Hofmeyr, Steven A., 176
Hollinger, Richard, 15
Home Box Office, 3

Honeyman, P., 210
Honeypots, 117
Hong Kong Blondes, 62, 65
Honkers Union (China), 125
Hospitals, virus attacks and, 22
Host computers, distributed denial of
    service attacks and, 42–43
"Hot seat" play, multiplayer on-line
    games and, 222
Howard, Michael, 172, 181, 182, 185,
    189, 193
Howe, Daniel, 141
Hubin, Don, 248
Human rights
    electronic civil disobedience and, 64
    hactivism and, 65, 88, 93–94
    hactivists, oppressive govern-
        ments and, 62
Hupp, Jon, 16
Hurwitz survey, software vendors
    and, 262
Huschle, Brian J., 79
Husseing, Fouad, 134
Hydroelectric dams, virus attacks
    and, 22

I
IBM, 25
iDefense, 129
Idle system argument, computer
    break-ins and, 55
IDSs. See Intrusion detection systems
ILOVEYOU virus, 31, 257
IMP program, 17–18
Indonesia, hactivism and human
    rights violations in, 65
Indonesian Government Web sites,
    East Timor occupation, hac-
    tivism and, 62
Information
    harm caused by, 255
    product liability and, 256
Information America, 14

Information control, struggle
    between centralizing/decen-
    tralizing forces and, 12
Information hiding, 205. See also
    Steganography
Information overload, 158
Information ownership, criminality
    questions and, 24
Information technology, formal edu-
    cation in, 127, 128, 134–135
Informed consent, 149, 150, 166
    cookie management and,
        153–154, 157–158
    criteria for, on-line, 155
    critical protections afforded by, 153
    retrospective analysis of, 156
    value-sensitive design and, 141
Inner Circle, 10
Innes, Harold, 12
Innocent third parties
    hactivism and harm caused to,
        89–90
    impacts of active responses on,
        111–112
Insecure software products, economic
    consequences related to, 197
Insider attacks, 180
Instantaneous disclosure, 259
Integrity
    computer security and, 30
    data security and, 30–31
    ensuring, 31, 176–177
    following, 178
Intellectual property, 194, 195, 203
    establishing a presumption in
        favor of, 239–244
    hacker ethic and, 52
    hactivism and, 67
    labor theory of acquisition and, 240
    overriding presumptions in favor
        of, for arguments in favor of
        hacking, 244–250
    watermarking and, 216
Intermediate active defense
    responses, 114–116

Intermediate level of active
    response, 102
International Federation of
    Information Processing, 18
International Information Hiding
    Workshop, 214
Internet
    digital activism and, 62
    "electronic agora" and, 69
    hactivists and commodification
        of, 62
    harm caused by information pub-
        lished on, 256–257
    phenomenal growth of, 143
Internet Black Tigers, 129
Internet Café, on-line games played
    in, 231
Internet development
    concept of profession and, 144–145
    Internet-appropriate model of
        professionalism and, 148
    Internet professional ethics and,
        148–149
    professional approach addressing
        broad impact of, 147–148
    professionalization of?, 147
    transition to professionalism
        and, 144
Internet Explorer, 156
Internet Explorer 5.x, 163
Internet Haganah, 131
    jihad cyberattacks and, 130
Internet Islamic Brigades, 130
Internet professional ethics, from
    Internet development to,
    148–149
Internet professionalism, description
    of, 149–150
Internet service providers, steno-
    graphic communication
    and, 210
Internet Worm program (1988), 49,
    53, 54
Internet worms, 32, 176. See also
    Worms
InterNIC, 64, 92

Intrusion detection systems, 176
Investigative journalism, 12
Iran Contra affair, 12
Irhabi 007, 131
Iron Guard, 129
Islamic Hacker Army, 134
Israeli-Palestinian conflict, cyberat-
    tacks and, 129
Israeli viruses, 19
IT. See Information technology
Items, on-line games and access to,
    228
Iterative waterfall (or lifecycle)
    process, security considera-
    tions incorporated into, 182
Ivkovich, Rick, 6

J
Jackson, Steve, 14
Jajodia, Sushil, 179
James, Henry, 224
Jamestown Foundation, 130, 132
Jefferson, Thomas, 239
Jihadists
    cyberattacks and, 137
    general experience with cyber-
        space and, 135
Jim Crow laws, 77, 78, 92
Joint Task-Force Computer Network
    Defense, 66
Jonsson, Erland, 181
Judgment, SE Code of Ethics, princi-
    ple 3, 197, 198
Just, Mike, 178
Just-in-time interventions
    cookie events and, 158
    Mozilla cookie watcher and, 162
Jyllands-Posten, cyberattacks against,
    130, 131, 132

K
Kaotik Team, 65
Karn, Philip R., 21
Kashpureff, Eugene, 64, 92
Kerebos, 179

Key-stroke monitoring technologies, 40
Khalil, Ziyad (pseud. Ziyad Sadaqa), 135
Kiesler, Sara, 8
Kimppa, Kai, 203
Kizza, Joseph M., 30
Kohno, Tadayoshi, 179
Kosovo conflict, cyberattacks and, 129

L
Labor theory of acquisition, 240
LambdaMOO case, 223n
Lambeth, Mark, 248
Lampson, Butler, 179
Landreth, Bill, 10
Laplante, Phillip, 182
Law, profession of, 144
Law enforcement agencies, digital intrusions and, 101
Law enforcement efforts, inadequacy of, 121–122
Lawton, George, 187
Least privilege principle, following, 178–179
LeBlanc, David, 172, 181, 182, 185, 189, 193
Legion of Doom, 49
Legion of the Underground, 66
Legislation
    computer crime, 68
    computer viruses and, 55
    for insecure code, 196
    super-DMCA, 215
    against use of steganography, 210
Lehigh University, 19
Lehigh virus, 19
Lessig, Lawrence, 148
Levy, Steven, 5, 68
    tenets of hacker ethic summarized by, 94
Liability, 194
    disclosure debate and, 261
    information and, 256
    for insecure software, 195–196

Liberation Tigers of Tamil Eelan, 127, 129
Liberty-Political/Military, 127
Licensing proposals, for security professionals, 122
LIFE, 18
Limited disclosure, 259, 263
Lincoln, Abraham, 245
Lindqvist, Ulf, 181
Lineage II, 228
Liston, Tom, 215
Locke, John, 240, 241, 244
Logic bombs, 32
    defined, 15
Log-out sequences, nonsecure, 10
London subway bombings, 136
LOpht Heavy Industries, 66
LoU. See Legion of the Underground
Lower level design, security policies and, 184
LTTE. See Liberation Tigers of Tamil Eelan

M
MacDougall, John (Captain Midnight), 3–4
Mad Hacker (Nicholas Whiteley), 13
Madrid train bombings, 136
Magnus Ranstorp, 131
Maintainability, 174
    auditing and/or monitoring and, 176
    ensuring confidentiality, integrity, and accessibility and, 177
    failing securely and, 179
    least privilege principle and, 179
Maintainers, 183
    SE Code of Ethics and, 198
    security concerns and, 193
Maintenance, 182
    "penetrate and patch" mentality and, 186–190
Management, SE Code of Ethics, principle 5, 197, 198
Man-in-the-middle attack, 180
Manion, Mark, 47, 79, 91, 92, 96

"Many eyeballs" approach, to software development, 187, 190
Market value
    social nature of information argument and, 244–247
    vulnerability disclosures and, 262
Marri, Ali S., 135
Martin, David M., Jr., 177
Massachusetts Institute of Technology, 5, 20
Massively multiplayer games, 224
Mass media, hactivism and corporate domination of, 62
Masters of Disaster, 14
Mattord, Herbert J., 184
McAfee, John, 19
McCollum, Catherine D., 179
McConnell, Steve, 172
McGraw, Gary, 172, 174, 180, 181, 182, 184, 187, 189, 191
McHugh, John, 186
McLendon, Jean, 192, 193
Me Against the Terrorist! (Sumadra), 132
Medical records, data security and, 31
Medicine, profession of, 144
Melbourne University, 13
Melissa virus, 31, 172
Mental state, epistemic issues in justifying civil disobedience and, 83
Messenger's haircut, 205, 208
Mexican government Web sites, symbolic acts of electronic civil disobedience and, 61, 63
MHC. See Muslim Hackers Club
Michelangelo virus, 31
Microsoft, 133, 172, 185
    Internet Information Server, 257
    limited disclosure and, 263
    software development at, 193, 194
MICROSTRAN, 132
Military research, on steganalysis, 210
Miller, Keith, 203
MilwOrm, 64, 65, 92, 96

Minbar ahl al-Sunna wal-Jama (The Pulpit of the People of the Sunna), 132
Minimal distraction, 158
    informed consent and, 155
Minsky, Marvin, 9
Mir, Hadmid, 133
MIT. See Massachusetts Institute of Technology
Mitchell, Stevan D., 109, 121, 122
MMORPGs. See Massively multiplayer games
Modem, hacker's use of, 9
Mohammad, 130
Monitoring, implementing, 176
Moor, James H., 34, 38
Moore, Adam, 203
Moral dilemmas, around computer security, 40–43
Moral hackers, discussion of, 49
Moral issues
    fully secure computing environments and, 39
    on non-sufficiently secure computing environments, 37–39
Morality
    civil disobedience and, 74–86
    distinction between ethics and, 36
Morals, moral values and, 36–37
Morris, Desmond, 237n
Morris, Robert T., 20, 32, 53, 54, 171
Morrison, Perry, 1
Morris worm (1988), 171
Motion Picture Association of America, 212
Mozilla 0.8
    Gedanken prototype, screen shot of cookie manager tool in, 159f
    Gedanken prototype and, 158–160
Mozilla browser, 154
    informed consent in, 153–167
    potential integration of cookie watcher and cookie information dialog box into, 167

Mozilla cookie watcher prototype, 160–165
  description of, 160–162
  formative evaluation, 162–165
    methods, 163
    participants, 163
    results and discussion, 163–165
  implementation of, in Mozilla showing cookie watcher tool and cookie information dialog box, 161f
Mozilla cookie watcher prototype, revisited, 165
  description of, 165
  formative evaluation of, 165
  implementation of, in Mozilla showing revised cookie watcher tool and cookie information dialog box, 166
MSNBC, 61
Muhammad, Sheikh Omar Bakri, 134
Multilevel security, providing, 177–178
Multiplayer computer games, 222
Mumford, Lewis, 237
Muslim Hackers Club, 133

N
NASA, 13
National Academy of Sciences, 4
National Infrastructure Assurance Council, 66
National Infrastructure Protection Center, 66, 131, 132
National Review, 133
National security, Clipper Chip and, 40
National Westminster Bank, 11
Natural law theory, counterhacking and, 43
Naval Postgraduate School, 126, 127, 136
Nazi Germany, 77
Necessity principle, 104–105, 108, 118
  aggressive active defense responses and, 113–114
  intermediate active defense responses and, 114

justification for counterhacking based on, 42, 43
Negligence, vulnerability disclosures and, 262
Neidorf, Craig, 14
Neill, Colin J., 182
Netscape Navigator, 153, 154, 156
Netscape Navigator/Communicator 4.x, 163
Net surfers, 235
Network hackers, 7
Network intrusions, 180
Network security, 43
  threat of cyberterrorism and, 32–33
Network spoofing, 181
New Age terrorist groups, cyberterror capability of, 126
New York City Human Resources Administration, 6
NIPC. *See* National Infrastructure Protection Center
Noncommercial entities, hactivism and harm caused to, 89–90
Nonmalicious intrusions, hacker viewpoints on, 73
Nonrival good, information characterized as, 255
Nonrivalrousness of information argument, 247–248, 250
Non-sufficiently secure computing environments, moral issues related to, 37–39
Nonviolence
  civil disobedience and, 74, 75, 82, 83
  hactivism and, 63, 64, 65
Normative ethical relativism, support for universal human rights and, 94
Nozick, Robert, 246
NPS. *See* Naval Postgraduate School
NSA. *See* National Security Agency
Nuclear plants, virus attacks and, 22
Nuclear testing
  hactivism and, 96
  hactivist groups and, 62, 64, 65

O

Obscenity, 143
On-line games
  account scams, 226–229
  account sharing, 231–232
  consideration of, as potential
      Internet security threat,
      221–225
  example of actual on-line games-
      related security alert, 222f
  general security threat related
      to, 224–225
  information given to game hosting
      company, 225–226
  as "just entertainment," 221,
      223–224
  as "just for kids," 221, 222–223
  multiplayer, 222
  security in, 203, 221–232
  third-party software and, 229–231
  user education and, 230–231
Open source process, security impli-
      cations with, 187–188
Open source software develop-
      ment, 182
Operation Sundevil, 14
Operation Sundial, 68
Operation Virus, 21
Oppression, privacy rights and, 238
Osama Bin Laden Crew, 130
Outlaw, 14
Out of the Inner Circle (Landreth), 10
Overcrowding, consequences of, 237
Ownership rights, social nature of
      information argument and,
      244–247

P

PABXs. *See* Private automatic branch
      exchanges
Packet sniffing software, 229
"Packet sniffing" technologies, 40
Pair programming, eXtreme pro-
      gramming and, 189, 190
Pakistan Hackerz Club, 123, 130
Pakistani Brain virus, 18

Palestinian Islamic Jihad, 134
Pareto-superior move, 241
Participatory design, 155
Password hackers, 7
Passwords
  abuse of, in on-line games, 227–229
  guessing, 9, 10
  memorability of, 178
Pasteur, Louis, 235
Patches, 262
  arguments against disclosure
      and, 261
Patent Act of 1790, 239
Patent law, in United States, 194, 195
Patents, 239
Paulk, Mark, 188
PC. *See* Personal computer
PCCIP. *See* President's Commission on
      Critical Infrastructure
      Protection
Peace virus, 20
Peer review, code inspection and, 185
Peer-to-peer architecture, multi-
      player on-line games and, 222
Penalties
  for hacking, 13–15
  for hactivism, 65
"Penetrate and patch" mentality,
      insecure environment and,
      186–190
Peripheral awareness
  of cookie events, 158
  Mozilla cookie watcher and, 162
Personal computer, hacker's use of, 9,
      10
Pfleeger, Shari, 186
PGP. *See* Pretty Good Privacy
PHC. *See* Pakistan Hackerz Club
Philadelphia Newspapers, 6
Philber Optic, 14
Phishing, 214
Phone hacking, reemergence of, 6
Phone "phreaks," 5
Phrack and Pulhas, 66
Pitterman, Bill, 193
Plagiarism, 143

Playboy Channel, 4
PLO, 127
Policing, in-game, 229
Political activism, 73, 87. *See also* Hactivism
Political activists, steganography and rights of, 217
Political agenda, electronic civil disobedience and plausibility of, 92–95
Political causes, hactivism and advancement of, 62
Political decentralization, hactivism and, 61
Political oppression, hactivists and, 69
Popp, Joseph, 22
Pornography, 143
Portability, team culture issues and, 191
Potter, Bruce, 179
Power, electronic opposition groups and, 63
Power, Richard, 31
Power grid, cyberterrorists and, 197
Preemptive attacks, moral issues and, 42, 43
President's Commission on Critical Infrastructure Protection, 66
Pretty Good Privacy, encryption algorithm, 208
PricewaterhouseCoopers, 222
Principle of least privilege, following, 178–179
Printer manufacturers, embedded serial numbers issue and, 216–218
Privacy, 203. *See also* Confidentiality
analysis of threat steganography has on, 216–218
cookies and, 177
in cyberspace, 31
distinguishing between security violations and violations of, 35–36
establishing a presumption in favor of, 236–239

hacker ethic and, 52
hactivists and, 69
informed consent and, 153
overriding presumptions in favor of, for arguments in favor of hacking, 244–250
role of steganography and, 206–209
security *vs.*, 34–36
Privacy and Freedom (Westin), 236
Privacy rights, justifying, 237
Private automatic branch exchanges, 6
Private entities
active response continuum and, 100
hactivism and harm caused to, 89–90
ProCD v. Zeidenberg, 256n
Proctor and Gamble, 6
Product, 256n
SE Code of Ethics, principle 1, 196, 197
team ownership of, 193
Product liability, information and, 256
Profession, concept of, 144–148
ethical obligations of professionals, 146–147
models of professional's relation to their clients, 145–146
Profession, SE Code of Ethics, principle 6, 197, 199
Professional ethics, 147, 149
Professionalism, Internet-appropriate model of, 148
Professional issues, production of secure software and, 194–199
Professionals
ethical obligations of, 146–147
relationship of, to clients, 145–146
Programmers, self-taught, 145
Project goals, tensions between security goals and, 173–180
Property law, vilification of hactivism and, 67
Proprietary information, data security and, 31

Prototyping, requirements gathering and, 182
Provos, Niels, 210, 215
Public, SE Code of Ethics, principle 2, 196, 198
Public entities, hactivism and harm caused to, 89–90
Public key cryptography, 212
Punishment
    unjustified acts of civil disobedience and, 80–81
    unjustified hactivism and, 97–98
Punishment principle, 107–109

Q
Quality assurance practices, security considerations and, 185
Quantum computing, 200

R
Race-based segregation, 83
Racial injustice, civil disobedience and, 85
Racism, hactivism and, 64
RAND Corporation, 20, 66
RATS. See Rough Auditing Tool for Security
Raymond, Eric S., 182, 187
Razzak, Mohammad Afroze Abdul, 133
Recording Industry Association of America, 214, 215
Refactoring, eXtreme programming and, 189
Reimerdes case (2001), 264
Release planning, eXtreme programming and, 189
Reliability, 174
    using community resources and, 179
Religious terrorist groups, cyberterror capability of, 126
Repressive regimes
    digital intrusions and, 93
    privacy rights and, 238
Requirements analysis, 182, 183

Requirements document, security policies incorporated into, 184
Responsibility
    civil disobedience and acceptance of, 79–80, 84, 86
    hactivists and acceptance of, 91–92
    Internet professional ethics and, 150, 151
Responsible disclosure, 259
    arguments for, 260
Retaliation principle, 106–107, 108
Retributivist theories, justifying punishment and, 108
Retrospective analysis, of cookies, browsers, and informed consent, 156
Reusability, 174
    auditing and/or monitoring and, 176
    ensuring confidentiality, integrity, and accessibility and, 177
    portability and, 191
    reluctance to trust and, 179
Revolutionary Armed Forces of Colombia, 127
Revolutionary terrorist groups, cyberterror capability of, 126
RIAA. See Recording Industry Association of America
Rice v. Paladin, 264n
"Right to know" problems, disclosing software vulnerabilities and, 263–264
Risk assessments, performing, 183–184
Risk management
    conflicts inherent in, 173
    risk assessment and, 183
    software process and, 181
Rogue computer programs, 32
Role-playing, in on-line games, 223n
Rose Bowl football game (1961), stunt-card "switcheroo" at, 6
Rosenberg, Richard S., 31
Ross, David, 41
Rossiter, Clinton, 237
Rough Auditing Tool for Security, 185

Russian Stock Exchange, 127
Russian viruses, 19

S
Saboteurs, 22
Sadaqa, Ziyad (pseud.). *See* Khalil,
    Ziyad (pseud. Ziyad Sadaqa)
"Safe" coding practices, coding per-
    formed in accordance with,
    184–185
Saloomey v. Jeppesen, 256n
Samudra, Imam, 132
Satellite hacking, as felony, 4
Satellites, malicious interference
    with, 3
SCADA. *See* Supervisory Control and
    Data Acquisition
Scanning ports, 100
Schifreen, Robert, 11
Schneier, B., 210, 211
Scholarship, steganography and,
    214–215
Scoch, John, 16
Scorpion, 14
Scotland Yard, 14
"Script kiddies," 186
Seattle, World Trade Organization
    protests in (1999), 85
Second Intifada, cyberattacks and, 129
Secure software, professional and
    ethical issues around pro-
    duction of, 194–199
Security, 171, 172. *See also* Software
    vulnerability
  "big three" in, 176
  building into workplace culture,
    193–194
  concept of, in computing con-
    text, 29–33
  distinguishing between privacy vio-
    lations and violations of, 35–36
  future issues, 199–200
  hacker ethic and, 52
  maintenance for, 186–190
  multilevel, 177–178
  on-line games and, 203, 221–232

open source process and, 187–188
  privacy *vs.,* 34–36
  quality assurance practices and, 185
  "safe" coding practices and, 184–185
  software processes and, 180–190
  steganoraphy and enhancement
    of, 211
  XP and, 187, 188–190
Security and social benefits argu-
    ment, 249–250
Security arguments, computer break-
    ins and, 53–55
Security goals
  software project goals and, 173–175
  tensions between project goals
    and, 173–180
Security "holes," disclosing informa-
    tion about, 257
Security personnel
  SE Code of Ethics and, 198
  team ownership of process and, 193
Security policies
  consideration of, from the start, 183
  incorporation of, into require-
    ments documents, 184
Security precautions, tacit consent
    and, 119, 120
Security professionals, licensing pro-
    posal for, 122
"Security snake oil," 198
Security testing, testing phase and,
    185–186
SEI. *See* Software Engineering
    Institute
Selby, Richard W., 194
Self, SE Code of Ethics, principle 8,
    197, 199
Self-defense, hacking back and, 40
Self-replicating software, 20
Sensitive information, data security
    and, 31
Serial numbers, embedded,
    steganography and, 216–218
Server, 177n
Shahbaz, Ibn, 130
Simmons, John, 244

Simple unstructured cyberterror
capability, 126, 136
Simplicity, 174
auditing and/or monitoring and, 176
ensuring confidentiality, integrity,
and accessibility and, 177
least privilege principle and, 179
multilevel security and, 177
team culture issues and, 191
trustworthy authentication and, 178
Sit-ins, 62, 81, 85, 92
electronic, 63
virtual, 129
Slammer worm, 125, 176
Smith, David, 172
Smithsonian Institution, 13
Sniffing, 102, 117
on-line games and, 229
Social engineering attacks, 180
Social informatics, 154
Social justice, hacktivism and, 61
Social nature of information argument, 244–247, 250
Social protector argument, computer
break-ins and, 56–57
Social security numbers, 90
Softwar: La Guerre Douce (Breton and
Beneich), 21
Software
secure code and cost of, 1
self-replicating, 20
Software and Electrical Engineering
company, 21
Software developers, 171, 180
Software development
congruence in, 192
impact of computer security con-
cerns on, 171–200
"many eyeballs" approach to,
187, 190
Software Engineering Code of
Ethics, 194
Software engineering community,
security wake-up calls and,
172
Software Engineering Institute, 188n

Software Engineering (SE) Code of
Ethics, three levels of ethical
obligation within, 196
Software engineers, 171
SE Code of Ethics and, 197, 198, 199
Software piracy, hacking vs., 7
Software process
effective and sensible, 192–193
risk management and, 181
security and, 180–190
team ownership of, 193
Software project goals
security goals and, 173–175
types of, 174
Software vendors, disclosure debate
and, 261, 262
Software viruses. See Viruses
Software vulnerability, 255–265
choice of silence: costs in free-
dom of choice and free
speech, 263–265
clash of interests in disclosure
debate, 261–263
debate about disclosure, 258–261
Somayaji, Anil, 176
Sony, 222
Spafford, Eugene H., 30, 38, 41, 42, 47,
187, 189
Spam, 214
Spam laws, on-line gaming and,
225, 226
Special Oversight Panel on Terrorism
of the Committee on Armed
Services, 48, 123
Speer, Mathias, 10
Spinello, Richard A., 31, 249
Spiral process, 182
Spooner, Lysander, 246
Spyware, 235
Sri Lankan embassies, 129
Stallman, Richard, 52
Stanford University, 5
break-ins at, 10
MBA Program break-ins at, 35–36
State authority, punishment princi-
ple and, 108–110

Steganalysis, 207
    analysis of threat related to government regulation of, 212–214
Steganography, 203
    analysis of, as a security threat: terrorist example, 209–211
    analysis of threat posed by, on privacy and anonymity, 216–218
    analysis of threat that comes from government regulation of, 212–214
    description of, 205–206
    in the digital age, 205–219
    digital rights management and, 215–216
    information hiding with, 205
    role of, in providing privacy and anonymity, 206–209
        ethical challenges with, 207–209
    scholarship and, 214–215
    threat to free and open society and abuse of, 218
Steve Jackson Games, 14
Stoll, Clifford, 13, 49
Streaming video, 195
Strickland, Karl, 14
"Strict liability" law, 195
strncpy function (C language), 191n
Student hacker argument, computer break-ins and, 55–56
Suicide bombings, 130
Suitomo Bank, 6
"Super-DMCAs," 209, 214
Supervisory Control and Data Acquisition, 128
System development, team culture issues and, 191
System resources, system security and vulnerability of, 31–32
System security, 43. See also Security
    vulnerability of system resources and, 31–32
Systems Security Engineering, 181

T
Tacit consent, 119–121
Tagging, 65, 90
Taliban, 94
Tamil Tigers, 129
Tarnoff, David, 141
Tavani, Herman, 1
Team culture issues, 190–194
    creating congruent culture without blaming, 193
    description of, 190–192
    effective and sensible software process and, 192–193
    managing workplace demons, 193–194
    team ownership of product, 193
    team ownership of the process, 193
Team ownership, of process and product, 193
Team Software Process, 181
Team spirit, creating, 192
Technical ethics, 149
Technical investigations, value-sensitive design and, 154
Telcordia, 193
Telecommunications, hactivism and corporate domination of, 62
Tempest, defined, 16
Tennessee Valley Authority, 6
Terrorism, blurring distinction between activism and, 97–98
Terrorist attacks of September 11, 2001, 48, 123, 130, 136
    cyberattacks and, 133
    security community in aftermath of, 172
    security technologies and, 40
    steganography and, 209–210, 212
Terrorist example, analysis of steganography as security threat and, 209–211
Terrorists
    hackers as security resources and, 12
    steganography and, 206
Terrorist 007, 131

Testers, 173, 180, 183, 190
  SE Code of Ethics and, 198
  security concerns and, 193
  team culture issues and, 191
  team ownership of process and, 193
  tension between developers and,
    185
Testing, 182
  eXtreme programming and, 189
Testing phase, security testing and,
    185–186
They still have their copy argument,
    235, 247–248, 250
Third-party cookies, 159, 161, 164, 165
Third-party software, on-line
    games, 229–231
  as security threat, 229–230
  solutions to problems with, 230–231
39 Principles of Jihad, The, 134
"Tiger team," 11
Time bomb, defined, 15
Timeliness, 174
  auditing and/or monitoring and, 176
  ensuring confidentiality, integrity,
    and accessibility and, 177
  team culture issues and, 191
Tracebacks, 102
  implementing, 99
  intermediate measures and, 114,
    115–116
Traceback technologies, improving
    reliability and efficacy of, 116
Trade secrets, 239
Trans Union, 14
Trap door, 15
Triumph without Victory: The
    Unreported History of the
    Persian Gulf War, 21
Trojan horses, 1, 32. See also Worms;
    Viruses
  defined, 15
  on-line gaming and, 229
Trust, being reluctant to, 179

"Trust (and Mistrust) in Secure
    Applications" (Viega, Kohno,
    and Potter), 179
TRW, 14
Turkel, Sherry, 8
Twelve Nasty Tricks virus, 20

U
UCITA. See Uniform Computer
    Information Transactions
UIs. See User interfaces
Unauthorized code, games with
    inbuilt detection of, 230
Underwriters Laboratory, 145
Unemployment rate, 91
Uniform Computer Information
    Transactions, 196, 197
United Nations, 126
UNITY, 129
University computer laboratories,
    hackers, log-on details and, 10
UNIX operating system, break-ins
    and, 10
Uplink video piracy, 4
U.S. Defense Department, 14
U.S. Department of Commerce, 208
U.S. House of Representatives, 32
U.S. International Traffic in Arms
    Regulations, 208, 214
U.S. National Security Agency, 22, 66,
    210, 212
U.S. News and World Report, 21
U.S. Secret Service, 14
Usability, 174
  ensuring confidentiality, integrity,
    and accessibility and, 177
  failing securely and, 179
  least privilege principle and, 179
  reluctance to trust and, 179
  team culture issues and, 191
  trustworthy authentication and, 178
  using community resources and,
    179
User anonymity, privacy in cyber-
    space and, 39

User education, on-line games and, 230–231
User friendliness, team culture issues and, 191
User interfaces, 158
Usernames, abuse of, in on-line games, 227–229
User stories, eXtreme programming and, 188, 189
Utilitarian justifications
    for counterhacking activities, 42
    of intellectual property, 239
Utilitarians, computer break-ins and views of, 41, 42

V
Vaccines, 21
    defined, 16
Value-sensitive design, 141, 153
    defined, 154
    four overarching goals with, 156–158
    Gedanken prototype, 158–160
    Mozilla cookie watcher prototype, 160–165
    Mozilla cookie watcher prototype, revisited, 165
    retrospective analysis of cookies, browsers, and informed consent, 156
    viability of, in real-world, large-scale software system, 167
Vandalism, 30, 85
Vandalware, 51, 56
VDTs. See Virtual data toolkits
Vendors
    disclosure about software vulnerability and, 259
    disclosure debate and, 261, 262
    security arguments and, 54
Verton, Dan, 135
Video monitoring, 235
Viega, John, 172, 174, 179, 180, 181, 182, 184, 187, 189, 191
Vigilantism, moral presumption against, 108, 109, 110

Violence, digital information technologies and, 75
Virtual blockades, 63
Virtual data toolkits, 5
Virtual "possessions" (on-line games), offline money and, 228
Virtual sit-ins, 129
Virus attacks
    pervasiveness of, 22
    potentially life-threatening, 22
Viruses, 1, 143. See also Trojan horses; Worms
    attacks against critical infrastructure by, 125
    Barry Manilow virus, 20
    Code Red, 256–257
    defined, 15–16
    distinguishing from worms, 31
    ethical issues around, 23
    hacking and, 3–25
    ILOVEYOU virus, 257
    invasion of, 16–23
    Melissa virus, 172
    Michelangelo virus, 31
    Twelve Nasty Tricks virus, 20
Virus warfare, 21
Visual Basic, 158
Voluntariness, informed consent and, 155
von Lohmann, F., 213
VSD. See Value-sensitive design
Vulnerabilities, 173, 181, 257. See also Software vulnerabilities
    exploits and prevention of, 175–176
    patch mentality and, 186

W
Wallenberg, F., 216
Wallhacks, 229
Walz, Diane B., 192
Warren, Justice Earl, 34
Wassenaar Arrangement, 209
Waterfall process, security considerations incorporated into, 182
Watergate, 12

Watermarks, steganography and, 215–216
Wa-Tor, 18
Web development, 143
Web sites. *See also* Internet
    character of the hack and shutting down of, 90, 91
    defacements of, 123, 125, 129, 130, 136
    hactivism and harm caused to, 89–90
Weinberg, Gerald M., 192, 193
Wells, Don, 190
West German Chaos Computer Club, 12
Westin, Alan, 236
WGN-TV, overriding of, 4
Whistleblowers, steganography and rights of, 217
"White hat" hackers, 38
Whiteley, Nicholas (Mad Hacker), 13
Whitman, Michael E., 184
Williams, Laurie, 190
Wilson, David L., 187
"Wily hackers," 49
Wolf, Marty, 203
Women, in Afghanistan, 94
Woods, Neil, 14
Workplace culture issues. *See also* Team culture issues
    security and, 180
Workplace demons, managing, 193–194
World of Warcraft, 224, 227
World Trade Organization, 85
World Trade Organization servers, DoS attack on, by Electrohippies, 112

Worms, 1, 20, 143. *See also* Trojan horses; Viruses
    attacks against critical infrastructure by, 125
    Blaster worm, 176
    Code Red worm, 172, 186
    creation of, 16
    defined, 16
    distinguishing viruses from, 31
    early, 17
    Morris worm, 171
    Slammer worm, 176
Writing Secure Code (Howard and LeBlanc), 172
W3C, 145
WTO. *See* World Trade Organization
WTTW, overriding of, 4
wu-ftpd, 187

X
Xerox, 216
    Palo Alto Research Center, 16
XP. *See* eXtreme programming
X-Ploit, 64

Y
Yahoo, hacker attack of, 61, 63, 65
Youngblood, Dick, 145

Z
Zapata, Emiliano, 64
Zapatista rebellion (Mexico), hactivist groups and, 62
Zapatistas, 64
Zedillo, Erenesto, hactivist attack on Web site of, 64
Zero Spam, 214
Zimmerman, Phil, 208
Zone-h, 130